Library of
Davidson College

Introduction to
MATHEMATICAL
LINGUISTICS

ROBERT WALL
Department of Linguistics
University of Texas at Austin

Introduction to MATHEMATICAL LINGUISTICS

PRENTICE-HALL, INC., Englewood Cliffs, New Jersey

© 1972 by PRENTICE-HALL, INC.
Englewood Cliffs, New Jersey

All rights reserved. No part of this book may be reproduced in any form or by any means without permission in writing from the publisher.

Printed in the United States of America

ISBN: 0-13-487496-X

Library of Congress Catalog No.: 75-38044

10 9 8 7 6 5 4 3

PRENTICE-HALL INTERNATIONAL, INC., London
PRENTICE-HALL OF AUSTRALIA, PTY. LTD., Sydney
PRENTICE-HALL OF CANADA, LTD., Toronto
PRENTICE-HALL OF INDIA PRIVATE LIMITED, New Delhi
PRENTICE-HALL OF JAPAN, INC., Tokyo

To Vivian

and to Don and Pat

Contents

Preface   *xiii*

1 Elements of Set Theory   *1*

    Specification of Sets, 2
    Equality of Sets: The Axiom of Extension, 4
    Sets of Sets, 6
    Subsets, 6
    Members vs. Subsets, 7
    Power Sets, 8
        Exercises, 9
        References and Supplementary Reading, 10

**2 Symbolic Logic:
The Propositional Calculus**   *12*

    Propositions, 13
    The Logical Connectives, 15
        1. Conjunction, 15
        2. Disjunction, 16
        3. Negation, 17
        4. The Conditional, 18
        5. The Biconditional, 21
    More Complex Propositions, 22
    Tautologies and Contradictions, 25
    Logical Equivalence, 27
    Arguments, 34

Validity and Truth, 37
Rules of Inference, 38
Conditional Proof, 41
Indirect Proof, 44
  Exercises, 45

3 The Predicate Calculus   51

Terms, Predicates, Propositional Functions, 52
Quantifiers, 53
Bound and Free Variables, 56
The Domain of Discourse, 57
Set Specification and Predicates, 58
Representation of Universal and
  Existential Statements, 59
Tautology, Contradiction, and Logical Equivalence, 62
Arguments Involving Quantifiers, 65
  1. Universal Instantiation, 65
  2. Universal Generalization, 66
  3. Existential Generalization, 68
  4. Existential Instantiation, 68
Conditional Proof in the Predicate Calculus, 71
Arguments Containing Propositions
  with Two or More Quantifiers, 73
  Exercises, 76
  References and Supplementary Reading, 80

4 Further Aspects of Set Theory   81

Some Set-Theoretic Predicates, 81
Some Theorems about Sets, 83
Informal Style in Mathematical Proofs, 84
Set Operations, 87
  1. Union, 87
  2. Intersection, 89
  3. Relative Complementation, 91
  4. Absolute Complementation, 92
Venn Diagrams, 92
Set-Theoretic Equalities, 98
  Exercises, 102

5 Ordered Pairs, Cartesian Products, Relations, and Functions   104

Ordered Pairs, 104
Cartesian Products, 106
Relations, 107

Domain and Range of a Relation, 108
Universal, Null, and Identity Relations, 109
Complementary and Inverse Relations, 109
Properties of Relations, 110
   1. Reflexivity, 110
   2. Symmetry, 111
   3. Transitivity, 113
   4. Connexity, 114
Diagrams of Relations, 115
Properties of Complementary
   and Inverse Relations, 117
Equivalence Relations and Partitions, 121
Functions, 124
Inverse Functions, 127
Composites, 129
Identity Functions, 130
Inverses of Composites, 131
   Exercises, 133

6 Orders, Operations, Configurations, and Isomorphisms   137

Orders, 137
Terminology, 140
Trees, 144
   1. Dominance, 145
   2. Precedence, 147
   3. Labeling, 148
Operations, 152
Properties of Operations, 153
   1. Well-definition, 153
   2. Closure, 154
   3. Associativity, 154
   4. Commutativity, 154
   5. Idempotence, 154
   6. Distributivity, 155
   7. Identity Elements, 155
   8. Inverse Elements, 156
   9. Zero Elements, 157
Mathematical Configurations
   Involving Operations, 157
   1. Groups, 158
   2. Subgroups, 160
   3. Monoids, 162
   4. Submonoids, 163
   5. Semigroups, 163
Strings, 164
Isomorphisms, 166
   Exercises, 172

7 Infinite Sets — 174

Equivalent Sets and Cardinality, 174
Denumerability of Sets, 177
Nondenumerable Sets, 181
  Exercises, 186
  References and Supplementary Reading, 186

8 Recursion — 188

Recursive Definition, 188
Induction, 193
Axiomatic Systems, 197
Extended Axiomatic Systems, 199
Semi-Thue Systems, 202
  Exercises, 204
  References and Supplementary Reading, 206

9 Grammars of Formal Languages — 207

Formal Grammars, 207
Types of Grammars, 211
Types of Languages, 213
Grammars and Constituent-Structure Trees, 214
Right-Linear Grammars and Languages, 221
  1. *An Equivalent Formulation of Right-Linear Grammars*, 223
  2. *Type 3 Languages and Regular Sets*, 225
  3. *Inadequacy of Right-Linear Grammars for Natural Languages*, 231
Context-Sensitive Grammars and Languages, 234
  1. *Existence of a Decision Procedure for Membership in a Type 1 Language*, 234
  2. *Type 1 Languages and Recursive Sets*, 236
  3. *Some Undecidable Questions Concerning Type 1 Grammars and Languages*, 238
Context-Free Grammars and Languages, 238
  1. *Decidability of the Emptiness Question for Context-Free Grammars*, 239
  2. *Reductions of Context-Free Grammars*, 241
  3. *A Characterization Theorem for Context-Free Languages*, 247
  4. *Closure Properties of Context-Free Languages*, 249
  Exercises, 251
  References and Supplementary Reading, 252

10 Automata — 254

Finite Automata, 254
  1. *State Diagrams of Finite Automata*, 257
  2. *Deterministic vs. Nondeterministic Finite Automata*, 258

  3. *Formal Definition of Deterministic Finite Automata*, 259
  4. *Finite Automata and Type 3 Grammars*, 261
  5. *Finite Automata as Generators*, 264
  6. *Finite Automata and Regular Sets*, 265
  7. *Finite Automata and Equivalence Relations*, 267
 Turing Machines, 274
  1. *Formal Definition of Turing Machines*, 276
  2. *Equivalent Formulations of Turing Machines*, 278
  3. *Recursive vs. Recursively Enumerable Sets*, 279
  4. *Equivalence of Turing Machines and Type 0 Grammars*, 280
 Pushdown Automata, 282
 Linear-Bounded Automata, 285
  Exercises, 288
  References and Supplementary Reading, 288

11 Mathematical Characterization of Transformational Grammars   *290*

  References and Supplementary Reading, 297

Bibliography   *298*

Answers to Selected Exercises   *304*

Index of Symbols   *321*

General Index   *323*

Preface

This book covers the fundamentals of set theory, symbolic logic, and related topics that are prerequisite to the field of mathematical linguistics. As used here, 'mathematical linguistics' comprises the study of formal models of generative grammars and closely allied devices called abstract automata. It does not include the application of arithmetic and statistical techniques to language data, e.g., calculations of word frequencies in texts, percentages of cognate vocabulary in related languages (glottochronology), probabilities of occurrence of various syntactic constructions, etc., nor does it have to do directly with the use of digital computers in parsing, translating, checking grammars, or performing other operations of possible interest to linguists. Since all these endeavors are, in a broad sense, mathematical, it has been suggested that the first might be appropriately termed 'algebraic linguistics' to distinguish it from the others. It is algebraic in the sense that it is concerned with combining and manipulating discrete entities, e.g., the letters of an alphabet, rather than continuous entities such as lines and areas. The reader will indeed find that the mathematics found here resembles that in a typical high school algebra course more closely than it does, say, calculus or statistics.

Although the principal goal is to acquaint the reader with the study of formal grammars, the topics of the first eight chapters comprise a kind of basic literacy course in discrete mathematics. Anyone who is now unfamiliar with this material will find that it is very useful—in fact, practically essential—to a proper understanding of formalizations found in a wide range of current linguistic literature, from semantics to phonology. It also opens up a large part of the philosophical literature dealing with the relations between natural language and symbolic logic.

The first four chapters deal with set theory and symbolic logic, the most important unifying systems of all of mathematics. These topics are so closely interconnected that it is difficult to discuss one without assuming previous knowledge of the other. My solution to this problem, admittedly an uneasy compromise, is to introduce a few fundamental notions of set theory in Chapter 1, discuss symbolic logic in Chapters 2 and 3, and then continue with set theory in Chapter 4.

Chapters 5 and 6 present relations, functions, orders, operations, and mathematical configurations in a fairly standard way. The sections on constituent-structure trees and strings in these chapters, which are not ordinarily included in elementary treatments of discrete mathematics, reflect the linguistic orientation of the book and prepare the way for use of these concepts in later chapters. Infinite sets are discussed in Chapter 7 in preparation for the introduction of recursive devices for specifying infinite sets—recursive definitions, axiomatic systems, and semi-Thue systems—in Chapter 8. Formal grammars are presented in Chapter 9 as special forms of semi-Thue systems generating, in general, infinite languages as their theorems. Chapter 10 is a brief survey of abstract automata related to the formal grammars of Chapter 9. Finally, Chapter 11 reports some recent results pertaining to transformational grammars.

There is a lot of ground to cover between elementary set theory and the recursive enumerability of transformational languages, and so the treatment of some topics is necessarily very brief. To help the reader along, there are strategically placed problems and exercises and suggestions for further reading. In an advanced undergraduate or beginning graduate course meeting three hours each week, the material can be covered comfortably in two quarters or, with some condensation, in one semester.

I have used earlier versions of the manuscript in classes at the University of Texas and the Linguistic Institute at the University of Illinois. The students in those classes have helped immeasurably in pointing out mistakes, ambiguities, and unclarities in the presentation. Edmund Erde, Maurice Gross, Masa Muraki, Royal Skousen, and Arnold Zwicky have made many valuable suggestions for which I am very grateful. I am also indebted to Reed Bates, Ursula Fischer, Frances Karttunen, Neal Parker, and Diane Simison, who gave me much assistance in preparing the manuscript. The remaining errors are, of course, mine.

I should also like to express my gratitude to Linalice Carey, who did the lion's share of the typing, and to Pam Campbell, Mary Lou Gibson, Beverly Mollenauer, and Carol Starck, who did the rest. My thanks go to the University of Texas and the National Science Foundation for support under grant GU-1598 during the time this book was written.

A special debt of gratitude is owed to Anthony G. Oettinger, who first taught me mathematical linguistics and gave me much encouragement.

1

Elements of Set Theory

A *set* is an aggregation of discrete individuals regarded as a whole; for example, a flock of sheep or a baseball team or the "jet set." This concept is familiar to every speaker of a natural language. The English words 'flock,' 'team,' and many others like them seem to fulfill the rather specific function of referring to sets, and similar words are found in all languages. The individuals comprising a set are known as its *members*. Thus, Mars is a member of the set of planets in our solar system, and Brazil is a member of the set called the United Nations.

In mathematics the terms *set* and *member* are used in much the same way as in everyday language. There are, however, some points about which ordinary usage may be vague or equivocal, while the mathematical usage is—and must be—clear and unambiguous.

1. *The members of a set need not be concrete objects.* Abstractions such as the number 2, the equator, and the English phoneme /p/ are as appropriate for set membership as are the Empire State Building and the Amazon River. In particular, sets themselves as abstract objects may be members of other sets. It is just this property of sets—that they may both *have* members and *be* members—that gives this superficially simple concept generality and power enough to serve as the foundation of all mathematics that is now known. An everyday example of a set with sets as members is a baseball league whose members are teams, each team being a set of players.
2. *It is possible for a set to have only one member.* Although expressions such as 'a committee of one' are found in ordinary language, it might

seem more natural to regard a single individual and the set that contains only that individual as for all practical purposes identical. Mathematically the distinction is important. George Washington is not the same as the set having George Washington as its only member. The former was a man who was the first president of the United States, while the latter is a set, an abstract mathematical entity, whose birthday has never been celebrated. Halmos (1960; p. 4) emphasizes this point by the statement "a box that contains a hat and nothing else is not the same thing as a hat." A set with but one member is often called a *singleton*.

3. *It is possible for a set to have no members at all.* Such a set is called the *null set* or the *empty set*. This rather startling departure from everyday usage is essentially a mathematical convenience. If sets were restricted to having at least one member, many otherwise very general statements would have to be qualified and encumbered with exceptions in order to allow for the case in which an alleged set may turn out to be empty. As a matter of principle, mathematicians strive for generality even if this necessitates including certain so-called *trivial* cases.

4. *A set may have an infinite number of members.* The notion of infiniteness is considered in more detail in Chapter 7. For the present, we rely on an intuitive conception of what it means for a set to be infinite, viz., the members form a sequence that "never ends" and that cannot, in principle, be exhibited completely. Some examples are the set of whole numbers (*integers*) $\{1, 2, 3, 4, 5, \ldots\}$; the set of points inside a circle; and, according to most linguists, the set of grammatical sentences of English. However troublesome the concept of infiniteness may be in other contexts, it is fairly tractable mathematically and is involved in a great many problems of interest.

Specification of Sets

When a set is finite and its membership is known, it can be denoted in what is called *list notation*. The names of the members, written in a line and separated by commas, are enclosed in braces. For example, the set whose members are the first letter of the English alphabet, the first president of the United States, and the number 3 could be written

(1-1) $\{a,$ George Washington, $3\}$

Several things deserve mention here. First, in denoting a set we use the names or some other definite description of each of its members, but the set consists of *the objects named, not the names themselves*. In our example, the first president of the United States, whose name happens to be 'George

Washington,' is a member of the set. But it is the man who belongs to the set, not his name. Exactly the same set could have been specified in the following way,

(1-2) $\{a, \text{the first president of the United States}, 3\}$

by using an alternative designation for this individual. Of course a name may also be a legitimate member of a set, so to avoid confusion names considered as objects in their own right are put in single quotes. Thus we would write George Washington was the first president of the United States, but 'George Washington' is the name of the first president of the United States. The set

(1-3) $\{\text{'Plato', 'Socrates', 'Aristotle'}\}$

has as its members not three Greek philosophers but the names of three Greek philosophers.

Second, insofar as sets are concerned, it is an accidental feature of our writing system that the members are listed in a particular order from left to right. One might be led to suppose from the representation of the set in (1-1) that the element a is in some way first and that it precedes the element George Washington. In fact, nothing of the sort is implied. (In Chapter 5 we consider a different kind of set whose members are ordered.) A less misleading notation for this simple unordered set might be

(1-4) (George Washington a 3)

to emphasize that there is no order of precedence among the members. The list notation, however, is obviously more convenient to write and set in type, and so it is used despite the fact that the reader has the added burden of remembering that the order in which the members of a set are listed on the page is both arbitrary and irrelevant.

Another point about the list notation for sets is that writing the name of a member more than once does not change its status. Should we out of carelessness or perversity write

(1-5) $\{a, b, c, d, e, e, e, e\}$

we would have specified exactly the same set as by writing

(1-6) $\{a, b, c, d, e\}$

This is consistent with an important and fundamental principle of set theory: For a given individual and a given set, either that individual is a member of the set or else it is not, and those are the only possibilities. There is no such thing as halfway or multiple membership.

In addition to the list notation a set may also be specified by some property that all and only its members have. We employ this method when we speak of sets such as 'all the living ex-presidents of the United States' or 'all the positive integers less than 7.' The so-called *predicate notation* for this type of specification can be illustrated as follows:

(1-7) $\quad \{x \mid x \text{ is a living ex-president of the United States}\}$

The vertical line following the first occurrence of x is read 'such that.' The whole expression, then, can be read 'the set of all x such that x is a living ex-president of the United States,' or simply 'the set of all living ex-presidents of the United States.' Here x is a *variable symbol* that stands for no specific individual but might be thought of as pointing to all the appropriate candidates for membership in the set. In English 'anyone' and other similar pronouns often function like mathematical variables. For example,

(1-8) $\quad$ Anyone who is a living ex-president of the United States is entitled to a pension.

For finite sets either the list or the predicate notation may be used; thus:

(1-9) $\quad \{1, 2, 3, 4, 5, 6\}$

(1-10) $\quad \{x \mid x \text{ is a positive integer less than 7}\}$

although the predicate notation is clearly preferable if a set is very large, and a necessity for infinite sets. There is, however, a kind of pseudo-list notation for infinite sets that are presumed to be familiar to the reader. For example, the set of all positive integers is often denoted by

(1-11) $\quad \{1, 2, 3, 4, \ldots\}$

or something similar. The ellipsis at the end indicates that the list is not complete but is to be continued indefinitely in the same way as indicated by the examples given. An ellipsis is also sometimes used in the list notation for finite sets which are familiar but which are too long to be conveniently listed in full. For example,

(1-12) $\quad \{1, 2, 3, \ldots, 98, 99, 100\}$

denotes the set of positive integers from 1 to 100.

Equality of Sets: The Axiom of Extension

The symbol $\in$ stands for 'is a member of.' Thus, we may write

(1-13) $\quad c \in \{a, b, c\}$

(1-14) $\quad 5 \in \{x \mid x \text{ is a positive integer less than 7}\}$

Nonmembership is denoted by $\notin$:

(1-15) $d \notin \{a, b, c\}$

For convenience in referring to a set we may assign it a name, commonly an uppercase letter of the alphabet, by some phrase such as 'let $A = \{a, b, c\}$.' Having done this, we could write equivalently to (1-13)

(1-16) $c \in A$

Naming a set is a wholly arbitrary matter, subject only to the constraint that one must avoid notational collisions that would result from calling two different sets by the same name within a particular discussion. In widely separated contexts where there is little chance of confusion, however, a name previously used may be reassigned to another set.

The equals sign is also used to state that two distinct names or representations actually refer to the same set. Thus,

(1-17) $\{1, 2, 3, 4, 5, 6\} = \{x \mid x \text{ is a positive integer less than } 7\}$

asserts that these two specifications denote the same set. Similarly, if the sets on the left and the right of (1-17) had been named B and C, respectively, we could write equivalently to (1-17)

(1-18) $B = C$

Note that whereas naming a set is a matter of choice, a statement that two sets are equal, such as (1-17), is a statement about a matter of fact and is either true or false. When is such a statement true? The answer to this question is contained in the Axiom of Extension.

AXIOM OF EXTENSION: Two sets are equal if and only if they have the same members.

An *axiom* is a statement whose truth is assumed rather than proved. Just as the concepts of set and membership are taken as primitives in set theory, the Axiom of Extension is primitive in the sense that its truth is not derived from the truth of other statements. Like most mathematical axioms, the Axiom of Extension seems so self-evident that one wonders why it need be stated at all. In fact, this axiom makes a nontrivial assertion about sets; namely, that the *only* thing relevant to the identity of a set is its members. To say that two sets have the same members, then, is equivalent to saying that there is really only one set, which has, for whatever reason, been called by two different names. Such a situation can arise, for example, when sets specified by two different predicates turn out to have the same members, as in the following:

(1-19) $\{x \mid x \text{ may legally purchase liquor in Texas}\}$
(1-20) $\{x \mid x \text{ is at least 21 years old}\}$

As the law now stands, (1-19) and (1-20) specify the same set.

An immediate consequence of the Axiom of Extension is that the null set is unique. Since the identity of a set is completely determined by its members, there can be only one set with no members at all. Because it is unique, it is convenient to have a fixed name for this set, and $\emptyset$ is the one that has been almost universally adopted. The list notation for the null set, which would be { }, is never used.

Sets of Sets

As we noted earlier, sets may have sets as members. For example, from the sets $A = \{a, b\}$ and $B = \{c, d\}$ we could form the set having A and B as its only members:

(1-21) $\quad \mathscr{C} = \{A, B\}$

In specifying $\mathscr{C}$ one could also use the list notation for A and B instead of the names, thus:

(1-22) $\quad \mathscr{C} = \{\{a, b\}, \{c, d\}\}$

Such examples raise an issue about which the ordinary usage of 'set' and 'member' is far from clear: Are a, b, c, and d to be counted as members of $\mathscr{C}$? In everyday language, a player for a baseball team in the National League might be called a member of that league, and anyone who insists that only teams, not players, are its members risks being put in the set of hairsplitting pedants. In mathematics this technical distinction is always scrupulously observed. Thus in (1-22) the members of A and B are *not* counted as members of $\mathscr{C}$. $\mathscr{C}$ has just two members, A and B; that A and B also happen to be sets does not alter this fact.

Confusion often arises with a set such as $\{\emptyset\}$. Since this set does have a member, namely the null set, by the Axiom of Extension it cannot be equal to the null set, which has no members. Once again, a set's members, or absence of them, have no bearing on another set with the former as a member.

Often the degree of complexity of a set is indicated informally by the kind of letter used in naming it, as we have just done. Individuals are denoted by lowercase letters, sets of individuals by uppercase letters, and sets of sets by the more outlandish type fonts such as script capitals. There is no theoretical significance in these conventions, nor is there in the use of 'collection' or 'class' as synonyms for 'set' in order to avoid terminological monotony.

Subsets

Given any two sets A and B, if all the members of A are also members of B, A is said to be a *subset* of B. For example, {Earth, Venus, Mars} is a subset of the set of planets in our solar system, and $\{a, b\}$ is a subset of $\{a, b, c\}$. The set $\{a, d\}$ is not a subset of $\{a, b, c\}$ since d is a member of the former but not of the latter. The subset relation is denoted by $\subseteq$ or $\supseteq$, thus:

(1-23) $\quad \{a, b\} \subseteq \{a, b, c\}$

(1-24) $\quad \{a, b, c\} \supseteq \{a, b\}$

Note that the open side of the symbol points *away from* the subset. Locutions equivalent to 'A is a subset of B' are 'A is included in B,' 'B includes A,' and 'B is a superset of A.'

The definition of subset allows the trivial case in which the subset is the set itself. For any set A whatever, every member of A is also a member of A, so it is always true that $A \subseteq A$. To exclude the case of identical sets, the term *proper subset* is used. A is a proper subset of B (or, A is *properly included in B*) whenever A is a subset of B but A is not equal to B. Proper inclusion is denoted by the symbols $\subset$ and $\supset$, although some authors use these for ordinary inclusion and use $\subsetneq$ or $\subsetneqq$ for proper inclusion, respectively. We shall adhere to the notation first described, reserving $\subset$ to refer specifically to proper inclusion. The corresponding negations have a diagonal line through the symbol, thus:

(1-25) $\quad \{a, d\} \nsubseteq \{a, b, c\}$

(1-26) $\quad \{a, b\} \not\subset \{a, b\}$

A curious consequence of the definition of subset involves another trivial case: The null set is a subset of every set. That is, for any set A whatever, $\varnothing \subseteq A$. Since $\varnothing$ has no members, the statement that every member of $\varnothing$ is also a member of A holds, even if vacuously. For those who find this line of reasoning somewhat slippery, there is an alternative argument. How could $\varnothing$ fail to be a subset of A? According to the definition of subset, there would have to be some member in $\varnothing$ that is not also a member of A. This is impossible since $\varnothing$ has no members at all, and so we cannot maintain that $\varnothing \nsubseteq A$. Since the argument does not depend in any way on what particular set is represented by A, it is true that $\varnothing \subseteq A$ for every A.

Problem: Does $\varnothing \subseteq A$ hold when A is the null set?

Members versus Subsets

Members of sets and *subsets* of sets both represent relationships of a part to a whole, but these relationships are quite different, and it is important not to confuse them. Subsets, as the name suggests, are *always sets*, whereas members may or may not be. Mars is a member of the set {Earth, Venus,

Mars} but not a subset of it. The set containing Mars as its only member, {Mars}, *is* a subset of {Earth, Venus, Mars} because every member of the former is also a member of the latter. The crucial distinction is between Mars, the planet, and {Mars}, the set.

Sets with sets as members provide the most opportunities for confusion. Consider, for example, the set $A = \{b, \{c\}\}$. The members of A are b and $\{c\}$. From the considerations in the preceding paragraph we see that $b \nsubseteq A$ and $\{b\} \subseteq A$. Similarly, $\{c\} \nsubseteq A$ because c is not a member of A, and $\{\{c\}\} \subseteq A$ because every member of $\{\{c\}\}$, namely, $\{c\}$, is a member of A. The reader should also verify the following statements concerning this example: $\{b\} \notin A$; $c \notin A$; $\{\{c\}\} \notin A$; $\{b, \{c\}\} \subseteq A$; $\{b, \{c\}\} \notin A$; $\{\{b, \{c\}\}\} \nsubseteq A$.

Here is another illustration of the difference between membership and inclusion. We have seen that every set is necessarily a subset of itself (although not a proper subset), but it is difficult to imagine how a set might be a member of itself. Of course one could easily write $A \in A$, but it would not be true of any reasonable set that one could conceive of. Investigations of the formal properties of sets have shown that the notion of a set being a member of itself leads to such serious difficulties that it is best to exclude the possibility of self-membership from set theory entirely. Not only $A \in A$ but also situations such as $A \in B$ and $B \in A$; $A \in B$, $B \in C$, and $C \in A$; etc., must be ruled out for well-defined sets. In contrast, the simultaneous truth of $A \subseteq B$ and $B \subseteq A$ and similar cases involving the subset relationship present no such problem.

Another difference between subsets and members has to do with our previous remarks about sets of sets. We have seen that if $b \in X$ and $X \in \mathscr{C}$, it does not necessarily follow that $b \in \mathscr{C}$. The element b *could* be a member of $\mathscr{C}$, but if so this would be an accidental property of $\mathscr{C}$, not a necessary one. With inclusion, however, if $A \subseteq B$ and $B \subseteq C$, it is *necessarily true* that $A \subseteq C$; that is, if every member of A is also a member of B, and further if every member of B is also a member of C, then it must be true that every member of A is also a member of C. (The reader might wish to construct a few examples.)

Power Sets

One sometimes has occasion to refer to the set whose members are all the subsets of some given set. Suppose, for instance, that we have the set $A = \{a, b\}$. A has four subsets: $\{a\}$, $\{b\}$, $\{a, b\}$, and $\varnothing$ (recall that $\varnothing$ is a subset of every set). The set that has just these four sets as its members is called the *power set of A* and is denoted $\mathscr{P}(A)$.

(1-27) $\mathscr{P}(A) = \{\{a\}, \{b\}, \{a, b\}, \varnothing\}$

We may state the definition as follows:

DEFINITION: For any set *A*, a set *B* is a member of the *power set* of *A* if and only if *B* is a subset of *A*.

The notation 2^A is sometimes used instead of $\mathscr{P}(A)$. The motivation for this is the fact that if the number of members of *A* is *n*, the power set of *A* has 2^n, i.e., $\underbrace{2 \times 2 \times \cdots \times 2}_{n \text{ times}}$ members. For example, $A = \{a, b\}$ has 2 members, and $\mathscr{P}(A)$ has $2 \times 2 = 2^2 = 4$ members.

EXERCISES

1. Given the following sets:

   $A = \{a, b, c, 2, 3, 4\}$ $E = \{a, b, \{c\}\}$
   $B = \{a, b\}$ $F = \emptyset$
   $C = \{c, 2\}$ $G = \{\{a, b\}, \{c, 2\}\}$
   $D = \{b, c\}$

   Classify each of the following statements as true or false.

   (a) $c \in A$ (g) $D \subset A$ (m) $B \subseteq G$
   (b) $c \in F$ (h) $A \subseteq C$ (n) $\{B\} \subseteq G$
   (c) $c \in E$ (i) $D \subseteq E$ (o) $D \subseteq G$
   (d) $\{c\} \in E$ (j) $F \subseteq A$ (p) $\{D\} \subseteq G$
   (e) $\{c\} \in C$ (k) $E \subseteq F$ (q) $G \subseteq A$
   (f) $B \subseteq A$ (l) $B \in G$ (r) $\{\{c\}\} \subseteq E$

2. State all the relationships of equality and of subset holding between pairs of the following sets:

   $A = \{a, b, c, d\}$ $E = a, \{b, b, b\}$
   $B = \emptyset$ $F = \{a, b, \{b\}, c, d\}$
   $C = \{a, \{b\}, c, d\}$ $G = \{a, b, d, c\}$
   $D = \{\{a, d, c, b\}\}$

3. List the members of the following sets:

   (a) $\mathscr{P}(\{a, b, c\})$ (d) $\mathscr{P}(\{\varnothing\})$

   (b) $\mathscr{P}(\{a\})$ (e) $\mathscr{P}(\mathscr{P}(\{a, b\}))$

   (c) $\mathscr{P}(\varnothing)$

4. Consider the five languages English, Russian, Arabic, Japanese, and Swahili and people who speak one or more of these. What is the largest group of people such that no two persons in the group speak exactly the same combination of these languages?

5. Give an equivalent representation in list notation for each of the following sets.

   (a) $\{x \mid x$ is a positive integer greater than 4 but less than 10$\}$

   (b) $\{x \mid x$ is a letter that occurs in the word 'banana'$\}$

   (c) $\{x \mid x$ is a member of the null set$\}$

   (d) $\{x \mid x$ is a positive integer less than 4 but greater than 10$\}$

   (e) $\{x \mid x$ is a subset of the letters occurring in the word 'car'$\}$

   (f) $\{x \mid x$ is a proper subset of the letters occurring in the word 'car'$\}$

6. Give an equivalent representation in predicate notation for each of the following sets:

   (a) $\{2, 4, 6, 8, 10\}$

   (b) $\{1, 2, 3, 5, 7, 11, 13\}$

   (c) $\varnothing$

   (d) $\{\varnothing\}$

References and Supplementary Reading

There are many works that present the rudiments of set theory, usually as the basis for introducing other mathematical topics. Breuer (1958), Christian (1958), Zehna and Johnson (1962), and Stoll (1963) [or in a shorter paperback version Stoll (1961)] are suitable for beginners since they presuppose very little mathematical background. Lipschutz (1964), in the Schaum College Outline Series, is especially useful as a source of exercises, most with solutions. For those with somewhat more experience in mathematics, Halmos (1960) is unsurpassed in surveying the field with brevity, clarity, and wit. The completely formal "axiomatic" approach to set theory is well presented in Suppes (1960). A comprehensive survey of the various axiom systems that have been devised can be found in Quine (1969).

For works that apply many of the definitions given in this and later chapters to linguistic examples, see Cooper (1964), Ortiz and Zierer (1968), and Hockett (1967).

2

Symbolic Logic: The Propositional Calculus

In the preceding chapter we introduced the basic concepts of set theory. Before going on to more complicated, and more interesting, aspects of this theory, it will be helpful if we first acquire some familiarity with symbolic logic.

Logic has been studied over many hundreds of years and from many points of view. Nonetheless, if there is one unifying objective in all these investigations, it has been to distinguish correct or *valid* ways of reasoning from those that are incorrect or *invalid*. A successful system of logic should, for example, designate the argument in (2-1) as valid since from its premises (the two statements above the line) the conclusion, Socrates is mortal, follows as a necessary consequence. On the other hand, (2-2) should be characterized as invalid since its conclusion does not follow necessarily from its premises.

(2-1)
All men are mortal.
Socrates is a man.
Therefore, Socrates is mortal.

(2-2)
All cats are mammals.
All dogs are mammals.
Therefore, all cats are dogs.

Logic has sometimes been called "the science of reasoning," but this appellation can be misleading if we take it as referring to mechanisms or processes occurring in the brain. This is a problem left to psychology and neurophysiology; logic is concerned only with the relations between premises and conclusions of arguments, no matter how they may have originated.

In mathematics one starts with certain assumptions about the properties of the objects under study and then goes on to demonstrate that these objects have other properties as well. Such a demonstration must proceed by a series of logically valid deductive steps, and if so it constitutes a *proof* of the final statement in the chain. With an adequate system of logic one can check a putative proof to determine whether it is valid. It is important to note that logic supplies no recipes for *constructing* proofs, only for *verifying* them. Devising a valid path, if one exists, from a given set of premises to some desired conclusion depends on the intelligence, skill, and luck of the mathematician. An understanding of logic may be helpful in this creative process, but it does not guarantee success.

Over the past hundred years or so, a logical system has been devised that reduces the verification of certain kinds of proofs to a straightforward manipulation of symbols with little or no regard to their interpretation. Such manipulations can, in principle, be carried out by a digital computer or other mechanical device having negligible intelligence. This system of *symbolic logic* may be viewed as a language with its own vocabulary of symbols, its syntactic rules for combining these symbols into well-formed (grammatical) expressions, and its (semantic) rules for assigning meanings or interpretations to such expressions. Compared to any natural language, it is a highly restricted system; yet it is adequate as a language for formulating statements and arguments in mathematics. The rules of combination and interpretation in symbolic logic, unlike those of a natural language, are few in number, easily stated, and perfectly precise. Its statements are thus free from any vagueness or ambiguity.

In this chapter and the next we discuss in rather broad outline two areas of symbolic logic: the *propositional* (or *sentential*) *calculus* and the (first-order) *predicate calculus*. The extraordinarily interesting and complex relationships between symbolic logic and natural language, which have commanded the attention of linguists and philosophers for many years, will concern us only peripherally. We are primarily interested in symbolic logic as a tool to assist us in making mathematical statements and checking mathematical arguments.

Propositions

Propositions are characterized by being either true or false but not both true and false simultaneously. Thus we say that propositions have a *truth value*, and in allowing only true (t) and false (f) we adopt a so-called *two-valued logic*. Other systems are conceivable—for instance a four-valued logic in which propositions are categorized as *true, plausible, implausible,* or *false*—but such systems will not concern us here.

In natural languages, propositions are normally expressed by declarative sentences, e.g., Bill Jones has a red beard, that make assertions about which one may sensibly ask whether they are true or false. Such is not the case with questions (What's for dinner?), imperatives (Get out!), and exclamations (Good grief!), which are said not to express propositions at all. On the other hand, some sentences of declarative form can be used in certain situations not as statements but as requests, e.g., I would like three copies of this letter, when said by an employer to his secretary; and there are others, the so-called *performatives* (I hereby pronounce you man and wife.), in which the utterance does not state a proposition but rather constitutes in itself the act referred to [Austin (1962)]. Therefore, one must distinguish *sentences*, which are part of natural language, from the *propositions* they sometimes express.

Different sentences may express the same proposition, as in

(2-3)   (a)   Paris is the capital of France.

           (b)   The capital of France is Paris.

           (c)   France's capital is Paris.

           (d)   France has a capital, which is Paris.

and ambiguous sentences (I know a taller man than John.) express more than one proposition. Symbolic logic is a calculus of propositions, not of sentences. In order to apply its principles to natural language one must first analyze the sentences of ordinary discourse into their propositional structure. This task is seldom straightforward. Consider, for example, a sentence such as

(2-4)   Omaha is a rather progressive city.

This sentence seems to express a proposition, but because of the vagueness of the words 'progressive and 'rather' it is not clear just what would count as evidence for its truth or falsity. In mathematics one must avoid terms with hazy or imprecise meanings, and one way to do this is to give them a restricted "technical" meaning. For example, in the preceding chapter in appropriating 'set' and 'member' into mathematics we attempted to clarify and sharpen the range of application of these terms. Such restrictiveness limits the language of mathematical statements to a small subset of a natural language but at the same time allows it to be represented by a system as simple as that of symbolic logic.

Despite our emphasis on the differences between sentences and propositions, we shall often ignore the distinction henceforth and write, for example, "the proposition 'John is tall' " instead of the cumbersome but more accurate "the proposition expressed by the sentence 'John is tall.' "

The Logical Connectives

Just as the connectives 'and,' 'because,' 'although,' 'unless,' 'if... then,' etc., can be used to conjoin English sentences, there is a group of logical connectives that may conjoin propositions. The five most commonly encountered are called 'and,' 'or,' 'not,' 'if... then,' and 'if and only if.' The way in which each is used parallels, but only approximately, the usage of the corresponding connectives in natural language. One important difference is that the logical connectives are *truth functional;* i.e., the truth value of a compound proposition is uniquely determined by the truth values of the propositions joined by the connective. The way in which the truth value of the larger proposition is determined from its components forms the substance of the definition of each of the connectives.

1. *Conjunction*

The logical conjunction of two propositions corresponds approximately to the ordinary usage of 'and' in conjoining sentences. From the sentences 'Paris is the capital of France,' and 'Detroit is in Michigan,' we may form the compound sentence 'Paris is the capital of France, and Detroit is in Michigan,' and this is true just in case both component sentences are true. If one or both of the component sentences are false, as in the following examples,

(2-5)   Paris is the capital of France, and Detroit is in Italy.

(2-6)   Paris is the capital of Denmark, and Detroit is in Italy.

the entire sentence is false. The logical connective *conjunction* is defined accordingly:

> **DEFINITION: If p and q are any two propositions, the *conjunction* of p and q (denoted $p \land q$) is a proposition that is true just in case both p and q are true; otherwise it is false.**

This definition is represented graphically in the *truth table* shown in Fig. 2-1. On the left of the double line are the four possible combinations of truth values that two propositions may have; on the right are the truth values for the conjunction in each of the four cases.

Any two propositions whatever may stand in place of p and q in the formula $p \land q$; they need not be semantically related. Although in normal discourse we do not form conjunctions like 'The dog is barking and two is an even number,' they are not prohibited in the propositional calculus. We may even conjoin a proposition with itself: 'Two is an even number and two is an even number.' Logical conjunction also differs from 'and' in that the former

p	q	$p \wedge q$
t	t	t
t	f	f
f	t	f
f	f	f

Figure 2-1

Truth table defining logical conjunction

does not have a temporal interpretation that is seen in such sentences as 'Bill took a shower and he got dressed' versus 'Bill got dressed and he took a shower.' As we shall see presently, the propositions $p \wedge q$ and $q \wedge p$ always have the same truth value, i.e., the same *logical meaning*.

The sentence 'Harry is handsome, but George has a lot of money' could also be logically represented as $p \wedge q$ since it is true when both conjuncts are true and false otherwise. Note, however, that whatever differences in meaning there are between 'and' and 'but' are lost in the logical representation.

2. Disjunction

Disjunction, also called *alternation*, corresponds roughly to the English connective 'or,' but once again the range of usage in ordinary language is wider. 'Or' sometimes means 'one or the other but not both' as would be the usual interpretation of 'You may have coffee or you may have tea.' This is 'or' in the *exclusive* sense. The *inclusive* 'or' meaning 'one or the other and possibly both' occurs in a sentence such as 'Applicants for the scholarship must be orphans or they must have a physical disability,' where it is surely intended that applications would also be accepted from those who had suffered both misfortunes. Logical disjunction has the *inclusive* sense.

DEFINITION: The *disjunction* (*alternation*) of any two propositions p and q (denoted $p \vee q$) is true whenever p is true or q is true or both; otherwise it is false.

The corresponding truth table is given in Fig. 2-2.

p	q	$p \vee q$
t	t	t
t	f	t
f	t	t
f	f	f

Figure 2-2

Truth table defining logical disjunction

As with conjunction, it is not necessary that the propositions connected by ∨ be semantically related.

The information contained in the two truth tables we have seen thus far allows us to make certain inferences about the truth values of the component propositions if we are given the truth value of a conjunction or disjunction. For example, if we know that $(p \wedge q)$ is true, we can say immediately from the definition of conjunction that both p and q must be true propositions; similarly, given that $(p \vee q)$ is false, we know that both p and q are false. Given that $(p \wedge q)$ is false, however, we can infer that at least one of the component propositions is false and possibly both are, but on the basis of this information alone we cannot tell which is the case.

Problem: What can be inferred about the truth or falsity of p and of q given that $(p \wedge q)$ is false while $(p \vee q)$ is true?

3. *Negation*

Whereas conjunction and disjunction connect two propositions, negation "connects" only one. The negation of a proposition p has a truth value opposite to that of p.

DEFINITION: The *negation* of any proposition p (denoted $\sim p$) is a proposition that is true when p is false and false when p is true.

The truth table for this connective is shown in Fig. 2-3. Note that only two columns and two rows are required since just one proposition is involved.

p	$\sim p$
t	f
f	t

Figure 2-3

Truth table defining logical negation

Logical negation thus corresponds to sentential negation, but once again the correspondence is not exact. While some declarative sentences can be negated by inserting 'not' into the proper place in the verb phrase, as in 'John is a philosopher' versus 'John is not a philosopher,' for others this fails:

(2-7)   Harry must go to Seattle tomorrow.

(2-8)   Harry must not go to Seattle tomorrow.

18 *Symbolic Logic: The Propositional Calculus*

The negation of (2-7) should be synonymous with 'It is not obligatory for Harry to go to Seattle tomorrow,' but (2-8) cannot have this interpretation. In such cases one can usually form the negation by prefixing 'it is not the case that' to the sentence, thus:

(2-9)   It is not the case that Harry must go to Seattle tomorrow.

This seems to yield a sentence with the required meaning, but it also raises a subtle philosophical point. The phrase 'it is not the case that' can be interpreted as asserting that the proposition following is false. The proposition p in $\sim p$ does not have to be false, however; all we can say is that the truth value of p is opposite to that of $\sim p$. To put the matter in another way, there is a difference between the proposition $\sim p$ and the proposition expressed by 'p is false.' The former is a proposition *about* something such as Paris, the moon, Harry, or whatever; the latter is *about* the proposition p, asserting that it is false. Surprisingly, the failure to make this distinction usually causes no great harm since both $\sim p$ and 'p is false' turn out always to have the same truth value! Suppose p is true. Then $\sim p$ has the value *false*, and 'p is false' is also false. On the other hand, if p is false, then $\sim p$ has the value *true* as does the proposition 'p is false.'

Problem: Do p and 'p is true' always have the same truth value?

4. The Conditional

The logical connective that corresponds to certain uses of 'if ... then' is called the *conditional*. It is defined as follows:

> **DEFINITION: Given any two propositions p and q, the *conditional* with p as *antecedent* and q as *consequent* (denoted $p \to q$) is a proposition that is false when p is true and q is false; otherwise, it is true.**

The corresponding truth table is shown in Fig. 2-4.

p	q	$p \to q$
t	t	t
t	f	f
f	t	t
f	f	t

Figure 2-4

Truth table defining the conditional

This logical connective has been the subject of much discussion because its definition departs in many respects rather radically from the usage of 'if . . . then' in ordinary language. As with the other connectives, propositions joined by the conditional may be unrelated in meaning. The sentence 'If China is in Asia, then two and two are four,' if uttered in everyday discourse, would probably be considered false or nonsensical, but in logic it is not only permissible but true as well (because both the antecedent and the consequent are true). Such a result strikes us as more puzzling here than with the other logical connectives because we expect a strong intrinsic connection between the sentences joined in natural language by 'if . . . then.' This connection may be of several kinds. For example, in the sentence that embodies the argument in (2-1),

(2-10)　　If all men are mortal and Socrates is a man, then Socrates is mortal.

the consequent follows from the antecedent as a logical consequence. This is said to be a *logical* use of 'if . . . then' or a case of *logical implication*. The implication is termed *causal* in the following sentence:

(2-11)　　If you wash this sweater in hot water, then it will shrink.

The intended meaning is that the circumstances described in the antecedent actually cause the occurrence of the event mentioned in the consequent. In causal implication the consequent does not follow from the antecedent by logical deduction; the truth or falsity of the implication can only be discovered by empirical investigation into the properties of the objects involved. 'If . . . then' may also be used in stating a definition:

(2-12)　　If a person is able to use both hands with equal ease, then he is ambidextrous.

Here the antecedent defines the term 'ambidextrous' in the consequent. Such a sentence is, in one sense, a proposal to attach a certain meaning to a term, and thus it cannot be called true or false; one can only agree or refuse to adopt it. A sentence having the form of a definition may also be taken as asserting that speakers of the language do in fact use the term in the sense indicated, however, and then the sentence has a truth value. Dictionary definitions are statements of the latter sort (describing usage), while definitions in mathematics, physics, economics, etc., generally have the former sense (assigning meaning).

Another kind of 'if . . . then' sentence that raises problems of logical analysis is the so-called *subjunctive conditional*:

(2-13)　　If Communist China were in the United Nations, then there would not now be war in Viet Nam.

This usage of 'if ... then' is not truth functional because for certain truth values of the antecedent and consequent the truth value of the subjunctive conditional is not determined. For example, at the time this is being written Communist China has not joined the United Nations and there is war in Viet Nam; yet reasonable men could still debate the truth or falsity of (2-13) in the light of factual evidence.

The conditional in logic (sometimes called the *material conditional*) is not restricted to any of these special senses. It does, however, capture a part of the meaning common to the logical, causal, and subjunctive uses of 'if ... then' and to the definitional form when it describes usage. In each of these cases a statement would be considered false if the antecedent were true and the consequent false (cf. the second line of Fig. 2-4). For example, if the sweater mentioned in (2-11) is washed in hot water and it does not shrink, then the statement is false. Similarly, should speakers of English cease to use the term 'ambidextrous' in the sense described in (2-12), then that assertion would no longer hold. And if it were the case that Communist China had entered the United Nations and there was now war in Viet Nam, then (2-13) could be rejected at once. Sentence (2-10) is different from the other examples in that there is no logically possible situation in which the antecedent can be true while the consequent is false. This is a very important characteristic of logical implication that we shall return to in a later section. To illustrate the point we are making about conditionals, however, let us change (2-10) by substituting a false statement for its consequent:

(2-14)   If all men are mortal and Socrates is a man, then Socrates is immortal.

The sentence then becomes false.

Thus, when the antecedent is true and the consequent is false, the conditional corresponds reasonably well to 'if ... then,' but in the other three lines of its truth table it may not. For example, consider the following three sentences:

(2-15)   If $2 + 2 = 5$, then Tokyo is in Japan.   (false antecedent and true consequent)

(2-16)   If $2 + 2 = 5$, then Tokyo is in Canada.   (both false)

(2-17)   If $2 + 2 = 4$, then Tokyo is in Japan.   (both true)

Whatever the status of these may be in natural language, the corresponding propositions having the conditional as the connective would all be true. It would take us rather far afield to attempt to justify this puzzling aspect of the conditional, and in any case there are many troublesome questions about it that have still not been satisfactorily answered. For further discussion the reader is referred to the references cited at the end of Chapter 3. For our purposes, it is sufficient to note that this particular assignment of truth values to the conditional leads to a simple and effective characterization of valid and invalid arguments in mathematics. It works, and that is all we really care about.

Other locutions that are frequently translated into the conditional are 'only if,' 'is a sufficient condition for,' and 'is a necessary condition for.' If we let p be the proposition 'John lives in Chicago' and q be 'John lives in Illinois,' all the following sentences could be represented by $p \rightarrow q$:

(2-18)   If John lives in Chicago, then he lives in Illinois.

(2-19)   John lives in Illinois if he lives in Chicago.

(2-20)   John lives in Chicago only if he lives in Illinois.

(2-21)   John's living in Chicago is a sufficient condition for his living in Illinois.

(2-22)   John's living in Illinois is a necessary condition for his living in Chicago.

Note that the correspondents of the antecedent and the consequent in $p \rightarrow q$ appear in the opposite order in (2-19) and (2-22) and that the order with 'only if' (2-20) is the same as in the 'if ... then' sentence (2-18). One cannot in general interchange the antecedent and consequent of a conditional without changing the meaning. Compare (2-23),

(2-23)   If John lives in Illinois, then he lives in Chicago.

which may be false, with (2-18), which is true.

5. *The Biconditional*

The last of the truth-functional connectives we shall consider is the biconditional. It is defined as follows:

> **DEFINITION:** Given any two propositions p and q, the *biconditional* (denoted $p \leftrightarrow q$) is true when p and q have the same truth values; otherwise, it is false.

The truth table is given in Fig. 2-5.

p	q	$p \leftrightarrow q$
t	t	t
t	f	f
f	t	f
f	f	t

Figure 2-5

Truth table defining the biconditional

English expressions translated by the biconditional are 'if and only if,' 'just in case that,' 'just if,' and 'is a necessary and sufficient condition for.' It is sometimes difficult to tell whether some statements in ordinary language should be represented by the conditional or the biconditional. For example, the sentence

(2-24)   I shall leave tomorrow if I get the car fixed.

might mean that getting the car fixed is a sufficient condition for leaving tomorrow (but I might leave tomorrow anyway), and it might also be intended to mean that getting the car fixed is not only a sufficient but also a necessary condition for leaving tomorrow (I won't leave unless the car gets fixed). The latter interpretation is forced when the connective is 'if and only if.'

(2-25)   I shall leave tomorrow if and only if I get the car fixed.

In mathematics this connective is frequently abbreviated 'iff.' Formal definitions of mathematical terms always employ it (cf. the definition of power set in Chapter 1). The usual form is

(2-26) X is called a Y (or is a Y) iff X has property P.

Using 'if' instead of 'iff' would leave open the possibility that X might also be called a Y (the term being defined) in other circumstances as well. The 'if and only if' makes it a proper definition by restricting X's being called Y to *only* those cases in which X has property P.

More Complex Propositions

Since the result of applying any of the five truth-functional connectives is itself a proposition, the process may be reiterated any number of times to form more complex expressions. For example, the conjunction of p and q may be joined by disjunction to the negation of r to give $(p \wedge q) \vee (\sim r)$. The parentheses are necessary here to avoid ambiguity. If we wrote $p \wedge q \vee \sim r$, this might be interpreted either as $(p \wedge q) \vee (\sim r)$ or as the conjunction of p with the disjunction of q and the negation of r; i.e., $p \wedge (q \vee (\sim r))$. In very long expressions, the nests of parentheses become confusing so various conventions have been adopted for omitting some of them. We shall use only one of these conventions: negation extends over the *shortest* following expression to which it can possibly apply. Thus, $\sim r \vee (p \wedge q)$ by this convention represents $(\sim r) \vee (p \wedge q)$, rather than $\sim(r \vee (p \wedge q))$. The latter expression must, of course, be written with both pairs of parentheses.

Since all the logical connectives are truth-functional, we can determine the truth value of an arbitrarily complex expression by beginning with the truth values of its *elementary* propositions (those that contain no connectives)

p	q	r
t	t	t
t	t	f
t	f	t
t	f	f
f	t	t
f	t	f
f	f	t
f	f	f

Figure 2-6

First step in constructing the truth table for $\sim(p \to (q \vee r))$

and proceeding stepwise to compute the truth values of successively larger parts of the expression. For example, suppose that we wish to determine the truth value of $\sim(r \vee (p \wedge q))$, given that p is true, q is false, and r is false. First, from the fact that p is true and q is false we ascertain that $p \wedge q$ is false. From this and the fact that r is false we conclude that $r \vee (p \wedge q)$ is also false. Finally, since $r \vee (p \wedge q)$ is false, $\sim(r \vee (p \wedge q))$ is true.

By repeating this procedure, we can go on to calculate the truth value of an expression for every possible combination of truth values that its elementary propositions may have. An orderly and convenient way to display the results is in a truth table. As an example, let us construct the truth table for $\sim(p \to (q \vee r))$. Since the expression contains three elementary propositions, each of which may be true or false, there are $2 \times 2 \times 2 = 8$ possible cases to be considered. We begin as in Fig. 2-6. Next we determine for each row the truth value of $q \vee r$. These are entered in a column to the right of the double vertical line as in Fig. 2-7. The next step is to calculate the truth

p	q	r	$q \vee r$
t	t	t	t
t	t	f	t
t	f	t	t
t	f	f	f
f	t	t	t
f	t	f	t
f	f	t	t
f	f	f	f

Figure 2-7

Truth table for $\sim(p \to (q \vee r))$ after entering truth values for $q \vee r$

p	q	r	$q \vee r$	$p \rightarrow (q \vee r)$	$\sim(p \rightarrow (q \vee r))$
t	t	t	t	t	f
t	t	f	t	t	f
t	f	t	t	t	f
t	f	f	f	f	t
f	t	t	t	t	f
f	t	f	t	t	f
f	f	t	t	t	f
f	f	f	f	t	f

Figure 2-8

Completed truth table for $\sim(p \rightarrow (q \vee r))$ showing intermediate steps

$\sim(p$	$\rightarrow$	$(q$	$\vee$	$r))$
		t	t	t
		t	t	f
		f	t	t
		f	f	f
		t	t	t
		t	t	f
		f	t	t
		f	f	f

(a)

$\sim(p$	$\rightarrow$	$(q$	$\vee$	$r))$
		t	**t**	t
		t	**t**	f
		f	**t**	t
		f	**f**	f
		t	**t**	t
		t	**t**	f
		f	**t**	t
		f	**f**	f

(b)

$\sim(p$	$\rightarrow$	$(q$	$\vee$	$r))$
t	**t**	t	t	t
t	**t**	t	t	f
t	**t**	f	t	t
t	**f**	f	f	f
f	**t**	t	t	t
f	**t**	t	t	f
f	**t**	f	t	t
f	**t**	f	f	f

(c)

$\sim$	$(p$	$\rightarrow$	$(q$	$\vee$	$r))$
f	t	t	t	t	t
f	t	t	t	t	f
f	t	t	f	t	t
t	t	f	f	f	f
f	f	t	t	t	t
f	f	t	t	t	f
f	f	t	f	t	t
f	f	t	f	f	f

(d)

Figure 2-9

Steps in constructing the truth table for $\sim(p \rightarrow (q \vee r))$ by the shorter method

values for $p \rightarrow (q \vee r)$ from the first and fourth columns and enter them in a fifth column. Finally, from the fifth column we get the truth values for $\sim(p \rightarrow (q \vee r))$. The completed truth table is shown in Fig. 2-8. It indicates that $\sim(p \rightarrow (q \vee r))$ is false in all cases except when p is true and q and r are false.

There is a technique for writing truth tables in more compact form, although the probability of making a clerical error is somewhat greater. The procedure is much the same as that just described except that the truth values of the elementary propositions are entered directly under the corresponding symbols in the whole formula [Fig. 2-9(a)], and the truth values for the intermediate expressions are entered under the main connective of that expression [Fig. 2-9(b), (c), and (d)]. To make the figures clearer, we have enclosed in rectangles the columns just calculated at each point. The truth values for the whole expression appear in Fig. 2-9(d) in the leftmost column.

In this procedure, if an elementary proposition occurs in an expression more than once, the same column of truth values is entered under each occurrence. For example, in constructing the truth table for $p \vee \sim(p \rightarrow q)$ we would begin as in Fig. 2-10. Note that the first two columns are identical.

$$p \vee \sim(p \rightarrow q)$$

t	t	t
t	t	f
f	f	t
f	f	f

Figure 2-10

Initial step in the construction of the truth table for $p \vee \sim(p \rightarrow q)$

This must be so since each row of a truth table represents one possible assignment of truth values to the elementary propositions, and in each case a particular proposition is either true or false, but not both.

Tautologies and Contradictions

Certain logical expressions are of particular interest because they are always true whatever the truth values of their elementary propositions. Such expressions are called *tautologies*. A simple example, $p \vee \sim p$, is shown in the truth table in Fig. 2-11.

p	$\sim p$	$p \vee \sim p$
t	f	t
f	t	t

Figure 2-11

Truth table for the tautology $p \vee \sim p$

Substituting a specific statement for p yields sentences such as

(2-27)   It is raining or it is not raining.

(2-28)   Either Columbus discovered America or he didn't.

These are true regardless of the truth values of the propositions 'It is raining' and 'Columbus discovered America.' Tautologies are said to be *analytically* or *logically true* since their truth is a consequence only of the definitions of the logical connectives. They are distinguished from empirically true propositions, e.g., Chicago is in Illinois, whose truth depends on the state of things in the real world. This last proposition could become false if, for example, the boundaries of Illinois were redrawn, but no modification of the physical world could possibly falsify (2-27) or (2-28).

An analytically or logically false proposition is called a *contradiction*. (Purists insist on the term *self-contradiction*.) A simple example is $p \wedge \sim p$ as shown in the truth table in Fig. 2-12.

Tautologies and contradictions are related in a straightforward way. The negation of a tautology is a contradiction, because if a proposition is always true, its negation is always false. Similarly, the negation of a contradiction is a tautology. Referring to the examples of Fig. 2-11 and 2-12, we see that $\sim(p \vee \sim p)$ is a contradiction and $\sim(p \wedge \sim p)$ is a tautology. Propositions which are neither tautologies nor contradictions, i.e., which are sometimes

p	$\sim p$	$p \wedge \sim p$
t	f	f
f	t	f

Figure 2-12

Truth table for the contradiction $p \wedge \sim p$

true and sometimes false, are called *contingent propositions* or *contingencies*. Figure 2-8 shows, for example, that $\sim(p \to (q \lor r))$ is contingent.

An important property of tautologies and contradictions is that any propositions whatever may be substituted for the elementary propositions without affecting the truth value of the original expression. For example, if in the tautology $p \lor \sim p$ we replace p by $q \to r$, the resulting expression $(q \to r) \lor \sim(q \to r)$ is still a tautology, as shown in Fig. 2-13. The substitution of any proposition Q for p in $p \lor \sim p$ produces a proposition of the form

q	r	$q \to r$	$\sim(q \to r)$	$(q \to r) \lor \sim(q \to r)$
t	t	t	f	t
t	f	f	t	t
f	t	t	f	t
f	f	t	f	t

Figure 2-13

Truth table showing that $(q \to r) \lor \sim(q \to r)$ is a tautology

$Q \lor \sim Q$. Whatever the truth value of Q in any particular line, the truth value of $\sim Q$ is the opposite; thus, one must be true and the other false. The disjunction of Q and $\sim Q$ is therefore true on every line of the truth table. Since Q may be any proposition at all, elementary or complex, we see that tautologous expressions are true by virtue of their *logical form*, i.e., the arrangement of propositions and connectives, and not because of the particular propositions they are made of. The same considerations apply, *mutatis mutandis*, to contradictions.

Problem: If a tautology is substituted for p in $p \land \sim p$, is the resulting expression a contradiction?

Logical Equivalence

Two propositions are said to be logically equivalent if and only if they have the same truth value for every uniform assignment of truth values to their elementary propositions. By 'uniform' we mean that no elementary proposition is assigned different truth values in the two expressions. For example, $\sim(p \lor q)$ and $\sim p \land \sim q$ are logically equivalent since the fourth and seventh

Symbolic Logic: The Propositional Calculus

p	q	$p \vee q$	$\sim(p \vee q)$	$\sim p$	$\sim q$	$\sim p \wedge \sim q$
t	t	t	f	f	f	f
t	f	t	f	f	t	f
f	t	t	f	t	f	f
f	f	f	t	t	t	t

Figure 2-14

Composite truth table showing the logical equivalence of $\sim(p \vee q)$ and $\sim p \wedge \sim q$

columns are identical in the composite truth table of Fig. 2-14. Some very simple examples of logically equivalent propositions are p, $p \wedge p$, $p \vee p$, and $\sim\sim p$, as shown in Fig. 2-15. To denote logical equivalence of two propositions we use the symbol $\equiv$; thus, $\sim(p \vee q) \equiv \sim p \wedge \sim q$; $p \equiv \sim\sim p$. Note carefully that $\equiv$ is a different sort of symbol from $\wedge$, $\vee$, $\rightarrow$, etc. $P \equiv Q$ is a statement about propositions P and Q, and to determine whether it is correct we must examine the entire truth tables of P and Q. Thus, given the fact that P and Q are both true, we know that $P \wedge Q$ is true, but we cannot tell from this fact alone whether $P \equiv Q$.

Expressions that are made up of different elementary propositions are not in general logically equivalent, although in special circumstances they may be. For example, $p \wedge q$ and $p \wedge r$ are not logically equivalent because there is a uniform assignment of truth values to the elementary propositions (say, p, true; q, false; and r, true) that makes one true and the other false. $p \wedge (q \vee \sim q)$ and $p \wedge (r \vee \sim r)$ are logically equivalent, however, since, as Fig. 2-16 shows, they have the same truth value for every combination of truth values for p, q, and r. It is easy to see that this comes about because $q \vee \sim q$ and $r \vee \sim r$ are both tautologies, and thus they contribute to the truth values of $p \wedge (q \vee \sim q)$ and $p \wedge (r \vee \sim r)$ in exactly the same way, regardless of the truth values of q and r. We can also say that any two tautologies or any two contradictions are logically equivalent, even though they

p	$p \wedge p$	$p \vee p$	$\sim p$	$\sim\sim p$
t	t	t	f	t
f	f	f	t	f

Figure 2-15

Composite truth table showing the logical equivalence of
p, $p \wedge p$, $p \vee p$, and $\sim\sim p$

p	q	r	$q \vee \sim q$	$p \wedge (q \vee \sim q)$	$r \vee \sim r$	$p \wedge (r \vee \sim r)$
t	t	t	t	t	t	t
t	t	f	t	t	t	t
t	f	t	t	t	t	t
t	f	f	t	t	t	t
f	t	t	t	f	t	f
f	t	f	t	f	t	f
f	f	t	t	f	t	f
f	f	f	t	f	t	f

Figure 2-16

Composite truth table showing the logical equivalence of
$p \wedge (q \vee \sim q)$ and $p \wedge (r \vee \sim r)$

might not contain the same elementary propositions, since their truth values are independent of the elementary propositions they contain; thus, $q \vee \sim q \equiv r \vee \sim r$; $p \wedge \sim p \equiv \sim(q \vee \sim q)$.

Logically equivalent formulas are important in logic because they may freely replace one another in any expression without altering its truth value. Because logically equivalent expressions, by definition, always have the same truth value for any given assignment of the truth values of the component elementary propositions, substitution of one logically equivalent expression for another could not possibly alter the truth value of any larger expression in which it might be embedded. For example, in the expression $q \vee p$, replacement of p by the logically equivalent $p \wedge p$ yields an expression, $q \vee (p \wedge p)$, whose truth value is the same as $q \vee p$. Thus, substitution of logical equivalents always preserves truth value, and so the expression resulting from the substitution is logically equivalent to the original expression. In our example, because $p \equiv p \wedge p$, it follows that $q \vee p \equiv q \vee (p \wedge p)$.

It is convenient to have at hand a small number of logical equivalences from which all others can be derived. Table 2-1 gives those most frequently used, together with their traditional names. This list is redundant in that some of the equivalences can be derived from others, but it is a convenient set to work with. Because they are referred to repeatedly in the remainder of the book, it is worthwhile to memorize them. (This task will be simplified by noting that most of the laws consist of pairs of similar-looking expressions; one with disjunction, the other with conjunction.)

The truth of the Idempotent Laws has already been established by the truth table in Fig. 2-15. The Associative Laws state that whenever we combine three propositions by two successive conjunctions or disjunctions, it makes no difference which two we combine first. This can be readily verified

1. *Idempotent Laws*
(a) $p \vee p \equiv p$ (b) $p \wedge p \equiv p$

2. *Associative Laws*
(a) $(p \vee q) \vee r \equiv p \vee (q \vee r)$ (b) $(p \wedge q) \wedge r \equiv p \wedge (q \wedge r)$

3. *Commutative Laws*
(a) $p \vee q \equiv q \vee p$ (b) $p \wedge q \equiv q \wedge p$

4. *Distributive Laws*
(a) $p \vee (q \wedge r) \equiv (p \vee q) \wedge (p \vee r)$ (b) $p \wedge (q \vee r) \equiv (p \wedge q) \vee (p \wedge r)$

5. *Identity Laws*
(a) $p \vee F \equiv p$ (c) $p \wedge F \equiv F$
(b) $p \vee T \equiv T$ (d) $p \wedge T \equiv p$

6. *Complement Laws*
(a) $p \vee \sim p \equiv T$ (c) $p \wedge \sim p \equiv F$
(b) $\sim \sim p \equiv p$

7. *DeMorgan's Laws*
(a) $\sim(p \vee q) \equiv \sim p \wedge \sim q$ (b) $\sim(p \wedge q) \equiv \sim p \vee \sim q$

8. *Conditional Laws*
(a) $p \rightarrow q \equiv \sim p \vee q$ (c) $p \rightarrow q \equiv \sim(p \wedge \sim q)$
(b) $p \rightarrow q \equiv \sim q \rightarrow \sim p$

9. *Biconditional Laws*
(a) $p \leftrightarrow q \equiv (p \rightarrow q) \wedge (q \rightarrow p)$ (b) $p \leftrightarrow q \equiv (\sim p \wedge \sim q) \vee (p \wedge q)$

Table 2-1

Some fundamental logical equivalences
(T indicates a tautology; F, a contradiction)

p	q	r	$q \wedge r$	$p \vee (q \wedge r)$	$p \vee q$	$p \vee r$	$(p \vee q) \wedge (p \vee r)$
t	t	t	t	t	t	t	t
t	t	f	f	t	t	t	t
t	f	t	f	t	t	t	t
t	f	f	f	t	t	t	t
f	t	t	t	t	t	t	t
f	t	f	f	f	t	f	f
f	f	t	f	f	f	t	f
f	f	f	f	f	f	f	f

Figure 2-17

Truth table showing the logical equivalence of $p \vee (q \wedge r)$ and $(p \vee q) \wedge (p \vee r)$

by truth tables. Here is another opportunity to omit parentheses: since $(p \wedge q) \wedge r$ and $p \wedge (q \wedge r)$ are logically equivalent, it does no harm to write either of them as $p \wedge q \wedge r$.

The Commutative Laws indicate that the order of the propositions in a conjunction or a disjunction is immaterial. This, too, can be checked by constructing truth tables or, more quickly, by returning to the definitions of conjunction and disjunction and interchanging p and q. One of the Distributive Laws is verified in the truth table in Fig. 2-17; the other is similar. The form of these laws is like one of the laws of arithmetic involving multiplication and addition:

(2-29) $a \times (b + c) = (a \times b) + (a \times c)$

Since (2-29) is true for any numbers a, b, and c, multiplication is said to *distribute over* addition. Note that addition does not distribute over multiplication, however, because it is not always true that $a + (b \times c) = (a + b) \times (a + c)$. In symbolic logic, disjunction distributes over conjunction, and conjunction also distributes over disjunction.

The Identity Laws are easily verified by inspection. For example, if p is true, then $p \vee F$ is true, and if p is false, then $p \vee F$ is false; thus, $p \equiv p \vee F$. The Complement Laws have been validated in the truth tables of Fig. 2-11, 2-12, and 2-15. One of DeMorgan's Laws was used as an illustration of logical equivalence in Fig. 2-14; the other can be verified similarly by a truth table. DeMorgan's Laws have their counterparts in ordinary language. The negation of 'John is here, and Harry is here' is 'John isn't here, or Harry isn't here' (in the inclusive sense of 'or'). Similarly, the negation of 'John is here, or Harry is here' is 'John isn't here and Harry isn't here,' or more naturally, 'Neither John nor Harry is here.'

Verification of the Conditional and Biconditional Laws is left as an exercise. Line 8(b) in Table 2-1 contains the very useful equivalence of a conditional $p \rightarrow q$ and its *contrapositive* form $\sim q \rightarrow \sim p$. Compare the statements 'If it is raining, then the streets are wet' and 'If the streets aren't wet, then it isn't raining.'

The equivalences of Table 2-1 hold not only for elementary propositions but also when complex propositions are substituted for p, q, r, etc. To show this, we first establish the following theorem, which relates logical equivalences and tautologies.

THEOREM 2-1: For any propositions P and Q (elementary or complex), P and Q are logically equivalent if and only if $P \leftrightarrow Q$ is a tautology.

Proof: If P and Q are logically equivalent, they have the same truth values on corresponding lines of their truth tables Therefore, in every line of the truth table for $P \leftrightarrow Q$, either P and Q are both true or both false, and thus $P \leftrightarrow Q$ is always true. Conversely, if $P \leftrightarrow Q$ is a tautology, every assignment of truth values to the elementary propositions makes P and Q both true or both false but never makes one true and the other false. Thus, P and Q always have the same truth value and are logically equivalent.

As an example, take the logical equivalence given as 8(a) of Table 2-1: $p \to q \equiv \sim p \vee q$. By the theorem, $(p \to q) \leftrightarrow (\sim p \vee q)$ is a tautology, and this is verified in the following truth table:

p	q	$p \to q$	$\sim p$	$\sim p \vee q$	$(p \to q) \leftrightarrow (\sim p \vee q)$
t	t	t	f	t	t
t	f	f	f	f	t
f	t	t	t	t	t
f	f	t	t	t	t

Figure 2-18

Truth table showing that $(p \to q) \leftrightarrow (\sim p \vee q)$ is a tautology

It is easy to see that the identity of the third and fifth columns makes the biconditional a tautology and conversely that the tautologousness of the biconditional implies that $(p \to q)$ and $(\sim p \vee q)$ have the same truth value on every line. We now recall our previous remark that a tautology remains a tautology when its elementary propositions are replaced by any propositions whatever. Thus, if $P \leftrightarrow Q$ is a tautology, then $P' \leftrightarrow Q'$ is a tautology, where P' and Q' are obtained from P and Q, respectively, by uniform substitution of some or all of their elementary propositions. By Theorem 2-1, if $P' \leftrightarrow Q'$ is a tautology, then P' and Q' are logically equivalent, and thus logical equivalence is preserved by uniform substitution of elementary propositions. To return to the example of Fig. 2-18, if we substitute $(r \vee s)$ for p and $\sim s$ for q, $((r \vee s) \to \sim s) \leftrightarrow (\sim(r \vee s) \vee \sim s)$ is still tautologous and thus $(r \vee s) \to \sim s$ and $\sim(r \vee s) \vee \sim s$ are logically equivalent.

Problem: Verify that $\sim p \to (r \vee q) \equiv \sim(\sim p \wedge \sim(r \vee q))$ by showing that it can be obtained by uniform substitution from one of the equivalences in Table 2-1.

We now wish to show how the fundamental logical equivalences can be used to simplify complex expressions and to derive other logical equivalences. A few examples should serve to illustrate the technique. In the following derivations, each line is obtained from the one just before it by replacing all

Logical Equivalence

or part of the expression by another that is logically equivalent. The law that justifies each step is noted to the right.

Example 2-1: Simplify $\sim p \vee (p \wedge q)$.

1. $\sim p \vee (p \wedge q)$
2. $(\sim p \vee p) \wedge (\sim p \vee q)$ Distr.
3. $(p \vee \sim p) \wedge (\sim p \vee q)$ Comm.
4. $T \wedge (\sim p \vee q)$ Compl.
5. $(\sim p \vee q) \wedge T$ Comm.
6. $\sim p \vee q$ Ident.

Because all the lines are logically equivalent, we can conclude that $\sim p \vee (p \wedge q) \equiv \sim p \vee q$. If we wished, we could add this logical equivalence to our inventory in Table 2-1 and use it in other derivations.

Example 2-2: Show that $p \rightarrow (q \rightarrow p)$ is a tautology without using truth tables.

1. $p \rightarrow (q \rightarrow p)$
2. $p \rightarrow (\sim q \vee p)$ Cond.
3. $\sim p \vee (\sim q \vee p)$ Cond.
4. $\sim p \vee (p \vee \sim q)$ Comm.
5. $(\sim p \vee p) \vee \sim q$ Assoc.
6. $T \vee \sim q$ Compl.
7. $\sim q \vee T$ Comm.
8. T Ident.

Example 2-3: Derive $p \rightarrow q \equiv \sim q \rightarrow \sim p$ from other logical equivalences in Table 2-1.

1. $p \rightarrow q$
2. $\sim p \vee q$ Cond.
3. $q \vee \sim p$ Comm.
4. $\sim\sim q \vee \sim p$ Compl.
5. $\sim q \rightarrow \sim p$ Cond.

Example 2-4: Show that $(p \lor q) \land \sim(p \land q) \equiv \sim(p \leftrightarrow q)$.

1. $(p \lor q) \land \sim(p \land q)$
2. $(\sim\sim p \lor q) \land \sim(p \land q)$ Compl.
3. $(\sim\sim p \lor \sim\sim q) \land \sim(p \land q)$ Compl.
4. $\sim(\sim p \land \sim q) \land \sim(p \land q)$ DeM.
5. $\sim((\sim p \land \sim q) \lor (p \land q))$ DeM.
6. $\sim(p \leftrightarrow q)$ Bicond.

Arguments

Thus far we have shown how propositions are combined by truth-functional connectives, how truth tables can be used for calculating the truth value of any complex proposition from the truth values of its component elementary propositions, and how the fundamental logical equivalences allow us to reformulate expressions without altering their truth value. We are now ready to take up the problem of assessing the validity of arguments.

An *argument* consists of a number of propositions called *premises*, which are assumed, for the purpose of the argument, to be true, and another proposition, called the *conclusion*, whose truth is alleged to follow necessarily from the truth of the premises. An argument, as we have used the term, contains real propositions with semantic content; for example, (2-1) and (2-2). The endless variety of propositions and number of ways of combining them into arguments is more easily handled if the criterion of validity is stated not for arguments directly but for *argument forms* or *argument schemata*, which contain variable symbols such as p, q, r, etc., rather than specific propositions. When actual propositions are put in place of the symbols in an argument form (with the usual proviso that the same proposition must replace every occurrence of a particular symbol), we have a *substitution instance* of that argument form. For example, (2-30) is an argument form (the symbol $\therefore$ stands for 'therefore' and marks the conclusion), and (2-31) is a substitution instance of it.

(2-30)
$$\begin{array}{l} p \rightarrow q \\ \underline{p} \\ \therefore q \end{array}$$

(2-31) If Fred lives in Chicago, Fred lives in Illinois.
Fred lives in Chicago.
$\therefore$ Fred lives in Illinois.

We now state the definition of a valid argument form.

DEFINITION: An argument form is *valid* iff there is no uniform assignment of truth values to its elementary propositions that makes all the premises true and the conclusion false; if there is such an assignment, the argument form is *invalid*.

Thus, to check whether an argument form is valid or invalid we can construct a composite truth table for all the premises and the conclusion and check whether there is any line in which all the premises are true while the conclusion is false. If so, the argument form is invalid; otherwise, it is valid. This technique is illustrated for the argument form in (2-30) in the truth table of Fig. 2-19. We note that only in the first line both premises, p and

p	q	$p \rightarrow q$
t	t	t
t	f	f
f	t	t
f	f	t

Figure 2-19

Truth table for checking the validity of the argument form in (2-30)

$p \rightarrow q$, are true, and there the conclusion, q, is true also. Since Fig. 2-19 contains all possible uniform assignments of truth values to these propositions, we see that it is impossible for the premises to be true while the conclusion is false; thus, (2-30) is a valid argument form.

An example of an invalid argument form and a substitution instance of it are given in (2-32) and (2-33).

(2-32)
$$p \rightarrow q$$
$$q$$
$$\therefore p$$

(2-33)
If Witherspoon is a socialist, then he favors state control of the railroads.
Witherspoon favors state control of the railroads.
$\therefore$ Witherspoon is a socialist.

The invalidity of (2-32) is shown by the third line of Fig. 2-19, where $p \rightarrow q$ and q are both true while p is false.

The criterion for validity can be framed in a different way. If $P, Q, R, \ldots, Z$ are the premises of an argument form and A is the conclusion ($P, Q, R, \ldots, Z, A$ may be elementary or complex), the argument form is

36   Symbolic Logic: The Propositional Calculus

valid if and only if the expression $(P \land Q \land R \land \cdots \land Z) \to A$ is a tautology. This is equivalent to the preceding definition since if $(P \land Q \land R \land \cdots \land Z) \to A$ is tautologous, there is no uniform assignment of truth values to the elementary propositions that will make the antecedent (i.e., the conjunction of all the premises) true and the consequent (i.e., the conclusion) false. The composite truth table in Fig. 2-20 shows that $((p \to q) \land p) \to q$ is tautologous and therefore (2-30) is valid, while $((p \to q) \land q) \to p$ is not tautologous and thus (2-32) is invalid.

p	q	$p \to q$	$(p \to q) \land p$	$((p \to q) \land p) \to q$	$(p \to q) \land q$	$((p \to q) \land q) \to p$
t	t	t	t	t	t	t
t	f	f	f	t	f	t
f	t	t	f	t	t	f
f	f	t	f	t	f	t

Figure 2-20

Truth table relating the argument forms (2-30) and (2-32) to tautologies

A tautologous conditional is denoted by the symbol $\Rightarrow$, which is read 'logically implies.' Thus, since we have shown $((p \to q) \land p) \to q$ to be tautologous, we may state this fact by writing $((p \to q) \land p) \Rightarrow q$. In a valid argument form, then, the conjunction of the premises logically implies the conclusion, and by this we mean that if all the premises are true (and thus the conjunction of the premises is true), then the conclusion cannot be false.

Relating the validity of argument forms to tautologies allows us to use the previously established facts about substitution in tautologies to infer that any uniform substitution for the elementary propositions in a valid argument form produces an argument form that is also valid. Since all tautologies remain tautologies under uniform substitution, in particular so will tautologous conditionals, i.e., valid argument forms. For example, having determined that (2-30) is valid, we know that (2-34) is also valid since it is obtained from (2-30) by substituting $\sim(r \lor s)$ for p and $(t \to \sim u)$ for q.

$$\sim(r \lor s) \to (t \to \sim u)$$

(2-34) $\underline{\sim(r \lor s)\qquad\qquad\qquad}$

$\therefore t \to \sim u$

Applying these principles of argument forms to arguments containing real propositions is now relatively straightforward. An argument is said to be valid if and only if it is a substitution instance of a valid argument form. Since the passage from argument forms to arguments involves a uniform substitution (of real propositions for variables), we can be confident that a substitution instance of a valid argument form cannot be invalid. Thus, (2-31), being a substitution instance of a valid argument form, is a valid argument. One should note carefully, however, that the problem of analyzing an argument stated in natural language may still present serious difficulties. As we have said, making explicit the propositions expressed by ordinary language may not be a simple task. Furthermore, arguments often occur in ordinary discourse with one or more premises omitted, particularly if these are considered common knowledge or if they can be easily supplied from the context. Such an argument is called an *enthymeme*, and before its validity can be assessed the missing premise or premises must be supplied. In the following example the reader is expected to furnish the additional premise 'Socrates is a man.'

(2-35)
If Socrates is a man, then he is mortal.
∴ Socrates is mortal.

Validity and Truth

A valid argument cannot have true premises and a false conclusion. If one or more of the premises is false, however, nothing can be inferred *from the argument* about the truth value of the conclusion. For example, (2-36) and (2-37) are both substitution instances of the valid argument form (2-30) and both contain premises that happen to be false; yet the conclusion of (2-36) is true and that of (2-37) is false.

(2-36)
If Socrates is a boy scout, then Socrates is mortal.
Socrates is a boy scout.
∴ Socrates is mortal.

(2-37)
If Socrates is a man, then Socrates is a parachutist.
Socrates is a man.
∴ Socrates is a parachutist.

Thus, if an argument is valid, the mode of reasoning it represents is correct in that one will never be led from truth to falsity in going from premises to conclusion, but no guarantee is made of the actual truth of the premises. Similarly, the conclusion of an invalid argument is not necessarily false. The invalidity of an argument means only that the conclusion does not necessarily follow from the premises; the actual truth or falsity of the conclusion is an independent matter.

In this connection, one should also note the difference between logical equivalence and logical implication. Replacement of a proposition by another logically equivalent to it is a process that preserves *truth value;* both propositions are true, or both are false. Drawing a conclusion by logical implication, on the other hand, is an operation that *preserves truth but does not necessarily preserve falsity.* A true antecedent logically implies a true consequent, but a false antecedent logically implies a consequent that may be either true or false. Logical equivalence and logical implication are connected by the following relation:

(2-38) For any two propositions P and Q,
$P \equiv Q$ if and only if $(P \Rightarrow Q \land Q \Rightarrow P)$.

To prove this, we recall that $P \equiv Q$ if and only if $P \leftrightarrow Q$ is a tautology. By the Biconditional Laws (Table 2-1) $P \leftrightarrow Q$ is logically equivalent to $(P \rightarrow Q) \land (Q \rightarrow P)$, and therefore the latter is a tautology if and only if $P \leftrightarrow Q$ is a tautology. $(P \rightarrow Q) \land (Q \rightarrow P)$ is a tautology if and only if both halves of the conjunction are also tautologies. Therefore, P and Q are logically equivalent if and only if P logically implies Q and Q logically implies P.

Rules of Inference

Although the validity of any argument form may be determined by constructing a truth table, it is often inconvenient to do so, particularly if it contains a large number of elementary propositions. The argument form given in (2-39), which contains five elementary propositions, would require a truth table of 2^5 or 32 lines.

(2-39)
$p \rightarrow q$
$p \lor s$
$q \rightarrow r$
$s \rightarrow t$
$\sim r$
$\therefore t$

An alternative is to analyze the argument form into a sequence of simpler argument forms whose validity has already been established. These simple argument forms are known as *rules of inference.* The seven listed in Table 2-2 suffice for most of the arguments we shall encounter, and like the logical equivalences in Table 2-1 they should be memorized. As an exercise the reader may wish to check the validity of each one by a truth table.

We shall illustrate the procedure using the argument form in (2-39). From the premises $q \rightarrow r$ and $\sim r$, we derive $\sim q$, this argument being an instance of *Modus Tollens.* Because all the premises are assumed to be true,

~q, having been derived from two of them by a valid argument, can also be assumed to be true, and it can be added to the stock of premises for use in further steps. When demonstrating validity in this way, it is customary to number each line and to justify a line other than the premises by a reference to the numbers of the lines and the rule of inference used in deriving it. For

Argument Form	Example
	Modus Ponens (M.P.)
$p \to q$	If Fred lives in Chicago, Fred lives in Illinois.
p	Fred lives in Chicago.
∴ q	∴ Fred lives in Illinois.
	Modus Tollens (M.T.)
$p \to q$	If Fred lives in Chicago, Fred lives in Illinois.
~q	Fred doesn't live in Illinois.
∴ ~p	∴ Fred doesn't live in Chicago.
	Hypothetical Syllogism (H.S.)
$p \to q$	If Fred lives in Chicago, Fred lives in Illinois.
$q \to r$	If Fred lives in Illinois, Fred lives in the United States.
∴ $p \to r$	∴ If Fred lives in Chicago, Fred lives in the United States.
	Disjunctive Syllogism (D.S.)
$p \vee q$	Fred lives in Chicago, or Fred lives in New York.
~p	Fred doesn't live in Chicago.
∴ q	∴ Fred lives in New York.
	Simplification (Simp.)
$p \wedge q$	Roses are red, and violets are blue.
∴ p	∴ Roses are red.
	Conjunction (Conj.)
p	Roses are red.
q	Violets are blue.
∴ $p \wedge q$	∴ Roses are red, and violets are blue.
	Addition (Add.)
p	Roses are red.
∴ $p \vee q$	∴ Roses are red, or cigarettes are a health hazard.

Table 2-2
Rules of inference

example, after the derivation of $\sim q$, (2-39) would appear as follows:

(2-40)
1. $p \to q$
2. $p \lor s$
3. $q \to r$
4. $s \to t$
5. $\sim r$
6. $\sim q$ 3, 5M.T.

The absence of justification for lines 1–5 indicates that they are premises.

As the next step, we use lines 1 and 6 to derive $\sim p$, again by *Modus Tollens*, and add it as line 7. From $\sim p$ and $p \lor s$, s follows by Disjunctive Syllogism, and finally from s and $s \to t$ we derive t by *Modus Ponens*. The completed derivation appears as in (2-41):

(2-41)
1. $p \to q$
2. $p \lor s$
3. $q \to r$
4. $s \to t$
5. $\sim r$
6. $\sim q$ 3, 5M.T.
7. $\sim p$ 1, 6M.T.
8. s 2, 7D.S.
9. t 4, 8M.P.

This shows that (2-39) is a valid argument form; if the premises are true, then in (2-41) the conclusion, t, which was derived by a sequence of valid inferences, must be true as well. A derivation such as (2-41) is said to be a *proof* of t from the premises in lines 1–5. Since the premises also logically imply the propositions in lines 6, 7, and 8, these have also been proved, and in fact we could have stopped after any one of these lines and called the derivation a proof of $\sim q$, $\sim p$, or s; it all depends on where we focus our attention. Note, however, that given some premises and an alleged conclusion, we are not assured that there is some derivation leading from the premises to that conclusion (there won't be when the argument form is invalid), and even when there is one, we cannot be sure that we shall be able to find it. On the other hand, given an alleged proof such as (2-41), it is a simple matter to check whether it is in fact a proof by verifying the derivation of each line. Thus, as promised, we have found in symbolic logic a method of verifying proofs but not of discovering them.

Sometimes in a proof it is necessary to replace an expression by one logically equivalent in order to apply a rule of inference. Such a step is legitimate since logically equivalent expressions have the same truth value, and thus the validity of the argument will not be affected. Consider, for example, the following argument form:

(2-42)
$$p \to (q \lor r)$$
$$\sim r$$
$$\therefore p \to q$$

None of the rules of inference in Table 2-2 applies directly to (2-42), but by converting the first premise to $\sim p \lor (q \lor r)$ by the Conditional Laws, then to $(\sim p \lor q) \lor r$ by the Associative Laws, and then to $r \lor (\sim p \lor q)$ by the Commutative Laws we shall be able to apply Disjunctive Syllogism to deduce $\sim p \lor q$. This is logically equivalent to the conclusion by the Conditional Laws. Written in full, the proof would appear as follows:

(2-43)

1. $p \to (q \lor r)$
2. $\sim r$
3. $\sim p \lor (q \lor r)$ 1, Cond.
4. $(\sim p \lor q) \lor r$ 3, Assoc.
5. $r \lor (\sim p \lor q)$ 4, Comm.
6. $\sim p \lor q$ 2, 5 D.S.
7. $p \to q$ 6, Cond.

Conditional Proof

Certain arguments whose conclusions contain a conditional as the principal connective are more easily proved by the method of conditional proof. Suppose an argument has propositions $P, Q, R, \ldots, Z$ as premises and $A \to B$ as its conclusion. In a conditional proof we add the antecedent of the conditional, A, as a kind of temporary premise and then derive B as a conclusion. That is, instead of proving

$$P$$
$$Q$$
$$R$$
$$\vdots$$
$$Z$$
$$\overline{\therefore A \to B}$$

(2-44)

we prove

$$P$$
$$Q$$
$$R$$
$$\vdots$$
$$Z$$
$$A$$
$$\overline{\therefore B}$$

(2-45)

The argument form in (2-44) is valid if and only if $(P \wedge Q \wedge \cdots \wedge Z) \to (A \to B)$ is a tautology. The justification for conditional proof is that $(P \wedge Q \wedge \cdots \wedge Z) \to (A \to B)$ is logically equivalent to $((P \wedge Q \wedge \cdots \wedge Z) \wedge A) \to B$, as shown in (2-46).

(2-46)

1. $(P \wedge Q \wedge \cdots \wedge Z) \to (A \to B)$		
2. $\sim(P \wedge Q \wedge \cdots \wedge Z) \vee (A \to B)$		1, Cond.
3. $\sim(P \wedge Q \wedge \cdots \wedge Z) \vee (\sim A \vee B)$		2, Cond.
4. $(\sim(P \wedge Q \wedge \cdots \wedge Z) \vee \sim A) \vee B$		3, Assoc.
5. $\sim((P \wedge Q \wedge \cdots \wedge Z) \wedge A) \vee B$		4, DeM.
6. $((P \wedge Q \wedge \cdots \wedge Z) \wedge A) \to B$		5, Cond.

Thus, line 1 is a tautology if and only if line 6 is a tautology, and argument form (2-44) is valid if and only if (2-45) is valid.

As an example, we use the method of conditional proof on (2-42):

(2-47)
1. $p \rightarrow (q \vee r)$
2. $\sim r$
3. p C.P.
4. $q \vee r$ 1, 3 M.P.
5. $r \vee q$ 4, Comm.
6. q 2, 5 D.S.
7. $p \rightarrow q$

In line 3 we introduce p, the antecedent of the conclusion $p \rightarrow q$, as a temporary premise and indicate that this is the beginning of a conditional proof by C.P. We then derive q as a conclusion to the argument with the added premise p. In line 7 we return to the original argument form without p as a premise and state the conclusion $p \rightarrow q$. Lines 3–6 have been indented to indicate that they have a different status from the other lines of the proof. Lines 1 and 2, the original premises, are assumed to be true; however, lines 3–6 would be true only on the condition that p were true, and this we do not assume. With the premises given, we cannot conclude that q is true, but we can say that *if p* were true as well, then q would also be true; that is, $p \rightarrow q$. One must be careful not to use the lines that are derived from a temporary premise in subsequent derivations in the main argument after that temporary premise has been abandoned. The following "proof" is defective in just this way.

(2-48)
1. $(p \vee q) \rightarrow r$
2. $r \rightarrow s$
3. $\sim s \vee t$
4. p C.P.
5. $p \vee q$ 4, Add.
6. r 1, 5 M.P.
7. s 2, 6 M.P.
8. $p \rightarrow s$
9. t 3, 7 D.S. (erroneous)

At line 8, we return to the main argument, and p is no longer assumed. Therefore, line 7, whose truth is contingent on the truth of p, cannot be used to draw a valid inference at line 9.

Similar constraints hold when one conditional proof is embedded within another as in the following:

(2-49)
1. $p \to (q \land r)$
2. $q \to s$ C.P.
3. p C.P.
4. $q \land r$ 1, 3M.P.
5. q 4, Simp.
6. s 2, 5M.P.
7. $p \to s$
8. $(q \to s) \to (p \to s)$

The argument form has just one premise, $p \to (q \land r)$. The temporary premise $q \to s$ is added in line 2, and then subordinate to this assumption another premise is added in line 3. In deriving s in line 6 we can make use of everything that precedes, but when we conclude $p \to s$ in line 7, the temporary premise p is abandoned, and thus lines 3–6 can no longer be used. Lines 2 and 7 are now treated just as if no other conditional proof had intervened, and thus the conclusion, line 8, follows from the single premise in line 1. Clearly, indenting successive conditional proofs will help in keeping track of what propositions can be taken as true at any point in the derivation.

Indirect Proof

Derivations of the sort we have been considering, including conditional proofs, fall in the category of *direct* proofs: The conclusion is produced as the final line of the derivation by a series of valid deductions. In an *indirect* proof, or *reductio ad absurdum*, the negation of the desired conclusion is added to the premises and the resulting set of propositions is shown to lead to a contradiction. One can arrive at a contradiction by valid steps only if one or more of the premises is false. Since all the original premises are assumed to be true, the false premise must be the negation of the desired conclusion that was added. Therefore, the desired conclusion is true. As an example we take the argument form given in (2-50):

(2-50)
$p \lor q$
$q \to r$
$\sim r$
$\therefore p$

An indirect proof would proceed as follows:

(2-51)
1. $p \vee q$
2. $q \to r$
3. $\sim r$
4. $\sim p$ I.P. (Indirect Proof)
5. q 1, 4D.S.
6. r 2, 5M.P.
7. $r \wedge \sim r$ 3, 6Conj.
8. p

Line 7 is a contradiction, and therefore the premise introduced in line 4 is false if the other premises are true. Thus, p is true if lines 1–3 are true, and (2-50) is a valid argument form. As with conditional proof, it is helpful to indent the lines of an indirect proof to show that they represent intermediate calculations and do not follow from the original premises. Indirect proofs can have other indirect proofs and conditional proofs embedded in them, and likewise they can be embedded in conditional proofs. In all such cases, lines from a more deeply embedded section cannot be assumed true in a less deeply embedded section.

Indirect proofs are used very frequently in mathematics, where they are often much easier to construct than a direct proof. We have already encountered an instance of it in Chapter 1 in showing that the null set is a subset of every set. By assuming the negation of this statement, we were led to the conclusion that the null set has a member, which, taken with the definition of the null set, forms a contradiction. Thus, the assumption that the null set is not a subset of every set reduces to an absurdity and cannot be maintained.

EXERCISES

1. Symbolize each of the following statements using truth-functional connectives:

    (a) Fred has driven Fords for 20 years, but now he drives a Buick.
    (b) Clarence can be considered well educated only if he can read Chuvash.
    (c) Either this cat goes or I go!
    (d) Marsha won't go out with John unless he shaves off his beard and stops drinking.

(e) The stock market advances when public confidence in the economy is rising and only then.
(f) A necessary but perhaps not sufficient condition for negotiations to commence is for Barataria to cease all acts of aggression against Titipu.

2. Construct truth tables for each of the following expressions. Note whether any are logically equivalent.

(a) $p \vee \sim q$
(b) $\sim(\sim p \wedge q)$
(c) $(p \leftrightarrow q) \wedge p$
(d) $(p \rightarrow (q \vee \sim r)) \wedge (p \rightarrow (q \vee \sim r))$
(e) $((p \rightarrow q) \rightarrow p) \rightarrow q$

3. For each of the following, find an assignment of truth values to the elementary propositions that makes the whole expression false.

(a) $p \vee q$
(b) $(p \vee q) \rightarrow (p \wedge q)$
(c) $\sim(\sim q \vee p) \vee (p \rightarrow q)$
(d) $(((p \rightarrow q) \rightarrow r) \rightarrow s) \rightarrow (p \rightarrow q)$
(e) $((p \vee q) \wedge (r \wedge s)) \leftrightarrow (p \wedge q \wedge r \wedge s)$

4. Use the fundamental logical equivalences to simplify each of the following expressions.

(a) $\sim p \vee (p \wedge q)$
(b) $p \rightarrow (q \rightarrow p)$
(c) $(\sim p \wedge q) \vee \sim(p \vee q)$
(d) $\sim p \wedge ((p \wedge q) \vee (p \wedge r))$
(e) $(\sim p \wedge q) \leftrightarrow (p \vee q)$
(f) $((p \vee q) \wedge (r \vee \sim q)) \rightarrow (p \vee r)$

5. Does conjunction distribute over the conditional; i.e., is $(p \wedge q) \rightarrow (p \wedge r)$ logically equivalent to $p \wedge (q \rightarrow r)$?

6. Expressions in the propositional calculus may be written in "Polish parenthesis-free notation," which places the connective to the left of the propositions it connects rather than between them. In this notation the connectives are N (negation), A (alternation), K (conjunction), C

(conditional), and E (biconditional). The last four extend over the next two well-formed expressions to the right; negation extends over only one. The expressions in standard notation in the left column below would be written in Polish notation as shown in the right column.

Standard	Polish
$\sim p$	Np
$p \lor q$	Apq
$p \land q$	Kpq
$p \to q$	Cpq
$p \leftrightarrow q$	Epq
$(p \land q) \lor r$	$AKpqr$
$p \land (q \lor r)$	$KpAqr$

Observe that parentheses are unnecessary in Polish notation to distinguish between $(p \land q) \lor r$ and $p \land (q \lor r)$.

(a) Translate into Polish notation:

  (i) $((p \lor q) \land (q \lor r)) \land (p \lor s)$

  (ii) $(\sim p \land (\sim p \to q)) \to q$

  (iii) $(p \lor q) \to ((r \leftrightarrow s) \land p)$

(b) Translate into standard notation:

  (i) $ApCKNpNqKpEqr$

  (ii) $KANKAKEEpqrspqrs$

  (iii) $NCAKEpqrst$

(c) Express DeMorgan's Laws in Polish notation.

7. Determine by a truth table whether each of the following argument forms is valid:

(a) $p \to q$
   $\sim q$
   $\therefore \sim p$

(b) $p \to q$
   $\sim p$
   $\therefore \sim q$

(c) $(p \to q) \land (r \to q)$
   $p \lor r$
   $\therefore q$

8. The binary truth-functional connective *alternative denial* is defined as follows: For any propositions p and q, the alternative denial of p and q, denoted $p \mid q$, is false when p and q are both true; otherwise, it is true.

   (a) Construct the truth table for $p \mid q$.
   (b) Of the Idempotent, Associative, and Commutative Laws, which hold when the connective is alternative denial? Do any of the Identity Laws hold?
   (c) For each of the following, find logically equivalent expressions in which alternative denial appears as the only logical connective.

       (i) $\sim p$ (ii) $p \wedge q$ (iii) $p \vee q$

9. Show that each of the following argument forms is invalid by finding an assignment of truth values that makes all the premises true while the conclusion is false.

   (a) $\quad \begin{array}{l} q \vee \sim p \\ q \vee r \\ r \to s \\ \hline \therefore p \vee s \end{array}$

   (c) $\quad \begin{array}{l} p \to (q \vee r) \\ r \to (s \vee u) \\ \sim s \\ \hline \therefore p \to u \end{array}$

   (e) $\quad \begin{array}{l} (p \vee q) \leftrightarrow r \\ s \leftrightarrow (r \wedge u) \\ p \leftrightarrow s \\ p \vee q \\ \hline \therefore q \wedge p \end{array}$

   (b) $\quad \begin{array}{l} p \to q \\ r \to s \\ p \vee r \\ \hline \therefore q \wedge s \end{array}$

   (d) $\quad \begin{array}{l} (p \vee q) \to r \\ (u \to p) \to \sim s \\ r \to (q \vee s) \\ p \to (\sim u \to q) \\ \hline \therefore r \leftrightarrow q \end{array}$

   (f) $\quad \begin{array}{l} (p \to q) \to (r \to s) \\ \sim (r \to q) \\ \hline \therefore s \end{array}$

10. Give a formal proof of validity for each of the following argument forms. (A conditional or indirect proof will be much easier in some.)

(a)
$p \to q$
$q \to r$
$\sim r$
$\therefore \sim p$

(b)
p
$\sim r$
$(p \land \sim r) \to q$
$\therefore q$

(c)
$p \lor q$
$\sim q$
$r \to \sim p$
$\therefore \sim r$

(d)
$p \to \sim q$
$r \to q$
$\sim r \to s$
$\therefore p \to s$

(e)
$\sim p \lor q$
$\sim q \land r$
$\sim(p \lor q) \to s$
$\therefore r \land s$

(f)
$p \lor (q \land r)$
$\sim t$
$(p \lor q) \to (s \lor t)$
$\sim p$
$\therefore r \land s$

(g)
$p \leftrightarrow q$
$\sim p$
$(q \land \sim r) \lor t$
$(s \lor t) \to r$
$\therefore r \land \sim q$

(h)
$\sim p \to q$
$r \to (s \lor t)$
$s \to \sim r$
$p \to \sim t$
$\therefore r \to q$

(i)
$p \to (q \land r)$
$q \to s$
$r \to t$
$(s \land t) \to \sim u$
u
$\therefore \sim p$

(j)
$p \to q$
$r \to s$
$\sim q \lor \sim s$
p
$(t \land u) \to r$
$\therefore \sim t \lor \sim u$

(k)
$(p \land q) \to (p \to (r \land s))$
$(p \land q) \land u$
$\therefore r \lor s$

(l)
p
$(p \land q) \lor (p \land r)$
$(p \lor q) \to \sim r$
$\therefore p \leftrightarrow q$

11. Express the following arguments in symbolic form, and determine whether they are valid.

(a) The butler or the cook or the chauffeur killed the baron. If the cook killed the baron, then the stew was poisoned, and if the chauffeur killed the baron, there was a bomb in the car. The stew wasn't poisoned, and the butler didn't kill the baron. Therefore, the chauffeur killed the baron.

(b) If the subject has not understood the instructions or has not finished reading the sentence, then he has pressed the wrong button or has failed to answer. If he has failed to answer, then the timer hasn't stopped. The subject has pressed the right button, and the timer has stopped. Therefore, the subject has understood the instructions.

(c) If the pressure is 1 atm, the water is boiling only if the temperature is at least 100°C. If the pressure is 1 atm, then the water is frozen only if the temperature is at most 0°C. The pressure is 1 atm and either the temperature is at least 100°C or it is at most 0°C. The water is not boiling. Therefore, the temperature is at most 0°C.

(d) If I am honest, then I am naive. Either I am honest or naive, or else Sam was right and that magazine salesman is a crook. I am not naive, and that magazine salesman is certainly a crook. Therefore, Sam was right.

(e) A certain consonantal segment, if it occurs initially, is prevocalic, and if it is noninitial, it is voiceless. If it is either prevocalic or voiceless, it is continuant and strident. If it is continuant, then if it is strident, it is tense. If it is tense, then if it occurs initially, it is palatalized. Therefore, the segment is palatalized and voiceless.

12. Why is it possible in the following proof to derive a contradiction by valid rules of inference?

1. $p \wedge \sim q$	
2. $p \rightarrow r$	
3. $\sim q \rightarrow \sim r$	
4. p	1, Simp.
5. r	2, 4 M.P.
6. $\sim q$	1, Simp.
7. $\sim r$	3, 6 M.P.
8. $r \wedge \sim r$	5, 7 Conj.

13. Show that indirect proof is legitimate by showing that $((P \wedge Q \wedge \cdots \wedge Z) \wedge \sim A) \rightarrow F$ is logically equivalent to $(P \wedge Q \wedge \cdots \wedge Z) \rightarrow A$. ($F$ is a contradiction.)

3

The Predicate Calculus

The logical system developed in the preceding chapter does not suffice for the analysis of all arguments. For example, although we intuitively recognize (3-1) as valid,

(3-1)
All humans are mortal.
Socrates is a human.
∴ Socrates is mortal.

in the propositional calculus all the propositions of (3-1) are elementary (they contain no logical connectives), and thus (3-1) would have to be considered a substitution instance of the invalid argument form:

(3-2)
p
q
∴ r

It is clear that the validity of (3-1) depends crucially on the internal structure of its propositions and that a better representation of the form of (3-1) would be something like

(3-3)
All x's are y.
s is an x.
∴ s is y.

The predicate calculus, which we now introduce, allows us to take account of this finer structure of propositions.

Terms, Predicates, Propositional Functions

In the predicate calculus a proposition such as 'Socrates is a human' can be analyzed into a *term* 'Socrates' and a *predicate* 'is a human,' which asserts that the term has a certain property, in this case the property of belonging to the set of humans. A predicate is denoted by a capital letter and a term by a lowercase letter in parentheses following the symbol for the predicate. Thus, if s stands for 'Socrates' and H for 'is a human,' the proposition 'Socrates is a human' would be represented by $H(s)$. (Some authors omit the parentheses and write simply Hs.) Similarly, if M represents the predicate 'is mortal' (= 'is a member of the set of mortal things'), the conclusion of (3-1) would be denoted $M(s)$.

Terms that refer to specific individuals, e.g., Socrates, the number 3, Yankee Stadium, are called *constants*. We also allow expressions such as $H(x)$, in which x is a symbol for a *variable*, whose referent is not specified. Such expressions in which a property is predicated of a variable are called *propositional functions*. They differ from propositions in that a propositional function does not have a truth value, just as one could not decide whether the sentence 'Some unspecified thing is human' is true or false. When the variable in a propositional function is replaced by a constant, e.g., $H(s)$, however, the result is a proposition that does have a truth value. A variable symbol can therefore be thought of as a kind of "placeholder," marking the position in a propositional function where a constant may appear. Replacing a variable term by a constant is said to produce an *instantiation* of the propositional function; thus, $H(s)$ is an instantiation of $H(x)$.

Both propositions and propositional functions can be joined by the logical connectives $\wedge$, $\vee$, $\sim$, and $\leftrightarrow$. For example, $\sim H(s)$ denotes 'Socrates is not a human', and if P stands for the predicate 'is a philosopher,' the proposition 'Socrates is a human and Socrates is a philosopher' would be represented by $H(s) \wedge P(s)$. When propositional functions are connected, the variable symbols indicate whether the terms are identical or possibly distinct. For instance, $H(x) \wedge P(x)$ means that the *same* unspecified thing is both a human and a philosopher, but $H(x) \wedge P(y)$ predicates humanness of one individual and being a philosopher of an individual that is in general distinct from the former, although the possibility that they may be identical is not excluded. In an instantiation of $H(x) \wedge P(x)$ the same constant term must replace both occurrences of the variable symbol; thus, $H(s) \wedge P(s)$. The variables in $H(x) \wedge P(y)$ can be replaced by different constants, however, to give, for example, 'Socrates is human and Kant is a philosopher,' or by the same constant to give 'Socrates is human and Socrates is a philosopher.' This is a quite general condition on the use of variables in mathematics. In algebra, for example, the equation $x + x = 4$ has only one solution; namely, $x = 2$; but the equation $x + y = 4$ has many solutions; e.g., $x = 1$ and $y = 3$, $x = 0$ and $y = 4$; among which is the solution $x = 2$ and $y = 2$, where the variables take on identical values.

A term and a predicate in logic need not correspond to the subject and verb phrase, respectively, of a declarative sentence. 'John loves Mary,' for example, could be analyzed as a logical predicate 'John loves _____' and the term 'Mary.' Predicates may also be applied to more than one term, and so it is possible to regard 'loves' as a two-place or *binary* predicate having 'John' and 'Mary' as its terms. The proposition 'New York is between Boston and Philadelphia' could be taken as composed of a three-place or *ternary* predicate 'is between' and three terms. The order in which the terms occur is important of course, just as the order of subject and object is important in English sentences. If $L(x, y)$ represents the propositional function 'x loves y,' then both 'John loves Mary' and 'Mary loves John' are instantiations but are not identical propositions.

The previous remarks about variable symbols and identity of reference also apply here. 'John loves Mary' is not an instantiation of $L(x, x)$ because the terms must be identical, but 'John loves himself' is a legitimate instantiation of $L(x, x)$ and of $L(x, y)$. There is a further complication that arises from the fact that the terms are ordered. $L(x, y)$ and $L(y, x)$ must be distinguished when both occur in the same context. Thus, $L(x, y) \wedge L(y, x)$ and $L(x, y) \wedge L(x, y)$ are not the same propositional functions since 'John loves Mary and Mary loves John' is an instantiation of the former but not of the latter.

Quantifiers

There are two ways to convert a propositional function into a proposition. The first, which we have just considered, is to replace each occurrence of a variable symbol by a constant. The second is to prefix the expression by as many *quantifiers* as there are distinct variables in the propositional function. The *universal quantifier*, denoted by $\forall$, corresponds to phrases such as 'for each,' 'for all,' 'for every,' and 'for any.' The *existential quantifier*, denoted by $\exists$, has as its English counterparts 'there exists,' 'for some,' 'there is at least one,' etc. Wherever a quantifier occurs, it is associated with some variable, and we shall represent this in our notation by enclosing the symbols for the quantifier and its associated variable in parentheses; thus, $(\forall x)$, $(\exists y)$. The universal and existential quantifications of the propositional function $M(x)$ are written as in (3-4) and (3-5), respectively:

(3-4) $(\forall x)M(x)$

(3-5) $(\exists x)M(x)$

A common notational variant is to represent the universal quantifier simply by the variable enclosed in parentheses. By this convention, (3-4) would be written $(x)M(x)$.

If M represents the predicate 'is a man,' the meaning of (3-4) could be expressed by

(3-6)   For $\begin{Bmatrix} \text{all} \\ \text{every} \\ \text{each} \end{Bmatrix}$ x, x is a man.

(3-7)   For anything whatever, $\begin{Bmatrix} \text{that thing} \\ \text{it} \end{Bmatrix}$ is a man.

or in more ordinary English

(3-8)   Everything is a man.

The existentially quantified proposition (3-5) means

(3-9)   There $\begin{Bmatrix} \text{is} \\ \text{exists} \end{Bmatrix}\begin{Bmatrix} \text{an} \\ \text{at least one} \end{Bmatrix}$ x such that x is a man.

(3-10) For $\begin{Bmatrix} \text{some} \\ \text{at least one} \end{Bmatrix}$ thing, $\begin{Bmatrix} \text{that thing} \\ \text{it} \end{Bmatrix}$ is a man.

(3-11) Something is a man.

From (3-7) and (3-10) it is clear that variables in quantified expressions serve to mark coreference in much the same way as indefinite nouns and pronouns do in natural language. In the logical notation, however, coreference can be explicitly represented by identical variable symbols.

Propositional functions in two or more variables may become propositions by instantiation of some of the variables and quantification of the others. $L(x, y)$, 'x loves y,' gives 'John loves Mary' by instantiation of both x and y, but existential quantification of x and instantiation of y by 'Mary' gives

(3-12) $(\exists x)L(x, \text{Mary})$

which means 'There is at least one individual who loves Mary.' If both variables of $L(x, y)$ are quantified, there are eight possibilities:

(3-13) $(\forall x)(\forall y)L(x, y)$
(3-14) $(\forall y)(\forall x)L(x, y)$
(3-15) $(\exists x)(\exists y)L(x, y)$
(3-16) $(\exists y)(\exists x)L(x, y)$
(3-17) $(\forall x)(\exists y)L(x, y)$
(3-18) $(\exists y)(\forall x)L(x, y)$
(3-19) $(\forall y)(\exists x)L(x, y)$
(3-20) $(\exists x)(\forall y)L(x, y)$

(3-13) and (3-14) are logically equivalent (we have not yet given a precise definition of this for the predicate calculus) and mean that every individual loves every individual (including himself). (3-15) and (3-16) are also logically equivalent and can be translated as 'There is at least one individual who loves at least one individual (possibly himself).' In general, the order in which the quantifiers are written is immaterial when they are either all universal or all existential, and it is common practice to abbreviate $(\forall x)(\forall y)$ as $(\forall x, y)$, $(\exists x)(\exists y)(\exists z)$ as $(\exists x, y, z)$, etc. The order is significant, however, when both existential and universal quantifiers are present. (3-17), for example, asserts that for all x there is at least one y such that x loves y—in other words, every individual loves at least one individual (and possibly some individuals love themselves). It excludes the possibility that there is someone who doesn't love anyone at all. (3-18), which differs from (3-17) only in the order of quantifiers, asserts that there is at least one y such that, for all x, x loves y; that is, there is at least one individual who is loved by everyone (including himself). Thus, (3-17) and (3-18) cannot be logically equivalent since it is easy to construct a situation in which one is true and the other is false.

Exercise: Give the English equivalents of (3-19) and (3-20) and construct a situation in which they have different truth values.

English sentences involving the pronouns 'someone,' 'everyone,' 'something,' etc., are often ambiguous in ways that correspond to propositions with different orders of quantifiers. For example, the sentence

(3-21)   Everyone loves someone.

is perceived by most speakers to have both the sense of (3-17), 'Everyone has someone whom he loves,' and of (3-18), 'There is someone whom everyone loves,' although the former interpretation has been claimed to be somehow more "natural." It is curious that the passive form of (3-21)

(3-22)   Someone is loved by everyone.

which by most analyses should be synonymous with (3-21), seems to have the sense of (3-18) as its more "natural" interpretation, and in fact many speakers claim that for them it cannot have the interpretation of (3-17) at all. Extending such examples to include the quantifiers 'few,' 'many,' 'numerous,' etc., which occur in natural language but are not usually dealt with in symbolic logic, raises many intriguing problems still under active investigation by linguists and philosophers.

Bound and Free Variables

A variable that has been quantified no longer fulfills a "placeholding" function but rather serves to connect the quantifier to occurrences of that variable in the propositional function. In $(\forall x)M(x)$, for example, the two occurrences of x do not mark places where a constant can be substituted but only indicate the association of the quantifier and the propositional function. Occurrences of variable symbols used in this way are said to be *bound* by the quantifier; occurrences that are not bound are called *free*. Both occurrences of x are bound in $(\forall x)M(x)$, and similarly in $(\forall x)(\exists y)L(x, y)$ all occurrences of x and y are bound. The single occurrence of x in the propositional function $M(x)$ is free. $(\exists y)L(x, y)$ is a propositional function containing two bound occurrences of y and one free occurrence of x.

Consider now the expression $(\forall x)M(x) \wedge P(x)$. A question that naturally arises is, Are all occurrences of x considered bound, or is the occurrence in $P(x)$ left free? This uncertainty points up the necessity of specifying a quantifier's *scope*, that is, the portion of the expression following within which the quantifier binds occurrences of variables. By a convention similar to that adopted for negation, the scope of a quantifier is taken to be the shortest propositional function immediately following. Hence, in $(\forall x)M(x) \wedge P(x)$ the scope of $(\forall x)$ extends only through $M(x)$, and the variable in $P(x)$ is free. To specify that the scope includes both propositional functions we use another pair of parentheses; thus, $(\forall x)(M(x) \wedge P(x))$. This expression represents the universal quantification of the complex propositional function $M(x) \wedge P(x)$, while $(\forall x)M(x) \wedge P(x)$ is the conjunction of the proposition $(\forall x)M(x)$ and the propositional function $P(x)$. Our convention, then, allows us to save parentheses by writing $(\forall x)M(x) \wedge P(x)$ rather than $((\forall x)M(x)) \wedge P(x)$.

In connection with these examples, we note that a formula may contain both bound and free occurrences of the same symbol. There are some notational pitfalls here that must be clearly recognized if we are to use such expressions correctly in argument forms. Bound occurrences of variables are essentially marks of connection, and it would do just as well to write $(\forall \square)(M(\square) \wedge P(\square))$ instead of $(\forall x)(M(x) \wedge P(x))$. A free occurrence, on the other hand, stands for an unspecified term and can be replaced by a constant. Even if bound and free occurrences should happen to be denoted by the same letter, they are nonetheless distinct and should more properly be distinguished by using different letters to represent them. $(\forall x)M(x) \wedge P(x)$, for example, might have the approximate English rendering 'Everything is a man and some unspecified thing is a philosopher,' which would not be changed by writing instead $(\forall x)M(x) \wedge P(y)$, $(\forall x)M(x) \wedge P(z)$, etc. Likewise the choice of the symbol x in $(\forall x)M(x)$ is arbitrary, and the same proposition could equally well be denoted by $(\forall y)M(y)$, $(\forall z)M(z)$, etc. Thus, while it is not, strictly speaking, illegal to write $(\forall x)M(x) \wedge P(x)$, a more perspicuous notation would be $(\forall x)M(x) \wedge P(y)$ or $(\forall y)M(y) \wedge P(x)$. Analogous remarks can be made for expressions such as $(\forall x)M(x) \wedge (\forall x)P(x)$. Occurrences of x in the left and right halves of the conjunction are unrelated, so we could write equivalently, and less confusingly, $(\forall x)M(x) \wedge (\forall y)P(y)$. What we have said here applies to bound versus free occurrences and occurrences bound by different quantifiers. All free occurrences of a particular variable within the same expression *are* related, and one cannot change one of the symbols without changing all of them if an equivalent expression is to result. As we noted previously, $M(x) \wedge P(x)$ is quite a different propositional function from $M(x) \wedge P(y)$.

Other problematic examples concerning binding by quantifiers are $(\forall x)H(y)$, $(\exists x)H(s)$, $(\forall y)(\forall x)M(x)$, etc., in which the variable associated with the quantifier has no matching occurrences following. All such cases are disposed of by stipulating that a quantifier can be prefixed to an expression only if that expression contains some free occurrence of a variable that will thereby become bound. [Alternatively, we could accept such expressions as legitimate and by ignoring superfluous quantifiers regard $(\forall x)H(y)$, for example, as equivalent to $H(y)$.] This condition also ensures that a particular occurrence of a variable can be bound only once. For example, $(\exists x)$ cannot be prefixed to $(\forall x)(M(x) \rightarrow L(x, y))$ since all occurrences of x are already bound, although of course $(\exists y)$ could be added to bind the free occurrence of y.

With the notions of *bound* and *free* more or less precisely delineated, we can now state

> **DEFINITION:** An expression in the predicate calculus is a proposition if and only if all occurrences of its variables are bound. If any occurrence is free, the expression is not a proposition but a propositional function.

The Domain of Discourse

Instantiation of a propositional function is accomplished by replacing variables by constant terms. All individuals which can appear as constant terms within the context of a particular discussion comprise a set which is called the *domain* (or *universe*) *of discourse* for that discussion. This set, in effect, contains everything that we might want to talk about, and we can arbitrarily exclude from it things that are irrelevant for the purpose at hand. In a mathematical discussion, for example, the domain of discourse might contain positive integers, sets of positive integers, collections of such sets, etc. A linguistic discussion might presuppose a domain of discourse containing words, sentences, phrase markers, grammars, etc., but not, say, motorboats or guitars.

Quantification of a propositional function must always be made with reference to a domain of discourse. $(\forall x)H(x)$ does not mean, for example, that literally everything has the property denoted by $H(x)$ but that everything *in the domain of discourse* does. Similarly, $(\exists x)H(x)$ means that there is at least one individual in the domain of discourse with the specified property. As we have said, such expressions are propositions and are therefore true or false, but it is clear that one could not decide which is the case without a specification of the domain of discourse. If $M(x)$ stands for 'x is a mother,' then $(\exists x)M(x)$ is true if the domain of discourse is the set of all humans or the set of all women, but it is false if the domain of discourse is taken to be the set of all men. Usually the domain of discourse is clear from the context of a discussion, but if it is not, it can be specified and its name written as part of the quantifier; for example, if Q is the set of all humans, then $(\exists x \in Q)M(x)$ states that there is at least one true instantiation of $M(x)$ in this set. Observe that quantification is related to instantiation in the following way: Given a domain of discourse D and some propositional function $P(x)$, $(\forall x)P(x)$ asserts that all instantiations of $P(x)$ are true (the terms being drawn from D, of course), while $(\exists x)P(x)$ asserts that there is at least one individual in D that, when substituted for x, makes $P(x)$ true. Let a, b, c, etc., denote individuals in the universe of discourse. Then, $(\forall x)P(x)$ is true if $P(a)$ is true and $P(b)$ is true and $P(c)$ is true, etc., that is, if the conjunction of all instantiations of $P(x)$, namely $P(a) \wedge P(b) \wedge P(c) \wedge \cdots$, is true. $(\forall x)P(x)$ is false if one or more of the instantiations is false. Thus, universal quantification is a kind of generalized logical conjunction extending over the entire domain of discourse. The existential quantifier viewed in this way corresponds to a generalized form of disjunction since $(\exists x)P(x)$ is true if and only if $P(a)$ is true or $P(b)$ is true or $P(c)$ is true, i.e., if and only if $P(a) \vee P(b) \vee P(c) \vee \cdots$ is true.

Set Specification and Predicates

In the first chapter we remarked that a set could be specified by exhibiting its members as a list (when this is possible) or by stating a property that is true of all its members and only these. Since properties are stated by predicates, the latter method of specifying sets amounts to selecting all the individuals from the universe of discourse that make true instantiations of the predicate. The set of all men is thus the set composed of all the individuals in the universe of discourse that make a true proposition of 'x is a man.' Letting D be the domain of discourse and $M(x)$ be 'x is a man,' we could denote this set by

(3-23) $\{\forall x \in D \mid M(x) \text{ is true}\}$

In practice, (3-23) is usually abbreviated to

(3-24) $\{x \mid M(x)\}$

If we name this set A, the following expression is an equivalent specification of it:

(3-25) $(\forall x \in D)(x \in A \leftrightarrow M(x))$

that is, for every individual in the domain of discourse, that individual is a member of A if and only if it yields a true instantiation of $M(x)$.

The set of all individuals of which a predicate is true is called the *extension* of that predicate. For example, the set of men is the extension of the predicate 'is a man,' and the set $\{1, 2, 3, 4, 5\}$ is the extension of the predicate 'is a positive integer less than 6.' In these terms, the *proposition* $(\forall x)M(x)$ asserts that the extension of $M(x)$ is equal to the entire domain of discourse; that is, $\{x \mid M(x)\} = D$. The existentially quantified proposition $(\exists x)M(x)$ is equivalent to the assertion that the extension of $M(x)$ is not empty; that is, $\{x \mid M(x)\} \neq \varnothing$.

Representation of Universal and Existential Statements

Consider now the first premise of the argument (3-1):

(3-26)   All humans are mortal.

To represent this statement we need the predicate $H(x)$, 'is a human,' and the predicate $M(x)$, 'is mortal.' (3-26) asserts that every individual that makes $H(x)$ true also makes $M(x)$ true; i.e., there is no individual i in the domain of discourse for which $H(i)$ is true and $M(i)$ is false. Therefore we represent (3-26) as a conditional with $H(x)$ as antecedent and $M(x)$ as consequent.

(3-27) $(\forall x)(H(x) \rightarrow M(x))$

Since the scope of the universal quantifier in (3-27) extends over both propositional functions, the proposition is true if and only if all instantiations of $H(x) \rightarrow M(x)$ are true. This is the case if every human in the domain of discourse is also mortal. Note that the existence of nonhumans in the domain of discourse does not falsify $H(x) \rightarrow M(x)$, for then $H(x)$ is false and the conditional is true. In fact, (3-27) is true even if the domain of discourse contains no humans at all. The only condition that would falsify it is the existence of a human in the domain of discourse who is not mortal.

To represent the statement

(3-28)   Some humans are mortal.

we use the existential quantifier and connect the propositional functions by conjunction.

(3-29) $(\exists x)(H(x) \land M(x))$

To say that some humans are mortal is to say that there is at least one individual in the domain of discourse who is both a human and mortal. Such an individual produces a true instantiation of $H(x) \land M(x)$. (3-29) is false if there are no humans who are mortal and also if there are no humans or no mortal things, or neither, in the domain of discourse.

Observe that connecting the propositional functions by a conditional

(3-30) $(\exists x)(H(x) \rightarrow M(x))$

produces a quite different proposition. (3-30) asserts the existence of at least one individual that, *if* it is human, is also mortal. This statement, unlike (3-29), is true even if there are no humans in the domain of discourse. If every instantiation of $H(x)$ is false, then every instantiation of $H(x) \rightarrow M(x)$ is true.

The negation of (3-26)

(3-31)   Not all humans are mortal.

can be represented simply by

(3-32) $\sim(\forall x)(H(x) \rightarrow M(x))$

It is often convenient to represent such propositions in a logically equivalent form in which the negation has been moved over the quantifier. (3-31) is synonymous with

(3-33)   There is at least one human who is not mortal.

which can be represented by

(3-34) $(\exists x)(H(x) \land \sim M(x))$

Expressions (3-32) and (3-34) are connected by the following logical equivalence:

(3-35) $\sim(\forall x)P(x) \equiv (\exists x)\sim P(x)$

where $P(x)$ stands for any propositional function.

We can justify (3-35) informally by noting that to deny that everything has property $P(x)$ is the same as to assert that there is at least one thing that lacks this property. This line of reasoning is the one employed in refuting a universally quantified statement by offering a *counter-example*. In answer to someone's claim that every individual has property $P(x)$, we produce one individual not having this property, i.e., $(\exists x) \sim P(x)$, and this is equivalent to $\sim(\forall x)P(x)$, the negation of the original claim.

The equivalence of (3-32) and (3-34) is shown in the following derivation:

(3-36)
1. $\sim(\forall x)(H(x) \to M(x))$
2. $(\exists x) \sim (H(x) \to M(x))$ 1, Log. Equiv. by (3-35)
3. $(\exists x) \sim (\sim H(x) \lor M(x))$ 2, Cond.
4. $(\exists x)(\sim\sim H(x) \land \sim M(x))$ 3, DeM.
5. $(\exists x)(H(x) \land \sim M(x))$ 4, Compl.

The negation of (3-28) denies the existence of any individual who is both human and mortal; i.e.,

(3-37)   No human is mortal.

This can be represented by

(3-38) $\sim(\exists x)(H(x) \land M(x))$

which can also be transformed by a logical equivalence which is the counterpart of (3-35):

(3-39) $\sim(\exists x)P(x) \equiv (\forall x) \sim P(x)$

We shall henceforth refer to this and the logical equivalence in (3-35) as the Laws of Quantifier Negation.

Denying the existence of any individuals with property $P(x)$ is tantamount to asserting that all individuals lack this property. Using (3-39), we see that (3-38) is equivalent to

(3-40) $(\forall x)(H(x) \to \sim M(x))$

by the following derivation:

(3-41)
1. $\sim(\exists x)(H(x) \land M(x))$
2. $(\forall x) \sim (H(x) \land M(x))$ 1, Quant. Neg.
3. $(\forall x)(\sim H(x) \lor \sim M(x))$ 2, DeM.
4. $(\forall x)(H(x) \to \sim M(x))$ 3, Cond.

For many speakers the English sentence

(3-42)   All humans are not mortal.

is ambiguous and can have either the meaning of (3-32), i.e., 'Not every human is mortal,' or the meaning of (3-38), i.e., 'No human is mortal.' How the rules of English syntax give rise to this ambiguity and how (3-42) is related to 'all humans are immortal,' which is not ambiguous, are interesting linguistic questions that we shall not pursue here.

Tautology, Contradiction, and Logical Equivalence

As in the propositional calculus, a tautology in the predicate calculus is an expression that is always true, regardless of the truth values of its component propositions. Since propositions in the predicate calculus can be made up of predicates and constant terms, quantified propositional functions, and combinations of these, the definition of a tautology in this system must be modified to take into account all these ways of constructing propositions. Consider first propositions composed only of predicates, constant terms, and logical connectives; $H(s) \vee \sim H(s)$, for example. The truth value of the proposition $H(s)$ depends on the nature of the predicate denoted by H and on the particular individual denoted by s. If H is 'is human' and s is 'Socrates,' then $H(s)$ is true; but if H is 'is a Hindu' and s is 'Spinoza,' then $H(s)$ is false. Yet $H(s) \vee \sim H(s)$ is true, whatever H and s may represent, because one of the disjuncts must always be true and the other false. Thus, we can treat $H(s)$ and all such propositions containing only a predicate and constant terms just as we did the elementary propositions in the propositional calculus, and the criteria for tautology, contradiction, and logical equivalence remain the same as before. For example, $H(s) \wedge \sim H(s)$ is a contradiction, and the expressions $\sim(H(s) \wedge M(a))$ and $\sim H(s) \vee \sim M(a)$ are logically equivalent.

When quantifiers are present, the situation is a little more complicated. The truth value of $(\forall x)M(x)$, for example, depends not only on the predicate represented by M but also on the particular domain of discourse chosen. If M is 'is a man,' then $(\forall x)M(x)$ is true for a domain of discourse containing only adult human males and nothing else, but it is false for a domain of discourse consisting of all humans. We therefore say that a quantified expression is a tautology if and only if it is true regardless of the particular predicates it contains *and for every possible domain of discourse*. Showing that an expression is tautologous by this definition is not a straightforward matter of examining all possible cases as in the truth tables of the previous chapter, since there are an infinite number of conceivable domains of discourse. Logicians have devised a generalized form of truth table to deal with this problem, but a discussion of the technique would be too lengthy to present here. Instead, we shall justify the tautologies, logical equivalences, etc., containing quantifiers by informal arguments as we did previously in the case of the rules of Quantifier Negation.

Consider, for example, the formula $(\forall x)(P(x) \vee \sim P(x))$. This is a tautology since any substitution instance of it—$P(a) \vee \sim P(a)$, $P(b) \vee \sim P(b)$, etc.—is true, and therefore it is true for every possible domain of discourse. Actually, there is one minor difficulty; when the domain of discourse is empty, there are no individuals with which to form an instantiation, and $(\forall x)(P(x) \vee \sim P(x))$ is true vacuously (there are no individuals in the domain of discourse for which it is false). One doesn't usually quantify over an empty domain of discourse intentionally, but it could happen if a set A were chosen whose exact nature was not known, and it was later discovered to be empty. An empty domain of discourse is not very useful in most circumstances, and it does play havoc with some rules of inference to be introduced later, so we shall rid ourselves of this annoying possibility by issuing the following declaration: *The domain of discourse is never empty.* The loss of generality this entails is not serious since what we are assuming, after all, is that in every situation we encounter there does exist something to talk about.

$(\forall x)(P(x) \land {\sim}P(x))$ is a contradiction, having no true substitution instances in any domain of discourse (except the empty one, which we have agreed to disregard). $(\exists x)(P(x) \land {\sim}P(x))$ is also a contradiction for the same reasons. The expressions $(\forall x)P(x)$ and $(\forall x)(P(x) \lor P(x))$ are logically equivalent since all corresponding instantiations (the same constant term in both) have the same truth value, i.e., $P(a) \equiv (P(a) \lor P(a))$, $P(b) \equiv (P(b) \lor P(b))$, etc., whatever the domain of discourse. In general, there are logically equivalent quantified expressions corresponding to all the logical equivalences of the propositional calculus, and they can be formed very easily by substituting uniformly propositional functions in one variable $P(x)$, $Q(x)$, $R(x)$, etc., for the elementary propositions p, q, r, etc., and prefixing the result with either $(\forall x)$ or $(\exists x)$. For example, from $p \to q \equiv {\sim}p \lor q$ we can construct the logical equivalences $(\forall x)(P(x) \to Q(x)) \equiv (\forall x)({\sim}P(x) \lor Q(x))$ and $(\exists x)(P(x) \to Q(x)) \equiv (\exists x)({\sim}P(x) \lor Q(x))$. There are other logical equivalences in the predicate calculus, however, that are not simple analogs of those in the propositional calculus. The few listed in Table 3-1 are among the most useful in the sorts of arguments we shall encounter later on. The names attached to them are not standard (they have, in fact, no commonly accepted names) and are given only for convenience in referring to them.

1. *Laws of Quantifier Negation (Quant. Neg.)*
(a) ${\sim}(\forall x)P(x) \equiv (\exists x){\sim}P(x)$ (b) ${\sim}(\exists x)P(x) \equiv (\forall x){\sim}P(x)$

2. *Laws of Identical Quantifiers (Ident. Quant.)*
(a) $(\forall x)(\forall y)P(x,y) \equiv (\forall y)(\forall x)P(x,y)$
(b) $(\exists x)(\exists y)P(x,y) \equiv (\exists y)(\exists x)P(x,y)$

3. *Laws of Quantifier Distribution (Quant. Distr.)*
(a) $(\forall x)(P(x) \land Q(x)) \equiv (\forall x)P(x) \land (\forall x)Q(x)$
(b) $(\exists x)(P(x) \lor Q(x)) \equiv (\exists x)P(x) \lor (\exists x)Q(x)$
(c) $(\forall x)P(x) \lor (\forall x)Q(x) \Rightarrow (\forall x)(P(x) \lor Q(x))$
(d) $(\exists x)(P(x) \land Q(x)) \Rightarrow (\exists x)P(x) \land (\exists x)Q(x)$

Table 3-1

Some logical equivalences and logical implications in the predicate calculus

The Laws of Quantifier Negation, which we introduced previously, can be regarded as a generalized form of DeMorgan's Laws. Because a universally quantified expression can be regarded as a (possibly infinite) series of conjunctions, $P(a) \land P(b) \land P(c) \land \cdots$, and similarly an existentially quantified expression as a series of disjunctions, $P(a) \lor P(b) \lor P(c) \lor \cdots$, the equivalences in 1(a) and (b) of Table 3-1 could be written as (3-43) and (3-44), respectively.

(3-43) $\quad \sim(P(a) \land P(b) \land P(c) \land \cdots) \equiv \sim P(a) \lor \sim P(b) \lor \sim P(c) \lor \cdots$

(3-44) $\quad \sim(P(a) \lor P(b) \lor P(c) \lor \cdots) \equiv \sim P(a) \land \sim P(b) \land \sim P(c) \land \cdots$

Quantifier Negation can be used to carry a negation over any number of successive quantifiers as shown in the following example:

(3-45)
1. $\sim(\exists x)(\forall y)(\exists z)(L(x, y) \lor P(z))$
2. $(\forall x) \sim (\forall y)(\exists z)(L(x, y) \lor P(z))$ 1, Quant. Neg.
3. $(\forall x)(\exists y) \sim (\exists z)(L(x, y) \lor P(z))$ 2, Quant. Neg.
4. $(\forall x)(\exists y)(\forall z) \sim (L(x, y) \lor P(z))$ 3, Quant. Neg.

The Laws of Identical Quantifiers are easily verified by considering what the expressions mean. $(\forall x)(\forall y)P(x, y)$ asserts that every pair of individuals in the domain of discourse forms a true instantiation of $P(x, y)$. Therefore, it is immaterial whether one selects the instantiation of x first and y second or in the reverse order, which would be expressed by $(\forall y)(\forall x)P(x, y)$. A similar argument can be made for the formulas with the existential quantifier.

Expression 3(a) of Table 3-1 can be justified by examining the statements 'Everything has both property P and property Q' and 'Everything has property P and everything has property Q,' which cannot have different truth values. For example, everything in the domain of discourse is both human and male if and only if everything in the domain of discourse is human and everything in the domain of discourse is male. As an example of 3(b), if there is something in the domain of discourse that is human or male, or both, then there is something in it which is human or something in it which is male, or both. Conversely, if there is something which is human or something which is male, or both, then there is something which is either human or male, or both.

Observe carefully that 3(c) and (d) of Table 3-1 are logical implications, not logical equivalences. To illustrate 3(c), let $P(x)$ be 'is made of plastic' and $Q(x)$ be 'is a cube.' $(\forall x)P(x) \lor (\forall x)Q(x)$ means that either everything in the domain of discourse is made of plastic or everything in it is a cube, or both, and if this is true, then $(\forall x)(P(x) \lor Q(x))$, 'Everything is either made of plastic or is a cube, or is both,' cannot be false. It is possible, however, for the latter statement to be true and the former false if, for example, the domain of discourse consists of plastic cones and wooden cubes. Therefore, the implication does not hold in this direction.

Problem: Show that it is possible for $(\exists x)P(x) \wedge (\exists x)Q(x)$ to be true while $(\exists x)(P(x) \wedge Q(x))$ is false.

Arguments Involving Quantifiers

We need add very little to our logical apparatus to handle arguments containing quantified propositions. The basic idea is to strip away the quantifiers, apply rules of inference to the resulting propositions and propositional functions as if they were expressions in the propositional calculus, and then replace the quantifiers. We require two additional rules of inference for removing quantifiers—*universal instantiation* (U.I.) and *existential instantiation* (E.I.)—and two for replacing quantifiers—*universal generalization* (U.G.) and *existential generalization* (E.G.). To avoid certain incorrect deductions, it is also necessary to state some general restrictions on when these rules can be applied.

1. Universal Instantiation

A universally quantified propositional function is true if and only if *every* instantiation of that propositional function is true. Therefore, from $(\forall x)P(x)$ we can validly infer that *some particular instantiation* of $P(x)$ is true (it always being understood that the constant term chosen is a member of the domain of discourse). For example, from the proposition $(\forall x)(H(x) \to M(x))$, we may deduce $H(s) \to M(s)$, 'If Socrates is a human, then Socrates is mortal;' or $H(a) \to M(a)$, 'If Aristotle is a human, then Aristotle is mortal;' and so on for any instantiation by a member of the domain of discourse.

The rule of U.I. can be summarized as follows:

(3-46)
$$\frac{(\forall x)P(x)}{\therefore P(c)}$$

where P is any predicate and c is any constant term in the domain of discourse.

With U.I. we have sufficient apparatus to demonstrate the validity of argument (3-1). We prove that (3-47) is a valid argument form, of which (3-1) is a substitution instance.

(3-47)
$$\frac{(\forall x)(H(x) \to M(x))}{H(s)}$$
$$\therefore M(s)$$

Here is the proof:

(3-48)
1. $(\forall x)(H(x) \to M(x))$
2. $H(s)$
3. $H(s) \to M(s)$ 1, U.I.

Here we choose the constant s from the domain of discourse to form an instantiation of line 1.

4. $M(s)$ 2, 3, M.P.

Since $H(s)$ and $M(s)$ are propositions, the rule of *Modus Ponens* can be applied to lines 2 and 3 just as in the propositional calculus.

2. Universal Generalization

To prove that some proposition is true of every member of some class, one can arbitrarily select an individual from the class and prove that the statement holds for that individual. Then if the proof depends only on the fact that the individual is a member of the class and not on any additional properties it may have, it can be validly inferred that the conclusion holds for *all* individuals in the class. For example, in Chapter 1 we argued that every set has the null set as a subset. What we did, in effect, was to pick an arbitrary set X and show that the definition of subset allowed us to conclude $\varnothing \subseteq X$. Since no assumptions were made about X other than that it is a set, we generalized the result to all sets. This line of reasoning is made explicit in the rule of Universal Generalization: What is true of an arbitrarily selected individual is true of every individual in the domain of discourse. We reserve the symbol v to represent such an individual; if more than one is needed, we add subscripts: v_1, v_2, etc. Observe that v is a constant term, and so $P(v)$ is a proposition, not a propositional function. Yet v is like a variable in that it stands for no specific individual in the domain of discourse. Such terms have been called *nonspecific constants*, or *variable constants*.

U.G. can be summarized as follows:

(3-49)
$$\frac{P(v)}{\therefore (\forall x)P(x)}$$

where P is any predicate and v is an arbitrarily selected individual from the domain of discourse.

This rule is used in proving the validity of the argument form (3-50), of

Arguments Involving Quantifiers

which (3-51) is a substitution instance.

(3-50)
$$(\forall x)(R(x) \rightarrow Q(x))$$
$$(\forall x)(Q(x) \rightarrow W(x))$$
$$\therefore (\forall x)(R(x) \rightarrow W(x))$$

(3-51)
All rabbits are quadrupeds.
All quadrupeds are warm-blooded.
$\therefore$ All rabbits are warm-blooded.

The proof is as follows:

(3-52)
1. $(\forall x)(R(x) \rightarrow Q(x))$
2. $(\forall x)(Q(x) \rightarrow W(x))$
3. $R(v) \rightarrow Q(v)$ 1, U.I.

The first premise is instantiated by the arbitrarily selected constant v. Recall that every constant produces a true instantiation of a universally quantified proposition; thus, $R(v) \rightarrow Q(v)$ is a legitimate instantiation of line 1.

4. $Q(v) \rightarrow W(v)$ 2, U.I.

Here we have instantiated the second premise with the same constant we selected in line 3.

5. $R(v) \rightarrow W(v)$ 3, 4, H.S.
6. $(\forall x)(R(x) \rightarrow W(x))$ 5, U.G.

Since v has been arbitrarily selected, the proposition containing it can be universally generalized to the conclusion in line 6.

Here is another example of the use of U.I. to remove a universal quantifier and of U.G. to replace the quantifier afterward.

(3-53)
1. $(\forall x)(P(x) \wedge Q(x))$
2. $(\forall x)(R(x) \rightarrow \sim P(x))$
3. $P(v) \wedge Q(v)$ 1, U.I.
4. $R(v) \rightarrow \sim P(v)$ 2, U.I.
5. $P(v)$ 3, Simp.
6. $\sim\sim P(v)$ 5, Compl.
7. $\sim R(v)$ 4, 6, M.T.
8. $Q(v)$ 3, Simp.
9. $Q(v) \wedge \sim R(v)$ 6, 8, Conj.
10. $(\forall x)(Q(x) \wedge \sim R(x))$ 9, U.G.

3. Existential Generalization

When a proposition $P(a)$ is true, it constitutes a true instantiation of $P(x)$. Thus, given the truth of $P(a)$, we may conclude $(\exists x)P(x)$; that is, $P(x)$ has at least one true instantiation. For example, from 'Socrates is a human' one can validly infer 'There is at least one thing that is a human.' The rule of Existential Generalization is represented formally by

(3-54) $\quad \dfrac{P(c)}{\therefore (\exists x)P(x)}$

where P is any predicate and c is a constant term in the domain of discourse.
The following proof employs E.G.

(3-55)
1. $H(s)$
2. $(\forall x)(H(x) \to M(x))$
3. $H(s) \to M(s)$ 2, U.I.
4. $M(s)$ 1, 3, M.P.
5. $(\exists x)M(x)$ 4, E.G.

4. Existential Instantiation

A true existentially quantified proposition has at least one true instantiation. Therefore from $(\exists x)P(x)$ we can validly infer $P(w)$ for some constant w in the domain of discourse. In general some instantiations of $P(x)$ will be true and others false, so w cannot represent any arbitrary constant, but a constant (perhaps the only one in the domain of discourse) that makes $P(x)$ true. Thus, w is like the constant v introduced by U.I. in that it might not refer to a specific individual, but it is different in that the range of individuals to which it can possibly refer is not in general the entire domain of discourse but a subset of individuals that form true instantiations of the propositional function in question. Because of this restriction on a constant w introduced by E.I., we must be particularly careful in using this rule of inference. For example, suppose $(\exists x)P(x)$ and $(\exists x)Q(x)$ are two premises of an argument and that in the proof the former has been instantiated as $P(w)$ by the rule of E.I. It is now *not* valid to infer $Q(w)$ from $(\exists x)Q(x)$ because the same constant w that makes $P(x)$ true might not make $Q(x)$ true. The correct inference would be to use two different constants, w_1 and w_2, thus deriving $P(w_1)$ and $Q(w_2)$ from the premises. We therefore impose as a restriction on E.I. that the constant introduced cannot have occurred previously in the proof. The formal representation of E.I. is as follows:

(3-56) $\quad (\exists x)P(x)$

$\quad \therefore P(w)$

where P is any predicate and w is a constant with no previous occurrence in the proof.

Note also that the proposition $P(w)$ cannot be universally generalized to $(\forall x)P(x)$ because w has not been arbitrarily selected but rather selected from a possibly narrower class of individuals that happen to form a true instantiation of a particular propositional function.

Here is a proof involving the rule of E.I.:

(3-57)
1. $(\exists x)(P(x) \land Q(x))$
2. $P(w) \land Q(w)$ 1, E.I.
3. $P(w)$ 2, Simp.
4. $(\exists x)P(x)$ 3, E.G.

This step is valid since w is a constant that forms a true instantiation of $P(x)$.

5. $Q(w)$ 2, Simp.
6. $(\exists x)Q(x)$ 5, E.G.
7. $(\exists x)P(x) \land (\exists x)Q(x)$ 4, 6, Conj.

This argument demonstrates the validity of the logical implication 3(d) in Table 3-1.

The following proof illustrates an important point about the rules of E.I. and U.I.

(3-58)
1. $(\exists x)(T(x) \land P(x))$
2. $(\forall x)(P(x) \rightarrow H(x))$
3. $T(w) \land P(w)$ 1, E.I.
4. $P(w) \rightarrow H(w)$ 2, U.I.

Since $P(x) \rightarrow H(x)$ is made into a true proposition by every individual in the domain of discourse, it is legitimate to choose w to form the instantiation. The proof would be technically incorrect if we had first instantiated line 2 as

$P(w) \to H(w)$ by U.I. and then instantiated line 1 as $T(w) \land P(w)$ by E.I. since w would then have occurred in a previous line.

5. $P(w)$	3, Simp.
6. $H(w)$	4, 5, M.P.
7. $T(w)$	3, Simp.
8. $T(w) \land H(w)$	6, 7, Conj.
9. $(\exists x)(T(x) \land H(x))$	8, E.G.

Note that it would have been incorrect to derive $(\forall x)(T(x) \land H(x))$ from line 8 by U.G. because w was introduced by E.I.

A substitution instance of this argument form is the following:

(3-59)
Some toadstools are poisonous.
All poisonous things are harmful.
∴ Some toadstools are harmful.

The following "proof" is erroneous because the restriction on E.I. has been ignored.

(3-60)

1. $(\exists x)(C(x) \land V(x))$	
2. $(\exists x)(D(x) \land V(x))$	
3. $C(w) \land V(w)$	1, E.I.
4. $D(w) \land V(w)$	2, E.I. (*incorrect*)
5. $C(w)$	3, Simp.
6. $D(w)$	4, Simp.
7. $C(w) \land D(w)$	5, 6, Conj.
8. $(\exists x)(C(x) \land D(x))$	7, E.G.

This argument form is easily seen to be invalid by examining the following substitution instance.

(3-61)
Some cats are vicious.
Some dogs are vicious.
∴ Some cats are dogs.

In order for a quantifier to be removed by E.I. or U.I. it must stand at the left side of the expression with no other quantifier or connectives preceding it, and it must have the entire expression as its scope. Thus, $\sim(\forall x)(P(x) \land Q(x))$ cannot be instantiated as $\sim(P(v) \land Q(v))$ by U.I. because the negation sign precedes the quantifier. To instantiate this expression it should first be transformed to $(\exists x) \sim (P(x) \wedge Q(x))$ by Quantifier Negation and then E.I. can be applied to give $\sim(P(w) \wedge Q(w))$. Similarly, $P(c) \rightarrow (\exists x)Q(x)$ cannot be instantiated to $P(c) \rightarrow Q(w)$ by E.I. because the existential quantifier is not at the extreme left of the expression. Neither quantifier in $(\forall x)P(x) \wedge (\exists y)Q(y)$ can be removed by instantiation since neither has the entire expression within its scope.

In the reverse process, the quantifier is attached to the left of the proposition being generalized and takes that entire expression as its scope. Thus, $P(v) \vee Q(w)$ cannot be generalized to $P(v) \vee (\exists x)Q(x)$ by inserting a quantifier internally, and $P(v) \vee Q(v)$ cannot be generalized by U.G. to $(\forall x)P(x) \vee Q(v)$ in which the scope of the universal quantifier does not include $Q(v)$.

Conditional Proof in the Predicate Calculus

The method of Conditional Proof allows us to introduce a premise P, which is temporarily assumed to be true, and upon deriving Q from P and the original premises to state that $P \rightarrow Q$ is logically implied by the original premises. Since the truth of P is not asserted but only accepted provisionally for the sake of deriving $P \rightarrow Q$ and then abandoned, P may be any proposition at all. In the predicate calculus, the first line of a conditional proof can be a quantified proposition, e.g., $(\forall x)P(x)$ or $(\forall x)(\exists y)Q(x, y)$, or a predicate with constant terms, e.g., $P(s)$ or $L(a, b)$. In particular, the constant terms v and w may appear, e.g., $P(v)$, $L(w, v)$, where, as before, v is an arbitrarily selected constant and w is a constant that forms a true instantiation of some existentially quantified expression. In the following example the conditional proof begins with $P(v)$.

(3-62)

1. $(\forall x)((P(x) \vee Q(x)) \rightarrow R(x))$		
2. $(P(v) \vee Q(v)) \rightarrow R(v)$		1, U.I.
3. $P(v)$		C.P.
4. $P(v) \vee Q(v)$		3, Add.
5. $R(v)$		2, 4, M.P
6. $P(v) \rightarrow R(v)$		
7. $(\forall x)(P(x) \rightarrow R(x))$		6, U.G.

The following is a substitution instance of this argument form:

(3-63)   Everyone who is polite or quarrelsome is right-handed.
         ∴ Everyone who is polite is right-handed.

The temporarily assumed premise in the following conditional proof is $P(c)$, where c is a specific constant term.

(3-64)
1. $(\forall x)(P(c) \to Q(x))$
2. $P(c) \to Q(v)$ 1, U.I.
3. $P(c)$ C.P.
4. $Q(v)$ 2, 3, M.P.
5. $(\forall x)Q(x)$ 4, U.G.
6. $P(c) \to (\forall x)Q(x)$
7. $(\exists y)(P(y) \to (\forall x)Q(x))$ 6, E.G.

Note that in line 7 the existential quantifier has the entire conditional as its scope. To conclude $(\exists y)P(y) \to (\forall x)Q(x)$ from line 6 by E.G. would be technically incorrect (although in this case the two expressions happen to be logically equivalent) since the existential quantifier binds only the variable in the antecedent of the conditional.

An example of a substitution instance of this argument form is

(3-65)   If Chauncey is a priest, then everyone is qualified.

∴ There is someone such that, if he is a priest, everyone is qualified.

The derivation in (3-66) constitutes part of the proof of one of the Laws of Quantifier Distribution, 3(a) in Table 3-1.

(3-66)
1. $(\forall x)(P(x) \land Q(x))$ C.P.
2. $P(v) \land Q(v)$ 1, U.I.
3. $P(v)$ 2, Simp.
4. $(\forall x)P(x)$ 3, U.G.
5. $Q(v)$ 2, Simp.
6. $(\forall x)Q(x)$ 5, U.G.
7. $(\forall x)P(x) \land (\forall x)Q(x)$ 4, 6, Conj.
8. $(\forall x)(P(x) \land Q(x)) \to ((\forall x)P(x) \land (\forall x)Q(x))$

This illustrates another aspect of conditional proof, namely, that it may proceed from no premises except the one that begins the conditional proof. In such a case the truth of the derived conditional statement is independent of any other propositions, which is another way of saying that the conclusion is tautologous. To see this, recall that for any valid argument form

(3-67)
$$
\begin{array}{c}
P \\
Q \\
R \\
\cdot \\
\cdot \\
\cdot \\
\hline
\therefore A
\end{array}
$$

the conditional $(P \wedge Q \wedge R \wedge \cdots) \to A$ is a tautology. We could think of the first seven lines of (3-66) not as a conditional proof but as a direct proof of $(\forall x)P(x) \wedge (\forall x)Q(x)$ from the single premise $(\forall x)(P(x) \wedge Q(x))$, and thus $(\forall x)(P(x) \wedge Q(x)) \to ((\forall x)P(x) \wedge (\forall x)Q(x))$ is tautologous. In general, for every valid argument form (3-67) there is a corresponding conditional proof

(3-68)

1.	$(P \wedge Q \wedge R \wedge \cdots)$	C.P.
2.	P	1, Simp.
3.	Q	1, Simp.
4.	R	1, Simp.
	$\cdot$	
	$\cdot$	
	$\cdot$	
n.	A	
$n+1$.	$(P \wedge Q \wedge R \wedge \cdots) \to A$	

that takes all the premises as provisional rather than assumed and derives a tautologous conditional as a conclusion. In both cases the same statement is being made: The premises $P, Q, R, \ldots$ taken together logically imply the conclusion A. The difference is only in whether or not the premises are assumed to be true.

Arguments Containing Propositions with Two or More Quantifiers

To prove arguments containing multiply quantified propositions, e.g., $(\forall x)(\exists y)P(x, y)$ or $(\forall x)(P(x) \to (\exists y)Q(y))$, we employ essentially the same procedure as that used with singly quantified propositions: Remove the quantifiers by U.I. and E.I., apply the rules of inference to the resulting propositions, and then replace the quantifiers by U.G. and E.G. In applying U.I. or E.I. to multiply quantified expressions, the quantifiers are removed one by one, beginning with the leftmost quantifier, and, as before, only a quantifier having the entire expression as its scope is removable. The complication comes in making sure that distinct variables do not become confused during successive applications of U.I. or E.I. For example, from $(\forall x)(\forall y)P(x, y)$ we get $(\forall y)P(v, y)$ by U.I., but if we further instantiate this by v to get $P(v, v)$, then the information that $P(x, y)$ is a propositional function in two variables, not one, has been lost. $P(v, v)$ could be generalized by U.G. only to $(\forall x)P(x, x)$, not to $(\forall x)(\forall y)P(x, y)$, since we cannot bind some occurrences of the same variable by one quantifier and some by another. In instantiating $(\forall x)(\forall y)P(x, y)$ we could use two different symbols, v_1 and v_2, say, each representing an arbitrarily chosen constant, which by being distinct preserve the form of the propositional function $P(x, y)$. Although it is *permitted* to use distinct symbols in such a case to instantiate distinct variables, it is not *necessary* to do so. $P(v, v)$, for example, is a legitimate instantiation of $(\forall x)(\forall y)P(x, y)$, and thus $(\forall x)(\forall y)P(x, y)$ logically implies $(\forall x)P(x, x)$. The latter does not imply the former, however, and thus in a proof if distinct variables are allowed to merge, the original distinction cannot be subsequently recaptured in the generalization steps.

Consider, for example, the following proof:

(3-69)

1. $(\forall x)(\forall y)(P(x, y) \to Q(y, x))$
2. $(\forall x)(\forall y)(Q(y, x) \to R(x))$
3. $(\forall y)(P(v_1, y) \to Q(y, v_1))$ 1, U.I.
4. $P(v_1, v_2) \to Q(v_2, v_1)$ 3, U.I.
5. $(\forall y)(Q(y, v_1) \to R(v_1))$ 2, U.I.
6. $Q(v_2, v_1) \to R(v_1)$ 5, U.I.

The instantiations in lines 5 and 6 could have been made with any constants whatever, but the choice of v_1 and v_2, the same constants used in lines 3 and 4, allows H.S. to be applied to lines 4 and 6.

7. $P(v_1, v_2) \to R(v_1)$ 4, 6, H.S.
8. $(\forall y)(P(v_1, y) \to R(v_1))$ 7, U.G.
9. $(\forall x)(\forall y)(P(x, y) \to R(x))$ 8, U.G.

The order in which v_1 and v_2 are generalized in lines 8 and 9 is immaterial since both quantifiers are universal and, of course, the particular choice of

Arguments Containing Propositions with Two or More Quantifiers

variable symbols—x for v_1 and y for v_2—is arbitrary. The conclusion could equally well be written $(\forall y)(\forall x)(P(y, x) \to R(y))$.

If the premises had been instantiated everywhere by v, then line 7 would have been $P(v, v) \to R(v)$, which can be generalized in one step to $(\forall x)(P(x, x) \to R(x))$. Again, this is a valid conclusion from the premises but a weaker one than the conclusion actually derived in (3-69).

As another example of an argument involving multiply quantified propositions, consider the following:

(3-70) Whoever forgives at least one person is a saint.
There are no saints.

∴ No one ever forgives anyone.

We represent 'x forgives y' by $F(x, y)$ and 'x is a saint' by $S(x)$.

(3-71)
1. $(\forall x)(\forall y)(F(x, y) \to S(x))$
2. $\sim(\exists x)S(x)$
3. $(\forall y)(F(v_1, y) \to S(v_1))$ 1, U.I.
4. $F(v_1, v_2) \to S(v_1)$ 3, U.I.
5. $(\forall x) \sim S(x)$ 2, Quant. Neg.
6. $\sim S(v_1)$ 5, U.I.
7. $\sim F(v_1, v_2)$ 4, 6, M.T.
8. $(\forall y) \sim F(v_1, y)$ 7, U.G.
9. $(\forall x)(\forall y) \sim F(x, y)$ 8, U.G.

Propositions containing both universal and existential quantifiers present a special problem in the order in which the quantifiers are reattached by E.G. and U.G. Suppose, for example, that $(\exists x)(\forall y)L(x, y)$ has been instantiated first by E.I. and then by U.I. to $L(w, v)$. The quantifiers can now be replaced, and either order of applying E.G. and U.G. yields a valid consequence. U.G. first and then E.G. produces the original expression, and generalizing in the opposite order gives $(\forall y)(\exists x)L(x, y)$, which is logically implied by $(\exists x)(\forall y)L(x, y)$. ('There is someone who loves everyone' implies 'Everyone is loved by at least one individual.') If we instantiate $(\forall x)(\exists y)L(x, y)$, however, where the universal stands before the existential quantifier, and then generalize, replacing the quantifiers in the opposite order yields an incorrect conclusion. $(\forall x)(\exists y)L(x, y)$, 'Everyone has someone whom he loves,' does not logically imply $(\exists y)(\forall x)L(x, y)$, 'There is at least one individual who is loved by everyone.' Thus, in order to generalize a proposition containing both v and w it is necessary to know the order in which these constants were originally introduced by U.I. and E.I. If U.I.

came before E.I., then the generalizations must be carried out in the order E.G. before U.G. If E.I. was applied before U.I., then either order of E.G. and U.G. is permitted. This restriction is illustrated in the proof of the following argument:

(3-72)
Every human has a father.
All Bulgarians are humans.
∴ Every Bulgarian has a father.

$H(x)$ represents 'x is a human;' $F(x, y)$, 'x is the father of y;' and $B(x)$, 'x is a Bulgarian' in the following proof.

(3-73)
1. $(\forall y)(\exists x)(H(y) \rightarrow F(x, y))$
2. $(\forall x)(B(x) \rightarrow H(x))$
3. $(\exists x)(H(v) \rightarrow F(x, v))$ 1, U.I.
4. $H(v) \rightarrow F(w, v)$ 3, E.I.
5. $B(v) \rightarrow H(v)$ 2, U.I.
6. $B(v) \rightarrow F(w, v)$ 4, 5, H.S.

Since v was introduced by U.I. before w was introduced by E.I. (lines 3 and 4), they must be generalized in the opposite order.

7. $(\exists x)(B(v) \rightarrow F(x, v))$ 6, E.G.
8. $(\forall y)(\exists x)(B(y) \rightarrow F(x, y))$ 7, U.G.

Generalizing in the other order would have given $(\exists x)(\forall y)(B(y) \rightarrow F(x, y))$, 'There is at least one individual who is the father of all Bulgarians.'

To handle propositions with three or more mixed universal and existential quantifiers would require additional restrictions on the rules of generalization, but we shall omit these refinements here since they are unnecessary for the arguments in the remainder of this book. The interested reader can consult the works on symbolic logic in the references at the end of this chapter for details.

EXERCISES

1. In each of the following expressions, identify all bound and free occurrences of variables.
   (a) $(\forall x)P(x) \lor Q(x, y)$
   (b) $(\exists y)(Q(x) \rightarrow (\forall z)P(y, z))$
   (c) $(\forall x) \sim (P(x) \rightarrow (\exists y)(\forall z)Q(x, y, z))$
   (d) $(\exists x)Q(x, y) \land P(y, x)$
   (e) $(\forall x)(P(x) \rightarrow (\exists y)(Q(y) \rightarrow (\forall z)R(y, z)))$

2. If $T(x)$ is the propositional function 'I touch x' and $G(x)$ is 'x turns to gold,' give English equivalents of the following propositions:

(a) $(\forall x)(T(x) \to G(x))$

(b) $(\forall x)(T(x) \to {\sim} G(x))$

(c) $(\forall x)(T(x) \land G(x))$

(d) $(\forall x)(T(x) \leftrightarrow G(x))$

(e) $(\exists x)(T(x) \land G(x))$

(f) $(\exists x)(T(x) \land {\sim} G(x))$

(g) ${\sim}(\exists x)(T(x) \land G(x))$

(h) ${\sim}(\forall x)(T(x) \to G(x))$

(i) $(\exists x)(T(x) \to G(x))$

(j) $(\exists x) {\sim} (T(x) \land G(x))$

3. Symbolize each of the following sentences using propositional functions, logical connectives, and quantifiers.

(a) Not all trees are deciduous.

(b) Some politicians are honest men.

(c) No ducks are amphibious.

(d) Every cloud has a silver lining.

(e) Only Rosicrucians experience complete happiness.

(f) Everything I like is immoral, illegal, or fattening.

(g) I like anything that is immoral, illegal, or fattening.

(h) Everyone is his own worst enemy.

(i) Everyone wants everyone to be rich.

(j) Everyone wants to be rich

4. As a representation of the sentence 'Everyone answered all the questions,' the expression $(\forall x)(\forall y)A(x, y)$ [where $A(x, y)$ represents 'x answered y'] is not adequate since the domain of discourse contains both people and questions. Thus, $(\forall x)(\forall y)A(x, y)$ also states that all questions answered all questions, all questions answered all people, etc. One possible correct representation is $(\forall x)(\forall y)((P(x) \land Q(y)) \to A(x, y))$, where $P(x)$ and $Q(y)$ represent 'x is a person' and 'y is a question,' respectively. In the

light of this discussion, find appropriate representations for the following statements:

(a) No one answered every question.

(b) For every question there was someone who answered it.

(c) Everyone answered at least one question.

(d) Some people didn't answer any questions.

(e) Everyone likes Mary except Mary herself. (*Hint:* Use the propositional function $E(x, y)$; 'x equals y.')

(f) Everyone but Fred answered at least one question.

(g) Everyone who answered at least one question attempted some question or other.

(h) No one answered any question that everyone attempted.

(i) Everyone who attempted a question answered it.

5. Prove the validity of the following argument forms:

(a) $\sim(\exists x)(P(x) \land Q(x))$
$(\exists x)(P(x) \land R(x))$
$\therefore \ (\exists x)(R(x) \land \sim Q(x))$

(b) $(\forall x)(P(x) \to Q(x))$
$(\exists x)(R(x) \land \sim Q(x))$
$\therefore \ (\exists x)(R(x) \land \sim P(x))$

(c) $(\forall x)(P(x) \to Q(x))$
$(\exists x)(P(x) \land R(x))$
$\therefore \ (\exists x)(R(x) \land Q(x))$

(d) $(\forall x)(P(x) \to Q(x))$
$\sim(\forall x)(P(x) \to R(x))$
$\therefore \ (\exists x)(\sim R(x) \land Q(x))$

(e) $(\forall x)(P(x) \to Q(x))$
$R(a)$
$P(a)$
$\therefore \ (\exists x)(R(x) \land Q(x))$

(f) $(\forall x)((P(x) \lor Q(x)) \to R(x))$
$(\forall x)((R(x) \lor S(x)) \to T(x))$
$\therefore \ (\forall x)(P(x) \to T(x))$

6. Construct proofs of the validity of the following arguments: [(b), (c), and (d) are from *Symbolic Logic* (published in 1896) by Lewis Carroll (C. L. Dodgson), the author of *Alice's Adventures in Wonderland*.]

(a) All linemen for the Green Bay Packers weigh at least 200 pounds. Matilda weighs less than 200 pounds. Therefore, Matilda isn't a lineman for the Green Bay Packers.

(b) Babies are illogical. Nobody who is despised can manage a crocodile. Illogical persons are despised. Therefore, babies cannot manage crocodiles.

(c) Everyone who is sane can do logic. No lunatics are fit to serve on a jury. None of your sons can do logic. Therefore, none of your sons is fit to serve on a jury.

(d) No ducks waltz. No officers ever decline to waltz. All my poultry are ducks. Therefore, my poultry are not officers.

(e) All cabdrivers and headwaiters are surly and churlish. Therefore, all cabdrivers are surly.

(f) All vowels are sonorants. All stops are obstruents. Nothing is both a sonorant and an obstruent. Therefore, nothing is both a vowel and a stop.

(g) No linguist believes in the parity principle. Everyone believes in the parity principle or is a behaviorist. Every dietician renounces behaviorism. My aunt is a dietician. Therefore, there is someone who is neither a linguist nor a behaviorist.

7. Find all the errors in the following "proof:"

   1. $(\forall x)((P(x) \vee Q(x)) \rightarrow (\exists y)P(y))$
   2. $(\exists x)(\exists y)(R(x, y) \rightarrow S(y, x))$
   3. $(\forall y)(\exists z)(P(y) \rightarrow R(y, z))$
   4. $(P(v) \vee Q(v)) \rightarrow (\exists y)P(y)$ 1, U.I.
   5. $(P(v) \vee Q(v)) \rightarrow P(v)$ 4, E.I.
   6. $(\exists z)(P(w) \rightarrow R(w, z))$ 3, U.I.
   7. $P(v) \rightarrow R(w, w)$ 6, E.I.
   8. $(\exists y)(R(w, y) \rightarrow S(y, v))$ 2, E.I.
   9. $R(w, w) \rightarrow S(w, v)$ 8, E.I.
   10. $(P(v) \vee Q(v)) \rightarrow R(w, w)$ 5, 7, H.S.
   11. $(P(v) \vee Q(v)) \rightarrow S(w, v)$ 9, 10, H.S.
   12. $(\forall x)((P(x) \vee Q(x)) \rightarrow S(w, x))$ 11, U.G.
   13. $(\exists y)(\forall x)((P(x) \vee Q(x)) \rightarrow S(y, x))$ 12, E.G.

References and Supplementary Reading

The presentation of the propositional and predicate calculi in this chapter and the preceding one follows Copi (1967) except for minor changes in notation. There is an abundance of other textbooks on symbolic logic that is aimed at a beginning audience. A few of these are Lee (1961), Leblanc (1966), Fisk (1964), Halberstadt (1960), Fitch (1952), Langer (1953), and Ambrose and Lazerowitz (1961). Reichenbach (1947) and Quine (1959) [also in a condensed version, Quine (1965)] cover all the fundamentals and contain useful discussions of the relations between logical connectives and their English counterparts. For those with some background in philosophy or mathematics there are excellent modern treatments in Kalish and Montague (1964) and Mates (1965). Tarski (1946), Rosser (1953), Lewis and Langford (1959), and Carnap (1958) are all classics in the field and do not gloss over the difficulties. Suppes (1957) combines in one volume an introduction to symbolic logic and the elements of set theory.

Massey (1970) is an introductory textbook with much valuable material on the axiomatic approach to the predicate and propositional calculi and to modal logic. A comprehensive treatment of modal logic can be found in Hughes and Cresswell (1968).

The foundation for all modern work in symbolic logic is *Principia Mathematica* by Whitehead and Russell, first published in 1910–1913 in three volumes. An abridged version of Volume I is now available in paperback as Whitehead and Russell (1961).

A comprehensive bibliography of symbolic logic up to 1936, compiled by Alonzo Church, was published in *Journal of Symbolic Logic* **1** (1936), 121–218; additions and corrections, *ibid.*, **3** (1938), 178–212. Supplementary material appears from time to time in the same journal. For a history of the development of logic from ancient times to the present, see Kneale and Kneale (1962).

4

Further Aspects of Set Theory

We have seen that a predicate can define a set, namely, the collection of all individuals for which the predicate is true. On the other hand, sets and members, being objects in the domain of discourse of mathematics can appear as terms in combination with predicates to form propositions—that is, propositions *about* sets and members. It is the purpose of this chapter to define certain predicates which apply to sets and to prove, using the rules of inference previously introduced, certain theorems which contain these predicates.

Some Set-Theoretic Predicates

Consider the sets $A = \{a, b, c\}$ and $B = \{b, c\}$. In this instance $b \in A$ is a true proposition, while $d \in B$ is false. Such propositions can be treated as instantiations of a two-place propositional function $x \in y$, 'x is a member of y,' in which the symbol $\in$ representing the predicate is written between the variables, following the order of the corresponding English sentence, rather than being written on the left. Other binary predicates of this sort with which we are already familiar are $\subseteq$, $\subset$, and $=$. In the case of the sets A and B above, $B \subseteq A$ and $B \subset A$ are propositions that are true, and $A \subseteq B$, $A = B$, and $A \subset B$ are false. There is no compelling reason to prefer the notation $A \subseteq B$ to $\subseteq(A, B)$, but for these predicates the latter is hardly ever used. To denote the propositional function 'X is a subset of Y,' we write '$X \subseteq Y$,' indicating informally by the uppercase letters that the variables are to be instantiated by sets. As before, we informally represent members of sets by lowercase letters.

Like other propositional functions, $X \subseteq Y$, $x \in Y$, etc., can be made into propositions by quantification or instantiation, e.g., $(\forall X)(\exists Y)X \subseteq Y$, $(\exists Y)a \in Y$, $b \in A$. The universe of discourse is usually assumed, implicitly, to contain all the specific sets and members that enter into the discussion, all possible collections of these, collections of these collections, etc. It is an unfortunate fact that one cannot assume, once and for all, a universe of discourse consisting of 'the set of all sets,' but accepting the existence of this set leads to a contradiction as a consequence of the set's containing not only itself but also its own power set as a member.

An example of a quantified proposition that is true of sets A and B above is $(\forall x)(x \in B \rightarrow x \in A)$; that is, for any member of the domain of discourse, if it is a member of B, then it is also a member of A. This is exactly the condition that holds when B is a subset of A:

(4-1) $\qquad B \subseteq A \leftrightarrow (\forall x)(x \in B \rightarrow x \in A)$

Generalizing this expression to any sets X and Y gives the definition of the predicate 'is a subset of' in the notation of the predicate calculus:

(4-2) $\qquad (\forall X, Y)(X \subseteq Y \leftrightarrow (\forall x)(x \in X \rightarrow x \in Y))$

This proposition, like a tautology, is always true, but for a different reason. (4-2) is true not by logical necessity but *by definition*. The expression $(\forall x)(x \in X \rightarrow x \in Y)$ defines the newly introduced expression $X \subseteq Y$ on the left of the biconditional. This essentially constitutes an agreement to consider $X \subseteq Y$ an abbreviation for $(\forall x)(x \in X \rightarrow x \in Y)$, and there can be no question as to the truth or falsity of an abbreviation. A defined predicate and the expression defining it are always freely interchangeable. Thus, wherever $B \subseteq A$ occurs, it can be replaced by $(\forall x)(x \in B \rightarrow x \in A)$, and vice versa.

The Axiom of Extension can be written as follows:

(4-3) $\qquad (\forall X, Y)(X = Y \leftrightarrow (\forall x)(x \in X \leftrightarrow x \in Y))$

This could be considered a definition of the set-theoretic predicate 'equals' in terms of the basic predicate 'is a member of,' or if it is assumed that 'equals' is also basic, then (4-3) is a proposition relating the predicates $=$ and $\in$. In the latter sense (4-3) is an axiom that would be assumed as one of the starting points in the formal development of set theory. Whether one wishes to call (4-3) an axiom or a definition is pretty much a matter of taste. Taking it as a definition, however, keeps the number of fundamental, unanalyzable predicates in set theory to just one, namely, 'is a member of.'

Some Theorems about Sets

Given (4-2) and (4-3), we can prove the following theorem relating the predicates = and $\subseteq$.

THEOREM 4-1: For any sets X and Y, X equals Y if and only if X is a subset of Y and Y is a subset of X.

In symbols,

(4-4) $\quad (\forall X, Y)(X = Y \leftrightarrow (X \subseteq Y \land Y \subseteq X))$

In the formal proof of Theorem 4-1 we take as the only premise the Axiom of Extension:

Proof:

1. $(\forall X, Y)(X = Y \leftrightarrow (\forall x)(x \in X \leftrightarrow x \in Y))$
2. $V_1 = V_2 \leftrightarrow (\forall x)(x \in V_1 \leftrightarrow x \in V_2)$ 1, U.I. (twice)
3. $V_1 = V_2 \leftrightarrow (\forall x)((x \in V_1 \to x \in V_2) \land (x \in V_2 \to x \in V_1))$
    2, Bicond.

(4-5)

4. $V_1 = V_2 \leftrightarrow ((\forall x)(x \in V_1 \to x \in V_2) \land (\forall x)(x \in V_2 \to x \in V_1))$
    3, Quant. Distr.
5. $V_1 = V_2 \leftrightarrow (V_1 \subseteq V_2 \land V_2 \subseteq V_1)$ 4, Def. of $\subseteq$

In step 5 we have replaced two subexpressions of line 4 by their abbreviated forms.

6. $(\forall X, Y)(X = Y \leftrightarrow (X \subseteq Y \land Y \subseteq X))$ 5, U.G. (twice)

This shows that Theorem 4-1 is a logical consequence of the Axiom of Extension, and thus it can be added to our stock of true statements for use in future proofs.

As another illustration of a proof of a set-theoretic proposition we demonstrate the transitivity of inclusion.

THEOREM 4-2: For any sets X, Y, and Z, if X is a subset of Y and Y is a subset of Z, then X is a subset of Z.

In symbols,

(4-6) $\quad (\forall X, Y, Z)((X \subseteq Y \land Y \subseteq Z) \to X \subseteq Z)$

Proof:

(4-7)

1. $V_1 \subseteq V_2 \land V_2 \subseteq V_3$ C.P.
2. $(\forall x)(x \in V_1 \to x \in V_2) \land (\forall x)(x \in V_2 \to x \in V_3)$
  1, Def. of $\subseteq$
3. $(\forall x)((x \in V_1 \to x \in V_2) \land (x \in V_2 \to x \in V_3))$
  2, Quant. Distr.
4. $(v \in V_1 \to v \in V_2) \land (v \in V_2 \to v \in V_3)$ 3, U.I.
5. $v \in V_1 \to v \in V_2$ 4, Simp.
6. $v \in V_2 \to v \in V_3$ 5, Simp.
7. $v \in V_1 \to v \in V_3$ 5, 6 H.S.
8. $(\forall x)(x \in V_1 \to x \in V_3)$ 7, U.G.
9. $V_1 \subseteq V_3$ 8, Def. of $\subseteq$
10. $(V_1 \subseteq V_2 \land V_2 \subseteq V_3) \to V_1 \subseteq V_3$
11. $(\forall X, Y, Z)((X \subseteq Y \land Y \subseteq Z) \to X \subseteq Z)$ 10, U.G. (three times)

Informal Style in Mathematical Proofs

A mathematician rarely presents proofs in the completely formal style we have been using since he can assume that his audience is familiar enough with logical equivalences and rules of inference to require only an outline of the essential steps. Such an informal proof should be easily expanded into a fully formal version that can be checked step by step if there is any doubt concerning its validity. Thus, the term 'informal' when applied to proofs does not mean 'sloppy' or 'fallacious,' only 'condensed.'

To illustrate, we give a proof of Theorem 4-2 as a mathematician might write it.

Proof:

(4-8)   Let X, Y, and Z be arbitrary sets such that $X \subseteq Y$ and $Y \subseteq Z$. Let x be an arbitrary member of X. Because $X \subseteq Y$, $x \in Y$; and because $Y \subseteq Z$, $x \in Z$. Therefore, $x \in X \to x \in Z$, and thus $X \subseteq Z$.

Observe that no explicit mention is made of U.I. and U.G., it being understood from the context and use of the word 'arbitrary' that the result is true of all sets. In the last two sentences of the proof it is assumed that the reader knows the definition of $\subseteq$ and the inferential rule of Hypothetical Syllogism. The whole is in the form of a conditional proof headed by the proposition

$X \subseteq Y \wedge Y \subseteq Z$, but it is left to the reader to draw the conclusion $(X \subseteq Y \wedge Y \subseteq Z) \to X \subseteq Z$ and to generalize it.

As a final example, we state the definition of 'proper subset' and give both formal and informal proofs of a theorem containing this predicate.

(4-9) $\quad (\forall X, Y)(X \subset Y \leftrightarrow (X \subseteq Y \wedge X \neq Y))$

The expression $X \neq Y$ is an alternative notation for $\sim(X = Y)$. Similarly, $X \nsubseteq Y, X \not\subset Y$, and $x \notin Y$ can be written in place of $\sim(X \subseteq Y), \sim(X \subset Y)$, and $\sim(x \in Y)$, respectively. The predicate $\subset$ in (4-9) is defined in terms of the predicates $\subseteq$ and $=$, which can in turn be expressed in terms of the predicate $\in$, thus:

(4-10) $\quad (\forall X, Y)(X \subset Y \leftrightarrow ((\forall x)(x \in X$

$\to x \in Y) \wedge \sim(\forall x)(x \in X \leftrightarrow x \in Y)))$.

All predicates in set theory are ultimately reducible to an expression containing $\in$ as its only predicate (and possibly $=$ also), although the expression may be so complex that it is of no practical use.

The theorem to be proved is

THEOREM 4-3: For any sets X and Y, if X is a proper subset of Y, there is some member of Y that is not a member of X. That is,

(4-11) $\quad (\forall X, Y)(X \subset Y \to (\exists x)(x \in Y \wedge x \notin X))$

Proof (formal):

(4-12)

1. $V_1 \subset V_2$		C.P.
2. $V_1 \subseteq V_2 \wedge V_1 \neq V_2$		1, Def. of $\subset$
3. $V_1 \neq V_2$		2, Simp.
4. $\sim(V_1 \subseteq V_2 \wedge V_2 \subseteq V_1)$		3, Theorem 4-1
5. $V_1 \nsubseteq V_2 \vee V_2 \nsubseteq V_1$		4, DeM.
6. $V_1 \subseteq V_2$		2, Simp.
7. $V_2 \nsubseteq V_1$		5, 6, D.S.
8. $\sim(\forall x)(x \in V_2 \to x \in V_1)$		7, Def. of $\subseteq$
9. $(\exists x) \sim (x \in V_2 \to x \in V_1)$		8, Quant. Neg.
10. $(\exists x) \sim (x \notin V_2 \vee x \in V_1)$		9, Cond.
11. $(\exists x)(x \in V_2 \wedge x \notin V_1)$		10, DeM.
12. $V_1 \subset V_2 \to (\exists x)(x \in V_2 \wedge x \notin V_1)$		
13. $(\forall X, Y)(X \subset Y \to (\exists x)(x \in Y \wedge x \notin X))$		12, U.G. (twice)

Proof (informal):

(4-13) Let X and Y be arbitrary sets such that $X \subset Y$. Then, by definition, $X \subseteq Y$ and $X \neq Y$. $X = Y$ iff $X \subseteq Y$ and $Y \subseteq X$. Therefore, since $X \neq Y$ and $X \subseteq Y$, it follows that $Y \nsubseteq X$, which implies that there is some x in Y that is not in X.

Problems:

1. Prove that for any two sets X and Y the proposition $X \subset Y \wedge Y \subset X$ is a contradiction.
2. Show that the null set is a subset of every set, i.e., $(\forall X)\ \varnothing \subseteq X$, by an indirect proof. $\sim(\exists x)x \in \varnothing$ can be used as the definition of the null set.
3. Prove, either formally or informally, that proper inclusion is transitive; i.e., $(\forall X, Y, Z)((X \subset Y \wedge Y \subset Z) \rightarrow X \subset Z)$.
4. Assume some nonvoid universe of discourse, I, which contains a number of sets. Consider the subset of I that is defined as follows:

$$B = \{X \in I \mid X \notin X\}$$

Thus, B is the collection of all those sets in I that are not members of themselves. Show that when we ask whether $B \in B$ a paradox results. That is, the assumption that $B \in B$ leads to the conclusion $B \notin B$ and vice versa.

This paradox, which was discovered by Russell in 1901, was a serious blow to the proponents of axiomatic set theory as the basis from which to construct all other concepts in mathematics. There are a number of ways to escape the paradox. One is to acknowledge that some propositions, e.g., $X \in X$, are not to be admitted into the theory as properly defining a set. This is done in many treatments. The problem, of course, is to determine just which propositions are or are not to be allowed. Russell excluded propositions such as $X \in X$ by a theory of "types" that placed individuals, sets of individuals, sets of sets, etc., in different logical classes. Objects of one type could be members only of a class of a higher type.

Note that one can draw another conclusion from Russell's Paradox. When we ask whether $B \in B$, we are implicitly assuming that B is a member of the domain of discourse. Since I was selected arbitrarily, except for being nonvoid, there seems to be no reason why B could not be a member of I. Yet we see that no matter how we select I, B cannot be a member of it. In particular, no domain of discourse can contain literally *every set* since B is an example of a set that cannot be in it. Thus, we must avoid choosing as a domain of discourse "the set of all sets." To put it another way, there is no set that contains everything.

5. Call adjectives which are correctly predicated of themselves 'autological' and those which are not, 'heterological.' For example, 'English' and 'short' are autological, but 'French' and 'long' are heterological. Show when we ask whether the adjective 'heterological' is heterological or autological we are led to a contradiction like that in Russell's Paradox. This is known as Grelling's Paradox.

Set Operations

We now introduce some operations that combine sets to produce new ones.

1. *Union*

DEFINITION: The *union* of any two sets X and Y, denoted $X \cup Y$, is the set which has as members all and only those elements which are in X or in Y or both.

(4-14) $\qquad X \cup Y \stackrel{\text{def}}{=} \{x \mid x \in X \lor x \in Y\}$

(The symbol $\stackrel{\text{def}}{=}$ indicates that the sets so connected are equal by definition.)
For example, if $A = \{a, b\}$, $B = \{c, d\}$, and $C = \{b, d\}$, then

(4-15) $\qquad A \cup B = \{a, b, c, d\}$

(4-16) $\qquad A \cup C = \{a, b, d\}$

(4-17) $\qquad B \cup C = \{b, c, d\}$

(4-18) $\qquad A \cup \emptyset = \{a, b\} = A$

(4-19) $\qquad B \cup \emptyset = \{c, d\} = B$

Equations (4-18) and (4-19) suggest a general result about set union, which is stated in the following theorem:

THEOREM 4-4: For any set X, $X \cup \emptyset = X$.

We give two proofs in order to illustrate the general methods used in proving theorems involving operations on sets. The first makes use of Theorem 4-1, which states that two sets are equal if and only if each is included in the other. Thus, to show that $X \cup \emptyset = X$, we prove that $X \cup \emptyset \subseteq X$ and then that $X \subseteq X \cup \emptyset$.

Further Aspects of Set Theory

Proof:

(4-20)

1. $v \in V \cup \emptyset$		C.P.
2. $v \in V \lor v \in \emptyset$		1, Def. of $\cup$
3. $(\forall x) x \notin \emptyset$		Def. of $\emptyset$
4. $v \notin \emptyset$		3, U.I.
5. $v \in V$		2, 4, D.S.
6. $v \in V \cup \emptyset \to v \in V$		
7. $V \cup \emptyset \subseteq V$		6, Def. of $\subseteq$
8. $v \in V$		C.P.
9. $v \in V \lor v \in \emptyset$		8, Add.
10. $v \in V \cup \emptyset$		9, Def. of $\cup$
11. $v \in V \to v \in V \cup \emptyset$		
12. $V \subseteq V \cup \emptyset$		11, Def. of $\subseteq$
13. $V \cup \emptyset \subseteq V \land V \subseteq V \cup \emptyset$		7, 12, Conj.
14. $V \cup \emptyset = V$		13, Theorem 4-1
15. $(\forall X) X \cup \emptyset = X$		14, U.G.

In the second proof we specify each set as the extension of a predicate and then demonstrate that the predicates are logically equivalent. Thus, they have the same extensions, and the sets are equal.

Proof:

(4-21) Choose arbitrarily a set V. In the predicate notation,

1. $V = \{x \mid x \in V\}$

and

2. $V \cup \emptyset = \{x \mid x \in V \lor x \in \emptyset\}$

We wish to show that $x \in V \equiv (x \in V \lor x \in \emptyset)$. Since $x \in \emptyset$ has no true substitution instances, $x \in V \lor x \in \emptyset$ is equivalent to $x \in V \lor F$, which is equivalent to $x \in V$. Thus, the two propositional functions $x \in V$ and $x \in V \lor x \in \emptyset$ are logically equivalent and we conclude, by the Axiom of Extension, that $V = V \cup \emptyset$. Because V was arbitrarily chosen, we may apply U.G. to obtain the desired conclusion.

Another theorem that is easily proved by either of the methods above is the following:

THEOREM 4-5: For any sets X and Y, $X \cup Y = Y \cup X$.

This theorem states that the operation of set-theoretic union is *commutative*, i.e., that both orders of writing the names of the sets around the operator specify the same set. We give two informal proofs.

Proof 1:

(4-22)   Assume $x \in X \cup Y$

Then $x \in X \vee x \in Y$ by definition of union, $x \in Y \vee x \in X$ by the Commutative Law for disjunction, and $x \in Y \cup X$, again by the definition of union. Thus, $X \cup Y \subseteq Y \cup X$. The proof that $Y \cup X \subseteq X \cup Y$ proceeds in exactly the same way except that the symbols X and Y are interchanged throughout. From $X \cup Y \subseteq Y \cup X$ and $Y \cup X \subseteq X \cup Y$ we conclude by Theorem 4-1 that $X \cup Y = Y \cup X$.

Proof 2:

(4-23) $X \cup Y = \{x \mid x \in X \vee x \in Y\}$

$= \{x \mid x \in Y \vee x \in X\} = Y \cup X$

$X \cup Y$ is the extension of the predicate $x \in X \vee x \in Y$, which is logically equivalent to the predicate $x \in Y \vee x \in X$, whose extension is $Y \cup X$. Thus $X \cup Y$ and $Y \cup X$ are the same set.

Problems:

1. Prove that for any set X, $X \cup X = X$, i.e., that union is idempotent.
2. Prove for any sets X, Y, and Z that $(X \cup Y) \cup Z = X \cup (Y \cup Z)$, i.e., that union is associative.

2. Intersection

DEFINITION: The *intersection* of any two sets X and Y, denoted $X \cap Y$, is the set of exactly those members that belong to both X and Y.

(4-24) $X \cap Y \stackrel{\text{def}}{=} \{x \mid x \in X \wedge x \in Y\}$

We illustrate with $A = \{a, b\}$, $B = \{c, d\}$, and $C = \{b, d\}$.

(4-25) $A \cap B = \emptyset$
(4-26) $A \cap C = \{b\}$
(4-27) $B \cap C = \{d\}$
(4-28) $A \cap \emptyset = \emptyset$

When two sets have no members in common, as in (4-25) and (4-28), their intersection is the null set, and the sets are said to be *disjoint*.

From the definition of intersection it is apparent that any set intersected with the null set yields the null set. This is stated in the following theorem:

THEOREM 4-6: $(\forall X) X \cap \emptyset = \emptyset$.

Proof: The proof is indirect. Assume $(\exists x) x \in X \cap \emptyset$. Then by definition of intersection, $(\exists x)(x \in X \wedge x \in \emptyset)$. But this is false since for no x is $x \in \emptyset$, and so the expression has no true substitution instances. Therefore, the assumption $(\exists x) x \in X \cap \emptyset$ is false, and we conclude $\sim(\exists x) x \in X \cap \emptyset$, i.e., that $X \cap \emptyset$ has no members. By the Axiom of Extension, there is only one such set—the null set; therefore, $X \cap \emptyset = \emptyset$.

Intersection, like union, is idempotent, commutative, and associative. These facts are stated in Theorems 4-7, 4-8, and 4-9, the proofs of which are left as exercises for the reader.

THEOREM 4-7: $(\forall X) X \cap X = X$.

THEOREM 4-8: $(\forall X, Y) X \cap Y = Y \cap X$.

THEOREM 4-9: $(\forall X, Y, Z) X \cap (Y \cap Z) = (X \cap Y) \cap Z$.

The following three theorems are useful in establishing a connection between set inclusion and union or intersection.

THEOREM 4-10: $(\forall X, Y) X \subseteq X \cup Y$.

Proof: Assume $x \in X$. Then $x \in X \vee x \in Y$, by addition. Thus, $x \in X \to (x \in X \vee x \in Y)$ or, by the definition of union, $x \in X \to x \in X \cup Y$. Since x is arbitrary, $(\forall x)(x \in X \to x \in X \cup Y)$, which by the definition of inclusion is equivalent to $X \subseteq X \cup Y$.

THEOREM 4-11: $(\forall X, Y) X \cap Y \subseteq X$.

Proof: Assume $x \in X \cap Y$. Then by definition of intersection, $x \in X \wedge x \in Y$. Simplification gives $x \in X$, and thus $x \in X \cap Y \to x \in X$. Universal generalization of x and the definition of subset gives $X \cap Y \subseteq X$.

THEOREM 4-12: $(\forall X, Y) X \cap Y \subseteq X \cup Y$.

Proof: This is left as an exercise for the reader.

3. Relative Complementation

DEFINITION: For any two sets X and Y, the *relative complement of Y with respect to X*, denoted $X - Y$, is the set of just those members that are in X but not in Y.

(4-29) $\quad X - Y \stackrel{\text{def}}{=} \{x \mid x \in X \wedge x \notin Y\}$

Using once more the examples of $A = \{a, b\}$, $B = \{c, d\}$, and $C = \{b, d\}$, we have

(4-30) $\quad A - B = \{a, b\} = A$

(4-31) $\quad A - C = \{a\}$

(4-32) $\quad B - C = \{c\}$

(4-33) $\quad C - \varnothing = \{b, d\}$

In general $X - Y$ is not the same set as $Y - X$, so relative complementation is not commutative. Compare (4-30) through (4-33) with the following:

(4-34) $\quad B - A = \{c, d\} = B$

(4-35) $\quad C - A = \{d\}$

(4-36) $\quad C - B = \{b\}$

(4-37) $\quad \varnothing - C = \varnothing$

Further, in contrast with union and intersection, relative complementation is not idempotent since, for any set X, $X - X = \varnothing$; that is, the set of all elements that are in X but not in X is empty.

It can be proved that relative complementation is not associative by exhibiting a counter-example. Recall that to disprove $(\forall x) P(x)$ it suffices to show that $(\exists x) \sim P(x)$. We use the sets A, B, and C in the examples above to show that $(A - B) - C \neq A - (B - C)$.

(4-38)
$$A - B = \{a, b\}$$
$$(A - B) - C = \{a, b\} - \{b, d\} = \{a\}$$
$$B - C = \{c\}$$
$$A - (B - C) = \{a, b\} - \{c\} = \{a, b\}$$
$$\therefore (A - B) - C \neq A - (B - C)$$

4. Absolute Complementation

DEFINITION: For any set X, the *absolute complement* of X (or simply the *complement* of X), denoted X', is the relative complement of X with respect to the domain of discourse.

If we denote the domain of discourse by I, this definition can be symbolized as

(4-39) $\quad X' \stackrel{\text{def}}{=} I - X$

or equivalently

(4-40) $\quad X' \stackrel{\text{def}}{=} \{x \mid x \notin X\}$

since the expression on the right side of (4-40) means 'the set of all elements in the domain of discourse not in X.'

In set-theoretic contexts the domain of discourse is often referred to as *the universal set*, although the definite article 'the' is misleading since this set varies in composition from discussion to discussion and is therefore not a unique set like the null set. (Recall that the natural choice for a truly universal set, 'the set of all sets,' does not exist.) Despite the nonuniqueness of the universal set it is convenient to have a fixed symbol to represent it, and we choose I for this purpose (many authors use U). By definition, I contains all the members and sets under discussion and so, for any set X, both $X \subseteq I$ and $X \in I$.

As a consequence of the definitions of the universal set and absolute complementation, we have

(4-41) $\quad I' = I - I = \emptyset$

(4-42) $\quad \emptyset' = I - \emptyset = I$

Relative and absolute complementation are also connected as shown in the following theorem:

THEOREM 4-13: $(\forall X, Y) X - Y = X \cap Y'$.

Proof:

$$X - Y = \{x \mid x \in X \land x \notin Y\} = \{x \mid x \in X\} \cap \{x \mid x \notin Y\} = X \cap Y'$$

Venn Diagrams

A useful pictographic representation of set operations is provided by Venn diagrams (sometimes called Venn-Euler diagrams) in which sets are represented by closed figures (usually a circle, although this is not essential) and

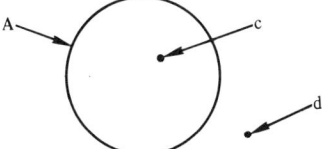

Figure 4-1

A Venn diagram

individuals by points lying either within or outside the enclosed area. In Fig. 4-1, the set A is indicated by the circle, and all the points inside A represent members of A. The point labeled c is one, and thus $c \in A$. The point d lies outside A, so $d \notin A$.

To show explicitly that the sets being diagramed are contained in a domain of discourse, a rectangle is drawn around the whole diagram as in Fig. 4-2. Here the unshaded circle represents the set A, and the shaded area, which is the rest of the universal set, represents the set A', the absolute complement of A.

Set inclusion is represented by drawing one closed figure inside another. In Fig. 4-3 the set B is shown as properly included in A (all the members of B are also members of A), but A and B are not equal. If A and B happened to be equal, the circles representing them would coincide exactly in the Venn diagram to express the fact that A and B have exactly the same members.

The intersection of two sets would be represented as in one of the diagrams in Fig. 4-4.

In Fig. 4-4(a) the two sets are shown as having some, but not all, members in common. The shaded area represents the set $A \cap B$. When $A = B$, the result is as in Fig. 4-4(b); the sets have all members in common, so $A \cap B = A = B$. Figures 4-4(c) and (d) represent the cases in which $B \subset A$ and $A \subset B$, respectively. It is easily seen that when $B \subset A$, $A \cap B = B$, and correspondingly when $A \subset B$, $A \cap B = A$. In Fig. 4-4(e) the sets are disjoint and so have no members in common. The absence of shading indicates that the intersection is the null set; i.e., $A \cap B = \varnothing$.

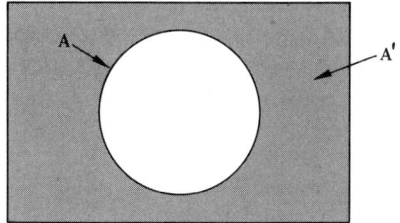

Figure 4-2

Venn diagram showing a set A and its complement A'

94 *Further Aspects of Set Theory*

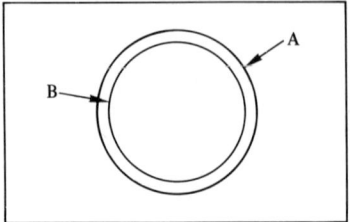

Figure 4-3

Venn diagram showing a set B properly included in a set A

These diagrams depict the five logically possible cases involving two sets. Of these, Fig. 4-4(a) represents the most general case since all the others make additional assumptions about the sets. This is easily seen when we

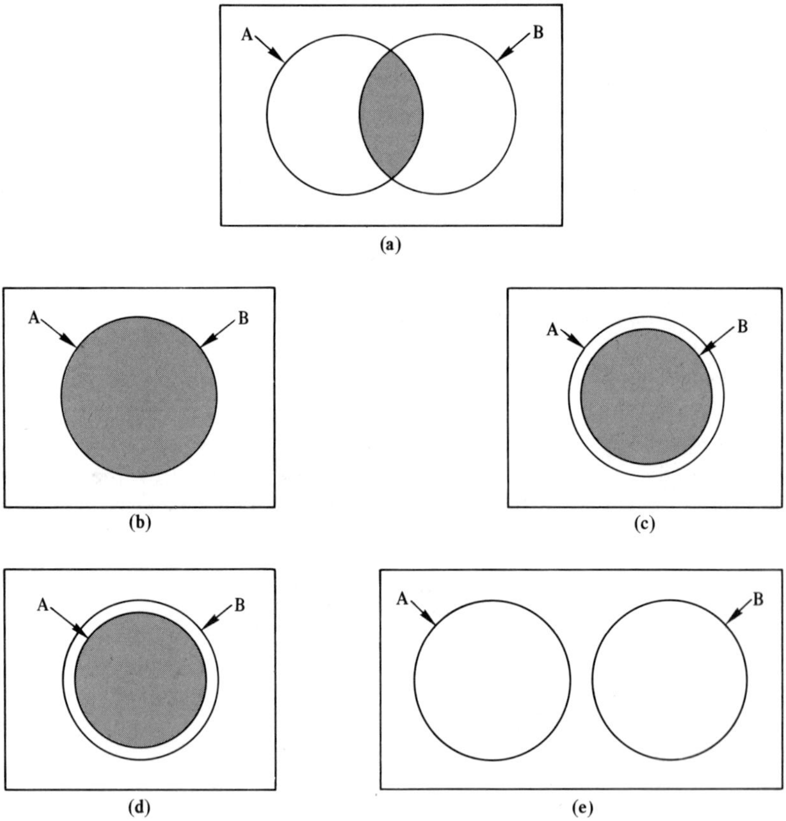

Figure 4-4

Venn diagrams showing the logical possibilities for the intersection of two sets examine more closely the meaning of Venn diagrams. A point is either inside an area representing a set or it is outside, and these are the only logical possibilities. In this way Venn diagrams capture the essential feature of set membership—that it is an all-or-none matter. Given an element x and a set A, either $x \in A$ or $x \notin A$, but not both. With two sets A and B, which may in general be distinct, there are four logical possibilities for any given element x:

(4-43)
1. $x \in A \land x \in B$
2. $x \in A \land x \notin B$
3. $x \notin A \land x \in B$
4. $x \notin A \land x \notin B$

The numbered expressions in (4-43) correspond to the numbered areas in the Venn diagram in Fig. 4-5. For example, an element for which line 1 of (4-43) is true is in the area labeled 1. These numbers also correspond to the

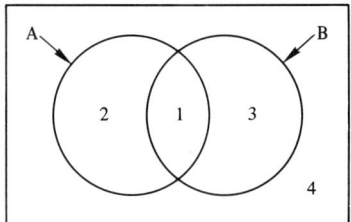

Figure 4-5

Venn diagram with areas numbered to correspond to the expressions in (4-43)

four lines of the partial truth table in Fig. 4-6.

The Venn diagrams (b) through (e) in Fig. 4-4 are now seen to exclude certain of these possibilities—for example, Fig. 4-4(c) does not allow

	$x \in A$	$x \in B$
1.	t	t
2.	t	f
3.	f	t
4.	f	f

Figure 4-6

Partial truth table with lines corresponding to the numbered areas of Fig. 4-5

$x \notin A \wedge x \in B$—and thus they involve additional restrictive assumptions. This is why diagrams of the form shown in Fig. 4-4(a) are used in illustrating set-theoretic operations in their full generality.

Problem: Which of the logical possibilities in (4-43) are excluded by the diagrams in Fig. 4-4(b), (d), and (e)?

The Venn diagram for the union of two sets is shown in Fig. 4-7. The shaded area represents the set whose members are in A or B or in both; i.e., $A \cup B$.

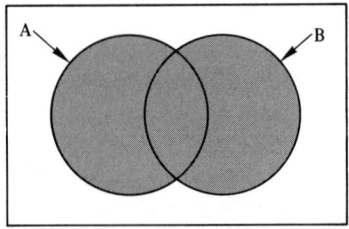

Figure 4-7

Venn diagram for $A \cup B$

The relative complement of B with respect to A is indicated by the shaded area in Fig. 4-8.

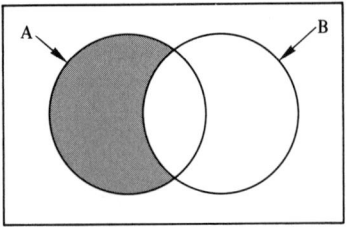

Figure 4-8

Venn diagram for $A - B$

Problem: Draw Venn diagrams for $A \cup B$ and $A - B$ corresponding to Fig. 4-4(b) through (e).

Venn diagrams can be used in demonstrating set-theoretic equalities. As an example, we shall show that $A - B = A \cap B'$. The Venn diagram for $A \cap B'$ is constructed in two steps; in Fig. 4-9(a), the shaded area represents B' and in Fig. 4-9(b) the crosshatched area represents the intersection of A

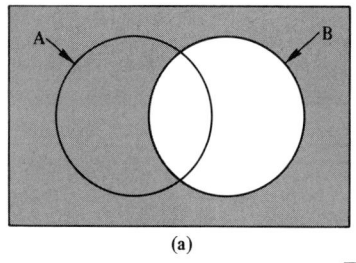
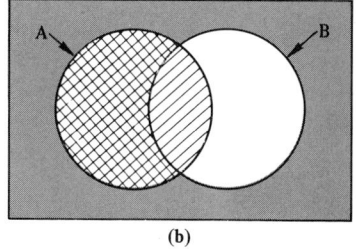

(a) (b)

Figure 4-9
Steps in the construction of the Venn diagram for $A \cap B'$

with B'. This area is seen to be the same as the shaded area of Fig. 4-8. Thus, the diagrams provide a rather convincing visual demonstration that $A - B$ and $A \cap B'$ are equal.

When three sets are involved, the most general case is diagramed as shown in Fig. 4-10. Each set shares some members with each of the others, but no

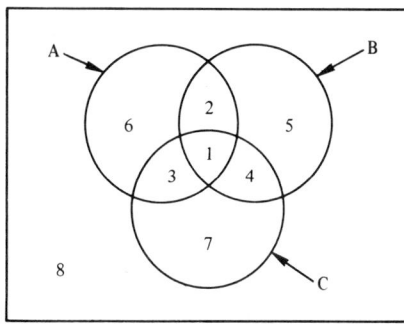
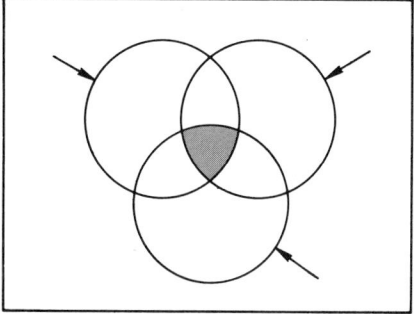

Figure 4-10
Venn diagram for the general case of three sets

Figure 4-11
Venn diagram of $A \cap B \cap C$

two are equal or disjoint, nor is any set included in another. The diagram divides the universal set into eight areas, corresponding to the eight logical possibilities for membership when there are three distinct sets.

In Fig. 4-11 the shaded area represents the intersection of A, B, and C. It is easy to show by stepwise construction of the appropriate diagrams that this area represents both $(A \cap B) \cap C$ and $A \cap (B \cap C)$ and thus that intersection is associative.

Problem: Show by means of Venn diagrams that union is associative; i.e., $A \cup (B \cup C) = (A \cup B) \cup C$.

If the number of distinct sets exceeds three, the construction of Venn diagrams becomes more difficult. It is no longer possible to divide the universal set into 16, 32, 64, etc., areas by means of circles; however, the Venn diagram for four sets in the general case could be drawn as in Fig. 4-12.

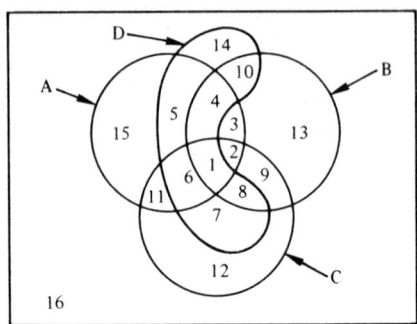

Figure 4-12

Venn diagram for four sets

Set-Theoretic Equalities

With five or more sets, Venn diagrams become so complex as to be effectively useless. The situation is analogous to that we encountered previously with truth tables where more than four or five propositions render them too cumbersome to be practical. We avoid this difficulty with sets in much the same way as we did in the propositional calculus: We establish some fundamental equalities among simple set-theoretic expressions that can be applied in stepwise fashion to prove more complex expressions equivalent. These are given in Table 4-1.

The close similarity of this table and Table 2-1 is noteworthy. There is a correspondence between union, intersection, and complementation and disjunction, conjunction, and negation, respectively, which arises from the way in which the set-theoretic operations are defined; i.e., union is defined in terms of disjunction, intersection in terms of conjunction, etc. Each of the equalities in Table 4-1, except the Consistency Principle, can be proved by using the corresponding logical equivalence in Table 2-1. For example, to prove 7(a) we note that $(X \cup Y)' = \{x \mid \sim(x \in X \vee x \in Y)\}$ by the definitions of union and complement. The set $\{x \mid x \notin X \wedge x \notin Y\}$ is identical to $\{x \mid \sim(x \in X \vee x \in Y)\}$ because the predicates are logically equivalent by DeMorgan's Laws (for propositions). Finally, by the definitions of complement and intersection, $\{x \mid x \notin X \wedge x \notin Y\} = X' \cap Y'$.

Observe also the analogy between the null set and a contradiction and between the universal set and a tautology. This arises from the fact that the

1. *Idempotent Laws*
(a) $X \cup X = X$ (b) $X \cap X = X$

2. *Commutative Laws*
(a) $X \cup Y = Y \cup X$ (b) $X \cap Y = Y \cap X$

3. *Associative Laws*
(a) $(X \cup Y) \cup Z = X \cup (Y \cup Z)$ (b) $(X \cap Y) \cap Z = X \cap (Y \cap Z)$

4. *Distributive Laws*
(a) $X \cup (Y \cap Z) = (X \cup Y) \cap (X \cup Z)$
(b) $X \cap (Y \cup Z) = (X \cap Y) \cup (X \cap Z)$

5. *Identity Laws*
(a) $X \cup \emptyset = X$ (c) $X \cap \emptyset = \emptyset$
(b) $X \cup I = I$ (d) $X \cap I = X$

6. *Complement Laws*
(a) $X \cup X' = I$ (c) $X \cap X' = \emptyset$
(b) $(X')' = X$

7. *DeMorgan's Laws*
(a) $(X \cup Y)' = X' \cap Y'$ (b) $(X \cap Y)' = X' \cup Y'$

8. *Consistency Principle*
(a) $X \subseteq Y$ iff $X \cup Y = Y$ (b) $X \subseteq Y$ iff $X \cap Y = X$

Table 4-1

Some fundamental set-theoretic equalities

propositional function $x \in \emptyset$ has no true instantiations and that all instantiations of $x \in I$ are true. The analogy fails, however, in the case of $\rightarrow$, $\leftrightarrow$, $\subseteq$, and $=$. The conditional and the biconditional connect propositions and the result is a proposition. When sets are connected by $\subseteq$ and $=$, the result is not a set, as in the case of union, intersection, or complementation, but a *proposition* about the sets so connected. One could define set theoretic operators, say $\rightarrow$ and $\leftrightarrow$, as $X \rightarrow Y \stackrel{\text{def}}{=} \{x \mid x \in X \rightarrow x \in Y\}$ and $X \leftrightarrow Y = \{x \mid x \in X \leftrightarrow x \in Y\}$, and thus preserve the analogy, but these operators would be quite different from the predicates $\subseteq$ and $=$.

Problem: Express $X \rightarrow Y$ and $X \leftrightarrow Y$ in terms of the standard operators union, intersection, and complementation.

The Consistency Principle, so called because it concerns the mutual consistency of the definitions of union, intersection, and subset, is easily verified by inspection of the Venn diagrams in Fig. 4-4. When $A \subseteq B$ [Fig. 4-4(b) and (d)], $A \cap B = A$ and $A \cup B = B$. Conversely, $A \cap B = A$ and $A \cup B = B$ only when $A \subseteq B$.

We now illustrate the use of the equalities given in Table 4-1 for manipulating set-theoretic expressions. The procedure is quite similar to that for logical expressions.

Example 4-1: Simplify the expression $(A \cup B) \cup (B \cap C)'$.

1. $(A \cup B) \cup (B \cap C)'$
2. $(A \cup B) \cup (B' \cup C')$ DeM.
3. $A \cup (B \cup (B' \cup C'))$ Assoc.
4. $A \cup ((B \cup B') \cup C')$ Assoc.
5. $A \cup (I \cup C')$ Compl.
6. $A \cup (C' \cup I)$ Comm.
7. $A \cup I$ Ident.
8. I Ident.

Example 4-2: Show that $(A \cap B) \cap (A \cap C)' = A \cap (B - C)$.

1. $(A \cap B) \cap (A \cap C)'$
2. $(A \cap B) \cap (A' \cup C')$ DeM.
3. $A \cap (B \cap (A' \cup C'))$ Assoc.
4. $A \cap ((B \cap A') \cup (B \cap C'))$ Distr.
5. $(A \cap (B \cap A')) \cup (A \cap (B \cap C'))$ Distr.
6. $(A \cap (A' \cap B)) \cup (A \cap (B \cap C'))$ Comm.
7. $((A \cap A') \cap B) \cup (A \cap (B \cap C'))$ Assoc.
8. $(\emptyset \cap B) \cup (A \cap (B \cap C'))$ Compl.
9. $(B \cap \emptyset) \cup (A \cap (B \cap C'))$ Comm.
10. $\emptyset \cup (A \cap (B \cap C'))$ Ident.
11. $(A \cap (B \cap C')) \cup \emptyset$ Comm.
12. $A \cap (B \cap C')$ Ident.
13. $A \cap (B - C)$ Theorem 4-13

In each step a set has been replaced by an equal set, so we are justified in asserting that $(A \cap B) \cap (A \cap C)' = A \cap (B - C)$.

Example 4-3: Prove Theorem 4-12; $X \cap Y \subseteq X \cup Y$.

By the Consistency Principle this expression is true iff $(X \cap Y) \cap (X \cup Y) = X \cap Y$. We demonstrate the latter.

1. $(X \cap Y) \cap (X \cup Y)$
2. $((X \cap Y) \cap X) \cup ((X \cap Y) \cap Y)$ Distr.
3. $(X \cap (X \cap Y)) \cup ((X \cap Y) \cap Y)$ Comm.
4. $((X \cap X) \cap Y) \cup ((X \cap Y) \cap Y)$ Assoc.
5. $((X \cap X) \cap Y) \cup (X \cap (Y \cap Y))$ Assoc.
6. $(X \cap Y) \cup (X \cap Y)$ Idemp. (twice)
7. $X \cap Y$ Idemp.

Example 4-4: Show that $(A \cup C) \cap (B \cup C') \subseteq (A \cup B)$.

By the Consistency Principle it suffices to demonstrate that $((A \cup C) \cap (B \cup C')) \cup (A \cup B) = (A \cup B)$.

1. $((A \cup C) \cap (B \cup C')) \cup (A \cup B)$
2. $(A \cup B) \cup ((A \cup C) \cap (B \cup C'))$ Comm.
3. $((A \cup B) \cup (A \cup C)) \cap ((A \cup B) \cup (B \cup C'))$ Distr.
4. $(A \cup B \cup A \cup C) \cap (A \cup B \cup B \cup C')$ Assoc.

Since union is associative, extra parentheses are unnecessary in line 4.

5. $(A \cup B \cup C) \cap (A \cup B \cup C')$ Comm.; Idemp.

Several steps involving applications of the Commutative and Idempotent Laws have been suppressed in going from line 4 to line 5. There is no harm in omitting such steps if they are easy for the reader to reconstruct when necessary.

6. $(A \cup B) \cup (C \cap C')$ Distr.
7. $(A \cup B) \cup \emptyset$ Comp.
8. $A \cup B$ Ident.

EXERCISES

1. Given the following sets,

$A = \{a, b, c, 2, 3, 4\}$ \qquad $E = \{a, b, \{c\}\}$

$B = \{a, b\}$ \qquad $F = \varnothing$

$C = \{c, 2\}$ \qquad $G = \{\{a, b\}, \{c, 2\}\}$

$D = \{b, c\}$

list the members of each of the following:

(a) $B \cup C$ \qquad (g) $A \cap E$ \qquad (m) $B - A$

(b) $A \cup B$ \qquad (h) $C \cap D$ \qquad (n) $C - D$

(c) $D \cup E$ \qquad (i) $B \cap F$ \qquad (o) $E - F$

(d) $B \cup G$ \qquad (j) $C \cap E$ \qquad (p) $F - A$

(e) $D \cup F$ \qquad (k) $B \cap G$ \qquad (q) $G - B$

(f) $A \cap B$ \qquad (l) $A - B$

2. Given the sets as in Exercise 1, assume that the universe of discourse I is the union of all the sets A to G. List the members of the following sets:

(a) $(A \cap B) \cup C$ \qquad (h) $D' \cap E'$

(b) $A \cap (B \cup C)$ \qquad (i) $F \cap (A - B)$

(c) $(B \cup C) - (C \cup D)$ \qquad (j) $(A \cap B) \cup I$

(d) $A \cap (C - D)$ \qquad (k) $(C \cup D) \cap I$

(e) $(A \cap C) - (A \cap D)$ \qquad (l) $C \cap D'$

(f) G' \qquad (m) $G \cup F'$

(g) $(D \cup E)'$ \qquad (n) $(B \cap C)'$

3. Show that the Distributive Laws for union and intersection are true by constructing Venn diagrams for $A \cup (B \cap C)$ and $(A \cup B) \cap (A \cup C)$ and for $A \cap (B \cup C)$ and $(A \cap B) \cup (A \cap C)$.

4. The *symmetric difference* of two sets A and B, denoted $A + B$, is defined as the set whose members are in A or in B but not in both A and B.

$$A + B \overset{\text{def}}{=} \{x \mid (x \in A \vee x \in B) \wedge \sim(x \in A \wedge x \in B)\}$$

Equivalently, symmetric difference may be defined in terms of union, intersection, and complementation as follows:

$$A + B \stackrel{\text{def}}{=} (A \cup B) - (A \cap B)$$

(a) Draw the Venn diagrams for the symmetric difference of two sets in all the five possible cases.
(b) Show that $A + B = (A - B) \cup (B - A)$ by means of the set-theoretic equalities in Table 4-1. Verify that the Venn diagrams for $(A - B) \cup (B - A)$ are equivalent to those in (a).
(c) Prove that symmetric difference is commutative; i.e.,

$$(\forall X, Y)(X + Y = Y + X).$$

(d) Express each of the following in terms of union, intersection, and complementation, and simplify:

(i) $A + A$
(ii) $A + I$
(iii) $A + \emptyset$
(iv) $A + B$, where $A \subseteq B$
(v) $A + B$, where $A \cap B = \emptyset$

5. Give a formal proof of each of the following:

(a) If $A \subseteq B$ and $B \subset C$, then $A \subset C$.
(b) If $A \subseteq B$ and $A \not\subseteq C$, then $B \not\subseteq C$.

6. Give informal proofs of each of the following statements that are true; if a statement is false, give a counter-example.

(a) If $A \neq B$ and $B \neq C$, then $A \neq C$.
(b) $(A - B) \subseteq A$.
(c) $A \cap (B - A) = \emptyset$
(d) $A \cup (B - A) = B$
(e) If $A \subseteq B$ and $C \subseteq D$, then $(A \cup B) \subseteq (C \cup D)$.

7. Demonstrate the truth of each of the following statements.

(a) $(A - B) + (B - A) = A + B$
(b) $((A - B) \cup (B - A) = \emptyset)$ iff $A = B$
(c) $B' \supseteq A$ iff A and B are disjoint.
(d) $(A + B) \subseteq B$ iff $A \subseteq B$
(e) $A \subseteq B$ iff $A \cup (B - A) = B$

8. Prove

(a) $\mathcal{P}(A) \cap \mathcal{P}(B) = \mathcal{P}(A \cap B)$
(b) $\mathcal{P}(A) \cup \mathcal{P}(B) \subseteq \mathcal{P}(A \cup B)$

5

Ordered Pairs, Cartesian Products, Relations, and Functions

A fundamental property of the sets we have discussed thus far is that in any given set all the members have equal status. The set $\{a, b\}$ could be denoted equivalently as $\{b, a\}$ since there is no order of precedence defined on the members. In order to build more complex mathematical structures it is convenient to have the notion of order defined among the elements of a set. Here we are faced with a choice: The concept of order among the members of a set could be taken as an undefined primitive along with 'set' and 'member,' or an ordered set could be defined in terms of notions already available. Either course would be acceptable, but mathematicians have chosen the latter in order to keep the number of irreducible concepts in set theory to a minimum. Once order has been defined, however, and we have shown that the definition agrees with our intuitive conception, the notion can be used just as if it were a primitive, that is, without referring back to its definition at every point.

Ordered Pairs

We start with ordered pairs—ordered sets with just two members—and then extend the notion of order to sets having any finite number of members.

> **DEFINITION:** An *ordered pair* with a as *first coordinate* and b as *second coordinate*, denoted (a, b), is equal to the set $\{\{a\}, \{a, b\}\}$.

Ordered sets are distinguished notationally from unordered sets by being written with parentheses rather than braces enclosing the members. By this definition an ordered pair is a particular sort of unordered set with two members, each of which is in turn an unordered set. It remains to show that this definition captures the essential features of what we would intuitively call an ordered pair.

The set $\{\{a\}, \{a, b\}\}$ has two members: $\{a\}$ and $\{a, b\}$. There is only one element, namely a, that is a member of both these sets, and it is taken as the *first coordinate* of the ordered pair. The remaining element, b, is then the *second coordinate*. It is easy to see that from any ordered pair written in the form (x, y) one could construct the unique unordered set to which it is equal, and, conversely, from the set $\{\{x\}, \{x, y\}\}$ one could always determine the first and second coordinates of the ordered pair.

Let us consider the unordered sets $\{a, b\}$ and $\{x, y\}$ and ask under what conditions they are equal. Since two sets are equal if and only if they have the same members, $\{a, b\}$ is equal to $\{x, y\}$ if

1. $a = x$ and $b = y$

or if

2. $a = y$ and $b = x$

If it happens that a, b, x, and y are all equal, i.e., both conditions 1 and 2 are true, then of course the sets are also equal. Now, under what conditions would we want to call the ordered sets (a, b) and (x, y) equal? A little thought should convince us that it is only when $a = x$ and $b = y$, i.e., when their first coordinates are identical and their second coordinates are identical. The following theorem states that our definition of ordered pairs has the required characteristics.

THEOREM 5-1: For any ordered pairs (a, b) and (x, y), $(a, b) = (x, y)$ iff $a = x$ and $b = y$.

Proof:
(a) The proof in one direction is immediate. If $a = x$ and $b = y$, then the sets $\{a\}$ and $\{x\}$ are equal because they have the same members. Similarly, the sets $\{a, b\}$ and $\{x, y\}$ are equal. Thus, $\{\{a\}, \{a, b\}\}$ and $\{\{x\}, \{x, y\}\}$ are equal, and therefore $(a, b) = (x, y)$.
(b) The proof in the other direction begins by a demonstration that an ordered pair (a, b) is a singleton (a set with exactly one member) if and only if $a = b$. First, suppose $a = b$. Then (a, b) is equal to $\{\{a\}, \{a, a\}\}$, which reduces to $\{\{a\}, \{a\}\}$ and then to the singleton $\{\{a\}\}$. Conversely, if (a, b) is a singleton, then $\{a\} = \{a, b\}$, and since $b \in \{a\}$, it must be the case that $b = a$. Now we assume that $(a, b) = (x, y)$ and show that $a = x$ and $b = y$. For the first case, suppose $a = b$. Then from the previous result (a, b) is a singleton, and since it is equal to (x, y), then (x, y) is also a singleton. Therefore, $x = y$, and from

$(a, b) = (x, y)$ it follows that $\{\{a\}\} = \{\{x\}\}$, whence $a = x$. Since $a = b$, $a = x$, and $x = y$, a, b, x, and y are all equal. For the second case, assume $(a, b) = (x, y)$ and $a \neq b$. Then (a, b) and (x, y) each contain just one singleton, $\{a\}$ and $\{x\}$, respectively, so $a = x$. The remaining members of (a, b) and (x, y) must be equal, so $\{a, b\} = \{x, y\}$. Since $b \in \{x, y\}$, b must be equal either to x or to y. But if $b = x$ and $x = a$, then $b = a$, contrary to our assumption. Therefore, b must be equal to y, and so we have $a = x$ and $b = y$. We have now considered the only two possible cases, $a = b$ and $a \neq b$; thus the proof is complete.

Ordered triples, quadruples, etc., are defined in terms of ordered pairs. The ordered triple with a as first, b as second, and c as third coordinate is, by definition, $((a, b), c)$, that is, the ordered pair with the ordered pair (a, b) as its first coordinate and c as its second coordinate. Similarly, the ordered quadruple given by $(((a, b), c), d)$ has a first, b second, c third, and d fourth. It is customary to omit all but the outermost parentheses in writing ordered triples, quadruples, etc.; thus, (a, b, c), (a, b, c, d). It would not do, however, to define an ordered triple (a, b, c), say, as $\{\{a\}, \{a, b\}, \{a, b, c\}\}$ since then the ordered triple $(a, a, a) = \{\{a\}, \{a, a\}, \{a, a, a\}\} = \{\{a\}\}$ would be indistinguishable from the ordered pair (a, a).

Problem: Show that $((a, a), a)$ is a set that is distinct from (a, a).

Cartesian Products

Given any two sets A and B, the set whose members are all the possible ordered pairs with first coordinates from A and second coordinates from B is called the *Cartesian product of A and B* and is denoted $A \times B$ (read 'A cross B').

DEFINITION: $A \times B \stackrel{\text{def}}{=} \{(x, y) \mid x \in A \land y \in B\}$.

For example, if $A = \{a, b, c\}$ and $B = \{1, 2\}$, then

(5-1) $A \times B = \{(a, 1), (a, 2), (b, 1), (b, 2), (c, 1), (c, 2)\}$
(5-2) $B \times A = \{(1, a), (1, b), (1, c), (2, a), (2, b), (2, c)\}$
(5-3) $B \times B = \{(1, 1), (1, 2), (2, 1), (2, 2)\}$
(5-4) $A \times A = \{(a, a), (a, b), (a, c), (b, a), (b, b), (b, c), (c, a), (c, b),$
$(c, c)\}$

The Cartesian product of two sets is itself a simple unordered set; although each of its members is an ordered pair, the members themselves are not ordered with respect to each other. $A \times B$ and $B \times A$ are, in general, distinct sets, however, since their memberships are different whenever A and B are different, as in the example above.

Cartesian products of three or more sets can be defined analogously:

(5-5) $\quad (A \times B) \times C = \{((x, y), z) \mid x \in A \land y \in B \land z \in C\}$

Although technically speaking $(A \times B) \times C$ and $A \times (B \times C)$ are distinct sets (since the former is a set of ordered triples by our definition and the latter is not), it is usual to ignore the difference by writing both as $A \times B \times C$ and to say that this denotes a set of ordered triples of the form (x, y, z). Similarly, $A \times B \times C \times D$ is taken as "the" Cartesian product having ordered quadruples of the form (w, x, y, z) as members, etc.

If $A \times B \times C \times \cdots \times N$ is a Cartesian product and x_1 is the number of members in A, x_2 is the number of members in $B, \ldots,$ and x_n is the number of members in N, then the Cartesian product has $x_1 \cdot x_2 \cdot \ldots \cdot x_n$ members. In our previous example, A has three members and B has two; thus the Cartesian product $A \times B$ contains $3 \cdot 2 = 6$ members.

One detail should be taken care of before proceeding. If one or more of the sets comprising a Cartesian product is empty, the Cartesian product is itself the null set. This result is a consequence of the definition since if either A or B is empty, then the predicate $x \in A \land y \in B$ is always false and thus $\{(x, y) \mid x \in A \land y \in B\}$ is empty. The same result holds for Cartesian products of any number of sets.

Relations

To say that John is Bill's father or that 6 is greater than 3 is to assert that one object stands in a certain relation to another. To put it in the language of the predicate calculus, $F(\text{John, Bill})$ is claimed to be a true substitution instance of the propositional function $F(x, y)$, 'x is the father of y,' and similarly for $G(6, 3)$, '6 is greater than 3.' Stated in another way, the ordered pairs (John, Bill) and (6, 3) are instances in which the relations of 'fatherhood' and 'being greater than,' respectively, hold between the first and second coordinates. The set of all ordered pairs in which the first coordinate stands in a particular relation to the second is said to specify that relation or, as the mathematician would have it, the set *is* the relation. For example, given a domain of discourse, I, containing, say, all human beings, the Cartesian product $I \times I$ is formed. The predicate $F(x, y)$, 'x is the father of y' is true of certain ordered pairs in $I \times I$ and false for others. The set of pairs for which $F(x, y)$ is true, that is, the extension of the predicate $F(x, y)$, can be called the relation of fatherhood R_f.

(5-6) $\quad R_f = \{(x, y) \in I \times I \mid F(x, y)\}$

or, simply,

(5-7) $\quad R_f = \{(x, y) \mid F(x, y)\}$

if the domain of discourse is understood.

To take another example, consider the relation of 'greater than' holding between pairs of numbers in the set $B = \{1, 2, 3\}$. The expression $G(x, y)$ stands for 'x is greater than y.'

(5-8) $\quad R_g = \{(x, y) \in B \times B \mid G(x, y)\} = \{(3, 1), (3, 2), (2, 1)\}$

In mathematics a relation is taken to be any set of ordered pairs whatever. For example, the set $\{(2, 1), (3, 3), (1, 3)\}$, because it is a set of ordered pairs, is considered a relation, and it is only accidental that there is no common English expression such as 'greater than' or 'father of' that serves as a name for this particular relation. (We could, of course, invent one.) Thus, any subset of a Cartesian product is a relation holding between the first and second coordinate of each ordered pair. As with any set, a relation can be specified by exhibiting all its members as a list, when this is possible, or by giving a predicate that is true of each ordered pair in the relation.

A relation may also be ternary, quaternary, etc., when it is made up of ordered triples, quadruples, etc. Ternary relations are specified by three-place predicates such as $B(x, y, z)$, 'x is between y and z,' quaternary relations by four-place predicates, etc. In this chapter we shall be exclusively concerned with binary relations.

A (binary) relation R that is a subset of $A \times B$ is said to be a relation *from A to B*. When only one set figures in the Cartesian product, e.g., $A \times A$, the relation is said to be a relation *in A*. In our examples above, the relation R_f is a relation in I, the set of human beings. If M is the set of all males and F the set of all females, then the relation 'husband of' is a relation from M to F.

If R is a relation and (a, b) is one of the ordered pairs in R, i.e., a stands in the relation R to b, this can be denoted either by $(a, b) \in R$ or by aRb. The latter is most often used when the relation has an accepted mathematical abbreviation such as $<$ (less than), $=$ (equals), $\geq$ (is greater than or equal to), $\in$ (is a member of), and so on. Thus, $3 < 5$, $x = y$, $7 \geq 2$, $a \in \{a\}$, etc. This system of notation is just the one mentioned in Chapter 4, where it was pointed out that we customarily write $A \subseteq B$ instead of $\subseteq(A, B)$, for example.

Domain and Range of a Relation

If R is a relation, then the set whose members are all the first coordinates of the ordered pairs in R is called the *domain* of R, abbreviated dom R. The set of all second coordinates is called the *range* of R and is abbreviated ran R. More formally, if R is a relation from A to B, i.e., $R \subseteq A \times B$, then

(5-9) $\quad$ dom $R = \{x \mid (\exists y)(x, y) \in R\}$

(5-10) $\quad$ ran $R = \{y \mid (\exists x)(x, y) \in R\}$

As an example, for the relation 'greater than' in the set $B = \{1, 2, 3\}$ in expression (5-8), we have

(5-11) $\quad$ dom $R = \{3, 2\}$

(5-12) $\quad$ ran $R = \{2, 1\}$

In general the domain and range of a relation are not equal to the sets in the Cartesian product of which the relation is a subset. If R is a relation from A to B, then necessarily dom $R \subseteq A$ and ran $R \subseteq B$, but it is not always true that dom $R = A$ or that ran $R = B$.

Universal, Null, and Identity Relations

We have remarked that mathematical definitions are often formulated to include trivial cases, and this is true of the definition of a relation. A relation may be equal to the Cartesian product of which it is a subset, and a relation may be empty. Given two sets A and B, the Cartesian product $A \times B$ is called the *universal relation from A to B*. Correspondingly, $A \times A$ is the *universal relation in A*. The null set, which contains no ordered pairs at all, may be called the *null relation*. The null set is of course unique and calling it the null relation does nothing to change that fact, but within the context of relations it is often convenient to refer to it in this way.

If R is a relation in a set A such that R contains all and only the pairs (x, x) for all $x \in A$, R is called the *identity relation in A*. For example, if $A = \{1, 2, 3\}$, the identity relation in A is the set $\{(1, 1), (2, 2), (3, 3)\}$. An identity relation is often denoted by the letter *i* with the name of the relevant set as a subscript; thus, i_A for the identity relation in A. The notion of an identity relation is not defined for relations from A to B where A and B are distinct.

Complementary and Inverse Relations

If R is a relation from A to B, then $(A \times B) - R$ is called the *complement* of R and is denoted R'. The name 'complement' and the notation indicate that this is ordinary set complementation as it was presented in Chapter 4 with the universal relation from A to B playing the role of the universal set. Thus, R' contains all the ordered pairs in $A \times B$ that are not in R.

As an example, consider once again the relation R_g in (5-8). The complement of R_g contains all members of $B \times B$ that are not in R_g.

(5-13) $\quad R_g' = \{(1, 1), (1, 2), (1, 3), (2, 2), (2, 3), (3, 3)\}$

It happens that there is a common name for R_g'; viz., 'less than or equal to.' The relations 'greater than' and 'less than or equal to' being complementary, every ordered pair in the Cartesian product must belong to one relation or the other but not to both simultaneously. Note that the complement of the universal relation is the null relation and vice versa and that the complement of a complement is the relation itself; i.e., $(R')' = R$.

If R is a relation from A to B, the *inverse* relation, R^{-1}, has as its members all the ordered pairs in R with their first and second coordinates reversed. The inverse of relation R_g is

(5-14) $\quad R_g^{-1} = \{(1, 3), (1, 2), (2, 3)\}$

This is the relation 'less than' in the set $\{1, 2, 3\}$. Since the inverse of the inverse is the relation itself, i.e., $(R^{-1})^{-1} = R$, the relations 'greater than' and 'less than' are inverses of each other. Note that if R is a relation from A to B, i.e., $R \subseteq A \times B$, the inverse relation R^{-1} is a subset of $B \times A$, while the complement R' is a subset of $A \times B$.

Properties of Relations

Certain properties of relations are so frequently encountered that it is useful to have names for them. The properties we shall consider are *reflexivity, symmetry, transitivity,* and *connexity*. All these apply only to relations *in* a set, i.e., in $A \times A$ for example, not to relations from A to B.

1. *Reflexivity*

Given a set A and a relation R in A, R is reflexive if and only if all the ordered pairs of the form (x, x) are in R for every x in A.

DEFINITION: If $R \subseteq A \times A$, then R is *reflexive* iff

$(\forall x \in A)(x, x) \in R.$

As an example, take the set $A = \{1, 2, 3\}$ and the relation $R_1 = \{(1, 1), (1, 2), (2, 2), (3, 3), (3, 1)\}$ in A. R_1 is reflexive because it contains the ordered pairs $(1, 1)$, $(2, 2)$, and $(3, 3)$. The relation $R_2 = \{(1, 1), (2, 2)\}$ is nonreflexive since it lacks the ordered pair $(3, 3)$ and thus fails to meet the definitional requirement that it contain the ordered pairs (x, x) *for every x in A*. Another way to state the definition of reflexivity is to say that a relation R in A is reflexive if and only if i_A, the identity relation in A, is a subset of R.

If a relation contains no ordered pair (x, x) with identical first and second coordinates, it is said to be irreflexive. $R_3 = \{(1, 2), (3, 2)\}$ is an example of an irreflexive relation in A. Irreflexivity is a stronger condition than nonreflexivity since every irreflexive relation is nonreflexive but not conversely. We state the definitions for nonreflexivity and irreflexivity as follows:

DEFINITION: If $R \subseteq A \times A$, then R is *nonreflexive* iff

$$\sim(\forall x \in A)(x, x) \in R.$$

DEFINITION: If $R \subseteq A \times A$, then R is *irreflexive* iff

$$(\forall x \in A)(x, x) \notin R.$$

These definitions may also be stated in terms of the identity relation in A. A relation R in A is nonreflexive iff $i_A \not\subseteq R$; the relation is irreflexive iff $R \cap i_A = \varnothing$.

2. Symmetry

A relation R in A is symmetric if and only if for every ordered pair (x, y) in R the pair (y, x) is also in R.

DEFINITION: If $R \subseteq A \times A$, then R is *symmetric* iff

$$(\forall x, y)((x, y) \in R \rightarrow (y, x) \in R).$$

It is important to note that this definition does not say that every ordered pair in $A \times A$ must be in R; rather, it says that *if* an ordered pair (x, y) is in R, then for the relation to be symmetric the ordered pair (y, x) must be in R also, and, further, this must be true of every such pair in R. Here are some examples of symmetric relations in $\{1, 2, 3\}$.

(5-15) $\{(1, 2), (2, 1), (3, 2), (2, 3)\}$

(5-16) $\{(1, 3), (3, 1)\}$

(5-17) $\{(2, 2)\}$

(5-17) is a symmetric relation because for every ordered pair in it, i.e., (2, 2), it is true that the ordered pair with the first and second coordinates reversed, i.e., (2, 2), is in the relation. Recall that the variable symbols x and y in (x, y) may take on identical values.

A relation that fails the criterion for symmetry is called nonsymmetric.

DEFINITION: If $R \subseteq A \times A$, R is *nonsymmetric* iff

$$\sim(\forall x, y)((x, y) \in R \rightarrow (y, x) \in R).$$

This expression is logically equivalent to

(5-18) $\quad (\exists x, y)((x, y) \in R \wedge (y, x) \notin R)$

The following relations are nonsymmetric:

(5-19) $\quad \{(2, 3), (1, 2)\}$

(5-20) $\quad \{(3, 3), (1, 3)\}$

(5-21) $\quad \{(1, 2), (2, 1), (2, 2), (1, 1), (2, 3)\}$

If it is never the case for any (x, y) in R that $(y, x) \in R$, the relation is called asymmetric.

DEFINITION: If $R \subseteq A \times A$, R is *asymmetric* iff

$$(\forall x, y)((x, y) \in R \rightarrow (y, x) \notin R).$$

This definition excludes the presence of any pairs (x, x) in R if it is to be asymmetric. The following are examples of asymmetric relations:

(5-22) $\quad \{(2, 3), (1, 2)\}$

(5-23) $\quad \{(1, 3), (2, 3), (1, 2)\}$

(5-24) $\quad \{(3, 2)\}$

A relation which is otherwise asymmetric but which may contain pairs of the form (x, x) is called antisymmetric.

DEFINITION: If $R \subseteq A \times A$, then R is *antisymmetric* iff

$$(\forall x, y)(((x, y) \in R \wedge (y, x) \in R) \rightarrow x = y).$$

This definition says that *if* both (x, y) and (y, x) are in R, then $x = y$, but it does not specify $(x, x) \in R$ for all $x \in A$. In other words, the relation is not required to be reflexive in order to be antisymmetric. A further consequence of the definition is that every asymmetric relation is antisymmetric but not vice versa. In an asymmetric relation, if $(x, y) \in R$, then $(y, x) \notin R$. Thus, for every pair (x, y) in an asymmetric relation, the antecedent of the conditional $((x, y) \in R \land (y, x) \in R) \to x = y$ is false, and so the relation satisfies the definition of antisymmetry.

The following relations are antisymmetric:

(5-25) $\{(2, 3), (1, 1)\}$

(5-26) $\{(1, 1), (2, 2)\}$

(5-27) $\{(1, 2), (2, 3)\}$

3. Transitivity

A relation R is transitive if and only if for all ordered pairs (x, y) and (y, z) in R, the pair (x, z) is also in R.

DEFINITION: If $R \subseteq A \times A$, R is *transitive* iff

$$(\forall x, y, z)(((x, y) \in R \land (y, z) \in R) \to (x, z) \in R).$$

Because there is no necessity for x, y, and z all to be distinct, the following relation meets the definition of transitivity,

(5-28) $\{(2, 2)\}$

where $x = y = z = 2$.

The relation given in (5-29) is not transitive,

(5-29) $\{(2, 3), (3, 2), (2, 2)\}$

because $(3, 2)$ and $(2, 3)$ are members, but $(3, 3)$ is not.

Here are some more examples of transitive relations:

(5-30) $\{(1, 2), (2, 3), (1, 3)\}$

(5-31) $\{(1, 2), (2, 1), (1, 1), (2, 2)\}$

(5-32) $\{(1, 2), (2, 3), (1, 3), (3, 2), (2, 1), (3, 1), (1, 1), (2, 2), (3, 3)\}$

A relation that fails the definition of transitivity is nontransitive.

DEFINITION: If $R \subseteq A \times A$, R is *nontransitive* iff

$$\sim(\forall x, y, z)(((x, y) \in R \land (y, z) \in R) \to (x, z) \in R).$$

Relation (5-29) is nontransitive, as are the following two:

(5-33) $\{(1, 2), (2, 3)\}$

(5-34) $\{(1, 2), (2, 3), (1, 3), (3, 1)\}$

A relation is intransitive if and only if for all ordered pairs (x, y) and (y, z) in R the pair (x, z) is not in R.

DEFINITION: If $R \subseteq A \times A$, R is *intransitive* iff

$$(\forall x, y, z)(((x, y) \in R \land (y, z) \in R) \to (x, z) \notin R).$$

The following relations are intransitive:

(5-35) $\{(1, 2), (2, 3)\}$

(5-36) $\{(3, 1), (1, 2), (2, 3)\}$

(5-37) $\{(3, 2), (1, 3)\}$

4. Connexity

A relation R in A is connex (or connected) if and only if for every two distinct elements x and y in A, $(x, y) \in R$ or $(y, x) \in R$, or both.

DEFINITION: If $R \subseteq A \times A$, R is *connex* iff

$$(\forall x, y \in A)(x \neq y \to (x, y) \in R \lor (y, x) \in R).$$

Note that the definition of connexity refers, as does the definition of reflexivity, to all the members of the set A. Further, the pairs (x, y) and (y, x) mentioned in the definition are explicitly specified as containing nonidentical first and second coordinates. Pairs of the form (x, x) are not prohibited in a connex relation, but they are irrelevant in determining connexity.

The following relations in $\{1, 2, 3\}$ are connex:

(5-38) $\{(1, 2), (3, 1), (3, 2)\}$

(5-39) $\{(1, 1), (2, 3), (1, 2), (3, 1), (2, 2)\}$

The following relations in $\{1, 2, 3\}$, which fail the definition, are nonconnex:

(5-40) $\{(1, 2), (2, 3)\}$

(5-41) $\{(1, 3), (3, 1), (2, 2), (3, 2)\}$

It may be useful at this point to give some examples of relations specified by predicates and to consider their properties of reflexivity, symmetry, transitivity, and connexity.

Example 5-1: R_f is the relation of 'fatherhood' in the set I of all human beings. R_f is irreflexive (no one is his own father); asymmetric (if x is y's father, then it is never true that y is x's father); intransitive (if x is y's father and y is z's father, then x is z's grandfather but not z's father); and nonconnex (there are distinct individuals x and y in I such that neither 'x is the father of y' nor 'y is the father of x' is true).

Example 5-2: R_g is the relation 'greater than' defined in the set $N = \{1, 2, 3, 4, \ldots\}$ of all the positive integers. N contains an infinite number of members and so does R, but we are able to determine the relevant properties of R from our knowledge of the properties of numbers in general. R is irreflexive (no number is greater than itself); asymmetric (if $x > y$, then $y \not> x$); transitive (if $x > y$ and $y > z$, then $x > z$), and connex (for every distinct pair of integers x and y, either $x > y$ or $y > x$).

Example 5-3: R_a is the relation defined by 'x is the same age as y,' in the set I of all living human beings. R_a is reflexive (everyone is the same age as himself); symmetric (if x is the same age as y, then y is the same age as x); transitive (if x and y are the same age and so are y and z, then x is the same age as z); and nonconnex (there are distinct individuals in I who are not of the same age).

Diagrams of Relations

It may be helpful in assimilating the notions of reflexivity, symmetry, etc., to introduce a diagrammatic representation of relations. The elements of the relevant set are represented by labeled points (the particular spatial arrangement of them is inessential); then, if x is related to y, i.e., if (x, y) is a member of the relation, we connect the corresponding points in the diagram by an arrow pointing from x to y. If both (x, y) and (y, x) are in the relation, the arrow is made bidirectional. As a particular case, if (x, x) is in the relation, a bidirectional arrow is drawn connecting x to itself (an 'identity loop'). The diagram in Fig. 5-1, which represents the relation in (5-42), illustrates the technique.

(5-42) $R = \{(1, 2), (2, 1), (2, 2), (1, 1), (2, 3), (3, 3)\}$

Figure 5-1.

Diagram representing the relation in (5-42).

Fig. 5.2

Diagrams of (a), an asymmetric relation, and (b), an antisymmetric relation

It is apparent from the diagram of Fig. 5-1 that the relation is reflexive since every element is connected to itself by an identity loop. In the diagram of a nonreflexive relation there will be some elements without identity loops, and in an irreflexive relation no elements will have them.

In a symmetric relation every ordered pair (x, y) is matched by the pair (y, x). In the corresponding diagram this means that every arrow is bidirectional (note, in particular, that the identity loops are bidirectional). The relation in (5-42) is seen to be nonsymmetric since in Fig. 5-1 the arrow connecting 2 to 3 is unidirectional only. An asymmetric relation has a diagram containing no bidirectional connections [Fig. 5-2(a)], and in an antisymmetric relation bidirectional connections, if there are any, are restricted to identity loops [Fig. 5-2(b)].

Transitivity is somewhat harder to determine from the diagrams. In a transitive relation for every pair (x, y) and (y, z) in the relation, the pair (x, z) is also present. In terms of these diagrams this condition becomes "if there is an arrow from x to y and one from y to z, then there is also an arrow leading directly from x to z." In Fig. 5-2(a), for example, 1 is connected to 3, 3 is connected to 2, and 1 is also directly connected to 2. These connections thus meet the definition of transitivity, and since in all other cases the definition is satisfied vacuously, the relation represented by this diagram is transitive. The relation diagramed in Fig. 5-2(b) is not transitive because (1, 2)

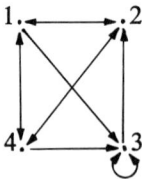

Fig. 5.3

Diagram of a connex relation

and (2, 3) are in the relation but (1, 3) is not. The relation is not intransitive, however, since the two pairs (4, 4) and (4, 3), among others, are instances of (x, y), (y, z), and (x, z) all being in the relation.

Connexity is easily determined from a diagram. A relation is connex if and only if in the corresponding diagram every pair of distinct points is connected in some way. For example, the relation represented in Fig. 5-3 is connex, but those in Fig. 5-1 and 5-2 are not.

Properties of Complementary and Inverse Relations

Given that a relation R has certain properties of reflexivity, symmetry, transitivity, and connexity, one can often make general statements about these properties also for the complementary relation R' and the inverse relation R^{-1}. For example, take a relation R in A that is reflexive. By the definition of reflexivity, for every x in A, $(x, x) \in R$. Since R^{-1} has all the ordered pairs of R with first and second coordinates reversed, then every pair (x, x) in R will also be in R^{-1}, and so the inverse of R is reflexive. The complementary relation R' contains all the ordered pairs in $A \times A$ that are not in R. Since R contains every pair of the form (x, x) for x in A, R' contains none of them; the complementary relation, therefore, is irreflexive. These observations are stated formally in the following theorem:

THEOREM 5-2: If R is a relation in a set A, then

(a) R is reflexive iff R^{-1} is reflexive.
(b) R is reflexive iff R' is irreflexive.

Proof:

(a)
1. $(\forall x \in A)(x, x) \in R$ C.P.
2. $(\forall x, y)((x, y) \in R \leftrightarrow (y, x) \in R^{-1})$ Def. of R^{-1}
3. $(v, v) \in R$ 1, U.I.
4. $(v, v) \in R \leftrightarrow (v, v) \in R^{-1}$ 2, U.I. (twice)
5. $((v, v) \in R \rightarrow (v, v) \in R^{-1}) \land$
   $((v, v) \in R^{-1} \rightarrow (v, v) \in R)$ 4, Bicond.
6. $(v, v) \in R \rightarrow (v, v) \in R^{-1}$ 5, Simp.
7. $(v, v) \in R^{-1}$ 3, 6, M.P.
8. $(\forall x \in A)(x, x) \in R^{-1}$ 7, U.G.
9. $(\forall x \in A)(x, x) \in R \rightarrow (\forall x \in A)(x, x) \in R^{-1}$

Thus, if R is reflexive, then the inverse of R is reflexive also. The proof in the other direction is now immediate. If R^{-1} is reflexive, then the inverse of R^{-1}, namely R, is reflexive. This completes the proof of part (a) of Theorem 5-2.

(b)
1. $(\forall x \in A)(x, x) \in R$ C.P.
2. $(\forall x, y)((x, y) \in R \leftrightarrow (x, y) \notin R')$ Def. of R'
3. $(v, v) \in R$ 1, U.I.
4. $(v, v) \in R \leftrightarrow (v, v) \notin R'$ 2, U.I. (twice)
5. $((v, v) \in R \rightarrow (v, v) \notin R') \wedge$
   $((v, v) \notin R' \rightarrow (v, v) \in R)$ 4, Bicond.
6. $(v, v) \in R \rightarrow (v, v) \notin R'$ 5, Simp.
7. $(v, v) \notin R'$ 3, 6, M.P.
8. $(\forall x \in A)(x, x) \notin R'$ 7, U.G.
9. $(\forall x \in A)(x, x) \in R \rightarrow (\forall x \in A)(x, x) \notin R'$

Thus, if R is reflexive, the complement of R is irreflexive. A similar series of steps justifies the converse and hence the iff in part (b) of Theorem 5-2.

From these results two others follow at once.

COROLLARY 5-1: R is nonreflexive iff R^{-1} is nonreflexive.

Proof: $p \leftrightarrow q$ is logically equivalent to $(p \rightarrow q) \wedge (q \rightarrow p)$. Replacing each conditional by its contrapositive gives $(\sim q \rightarrow \sim p) \wedge (\sim p \rightarrow \sim q)$, which is logically equivalent to $\sim p \leftrightarrow \sim q$. Thus, Corollary 5-1 is logically equivalent to Theorem 5-2(a).

COROLLARY 5-2: R is irreflexive iff R' is reflexive.

Proof: Theorem 5-2(b) and the fact that $(R')' = R$.

Conclusions that follow from a theorem by a few very simple and (allegedly) obvious steps are called *corollaries*. The distinction in terminology, however, is not intended to imply any difference in truth value, since both theorems and corollaries are true (provided of course that the premises are true and the proof is valid). The terms reflect the mathematician's attitude toward the results, a theorem being considered of greater importance or generality than a corollary, which is regarded as an ancillary truth of usually no more than passing interest.

Consider now the property of symmetry. If a relation R is symmetric, then for every (x, y) in R, (y, x) is in R also. By the definition of the inverse relation, $(x, y) \in R$ implies $(y, x) \in R^{-1}$, and $(y, x) \in R$ implies $(x, y) \in R^{-1}$. Thus, if R is symmetric, R^{-1} is symmetric also. The converse of this statement is true because $(R^{-1})^{-1} = R$. In fact, we can prove an even stronger result, namely, that R is a symmetric relation if and only if R and its inverse are identical.

THEOREM 5-3: For any relation $R \subseteq A \times A$, R is symmetric iff $R = R^{-1}$.

Proof (informal):

(a) (only if) Assume R is symmetric and $(x, y) \in R$. Therefore, (y, x) is also in R and hence (x, y) is in R^{-1}. Thus, $R \subseteq R^{-1}$. To show that $R^{-1} \subseteq R$, assume the negation, i.e., that there is some (a, b) in R^{-1} that is not in R. But $(a, b) \in R^{-1}$ implies that $(b, a) \in R$, and because R is symmetric, (a, b) is in R, thus contradicting the assumption that (a, b) is not in R. Therefore, $R^{-1} \subseteq R$ and it follows that $R = R^{-1}$.
(b) (if) Assume $R = R^{-1}$. To show that R is symmetric, assume that it is not, i.e., that there is some (x, y) in R such that (y, x) is not in R. But $(x, y) \in R$ implies that $(y, x) \in R^{-1}$, and $(y, x) \notin R$ and $(y, x) \in R^{-1}$ contradicts the assumption that $R^{-1} = R$. Therefore, R is symmetric.

COROLLARY 5-3: R is nonsymmetric iff $R \neq R^{-1}$.

Proof: Theorem 5-3 and the logical equivalence of $p \leftrightarrow q$ and $\sim p \leftrightarrow \sim q$.

THEOREM 5-4: For any relation $R \subseteq A \times A$, R is symmetric iff R' is symmetric.

Proof: Let R be a symmetric relation in A. Assume that R' is not symmetric, i.e., that there is some (x, y) in R' such that $(y, x) \notin R'$. Since (y, x) is not in R', it is necessarily in the complement of R', namely R. Because R is symmetric, (x, y) is also in R. But (x, y) cannot be in both R and R'. Therefore, if R is symmetric, R' is symmetric also. The converse follows by substituting R' for R in the preceding statement and noting that $(R')' = R$.

THEOREM 5-5: For any relation $R \subseteq A \times A$, R is transitive iff R^{-1} is transitive.

Proof: Let R be a transitive relation. Assume R^{-1} is not transitive; i.e., for some x, y, and z, $(x, y) \in R^{-1}$ and $(y, z) \in R^{-1}$ but $(x, z) \notin R^{-1}$. (x, y) and (y, z) being in R^{-1} implies that (y, x) and (z, y) are in R, and because R is transitive, (z, x) is also in R. But $(x, z) \notin R^{-1}$ implies $(z, x) \notin R$. Therefore if R is transitive, R^{-1} is transitive also. The converse follows from the fact that $(R^{-1})^{-1} = R$.

THEOREM 5-6: If R is a transitive relation in A, then R' may be either transitive or nontransitive.

Proof: We need only give examples of transitive relations such that the complement of one is transitive and the complement of the other is nontransitive.
(a) Let $A = \{1, 2, 3\}$ and $R = \{(1, 2), (2, 3), (1, 3)\}$, which is transitive. Then, $R' = \{(1, 1), (2, 1), (2, 2), (3, 1), (3, 2), (3, 3)\}$, which is also transitive.
(b) Let $A = \{1, 2, 3\}$ and $R = \{(1, 1), (2, 2), (3, 3), (1, 3), (3, 1)\}$, which is transitive. Then, $R' = \{(1, 2), (2, 1), (2, 3), (3, 2)\}$, which is nontransitive, in fact, intransitive.

THEOREM 5-7: If R is a relation in A, R is connex iff R^{-1} is connex.

Proof: Let R be a connex relation in A. Assume that R^{-1} is not connex; i.e., there are distinct x and y in A such that neither (x, y) nor (y, x) is in R^{-1}. This implies that neither (y, x) nor (x, y) is in R, and therefore R is not connex, contrary to assumption. Therefore, if R is connex, R^{-1} is connex also. The converse follows from the fact that $(R^{-1})^{-1} = R$.

Theorems 5-2, 5-3, 5-5, and 5-7 (and corollaries of these) show that a relation R and its inverse R^{-1} have the same properties of reflexivity, symmetry, transitivity, and connexity. With complementary relations, while R and R' are both symmetric or both nonsymmetric, R is reflexive iff R' is

If R is	R^{-1} is	R' is
reflexive	reflexive	irreflexive
irreflexive	irreflexive	reflexive
symmetric	symmetric (and equal to R)	symmetric
asymmetric	asymmetric	symmetric if R is null; nonsymmetric otherwise
antisymmetric	antisymmetric	not determined with respect to symmetry
transitive	transitive	not determined with respect to transitivity
intransitive	intransitive	
connex	connex	not determined with respect to connexity

Table 5-1

Inferences from given properties of a relation to those of the inverse and complementary relations

irreflexive. If R is transitive, nothing can be inferred in general about the transitivity of R'. Similarly, the connexity of R implies nothing about the connexity of R'.

These facts are summarized in Table 5-1.

Equivalence Relations and Partitions

A relation that is reflexive, symmetric, and transitive is called an *equivalence relation*. The appropriateness of this term can be seen by considering some examples.

The relation R_a (Example 5-3) defined by the predicate 'x is the same age as y' in the set of all human beings is an equivalence relation because it is reflexive, symmetric, and transitive. Any two individuals x and y that stand in this relation to each other ((x, y) and (y, x) are both in R_a because R_a is symmetric) can be regarded as *equivalent with respect to age*, regardless of how they might differ in other respects. As another example, consider the relation R_p, 'being parallel' defined on straight lines. R_p is reflexive (every line is parallel to itself), symmetric (if line x is parallel to line y, then y is parallel to x), and transitive (if x and y are parallel and so are y and z, then x is parallel to z) and is thus an equivalence relation. In terms of R_p, all straight lines that are parallel to one another are regarded as equivalent.

For every equivalence relation there is a natural way to break up the set on which it is defined into mutually exclusive subsets called *equivalence classes*. R_a, for example, specifies a division of the set of all people into equivalence classes, each of which has as its members all those persons who are of the same age. Every pair of distinct equivalence classes is disjoint, because each person, having only one age, belongs to only one equivalence class. Furthermore, the division of the set of people is exhaustive since every person has some age and thus no one is left out of an equivalence class. This is so even if just one person happens to be 150 years old and consequently occupies an equivalence class by himself. In a similar way, the equivalence relation R_p specifies the division of the infinite set of all straight lines into equivalence classes, each one of which contains all the (infinite number of) lines which are all parallel to one another.

By dividing a set into mutually exclusive and collectively exhaustive subsets we effect what is called a *partitioning* of the set.

DEFINITION: **Given a nonempty set A, a *partition* of A is a collection of nonempty subsets of A such that**
1. For any two distinct subsets X and Y, $X \cap Y = \emptyset$.
2. The union of all the subsets in the collection equals A.

The notion of a partition is not defined if the set A is empty. The subsets that are members of a partition are called *cells* of that partition.

For example, let $A = \{a, b, c, d, e\}$. Then, $P = \{\{a, c\}, \{b, e\}, \{d\}\}$ is a partition of A because every pair of cells is disjoint: $\{a, c\} \cap \{b, e\} = \emptyset$, $\{b, e\} \cap \{d\} = \emptyset$, and $\{a, c\} \cap \{d\} = \emptyset$; and the union of all the cells equals A: $\{a, c\} \cup \{b, e\} \cup \{d\} = A$.

The following three sets are also partitions of A:

(5-43) $\quad Q = \{\{a, c, d\}, \{b, e\}\}$

(5-44) $\quad R = \{\{a\}, \{b\}, \{c\}, \{d\}, \{e\}\}$

(5-45) $\quad S = \{\{a, b, c, d, e\}\}$

S is the trivial partition of A into only one set. Note however that the definition of a partition is satisfied.

The following two sets are not partitions of A:

(5-46) $\quad C = \{\{a, b, c\}, \{b, d\}, \{e\}\}$

(5-47) $\quad D = \{\{a\}, \{b, e\}, \{c\}\}$

C fails the definition because $\{a, b, c\} \cap \{b, d\} \neq \emptyset$ and D because $\{a\} \cup \{b, e\} \cup \{c\} \neq A$.

There is a close correspondence between partitions and equivalence relations. Given a partition of a set A, the relation $R = \{(x, y) \mid x \text{ and } y \text{ are in the same cell of the partition}\}$ is an equivalence relation. Conversely, given a reflexive, symmetric, and transitive relation R in A, there exists a partition of A in which x and y are in the same cell if and only if x and y are related by R. The equivalence classes specified by R are just the cells of the partition. An equivalence relation in A is sometimes said to *induce a partition on A*.

As an example, consider the set $A = \{1, 2, 3, 4, 5\}$ and the equivalence relation

(5-48) $\quad R = \{(1, 1), (1, 3), (3, 1), (3, 3), (2, 2), (2, 4), (4, 2), (4, 5),$
$\quad\quad\quad (4, 4), (5, 2), (5, 4), (5, 5), (2, 5)\}$

which the reader can verify to be reflexive, symmetric, and transitive. In this relation 1 and 3 are related among themselves in all possible ways, as are 2, 4, and 5, but no members of the first group are related to any member of the second group. Therefore, R defines the equivalence classes $\{1, 3\}$ and $\{2, 4, 5\}$, and the corresponding partition induced on A is

(5-49) $\quad P = \{\{1, 3\}, \{2, 4, 5\}\}$

Given a partition such as

(5-50) $\quad Q = \{\{1, 2\}, \{3, 5\}, \{4\}\}$

the relation R_Q consisting of all ordered pairs (x, y) such that x and y are in the same cell of the partition is as follows:

(5-51) $\quad R_Q = \{(1, 1), (1, 2), (2, 1), (2, 2), (3, 3), (3, 5), (5, 3), (5, 5),$
$(4, 4)\}$

R_Q is seen to be reflexive, symmetric, and transitive, and it is thus an equivalence relation.

The fact that there is an equivalence relation corresponding to every partition of a set is stated in the following theorem.

THEOREM 5-8: Given a partition P of a set A, the relation R defined by $R = \{(x, y) \mid x \text{ and } y \text{ are in the same cell of } P\}$ is an equivalence relation.

Proof: For every x in A, x is in the same cell as itself. Thus, $(x, x) \in R$ for all x in A, and R is reflexive. If x and y are in the same cell of P, then y and x are in the same cell. Thus, if $(x, y) \in R$, then $(y, x) \in R$, and R is symmetric. Finally, if x and y are in the same cell and y and z are in the same cell, then x and z are in the same cell, because no element of A can be in more than one cell. Thus, R is transitive.

To prove the converse relation between partitions and equivalence relations we need to introduce the following notion:

DEFINITION: Given a relation R and an element x, the set of R *relatives* of x, denoted $[x]$, is the set of all elements y such that $(x, y) \in R$.

That is, the R relatives of x are all elements appearing as second coordinate in an ordered pair with x as first coordinate. For example, in the relation R_Q [(5-51)], the R_Q relatives of 1 are 1 and 2; the R_Q relatives of 3 are 3 and 5. In general, it is not necessary that $x \in [x]$, since x need not be paired with itself.

We now prove two lemmas. (A *lemma* is a preliminary result established in preparation for proving a theorem.)

LEMMA 5-1: If R is an equivalence relation in A, then for all x and y, $(x, y) \in R \rightarrow [x] = [y]$.

Proof: Assume $(x, y) \in R$. Then $(y, x) \in R$ also, because R is symmetric. Let z be an arbitrarily selected R relative of x; i.e., $z \in [x]$. By definition of R relative, $(x, z) \in R$. Since R is transitive, $(y, x) \in R$ and $(x, z) \in R$ implies that $(y, z) \in R$, and so z is also an R relative of y; i.e., $z \in [y]$. This result holds for any z; thus, $[x] \subseteq [y]$.

Now let v be any R relative of y; i.e., $(y, v) \in R$. Again, by transitivity of R, $(x, y) \in R$ and $(y, v) \in R$ implies $(x, v) \in R$, so v is an R relative of x. Therefore, $[y] \subseteq [x]$. Thus, we have proved that if $(x, y) \in R$, where R is an equivalence relation in A, x and y have the same R relatives.

LEMMA 5-2: If R is an equivalence relation in A, and x and y are elements of A such that $[x] \neq [y]$, then $[x]$ and $[y]$ are disjoint.

Proof: Take $[x] \neq [y]$ and assume $[x]$ and $[y]$ are not disjoint; i.e., there is some z such that $z \in [x]$ and $z \in [y]$. By definition of R relatives, $(x, z) \in R$ and $(y, z) \in R$. By Lemma 5-1, $(x, z) \in R$ implies that $[x] = [z]$, and $(y, z) \in R$ implies that $[y] = [z]$, and thus $[x] = [y]$, contradicting the assumption that $[x] \neq [y]$. Therefore, $[x]$ and $[y]$ are disjoint.

THEOREM 5-9: If R is an equivalence relation in A, then the distinct sets of R relatives $[x], [y], [z], \ldots, (x, y, z, \ldots$ in $A)$ are the cells of a partition in A.

Proof: Since R is reflexive, $(x, x) \in R$ for all x in A. Therefore, for all x in A, $x \in [x]$; i.e., every member of A is in some R relative class, and thus the union of all such classes is equal to A. By Lemmas 5-1 and 5-2, distinct R relative classes are disjoint. Thus, they form a partition of A.

Functions

A function is a special kind of relation. A relation R in $A \times B$ is a function if and only if it meets both of the following conditions:

1. The domain of R is equal to A.
2. Each element in the domain is paired with just one element in the range.

This amounts to saying that a subset of a Cartesian product $A \times B$ can be called a function just in case every member of A occurs exactly once as a first coordinate in the ordered pairs of the set.

As an example, consider the sets $A = \{a, b, c\}$ and $B = \{1, 2, 3, 4\}$. The following relations in $A \times B$ are functions:

(5-52) $P = \{(a, 1), (b, 2), (c, 3)\}$

(5-53) $Q = \{(a, 3), (b, 4), (c, 1)\}$

(5-54) $R = \{(a, 3), (b, 2), (c, 2)\}$

R is a function even though both b and c are paired with the same element, 2, in the range. Condition 2 above states only that each member of the domain must have just one partner in the set of ordered pairs; nothing prohibits different elements of the domain from having the same second coordinate.

The following relations in $A \times B$ are not functions:

(5-55) $\qquad S = \{(a, 1), (b, 2)\}$

(5-56) $\qquad T = \{(a, 2), (b, 3), (a, 3), (c, 1)\}$

(5-57) $\qquad U = \{(a, 2), (a, 3), (b, 4)\}$

S fails to meet condition 1 because the set of first coordinates, namely $\{a, b\}$, is not equal to A. T does not satisfy condition 2, since a is paired with both 2 and 3. In relation U both conditions are violated.

Functions can be diagramed in a way similar to that used for relations: The first coordinate is connected to the second coordinate of each ordered pair by an arrow. Of course when the function is from one set to another instead of in one set, there will be two sets in the diagram. In this representation, relations P, R, S, and T would appear as in Fig. 5-4.

By means of such diagrams it is easy to visualize the difference between relations in general and the restricted varieties of them that qualify as functions. A relation (from A to B) is represented by any pattern of arrows whatever connecting the elements of A to those in B. A function, however, has exactly one arrow emanating from each element of A.

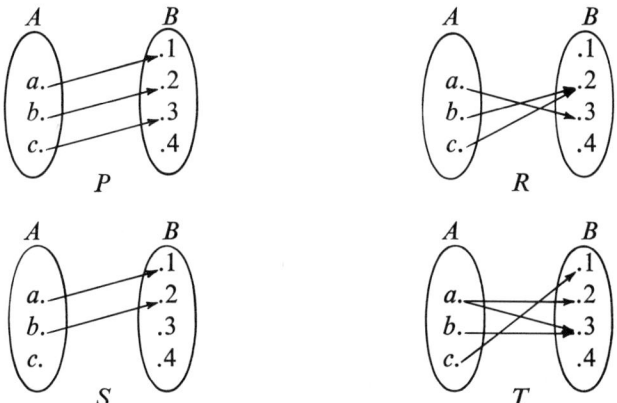

Figure 5-4

Representation of functions P and R and relations S and T

Much of the terminology used in talking about functions is the same as that for relations. We say that a function that is a subset of $A \times B$ is a function *from A to B*, while one in $A \times A$ is said to be a function *in A*. Frequently one sees the notation '$f: A \to B$' as an abbreviation for the statement '*f* is a function from *A* to *B*.' The set *B* is often called the *codomain* of the function. In some contexts it is useful to state specifically whether or not the range of a function from *A* to *B* is equal to the set *B*, i.e., whether the range is equal to the codomain. (We already know that the domain equals *A* as a necessary condition for being a function.) Accordingly, we have the following definition of *into* and *onto* functions.

DEFINITION: If $f: A \to B$ and ran $f = B$, f is said to be a function from A onto B. If the range of f is a subset of B, f is a function from A into B.

Every onto function is, therefore, necessarily into, but into functions are not always onto. In the examples diagramed in Fig. 5-5, function *f* is from *A* onto *C*, *g* is from *A* onto *D*, while *h* is from *A* into *C* but not onto *C*.

Elements in the domain of a function are sometimes called *arguments* and their correspondents in the range, *values*. Of function *f* in Fig. 5-5, for example, one may say that it takes on the value 3 at argument *c*. The usual way to denote this fact is $f(c) = 3$, with the name of the function preceding the argument, which is enclosed in parentheses, and the corresponding value to the right of the equals sign. In the same way, one could state that $f(c) = h(b)$: The value of *f* at argument *c* is the same as the value of *h* at argument *b*. This can be read briefly as '*f* of *c* equals *h* of *b*.'

'Transformation,' 'map,' 'mapping,' and 'correspondence' are commonly used synonyms for 'function,' and often '$f(a) = 2$' is read as '*f* maps *a* into 2.' Such a statement gives a function the appearance of an active process that changes arguments into values. A term such as 'correspondence,' however, suggests a static picture of a function as a set of ordered pairs. It is important to recognize that from a mathematical point of view there is nothing essential involved in this terminological difference. A function is a

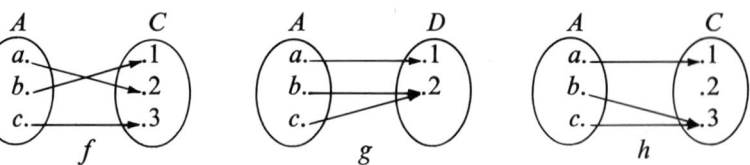

Figure 5-5

Illustration of onto and into functions

pairing of the members of two sets in a particular way, and subject to certain constraints (conditions 1 and 2 above). While it may sometimes be helpful to think of a function as a kind of machine that accepts an argument as input and emits its value as output, one should not be misled into thinking that functions are somehow essentially "active" in a way that sets, relations, etc., are not.

One reason that functions are so often thought of as processes is that for many of the functions commonly encountered in mathematics the pairing of arguments and values can be specified by a formula containing operations such as addition, multiplication, division, etc. For example, $f(x) = 2x + 1$ is a function that, when defined on the set of integers, pairs 1 with 3, 2 with 5, 3 with 7, and so on. In our usual notation we might write

(5-58) $\quad f = \{(x, y) \mid y = 2x + 1\} \quad$ (where x and y are integers)

That is, f consists of all ordered pairs of integers in which the second coordinate is one greater than twice the first coordinate. $2x + 1$ is a formula for computing the value of the function at each argument, but it is often also used informally as a name for the function, i.e., 'the function $2x + 1$.' Strictly speaking, however, the function is a set of ordered pairs, while the expression $2x + 1$ is a part of the predicate specifying the set.

Inverse Functions

For a function, as for relations generally, an inverse may be defined in which the members of each ordered pair are reversed. Because of the restricted properties of functions, however, the inverse of a function might not itself be a function. For example, the inverse of function R in Fig. 5-4

(5-59) $\quad R^{-1} = \{(2, b), (2, c), (3, a)\}$

is a relation but not a function because 2 is paired with both b and c. Similarly, P^{-1} is not a function since the domain does not equal the set B. (The inverse of a function from A to B is of course a relation from B to A.)

The inverse of function f in Fig. 5-5 is a function since the set of ordered pairs $\{(1, b), (2, a), (3, c)\}$ meets both conditions 1 and 2 above. In general, the inverse of a function f from A to B will also be a function just in case both the following conditions are met:

    3. No two distinct elements of A are paired with the same element of B.

    4. f is onto B.

If the function does not meet condition 3, then some distinct x and y in A are mapped into the same element z in B. Thus, the inverse will contain the ordered pairs (z, x) and (z, y) where $x \neq y$ and will fail to be a function because of condition 2. If the original function is not onto B, then there is some element of B that does not occur as a second coordinate of an ordered pair. The inverse, then, will lack this element as a first coordinate, and so the domain will not equal B.

A function meeting condition 3 is called *one-to-one*. Formally, a function f from A to B is one-to-one if and only if $(\forall x, y \in A)(x \neq y \rightarrow f(x) \neq f(y))$. P in Fig. 5-4 and f in Fig. 5-5 are examples of one-to-one functions. Function g in Fig. 5-5 is not one-to-one since distinct elements in the domain are mapped onto the same element ($g(b) = g(c) = 2$).

A function that is both one-to-one and onto (i.e., that meets both conditions 3 and 4) is called a *one-to-one correspondence*. Function f of Fig. 5-5 is an example.

THEOREM 5-10: Given a function f from A to B, f^{-1} is a function iff f is a one-to-one correspondence.

Proof: (a) Assume $f: A \rightarrow B$ is one-to-one and onto. We must show that f^{-1} meets conditions 1 and 2, i.e., that it is a function. Suppose f^{-1} fails condition 1, i.e., dom $f^{-1} \neq B$. Then there is some y in B such that for all x in A, $(y, x) \notin f^{-1}$. By the definition of inverse, there is some y in B such that for all x in A, $(x, y) \notin f$, so f is not onto. Contradiction: $\therefore f^{-1}$ meets condition 1.

Suppose now that f^{-1} fails condition 2; i.e., $(\exists x \in B)(\exists y, z \in A)((x, y) \in f^{-1} \wedge (x, z) \in f^{-1} \wedge y \neq z)$. Then $(y, x) \in f \wedge (z, x) \in f \wedge y \neq z$, so f is not one-to-one. Contradiction: $\therefore f^{-1}$ also meets condition 2 and is a function.

(b) Assume f^{-1} is a function. We must show that f is one-to-one and onto. Suppose f is not one-to-one; i.e., $(\exists x, y \in A)(\exists z \in B)((x, z) \in f \wedge (y, z) \in f \wedge x \neq y)$. Then $(z, x) \in f^{-1} \wedge (z, y) \in f^{-1} \wedge x \neq y$, so f^{-1} is not a function. Contradiction: Thus, f is one-to-one.

Finally, suppose f is not onto; i.e., $(\exists y \in B)(\forall x \in A)(x, y) \notin f$. Then $(\exists y \in B)(\forall x \in A)(y, x) \notin f^{-1}$, so dom $f^{-1} \neq B$ and f^{-1} is not a function. Contradiction: $\therefore f$ is onto.

COROLLARY 5-4: If $f: A \rightarrow B$ is a one-to-one and onto function, then f^{-1} is also.

Proof: The inverse of f^{-1}, namely f, is a function. Therefore, by Theorem 5-10, f^{-1} is one-to-one and onto.

Composites

Given two functions $f: A \to B$ and $g: B \to C$, we may form a new function, called the *composite* of f and g, which is from A to C and which may be characterized essentially as follows: If f maps x into y and g maps y into z, then the composite of f and g maps x into z. Here is a more formal definition:

DEFINITION: Given a function f from A to B and a function g from B to C, the composite of f and g (denoted $g \circ f$) is given by

$$\{(x, z) \mid (\exists y)((x, y) \in f \land (y, z) \in g)\}.$$

Figure 5-6 shows two functions f and g and their composite $g \circ f$.

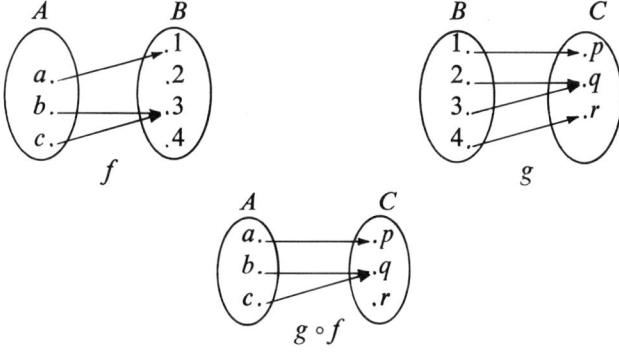

Figure 5-6

Diagram of the composite of two functions

Note that f is into, while g is onto and that neither is one-to-one. This shows that composites may be formed from functions that do not have these special properties. The essential point is that the range of the first function is a subset of the domain of the second; otherwise, there would be no y such that $(x, y) \in f$ and $(y, z) \in g$, and so the set of ordered pairs defined by $g \circ f$ would be null.

In the example of Fig. 5-6, f is the first function and g is the second in the composite. Order is crucial, since in general the composite of f with g, $(g \circ f)$, is not equal to the composite of g with f, $(f \circ g)$. The notation, $g \circ f$, which seems to read backward, results from the mathematician's custom of denoting the value of f at argument a by $f(a)$. The value of g at the argument $f(a)$ is then written $g(f(a))$. By the definition of composite, $g(f(a))$ and $(g \circ f)(a)$ denote the same value.

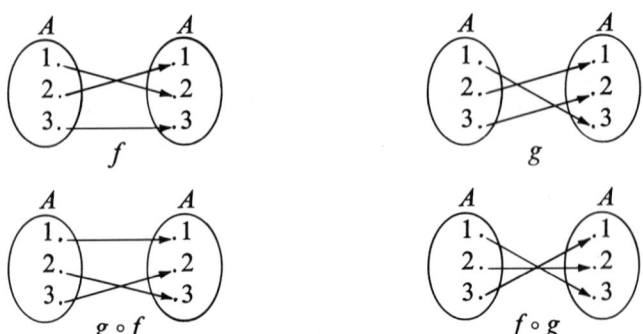

Figure 5-7

Diagrams of functions such that $g \circ f \neq f \circ g$

To show that composition of functions is not commutative, it suffices to produce one example in which $g \circ f \neq f \circ g$. Such an example is given in Fig. 5-7.

Although composition of functions is not commutative, it is associative, as shown in the following theorem:

THEOREM 5-11: Given any functions $f: A \rightarrow B$, $g: B \rightarrow C$, and $h: C \rightarrow D$, $h \circ (g \circ f) = (h \circ g) \circ f$.

Proof: $(h \circ (g \circ f))(a) = h((g \circ f)(a)) = h(g(f(a))) = (h \circ g)(f(a)) = ((h \circ g) \circ f)(a)$

Identity Functions

A function $f: A \rightarrow A$ such that $f = \{(x, x) \mid x \in A\}$ is called the *identity function in A* and is denoted i_A. This function maps every element of A into itself, and of course it is exactly the same as the identity relation in A. Because conditions 1 and 2 are satisfied, an identity relation is also a function.

Composition of a function f with the appropriate identity function gives a function that is equal to the function f itself. This is illustrated in Fig. 5-8.

Given a function $f: A \rightarrow B$ that is a one-to-one correspondence (thus the inverse is also a function), we have the following general equations:

(5-60) $\qquad f^{-1} \circ f = i_A$

(5-61) $\qquad f \circ f^{-1} = i_B$

These are illustrated in Fig. 5-9.

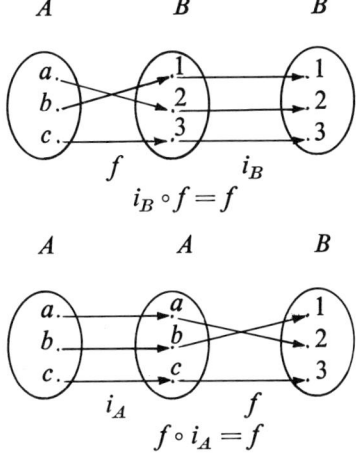

Figure 5-8

Diagrams illustrating composition with an identity function

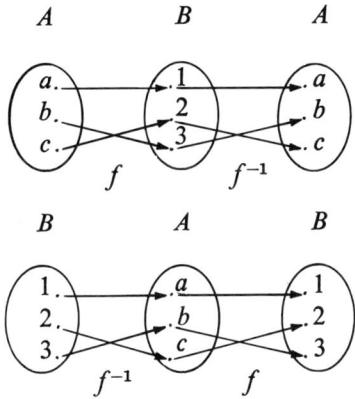

Figure 5-9

Diagrams illustrating the composition of a function with its inverse

Inverses of Composites

The inverse of a composite function is equal to the composite of the inverses of the functions *but in the reverse order*. In order for the inverses to be functions all the functions and the composites must be one-to-one correspondences. An illustrative example is given in Fig. 5-10.

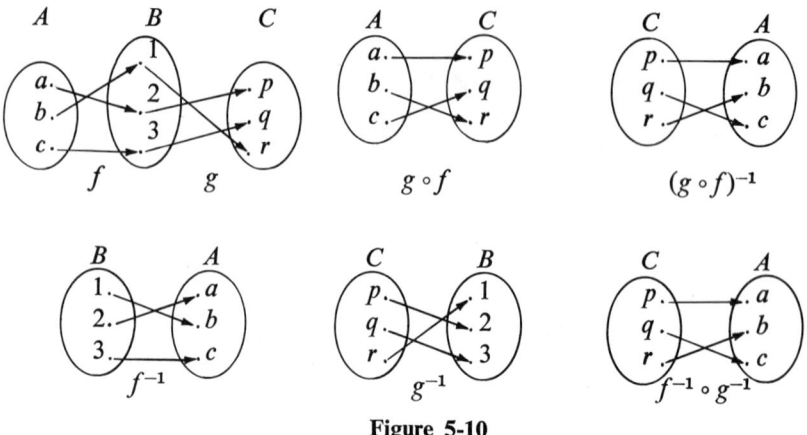

Figure 5-10

Diagrams illustrating that $(g \circ f)^{-1} = f^{-1} \circ g^{-1}$

THEOREM 5-12: Given functions $f: A \to B$ and $g: B \to C$ that are one-to-one correspondences, $(g \circ f)^{-1} = (f^{-1} \circ g^{-1})$.

Proof: Assume $(x, z) \in (g \circ f)^{-1}$. Then $(z, x) \in (g \circ f)$. By the definition of composite, $(\exists y \in B)((z, y) \in f \land (y, x) \in g)$. Thus, $(\exists y \in B)((y, z) \in f^{-1} \land (x, y) \in g^{-1})$, and so (x, z) is in the composite $f^{-1} \circ g^{-1}$. This shows that $(g \circ f)^{-1} \subseteq (f^{-1} \circ g^{-1})$. The proof of the reverse inclusion takes the same steps in the opposite order.

Many of the results shown for functions can be extended to relations generally. For example, one can define in an analogous way the composite of two relations.

DEFINITION: Given relations R from A to B and S from B to C, the *composite* of R and S, denoted $S \circ R$, is the set

$$\{(x, z) \mid (\exists y \in B)((x, y) \in R \land (y, z) \in S)\}.$$

Given a relation R from A to B, we also have $i_B \circ R = R$ and $R \circ i_A = R$, and given two relations R from A to B and S from B to C, $(S \circ R)^{-1} = R^{-1} \circ S^{-1}$. Composition of relations is likewise associative and noncommutative.

Problem: Show that for a relation R from A to B, the composite $R^{-1} \circ R$ is, in general, not equal to i_A.

The notion of a function, like that of a relation, is also easily generalized to include sets of ordered triples, quadruples, etc. If f is a set of ordered

n-tuples of the form $(x_1, x_2, \ldots, x_{n-1}, x_n)$, then it is said to be a function of $n - 1$ variables, and x_n is the value of the function at the argument $(x_1, x_2, \ldots, x_{n-1})$. A simple example of a function of two variables is $x^2 + y^2$, which when defined on the positive integers and zero consists of ordered triples $(0, 0, 0)$, $(1, 1, 2)$, $(1, 2, 5)$, $(3, 4, 25)$, etc. The order of the members of the n-tuples is crucial. For example, the function $x + 2y$ maps the pair $(1, 3)$ onto the value 7 but the pair $(3, 1)$ onto 5.

Sometimes in mathematical parlance the term 'function' is used to refer to a mapping from A to B even though it does not meet condition 1; i.e., the domain does not equal A. Such mappings are properly called *partial functions* or *restrictions* to emphasize that the domain is a proper subset of A. The most crucial property of functions, then, is that they meet condition 2, i.e., that each argument be assigned a single value. Incidentally, this requirement has the consequence that some things that are sometimes called functions in mathematics must now be regarded as relations but not functions. For example, the "function" $\sqrt{x}$ defined on the positive integers has two values, one positive and one negative, for each argument ($\sqrt{4} = +2$ or -2). By our definition then, $\sqrt{x}$ cannot be called a function. It could, however, be regarded as the union of two functions, f^+ and f^-, in the following way:

(5-62) $\quad f^+ = \{(0, 0), (1, 1), (4, 2), (9, 3), \ldots\}$

(5-63) $\quad f^- = \{(0, 0), (1, -1), (4, -2), (9, -3), \ldots\}$

EXERCISES

1. In the following problem, use the sets

$$A = \{b, c\} \quad \text{and} \quad B = \{2, 3\}$$

(a) Specify the following sets by listing their members:

(i) $A \times B$
(ii) $B \times A$
(iii) $A \times A$
(iv) $(A \cup B) \times B$
(v) $(A \cap B) \times B$
(vi) $(A - B) \times (B - A)$

(b) Classify each statement as true or false:

(i) $(A \times B) \cap (B \times A) = \emptyset$
(ii) $(A \times A) \subseteq (A \times B)$
(iii) $(c, c) \subseteq (A \times A)$
(iv) $\{(b, 3), (3, b)\} \subseteq (A \times B) \cup (B \times A)$
(v) $\emptyset \subseteq A \times A$
(vi) $\{(b, 2), (c, 3)\}$ is a relation from A to B.
(vii) $\{(b, b)\}$ is a relation in A.

2. Consider the following relation in $A \times (A \cup B)$, where $A = \{b, c\}$ and $B = \{2, 3\}$:

$$R = \{(b, b), (b, 2), (c, 2), (c, 3)\}$$

(a) Specify the domain and range of R.
(b) Specify the complementary relation R' and the inverse relation R^{-1}.
(c) Give the members of the identity relation in $(A \cup B) \times (A \cup B)$.

3. Given the set $A = \{1, 2, 3, 4\}$, classify each of the following relations and their inverses and complements as to reflexivity, symmetry, transitivity, and connexity. In each case make the strongest possible statement; for example, call a relation irreflexive whenever possible rather than just nonreflexive. If any of the relations happens to be an equivalence relation, show the partition that it induces on A.

$R_1 = \{(1, 1), (2, 1), (3, 4), (2, 2), (3, 3), (4, 4), (4, 1)\}$
$R_2 = \{(3, 4), (1, 2), (1, 4), (2, 3), (2, 4), (1, 3)\}$
$R_3 = \{(2, 4), (3, 1), (3, 4), (2, 2), (1, 3), (4, 3), (4, 2)\}$
$R_4 = \{(1, 1), (2, 4), (1, 3), (2, 2), (3, 1), (4, 4), (3, 3), (4, 2)\}$

4. Give the equivalence relation that induces the following partition on A:

$$P = \{\{1\}, \{2, 3\}, \{4\}\}$$

5. How many distinct partitions of $A = \{1, 2, 3, 4\}$ are possible?

6. Investigate whether each of the following relations is reflexive, symmetric, transitive, and connex. If any one is an equivalence relation, indicate the partition it induces on the appropriate set.

(a) $M = \{(x, y) \mid x$ and y are a minimal pair of utterances in English$\}$
(b) $C = \{(x, y) \mid x$ and y are phones of English that are in complementary distribution$\}$
(c) $F = \{(x, y) \mid x$ and y are phones of English that are in free variation$\}$
(d) $A = \{(x, y) \mid x$ and y are allophones of the same English phoneme$\}$
(e) S is the relation defined by 'X is a subset of Y.'
(f) P is the relation defined by 'X is a proper subset of Y.'
(g) Q is the relation defined by 'X is a set having the same number of members as Y.'

7. Prove: For any relation R in a set A, R is asymmetric iff $R \cap R^{-1} = \emptyset$.

8.* What is wrong with the following "proof" that reflexivity is a consequence of symmetry and transitivity?

$(x, y) \in R \Rightarrow (y, x) \in R$ by symmetry

$(x, y) \in R \land (y, x) \in R \Rightarrow (x, x) \in R$ by transitivity

9. Form the composites $R_2 \circ R_1$ and $R_1 \circ R_2$, where R_1 and R_2 are as given in Exercise 3. Are the composites equal?

10. Prove: For any relations R and S in $A \times A$, if S is reflexive, $R \subseteq (S \circ R)$.

11. Prove: For any relation R in $A \times A$, R is transitive iff $(R \circ R) \subseteq R$.

12. Prove: If R and S are both equivalence relations in A, $R \cap S$ is also an equivalence relation in A.

13. Let $A = \{a, b, c\}$ and $B = \{1, 2\}$. How many distinct relations are there from A to B? How many of these are functions? How many of the functions are onto? one-to-one? Do any of the functions have inverses that are functions? Answer the same questions for all relations from B to A.

14. Let $Z = \{0, 1, 2, 3, 4, \ldots\}$, the set of all positive integers and zero. Let f map every $x \in Z$ into $x + 1$, and let g map every $x \in Z$ into x^2. Show that f and g are functions and that each is one-to-one and into but not onto. Describe the functions $g \circ f$ and $f \circ g$. Are they one-to-one? onto?

15. Let P be the set of all consonantal phonemes in English and define R to be a relation in P such that $(x, y) \in R$ iff /xy/ is an acceptable two-constant initial cluster in English. Investigate whether R is reflexive, symmetric, transitive, and connex. From R, define a set of ordered triples T as follows:

$$T = \{(x, y, z) \mid (x, y) \in R \land (y, z) \in R\}$$

Does T bear any correspondence to the allowed initial three-consonant clusters of English?

16. The reader should now be prepared to read and discuss critically an article by Harary and Paper, 1957. This was one of the earliest papers

* From Garrett Birkhoff and Saunders MacLane, *A Survey of Modern Algebra*, rev. ed. (New York: The Macmillan Co., © 1953); reprinted by permission.

to appear in the literature applying notions from discrete mathematics to linguistic data. The authors state (p. 145), "It is our aim to provide a technique for describing and quantifying phonemic interaction, thereby sharpening the concept of distribution," and later (p. 151), "... new information is available about the real-world situation as a result of the application of a particular mathematical model." To what extent are Harary and Paper successful in accomplishing their objectives, and how much of the mathematical apparatus is essential to what they have done?

6

Orders, Operations, Configurations, and Isomorphisms

Orders

In Chapter 5 we defined the notion of an ordered pair and noted that this definition could be extended to ordered triples, quadruples, etc. In each of these the members form a linear sequence; e.g., in the ordered triple (a, b, c) the member a precedes both b and c; b follows a and precedes c; and c follows both a and b. A convenient way of representing this ordered triple is shown in Fig. 6-1, where an arrow connects each member to those which follow it.

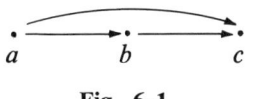

Fig. 6-1

Diagram of the ordering of the members of the triple (a, b, c)

Using the same system of representation, let us now diagram a different ordering of the same elements (Fig. 6-2). Here a precedes both b and c, but there is no order of precedence defined between b and c. No ordered triple containing the elements a, b, and c corresponds to the ordering shown in Fig. 6-2. Thus, to describe orderings such as these, we must extend the concept of an order beyond that of ordered n-tuples. The usual course is to define an order as a kind of relation, i.e., as a set of ordered pairs, in a manner suggested by the preceding diagrams. In each ordered pair the first coordinate is considered as preceding the second. A complete specification

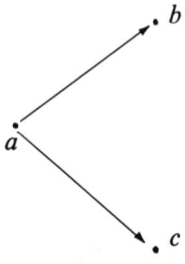

Fig. 6–2

Diagram of an ordering of three elements not representable as an ordered triple

of how each element is ordered with respect to all the others is given then by the entire collection of pairs. For example, the ordering in Fig. 6-2 would be given by the following relation:

(6-1) $\quad \{(a, b), (a, c)\}$

and the ordering in Fig. 6-1 by

(6-2) $\quad \{(a, b), (a, c), (b, c)\}$

It may seem circular to define an order in terms of ordered pairs, but there is in fact nothing illegitimate in this. Recall that an ordered pair is defined in terms of unordered sets and that a relation is just an unordered set of ordered pairs. An order defined as a type of relation is therefore ultimately reducible to unordered sets, and thus there is no circularity. It remains to be shown, however, that the definition we choose is a reasonable one, in the sense that it ascribes to orders the properties we intuitively expect them to have. Let us consider what these might be.

For any a, b, and c, if a precedes b and b precedes c, then it is necessarily also the case that a precedes c, at least if we are using the word 'precedes' in the normal way. Thus, if the ordered pairs (a, b) and (b, c) are in the order, then so is (a, c), or in other words an order is transitive. Next, if a and b are distinct elements and a precedes b, we ask if b can ever precede a. The answer is yes, if the elements are arranged in a "circular" order, i.e., with a preceding b, b preceding c, and c preceding a. If this is the case, then b also precedes a as a consequence of transitivity. The usual practice is to exclude circular orderings from the definition (if they are allowed, we have what is called a *preorder*) and to require that if a and b are distinct, then it is never the case that both a precedes b and b precedes a. This is a condition on *distinct* elements. When $a = b$, we have a choice that comes to this: Is an element allowed to precede (and follow) itself or not? It happens that either of the alternatives leads to a useful definition. If no element precedes itself, the order is called *strict* (or *strong*), and if every element precedes itself, the order is called *weak*. Thus, the relation of 'preceding' is irreflexive in strict orders and reflexive in weak orders. (One could of course choose to let some, but not all, of the elements precede themselves, but this does not ordinarily prove useful.) Further, in a strict order, the relation of 'preceding' is asymmetric. Since no element can precede itself, when a precedes b they are necessarily distinct, and therefore b does not precede a. In weak orders the relation is antisymmetric (a preceding b and b preceding a implies $a = b$). Accordingly, we have the following definitions:

DEFINITION: Given a set A, a binary relation R in A is a *weak order* iff R is reflexive, antisymmetric, and transitive.

DEFINITION: Given a set A, a binary relation R in A is a *strict* (or *strong*) *order* iff R is irreflexive, asymmetric, and transitive.

To illustrate, let $A = \{a, b, c, d\}$. The following relations are all weak orders in A:

(6-3)
$$R_1 = \{(a, b), (a, c), (a, d), (b, c), (a, a), (b, b), (c, c), (d, d)\}$$
$$R_2 = \{(b, a), (b, b), (a, a), (c, c), (d, d), (c, b), (c, a)\}$$
$$R_3 = \{(d, c), (d, b), (d, a), (c, b), (c, a), (a, a), (b, b), (c, c),$$
$$(d, d), (b, a)\}$$

These are represented in Fig. 6-3 according to the method of diagraming relations introduced in Chapter 5.

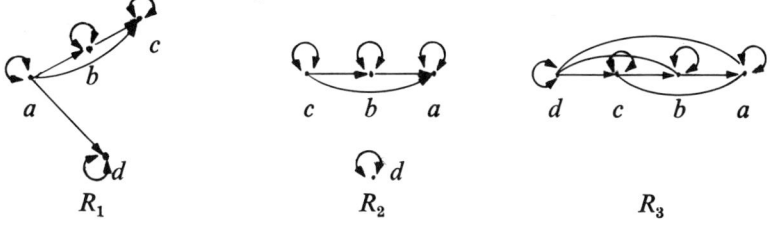

Figure 6-3

Diagrams of the orders in (6-3)

To these weak orders there correspond the strict orders S_1, S_2, and S_3, respectively:

(6-4)
$$S_1 = \{(a, b), (a, c), (a, d), (b, c)\}$$
$$S_2 = \{(b, a), (c, b), (c, a)\}$$
$$S_3 = \{(d, c), (d, b), (d, a), (c, b), (c, a), (b, a)\}$$

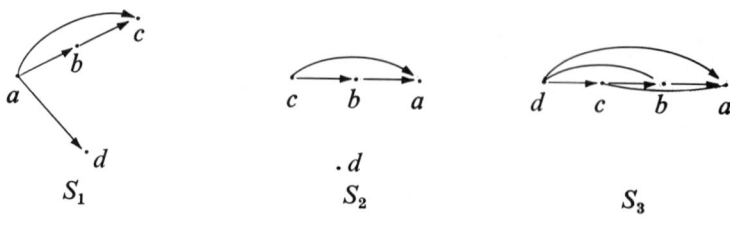

Figure 6-4

Diagrams of the orders in (6-4)

These can be gotten from the weak orders by removing all the ordered pairs of the form (x, x). The corresponding diagrams (Fig. 6-4) have no arrows connecting an element to itself (identity loops). Conversely, one can make a strict order into a weak order by adding all the pairs of the form (x, x) for every x in A.

Terminology

If R is an order, either weak or strict, and $(x, y) \in R$, we say that x *precedes* y, x *is a predecessor of* y, y *succeeds* (or *follows*) x, or y *is a successor of* x, these being equivalent locutions. To emphasize that the order is strict or weak, the appropriate modifier is added: Thus, x *strictly precedes* y, x *is a strict predecessor of* y, y *is a weak successor of* x, etc. To illustrate, in R_1, c is a weak successor of a, b, and c, while d weakly precedes only itself. In R_2, d weakly precedes and follows itself but, in S_2, d neither strictly precedes nor strictly follows any element.

A notion that is useful in discussing orders is that of an *immediate predecessor*. If x precedes y and x and y are distinct elements, then x is an immediate predecessor of y iff there is no element z, distinct from both x and y, which is between them in the ordering. Observe that the elements are all required to be distinct. Thus, no element can be an immediate predecessor of itself. In R_1 and S_1, b is between a and c; therefore, although a precedes c, a is not an immediate predecessor of c. In R_2 and S_2, c is an immediate predecessor of b, and b is an immediate predecessor of a.

In diagraming orders it is usually simpler and more perspicuous to connect pairs of elements by arrows only if one is an immediate predecessor of the other. The remaining connections can be inferred from the fact that the relation is transitive. In order to distinguish weak from strict orders, however, it is necessary to include the identity loops as well. Diagramed in this way, the orders in (6-3) and (6-4) would appear as in Fig. 6-5. Henceforth, we shall use only immediate predecessor diagrams for orders.

S_3 is a linear sequence and thus could be represented as an ordered n-tuple, in this case (d, c, b, a), while S_1 and S_2 are types of orders that cannot be so represented. The formal property that distinguishes the former from the latter two is connexity. In S_3 for every distinct x and y in A, either (x, y) or (y, x) is in S_3; that is, S_3 is connex. The diagrams in Fig. 6-4 show this most clearly. Every pair of distinct elements in S_3 is connected by an arrow, but, in S_1, d is connected neither to b nor to c, and, in S_2, d is not connected to any other element. If a connex order is diagramed by connecting only immediate predecessors as in Fig. 6-5, then the elements form a single chain, and hence such orders are said to be *linear*. The term '*total*' is also used with the same meaning. The general class of orders we have just introduced, i.e., transitive relations that are also either antisymmetric and reflexive or else asymmetric and irreflexive, are known as *partial orders*. Total orders are a special subclass of partial orders that happen, in addition, to be connex. It is an unfortunate consequence of this terminology that some orders can be correctly called both partial and total.

Mathematicians frequently refer to a set together with a partial order defined on that set as a *partially ordered set* (or if the order happens to be total, as a *totally ordered set*). For example, if we take the order R_1 in the set $A = \{a, b, c, d\}$, then the partially ordered set consisting of A together with R_1 is customarily written as an ordered pair (A, R_1). The motivation for this is that sometimes it is conceptually more natural to regard a set and an order defined with that set as its basis as distinct components of an overall mathematical structure. An ordered pair is simply a convenient way of putting the components together into a unit. Structures composed of one or more sets together with one or more relations defined on those sets are

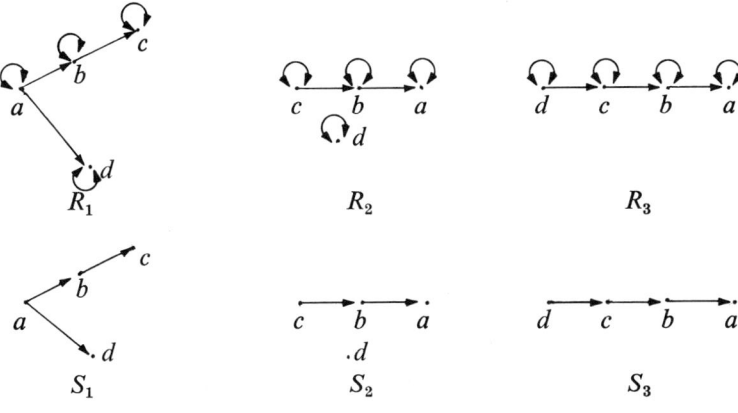

Figure 6-5

Immediate predecessor diagrams of the orders in (6-3) and (6-4)

known generally as *mathematical configurations*. Much of current mathematics is devoted to the study of one or another of the endless variety of possible mathematical configurations. When we introduce formal grammars in later chapters, they are formulated as a type of mathematical configuration.

Example 6-1: $D = \{1, 2, 3, 4\}$. The relation 'less than or equal to' in $D \times D$ is reflexive, antisymmetric, transitive, and connex, and it is thus a weak total order. The ordered pair $(D, \leq)$ is a (weakly) totally ordered set.

Example 6-2: $B = \{a, b, c\}$. The relation $\subset$ in $\mathscr{P}(B)$ is irreflexive, asymmetric, and transitive and thus $(\mathscr{P}(B), \subset)$ is a (strictly) partially ordered set.

The same diagram can be thought of as representing either a partial order or the corresponding partially ordered set. Immediate predecessor diagrams for $(D, \leq)$ and $(\mathscr{P}(B), \subset)$ are shown in Fig. 6-6.

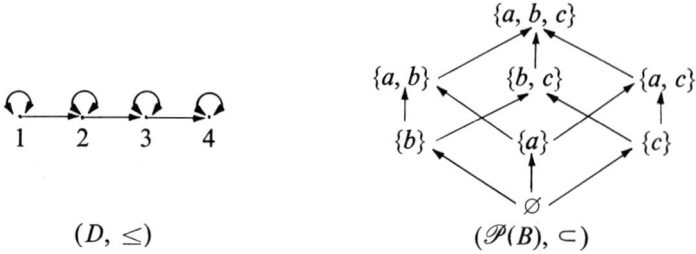

Figure 6-6

Immediate predecessor diagrams of the partially ordered sets of Examples 6-1 and 6-2

Partially ordered sets have corresponding strict and weak forms. The strictly totally ordered set corresponding to $(D, \leq)$ is $(D, <)$, where the relation 'less than or equal to' is replaced by 'less than.' Similarly, the weakly partially ordered set corresponding to $(\mathscr{P}(B), \subset)$ is $(\mathscr{P}(B), \subseteq)$.

There is a group of terms referring to elements that stand at the extremes of a partially ordered set.

DEFINITION: Given a partially ordered set (A, R), strict or weak:
1. An element x in A is *minimal* iff there is no element in A that strictly precedes x.
2. An element x in A is *least* iff x strictly precedes every other element of A.

3. An element x in A is *maximal* iff there is no element in A that strictly follows x.
4. An element x in A is *greatest* iff x strictly follows every other element of A.

For example, in R_1 and S_1, a is least because it strictly precedes every other element, and it is also minimal because no other element strictly precedes it. Both c and d are maximal, neither having a strict successor, but there is no greatest element in R_1 or S_1 since there is no element that strictly succeeds all the others in the orders. In R_2 and S_2, c and d are minimal, and a and d are maximal. There is no greatest element and no least element. In R_3 and S_3, d is both least and minimal, and a is both greatest and maximal. In the partially ordered set $(D, \leq)$ of Example 6-1, 1 is least and minimal, and 4 is greatest and maximal.

A least element is always minimal, since if x strictly precedes every other element in the order, then there is no other element that strictly precedes x. Similarly, a greatest element is always maximal. The converses do not hold, however. A minimal element is not necessarily a least element, and a maximal element is not necessarily greatest, as we have seen in the examples cited in the preceding paragraph. An order can have several maximal elements and several minimal elements, but there can be at most one greatest element and at most one least element.

THEOREM 6-1: Given a partially ordered set (A, R), a greatest element, if it exists, is unique, and a least element, if it exists, is unique.

Proof: Assume that x_1 and x_2 are distinct greatest elements. By definition of a greatest element, x_1 follows every other element, and in particular, it follows x_2. Thus, $(x_2, x_1) \in R$. Similarly, if x_2 is a greatest element, then it follows every other element, in particular, x_1. Thus, $(x_1, x_2) \in R$. Since x_1 is assumed to be distinct from x_2, R cannot be asymmetric or antisymmetric, contrary to the assumption that it is a partial order. Accordingly, x_1 and x_2 must be identical, and thus a greatest element, if there is one, is unique. The proof of the uniqueness of a least element proceeds analogously.

Problems: 1. Find the maximal, minimal, greatest, and least elements, if there are such, in $(\mathscr{P}(B), \subset)$ in Fig. 6-6. 2. Find a partial ordering of the set of all positive and negative integers and zero such that there are no maximal, minimal, greatest, or least elements.

Trees

A mathematical configuration of great importance in linguistics is a *constituent-structure tree* (or simply a *tree*), an example of which is shown in Fig. 6-7.

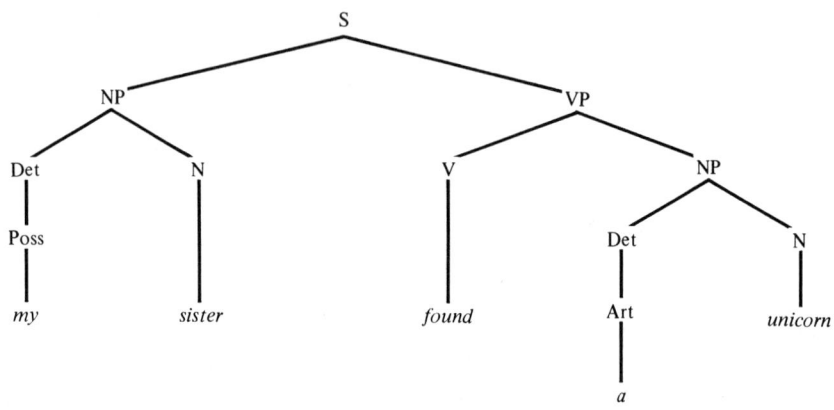

Figure 6-7

A typical constituent-structure tree

Such diagrams represent three sorts of information about the syntactic structure of a sentence:

1. The hierarchical grouping of the parts of the sentence into constituents.
2. The grammatical type of each constituent.
3. The left-to-right order of the constituents.

For example, Fig. 6-7 indicates that the largest constituent, which is labeled by *S* (for Sentence), is made up of a constituent which is a *N*(oun) *P*(hrase) and one which is a *V*(erb) *P*(hrase) and that the noun phrase is composed of two constituents: a *Det*(erminer) and a *N*(oun), etc. Further, in the sentence constituent the noun phrase precedes the verb phrase, the determiner precedes the noun in the noun phrase constituents, and so on. The tree diagram itself is said to be composed of *nodes*, or points, some of which are connected by lines called *branches*. Each node has associated with it a *label* chosen from a specified finite set of grammatical categories (*S*, *NP*, *VP*, etc.) and formatives (*my*, *sister*, etc.). As they are customarily drawn, a tree diagram has a vertical orientation on the page with the node labeled *S* at the top and the nodes labeled by the formatives at the bottom. Because a branch always connects a higher node to a lower one, it is an inherently directional connection. This directionality is ordinarily not indicated by an arrow, as in the preceding diagrams of relations and orders but only by the vertical orientation of the tree taken together with the convention that a branch extends *from* a higher node *to* a lower node. If branches were drawn as arrows rather than as lines, the relative vertical position of the nodes would be an irrelevant feature of the tree diagram, and the four diagrams in Fig. 6-8, for example, would represent identical trees.

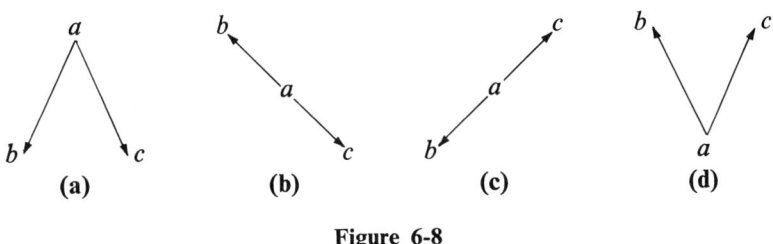

Figure 6-8

Equivalent representations for a tree using arrows as branches

The point here is to distinguish the character of the information represented by a tree diagram as customarily drawn from inessential features of the diagram that arise from the notational system used.

1. *Dominance*

We say that a node x *dominates* a node y if there is a connected sequence of branches in the tree extending from x to y. This is the case when all the branches in the sequence have the same orientation away from x and toward y. For example, in Fig. 6-7 the node labeled *VP* dominates the node labeled *Art*, since the sequence of branches connecting them is uniformly "descending" from the higher node *VP* to the lower node *Art*. The node labeled *VP* does not dominate the node labeled *Poss*, since the path by which they are joined first ascends from *VP* to *S* and then descends through *NP* and *Det*.

Given a tree diagram, we agree to represent the fact that x dominates y by the ordered pair (x, y). The set of all such ordered pairs for a given tree is said to constitute the *dominance relation* for that tree. Dominance is clearly a transitive relation. If x is connected to y by a sequence of descending branches and y is similarly connected to z, then x dominates z because they are also connected by a sequence of descending branches, specifically, by the sequence passing through y. As a technical convenience, it is usually assumed that every node dominates itself, i.e., that the dominance relation is reflexive. Further, if x dominates y, then y can dominate x only if $x = y$; or in other words, dominance is antisymmetric. Thus, the relation of dominance is a weak partial ordering of the nodes of a tree.

Applying the previously introduced terminology for partial orders, we can say that if x and y are distinct and x dominates y and there is no distinct node between x and y, then x *immediately dominates y*. In Fig. 6-7, the node labeled *VP* immediately dominates the node labeled *V* but not the node labeled *found*. A node is said to be the *daughter* of the node immediately dominating it, and distinct nodes immediately dominated by the same node are called *sisters*. In Fig. 6-7, the node labeled *VP* has two daughters, viz., the node labeled *V* and the rightmost node labeled *NP*. The latter two nodes are sisters. A node which is minimal in the dominance relation, i.e., which is not dominated by any other node, is called a *root*. In Fig. 6-7 there is one root, the node labeled *S*. Maximal elements are called *leaves*, and in Fig. 6-7 these are the nodes labeled by the formatives, *my*, *sister*, etc. Note that a tree diagram is ordinarily drawn upside down with respect to the terminology since the root is at the top and the leaves are at the bottom.

Mathematicians sometimes use the term 'tree' for a configuration with more than one root, e.g., that shown in Fig. 6-9. For a linguist, however,

Figure 6-9

A multiply rooted "tree"

a tree is invariably singly rooted, and he would consider the configuration in Fig. 6-9 a "forest" of trees. We shall adhere to the usage in linguistics, and accordingly we have the following condition that holds for every well-formed tree:

THE SINGLE ROOT CONDITION: In every well-formed constituent structure tree there is exactly one node that dominates every node.

The root node is, therefore, a least element (and necessarily also a minimal element) in the partial ordering specified by the dominance relation. We note, incidentally, that the Single Root Condition is met in the trivial case of a tree that has only one node, which is simultaneously root and leaf. The condition would not be met by an "empty" tree with no nodes at all, since it asserts that a node with the specified property exists in the tree.

2. Precedence

Two nodes are ordered in the left-to-right direction just in case they are not ordered by dominance. In Fig. 6-7 the node labeled V precedes (i.e., is to the left of) its sister node labeled NP and all the nodes dominated by this NP node; it neither precedes nor follows the nodes labeled S, VP, V, and *found*, i.e., the nodes that either dominate or are dominated by the V node. It is not logically necessary that the relations of dominance and left-to-right precedence be mutually exclusive, but this accords with the way in which tree diagrams are usually interpreted. For example, the trees shown in Fig. 6-10 are ordinarily taken to be equivalent despite the fact that the diagrams themselves differ in the left-to-right orientation of the nodes b and c with respect to the node a that immediately dominates them. It is only when two nodes do not stand in the dominance relation that their left-to-right positions with respect to each other becomes significant. In Fig. 6-10, for example, we could not interchange nodes b and c (which do not stand in the dominance relation with each other) without producing a tree different from the original.

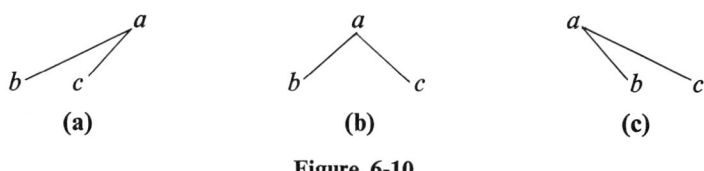

Figure 6-10

Equivalent tree representations on the assumption that the dominance and precedence relations are mutually exclusive

Given a tree, the set of all ordered pairs (x, y) such that x precedes y, i.e., x is to the left of y, is said to define the *precedence relation* for that tree. To ensure that the precedence and dominance relations have no ordered pairs in common, we add the Exclusivity Condition for well-formed trees:

THE EXCLUSIVITY CONDITION: In any well-formed constituent-structure tree, for any nodes x and y, x and y stand in the precedence relation P, i.e., either $(x, y) \in P$ or $(y, x) \in P$, if and only if x and y do not stand in the dominance relation D, i.e., neither $(x, y) \in D$ nor $(y, x) \in D$.

Like dominance, precedence is a transitive relation, but precedence is irreflexive rather than reflexive. The latter follows from the Exclusivity Condition, since for every node x, $(x, x) \in D$ and therefore $(x, x) \notin P$. If x precedes y, then y cannot precede x, and thus the relation is asymmetric.

148   *Orders, Operations, Configurations, and Isomorphisms*

Precedence, therefore, defines a strict partial order on the nodes of the tree.

One other condition on the dominance and precedence relations is needed in order to exclude certain configurations from the class of well-formed trees. An essential characteristic of a tree that distinguishes it from a partially ordered set in general is that no node can have more than one branch entering it or, to put it differently, every node has at most one node immediately dominating it. The structure shown in Fig. 6-11(a) has a node d with two immediate predecessors, b and c, and therefore it is not a tree. Another defining property of trees is that branches are not allowed to cross. Figure 6-11(b) illustrates the sort of structure that is forbidden. Both types of ill-formedness can be ruled out by adding the Nontangling Condition as a part of the definition of a tree.

Figure 6-11

Structures excluded as trees by the Nontangling Condition

THE NONTANGLING CONDITION: In any well-formed constituent-structure tree, for any nodes x and y, if x precedes y, then all nodes dominated by x precede all nodes dominated by y.

The configuration in Fig. 6-11(a) fails to meet this condition because b precedes c, b dominates d, and c dominates d, and therefore d ought to precede d. This is impossible, however, since precedence is irreflexive. In Fig. 6-11(b), b precedes c, b dominates d, and c dominates e. Thus, by the Nontangling Condition, d should precede e, but in fact the reverse is true.

3. Labeling

To complete the characterization of trees we must consider the labeling of the nodes. It is apparent from Fig. 6-7 that distinct nodes can have identical labels attached to them, e.g., the two nodes labeled *NP*. Since each node has exactly one label, the pairing of nodes and labels can be represented by a *labeling function L*, whose domain is the set of nodes in the tree and whose range is a set, presumably finite, of grammatical categories and formatives. The mapping is, in general, an *into* function.

The grammatical categories *S*, *NP*, *VP*, etc., are generally taken to be specified as a part of linguistic theory, i.e., as linguistic universals applicable to the description of every natural language. The formatives, on the other hand, are by and large language specific and distinct from the set of grammatical categories. Therefore, there is some justification for saying that the labeling function consists of two disjoint parts: a function L_1, which maps leaf nodes into a set of formatives F, and a function L_2, which maps nonleaf nodes into a set of grammatical categories G that is disjoint from F. Various additional refinements in the definition of the labeling function might also be proposed. For example, one might want to specify that the root node of every well-formed tree is labeled S or that only members of a specific set of lexical categories, *N*, *V*, *Adj*, etc., can be attached to nodes that immediately dominate leaves. The disadvantage of adding such restrictions to the definition is that substructures that one would want to call *subtrees* would be excluded from the class of trees. For example, it would be natural to call everything dominated by the *VP* node in Fig. 6-7 a subtree of the larger tree. Similarly, the configuration formed by just the nodes labeled *VP* and *V* in Fig. 6-7 would also be considered a subtree, and in this case the root is not labeled *S* and the leaf is not labeled by a formative. Accordingly, we adopt the following definition:

> **DEFINITION:** A (*constituent-structure*) *tree* is a mathematical configuration (N, Q, D, P, L), where
>
> N is a finite set, the set of *nodes*
> Q is a finite set, the set of *labels*
> D is a weak partial order in $N \times N$, the *dominance relation*
> P is a strict partial order in $N \times N$, the *precedence relation*
> L is a function from N into Q, the *labeling function* and such that the following conditions hold:
>
> 1. $(\exists x \in N)(\forall y \in N)(x, y) \in D$ Single Root Condition
> 2. $(\forall x, y \in N)(((x, y) \in P \vee (y, x) \in P) \leftrightarrow$
> $((x, y) \notin D \wedge (y, x) \notin D))$ Exclusivity Condition
> 3. $(\forall w, x, y, z \in N)(((w, x) \in P \wedge (w, y) \in D \wedge (x, z) \in D)$
> $\rightarrow (y, z) \in P)$ Nontangling Condition

Given this definition, one can prove theorems of the following sort concerning trees.

> **THEOREM 6-2:** Given a tree $T = (N, Q, D, P, L)$, every pair of sister nodes is ordered by P.

Proof: Take x and y as sisters immediately dominated by some node z. By the definitions of 'sister' and 'immediate domination,' x, y, and z must all be distinct. As an assumption to be proved false, let x dominate y. Therefore, x must dominate z. But z also dominates x, and x and z are distinct, so this violates the condition that dominance is antisymmetric. Therefore, x cannot dominate y. By a symmetrical argument, we can show that y does not dominate x. Thus, $(x, y) \notin D$ and $(y, x) \notin D$, and by the Exclusivity Condition it follows that $(x, y) \in P \vee (y, x) \in P$; i.e., x and y are ordered by P.

THEOREM 6-3: Given a tree $T = (N, Q, D, P, L)$, the leaves are totally ordered by P.

Proof: Let M be the set of leaves, and let R be the restriction of the relation P to the set M; i.e., $R = \{(x, y) \in M \times M \mid (x, y) \in P\}$. R is a strict partial order, since if there were any ordered pairs violating the conditions of irreflexivity, asymmetry, and transitivity in R, then because $R \subseteq P$, these pairs would also appear in P, and P would not be a strict partial order. By definition, a leaf dominates no node except itself, and therefore for every pair of distinct leaves x and y, $(x, y) \notin D$ and $(y, x) \notin D$. Thus, by the Exclusivity Condition $(x, y) \in P \vee (y, x) \in P$. Since x and y are leaves, $(x, y) \in R \vee (y, x) \in R$, by the definition of R, and thus R is connex. Therefore, R is a strict total order.

Every statement about the formal properties of a constituent-structure tree can be formulated in terms of the dominance and precedence relations and the labeling function. For example, one useful predicate on trees is that of *belonging to*. A node will be said to belong to the next highest S node that dominates it. Formally, the definition is as follows:

DEFINITION: Given a tree $T = (N, Q, D, P, L)$, node x **belongs to** node y iff
1. $x \neq y$
2. $(y, x) \in D$
3. $(y, S) \in L$
4. $\sim(\exists w \in N)((w, S) \in L \wedge w \neq y \wedge w \neq x \wedge (y, w) \in D \wedge (w, x) \in D)$

Parts 2 and 3 of this definition specify that the node to which x belongs is labeled S and dominates x. Part 4 prohibits any S node from standing between x and y in the dominance relation, and part 1 excludes the case of an S node belonging to itself. To illustrate, let us consider the tree in Fig. 6-12.

The node *Prn* belongs to the circled S node since this is the next highest S node dominating it. *Prn* does not belong to the highest S node (i.e., the

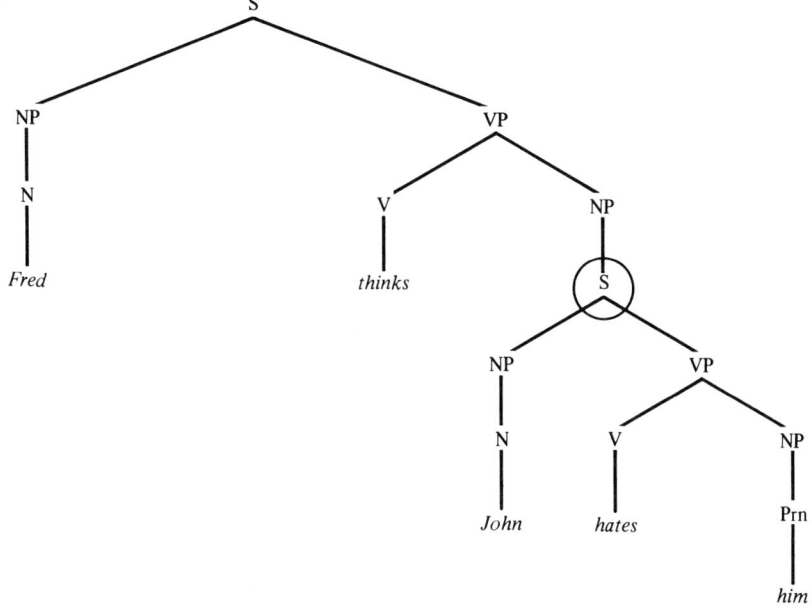

Figure 6-12

Tree illustrating the definitions of 'belonging to' and 'command'

root) of the tree because the circled *S* node is between the root and *Prn* in the dominance relation.

With this definition we can easily define some other predicates. Two nodes are called *clause mates* iff neither dominates the other and both belong to the same node. In Fig. 6-12 the nodes labeled *John* and *him* are clause mates since neither dominates the other and both belong to the circled *S* node. *Fred* and *him* are not clause mates since they do not belong to the same node, and *Prn* and *him* are not clause mates since *Prn* dominates *him*.

If we let $B(x, y)$ denote 'x belongs to y,' we can state the definition of clause mates as follows:

DEFINITION: Given a tree $T = (N, Q, D, P, L)$, nodes x and y are *clause mates* iff

$$(x, y) \notin D \land (y, x) \notin D \land (\exists z \in N)((x, z) \in B \land (y, z) \in B).$$

A node x is said to *command* a node y iff neither dominates the other and x belongs to a node z that dominates y (Langacker, 1969). In Fig. 6-12 the node labeled *Fred* commands the node labeled *him* since neither dominates the other and *Fred* belongs to the root node *S*, which also dominates *him*. The node *him* does not command *Fred*, however, since the node to which him belongs—the circled S node—does not dominate *Fred*. Note, further, that *John* commands *him* and vice versa. Formally, the definition is as follows:

DEFINITION: Given a tree $T = (N, Q, D, P, L)$, node x **commands** node y iff

$$(x, y) \notin D \land (y, x) \notin D \land (\exists z \in N)((x, z) \in B \land (z, y) \in D).$$

Problem: Prove that two nodes are clause mates iff each commands the other.

Operations

Conjunction, disjunction, and negation of propositions; union, intersection, and complementation of sets; composition of functions and relations; and addition, subtraction, multiplication, and division of numbers are all examples of mathematical operations. In each of these instances we can think of the operation as converting one or a pair of things of the appropriate sort into another thing of the same kind. For example, the union of two sets is a set, the sum of two numbers is a number, the negation of a proposition is again a proposition, and so on. Further, each operation is defined only for particular classes of mathematical objects. It makes no sense, for example, to speak of the quotient of two propositions or the negation of a function.

An operation is called *singulary*, *binary*, *ternary*, . . . , *n-ary*, according to the number of entities it requires. Negation of propositions, absolute complementation of sets, and formation of inverses of functions are examples of singulary operations. All the other operations we have considered thus far—set union, composition of functions, disjunction of propositions, etc.— are binary. Ternary and higher-order operations are sometimes encountered, but they will not concern us here.

A mathematical operation, like a function, need not be thought of as an active process but can be regarded simply as a set in which arguments are paired with values. For example, given a set of propositions $P = \{p, q, r, s, \sim p, \sim q, \sim r, \sim s, \ldots\}$, the set of ordered pairs each with a proposition as first coordinate and the negation of that proposition as second coordinate

(6-5) $\{(p, \sim p), (q, \sim q), (r, \sim r), (\sim p, p), (\sim q, q), (\sim r, r), \ldots\}$

could be taken as constituting a definition of the operation of negation on the set P. Binary operations can be considered as sets of ordered pairs whose first coordinates are themselves ordered pairs. For example, given the set of positive integers $N = \{1, 2, 3, 4, \ldots\}$, the operation of arithmetic addition could be given as

(6-6) $\quad + = \{((1, 1), 2), ((1, 2), 3), ((2, 1), 3), ((2, 2), 4), \ldots\}$

and arithmetic multiplication by

(6-7) $\quad \times = \{((1, 1), 1), ((1, 2), 2), ((2, 1), 2), ((2, 2), 4), \ldots\}$

or by the convention that allows us to write $((a, b), c)$ as (a, b, c),

(6-8) $\quad \times = \{(1, 1, 1), (1, 2, 2), (2, 1, 2), (2, 2, 4), \ldots\}$

that is, as a set of ordered triples.

In this way, addition and multiplication can be regarded as relations from $N \times N$ to N. These relations are, in fact, functions, since the domain is equal to $N \times N$ (a sum and a product exists for every pair of integers) and for each (x, y) in the domain of each function there is a unique z in the range that is the value (adding or multiplying two given integers yields a unique integer as sum or product). As given here, multiplication is an onto function, since for every integer z there exist integers x and y such that the product of x and y is z, but addition is into N, because there are no two positive integers having a sum of 1 (0 is not included in N).

> **Problem:** Show that subtraction and division are not functions from $Z \times Z$ to Z, where $Z = \{0, 1, 2, 3, \ldots\}$. (Recall that division by zero is not defined.)

Properties of Operations

We now give definitions of certain properties of interest in the case of binary operations. We shall use $*$ to denote a general binary operation not further specified, and we shall write equivalently

(6-9) $\quad (a, b, c) \in *$

(6-10) $\quad *(a, b) = c$

(6-11) $\quad a * b = c$

1. Well-definition

An operation $*$ from $A \times A$ to B is *well-defined* (*in A*) if and only if $(\forall x, y \in A)(\exists z \in B) x * y = z$; that is, the domain of the operation equals $A \times A$. As we have just seen, addition and multiplication are well-defined in the set of positive integers. Division is not well-defined in the set $Z = \{0, 1, 2, \ldots\}$ because there are no x and z in Z such that $x/0 = z$.

2. Closure

An operation $*$ from $A \times A$ to B is *closed* (*in A*) if and only if the range of $*$ is a subset of A. In other words, $*$ is closed in A just in case applying the operation to any pair of elements in A for which it is defined gives a value which is in A. Addition is closed in the set Z of positive integers and zero, since for every x and y in Z, the sum $x + y$ is a member of Z. Addition is not closed in the set $B = \{1, 2, 3, 4\}$ since $3 + 4 = 7$, for example, but $7 \notin B$. Subtraction is not closed in the set of positive integers, because $2 - 3 = -1$, for example, and -1 is not a positive integer. Subtraction is closed, however, in the set of all positive and negative integers and zero.

Well-definition and closure in appropriate sets are ordinarily considered the minimal standards for well-behaved operations. We shall not be concerned with any operations that do not have these properties.

3. Associativity

An operation $*$ from $A \times A$ to B is *associative* if and only if for all x, y, and z in A, $(x * y) * z = x * (y * z)$. In an associative operation it is immaterial in what order repeated applications of it are made. Set union, intersection, and symmetric difference; logical conjunction and disjunction; composition of functions; and arithmetic multiplication and addition are all associative. Examples of nonassociative operations are subtraction $[(6 - 3) - 2 \neq 6 - (3 - 2)]$ and division $[(\frac{12}{6})/2 \neq 12/(\frac{6}{2})]$.

4. Commutativity

An operation $*$ from $A \times A$ to B is *commutative* if and only if for all x and y in A, $x * y = y * x$. Familiar commutative operations are logical conjunction and disjunction; set intersection, union, and symmetric difference; and arithmetic addition and multiplication. Some noncommutative operations are subtraction, division, relative complementation of sets, and composition of functions.

5. Idempotence

An operation $*$ from $A \times A$ to B is *idempotent* if and only if for all x in A, $x * x = x$. Set union and intersection are idempotent, as are logical conjunction and disjunction, but most of the operations we have encountered thus far are not. Symmetric difference of sets is not idempotent since in general $A + A \neq A$. Similarly, arithmetic addition, multiplication, subtraction, and division, relative complementation of sets, and composition of functions are nonidempotent.

Problem: Show that composition of functions is not idempotent by exhibiting a set of functions in which composition is well-defined and closed (it is necessarily associative) and such that for some function f in the set $f \circ f \neq f$.

6. Distributivity

For two operations $*_1$ and $*_2$ both from $A \times A$ to B, $*_1$ distributes over $*_2$ if and only if for all x, y, and z in A, $x *_1 (y *_2 z) = (x *_1 y) *_2 (x *_1 z)$. We have seen that set union distributes over set intersection, and vice versa, but while arithmetic multiplication distributes over addition, $a \cdot (b + c) = (a \cdot b) + (a \cdot c)$, addition does not distribute over multiplication since in general $a + (b \cdot c) \neq (a + b) \cdot (a + c)$.

Problem: Which of the arithmetic operations of addition, subtraction, multiplication, and division distribute over the others?

The next three sections are concerned with members of a set that have special properties with respect to some operation defined on the set.

7. Identity Elements

Given an operation $*$ from $A \times A$ to B, an element e_l in A is a *left identity element (of $*$)* if and only if for all x in A, $e_l * x = x$. Similarly, e_r in A is a *right identity element (of $*$)* if and only if for all x in A, $x * e_r = x$. As we saw previously, for a function $f: A \to B$, $i_B \circ f = f$ and $f \circ i_A = f$; thus for the operation of composition of functions the identity functions i_B and i_A are a left and a right identity element, respectively. Subtraction defined on the set of positive and negative integers and zero has a right identity element, namely zero, since for all x, $x - 0 = x$, but there is no left identity element; i.e., there is no element y in the set such that for all x, $y - x = x$.

For commutative operations, every left identity element is also a right identity element, and vice versa. To see this, consider a left identity e_l. By definition $(\forall x \in A)(e_l * x = x)$. Because the operation is commutative, $e_l * x = x * e_l = x$, for all $x \in A$, and so e_l is also a right identity element. Similarly, every right identity is also a left identity. An element that is both a right and a left identity element is called a *two-sided identity* or simply an *identity element*. While commutativity of an operation is a sufficient condition for every right (or left) identity to be two-sided, it is not a necessary condition; a two-sided identity may exist for some operation that is not commutative. An example of this is found in the operation of composition of functions defined on some set of functions $F = \{f, g, h, \ldots\}$, each being a function in A. If i_A is one of the functions in F, it is a two-sided identity, since for each $x \in F$, $i_A \circ x = x \circ i_A = x$, but the operation of composition of functions is not in general commutative.

For addition the two-sided identity element is 0, since $(\forall x)(x + 0 = 0 + x = x)$ and for arithmetic multiplication it is 1, since $(\forall x)(x \cdot 1 = 1 \cdot x = x)$. Given some collection of sets, the identity element for intersection is I, the universal set, $(X \cap I = I \cap X = X)$, and for union it is the null set $(X \cup \emptyset = \emptyset \cup X = X)$. Relative complementation has $\emptyset$ as a right identity $(X - \emptyset = X)$ but has in general no left identity.

If for a given operation a two-sided identity exists, then this element is unique. This is stated in the following theorem:

THEOREM 6-4: Given an operation $*$ from $A \times A$ to B, there is at most one two-sided identity element in A.

Proof: Suppose there were two distinct two-sided identity elements, e_1 and e_2, in A. Then, because e_1 is an identity element, $(e_2 * e_1) = (e_1 * e_2) = e_2$, and because e_2 is an identity element, $(e_2 * e_1) = (e_1 * e_2) = e_1$. Therefore, $(e_2 * e_1) = (e_1 * e_2) = e_1 = e_2$, and the two elements e_1 and e_2 are equal.

8. *Inverse Elements*

Given an operation $*$ from $A \times A$ to B with a two-sided identity element e, a given element x in A is said to have a *right inverse* x_r if and only if $x * x_r = e$. A given element x in A is said to have a *left inverse* x_l if and only if $x_l * x = e$. If x^{-1} is both a left and a right inverse of x, i.e., if $x^{-1} * x = x * x^{-1} = e$, then x^{-1} is called a *two-sided inverse* of x. When the term 'inverse' is used without further qualification, we mean that it is two-sided. Note that inverses are always paired in the following way: y is a right inverse of x if and only if x is a left inverse of y, since both statements follow from $x * y = e$. One should observe also that the question of the existence of an inverse can be raised with respect to *each element in the set* on which the operation is defined. In contrast, an identity element, if it exists, is defined for the operation as a whole.

To illustrate, let addition be defined in the set Q of all positive and negative integers and zero. As we have seen, 0 is the two-sided identity element for this operation. Consider now the number 3, and let us ask if it has an inverse in the set Q; that is, is there an element x in Q that when added to 3 will yield zero? The number -3 is such an element, and, furthermore, it is both a right and left inverse since $3 + (-3) = (-3) + 3 = 0$. From this it also follows that 3 is a two-sided inverse of -3. For addition, every member of Q has an inverse since to each integer x (except 0) there corresponds a negative integer $-x$ such that $x + (-x) = 0$. The number 0 is its own inverse, since $0 + 0 = 0$.

As another example, consider the operation of intersection defined on some collection of sets. Since a two-sided identity exists, namely the universal set I, we may sensibly ask whether any of the sets in the collection have inverses; i.e., for some set A in I, is there a set A^{-1} such that $A \cap A^{-1} = I$? This equation can be satisfied only when $A = A^{-1} = I$. Thus, for set intersection defined on an arbitrary collection of sets the only element having an inverse is the universal set, which is its own inverse.

> *Problem:* Given an arbitrary collection of sets, what elements, if any, have inverses with respect to the operations of (1) union and (2) symmetric difference?

9. Zero Elements

Given an operation $*$ from $A \times A$ to B, an element 0_l is called a *left zero (of $*$)* if and only if for all x in A, $0_l * x = 0_l$. Similarly, 0_r is a *right zero (of $*$)* if and only if for all x in A, $x * 0_r = 0_r$. An element that is both a left and right zero is called a *two-sided zero* or, simply, a *zero*.

The terminology derives from the fact that the number zero functions as a zero element in arithmetic multiplication (for all x, $x \cdot 0 = 0 \cdot x = 0$). There is no zero element for subtraction or for division. The null set is a zero element for set intersection (for all X, $\emptyset \cap X = X \cap \emptyset = \emptyset$), and the universal set is the zero element for set union (for all X, $I \cup X = X \cup I = I$).

Mathematical Configurations Involving Operations

Let A be a set and $*$ a binary operation that is well-defined and closed in A. We consider the configuration $(A, *)$ and focus our attention on the following three properties that the configuration might have:

1. The operation is associative.
2. There is a two-sided identity element in A.
3. Every element of A has a two-sided inverse.

If $(A, *)$ has the first of these properties, it is called a *semigroup*. If it has both the first and second, it is called a *monoid* or a *semigroup with identity*. With all three properties the configuration is called a *group*. If in any of these cases the operation is also commutative, the name can be qualified by the words 'Abelian' or 'commutative.' Thus, a configuration consisting of a set together with an operation that is well-defined, closed, associative, and commutative is an Abelian semigroup.

1. Groups

Let $A = \{a, b, c\}$ and let $*$ be a binary operation whose ordered triples are exhibited in tabular form in (6-12).

(6-12)
$$\begin{array}{lll} a*a = a & b*a = b & c*a = c \\ a*b = b & b*b = c & c*b = a \\ a*c = c & b*c = a & c*c = b \end{array}$$

$(A, *)$ is an Abelian group since

1. $*$ is well-defined. Every element of $A \times A$ is assigned a value.
2. $*$ is closed in A. All values are in the set A.
3. $*$ is associative. We can verify the associativity of $*$ by checking every one of the twenty-seven possible expressions of the form $x * (y * z) = (x * y) * z$, where each of the variable symbols can take on the values a, b, and c. The two computations below illustrate the procedure.

$$\begin{array}{ll} a * (b * c) = (a * b) * c & b * (c * b) = (b * c) * b \\ \quad a * a = b * c & \quad b * a = a * b \\ \quad\quad a = a & \quad\quad b = b \end{array}$$

4. There is a two-sided identity element, namely a, in A. This can be seen in the left column and top row of (6-12).
5. Every element has a two-sided inverse. a is its own inverse, since $a * a = a$; and b and c are inverses of each other $(b * c = a, c * b = a)$.
6. $*$ is commutative. $a * b = b * a$, etc.

A common way to display the ordered triples of an operation is in a so-called *multiplication table* (Fig. 6-13). It is so named because of its resemblance to the array defining arithmetic multiplication that everyone memorizes in elementary school. The term 'multiplication table' is used despite the fact that the operation exhibited may have nothing whatever to do with multiplication.

*	a	b	c
a	a	b	c
b	b	c	a
c	c	a	b

Figure 6-13

Multiplication table for the operation ∗ of (6-12)

In order to interpret Fig. 6-13 correctly, one must know the convention that the elements in the column to the left of the vertical line mark the first coordinate of the ordered pair and the elements in the row above the horizontal line mark the second coordinate. The value associated with the pair (x, y) is given by the element at the intersection of the x row and the y column. Figure 6-13 shows, for example that $*(b, c) = a$.

It is easy to determine many of the properties of an operation by inspection of its multiplication table. The operation is well-defined if there is a value associated with every pair; that is, if there are no gaps in the array of values. The operation is closed in a set A if every one of the values is a member of A. An identity element, if it exists, is also easily found from the table. If a column of values is identical to the column to the left of the vertical line, then the element heading the column of values is a right identity; e.g., the column headed by a in Fig. 6-13. Similarly, if a row of values is identical to the row above the horizontal line, then the element heading the row of values is a left identity, e.g., the row headed by a in Fig. 6-13. An element that is both a left and a right identity is, of course, a two-sided identity. If the value at the intersection of the row headed by x and the column headed by y is the two-sided identity element, then x is a left inverse of y, and y is a right inverse of x. If there is an occurrence of the two-sided identity in every row, then every element has a right inverse, and, correspondingly, if there is an occurrence of the two-sided identity in every column, then each element has a left inverse. In Fig. 6-13 a occurs once in each row and once in each column, and therefore every element has both a left and a right inverse. Since in this case the left and right inverses for each element are identical, all inverses are two-sided.

If the operation is commutative and if the elements heading the rows and columns are listed in the same order, then the multiplication table is symmetrical around the diagonal line extending from the upper left corner to the lower right (Fig. 6-14). When the row and column headings are in the same order, the values corresponding to the arguments (x, y) and (y, x) occupy symmetrical positions with respect to this diagonal, and if the operation is commutative, the values at corresponding pairs of points are identical.

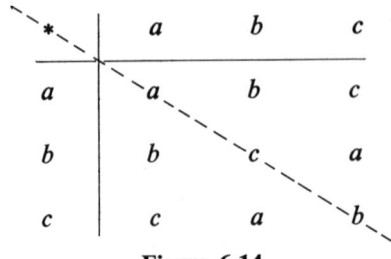

Figure 6-14

Commutativity of * indicated by symmetry around the diagonal

Associativity of an operation generally cannot be determined by a simple inspection of its multiplication table. Unless one knows on other grounds that the operation is or is not associative, the only recourse is to check all the possible expressions of the form $x * (y * z) = (x * y) * z$. The computational labors involved can sometimes be shortened if the operation is commutative and if there are inverses and an identity element. For example, if there is a two-sided identity e, any expression involving it can be omitted from the check because of the following equivalences:

(6-13)
$$e * (y * z) = (e * y) * z \quad \text{reduces to} \quad y * z = y * z$$
$$x * (e * z) = (x * e) * z \quad \text{reduces to} \quad x * z = x * z$$
$$x * (y * e) = (x * y) * e \quad \text{reduces to} \quad x * y = x * y$$

Similarly, if the operation is commutative, expressions in which the first and third variables take on the same value need not be checked since $x * (y * x) = (x * y) * x$ follows directly from the commutativity of the operation.

Problem: Verify that the configuration $(A, *)$ is an Abelian group, where $A = \{e, a, b, c\}$ and $*$ is defined by the multiplication table in (6-14).

(6-14)

*	e	a	b	c
e	e	a	b	c
a	a	e	c	b
b	b	c	e	a
c	c	b	a	e

2. Subgroups

Given a group $(A, *)$, we select a subset B of A and define a new operation $*_B$ consisting of just those triples in $*$ in which only members of B appear. If the resulting configuration $(B, *_B)$ is a group, it is said to be a *subgroup* of $(A, *)$. As an example, let $A = \{e, a, b, c\}$ and let $(A, *)$ be the group in (6-14). Take $B = \{e, a\}$. The multiplication table for the operation $*_B$ is shown in (6-15). By inspection of this table it can be seen that $(B, *_B)$

(6-15)

$*_B$	e	a
e	e	a
a	a	e

is a group: It is well-defined and closed in B, it contains an identity element, and every element has an inverse. Further, it is associative as a consequence of the fact that $*$ in (6-14) is associative. Therefore, $(B, *_B)$ is a subgroup of $(A, *)$.

Not every configuration obtained in this way from a subset of A is a group. For example, if we choose $C = \{e, a, b\}$, the multiplication table for $*_C$ in (6-16) shows that this operation is not well-defined, in particular, the ordered triples (a, b, c) and (b, a, c) are not members of $*_C$ since c is not a member of C.

(6-16)

$*_C$	e	a	b
e	e	a	b
a	a	e	
b	b		e

Therefore, the configuration $(C, *_C)$ is not a group and hence not a subgroup of $(A, *)$.

There are five subsets of A that, together with the appropriate operation, form subgroups of $(A, *)$ in (6-14). These are $\{e\}$, $\{e, a\}$, $\{e, b\}$, $\{e, c\}$, and $\{e, a, b, c\}$. The first forms the trivial subgroup consisting of just the identity element and the operation $*_{\{e\}} = \{(e, e, e)\}$. The set $\{e, a, b, c\}$ (equal to A) is another trivial case. Since $A \subseteq A$, $(A, *)$ is a subgroup of itself.

Problem: Verify that $\{e, b\}$ and $\{e, c\}$, together with the appropriate operations, are subgroups of $(A, *)$.

The *order* of any group $(A, *)$ is the number of members in the set A. The group in (6-14) is thus of order 4, and the group in Fig. 6-13 is of order 3. An important theorem of group theory states that the order of any subgroup exactly divides (i.e., without remainder) the order of the parent group. Consequently, only subgroups of order 1, 2, or 4 are possible for the group in (6-14), these being the integral divisors of 4. The theorem does not guarantee that every subset having the proper number of members will give rise to a subgroup—only that if a subgroup exists, its order is a divisor of the order of the group. An immediate consequence of this theorem is that a group $(G, *)$ of order 5 has only the trivial subgroups ($\{e\}$, $*_{\{e\}}$) and $(G, *)$ of orders 1 and 5, respectively, since 5 has no other divisors.

3. Monoids

Let $A = \{e, a, b, c\}$, and let $*$ be the operation defined by the multiplication table in (6-17). From inspection of the table we see that the operation

(6-17)

$*$	e	a	b	c
e	e	a	b	c
a	a	c	a	c
b	b	a	e	c
c	c	c	c	c

is well-defined and closed in A, is commutative, and has a two-sided identity, namely e. Showing that it is associative is, as usual, a more laborious task, but in this case it is simplified by the presence of a two-sided zero c. Whenever one of the variables in $(x * y) * z = x * (y * z)$ takes on the value c, the equation reduces to $c = c$.

Thus, $(A, *)$ can be described as an Abelian monoid. It is not a group since a and c do not have inverses.

Another example of a monoid is the set of positive integers and zero, $Z = \{0, 1, 2, 3, \ldots\}$, together with the operation of arithmetic addition. The multiplication table cannot be exhibited in full because it is infinite. The initial portion of it is shown in (6-18).

(6-18)

$+$	0	1	2	3	$\cdots$
0	0	1	2	3	$\cdots$
1	1	2	3	4	$\cdots$
2	2	3	4	5	$\cdots$
3	3	4	5	6	$\cdots$
$\cdot$	$\cdot$	$\cdot$	$\cdot$	$\cdot$	
$\cdot$	$\cdot$	$\cdot$	$\cdot$	$\cdot$	
$\cdot$	$\cdot$	$\cdot$	$\cdot$	$\cdot$	

We shall use our informal knowledge of the properties of arithmetic addition to show that $(Z, +)$ is a monoid. First, the operation is well-defined and closed in Z since every pair of members of Z has a sum that is in Z. We know that addition is associative and commutative and that 0 is a two-sided identity. No element except 0 has an inverse (the negative integers are not in Z), so $(Z, +)$ cannot be a group. It does, however, meet all the conditions for an Abelian monoid.

Problem: Show that the configuration $(Z, \cdot)$, where the operation is arithmetic multiplication, forms a monoid but not a group. Does it contain a zero element?

4. Submonoids

Submonoids are defined analogously to subgroups. Given a monoid $(A, *)$, a subset B of A, and the operation $*_B$ that is the subset of $*$ containing only those triples all of whose members are in B, then $(B, *_B)$ is a *submonoid* of $(A, *)$ if it meets the conditions for a monoid *and* if the identity element is the same as in $(A, *)$. The final qualification need not be added in defining subgroups since there it is an automatic consequence. It is possible to find subsets of a monoid that themselves form monoids, however, but with different identity elements. For example, from the monoid in (6-17) we can take the subset $\{c\}$ and the corresponding operation $*_{\{c\}}$ as shown in (6-19).

(6-19)

$*_{\{c\}}$	c
c	c

The operation $*_{\{c\}}$ is well-defined and closed in $\{c\}$, is associative, and has an identity element, namely c. Thus, $(\{c\}, *_{\{c\}})$ is a monoid, but it is not a submonoid of $(A, *)$ in (6-17) since the identity elements are different.

Problem: Show that $(E, +_E)$, where $E = \{0, 2, 4, 6, 8, \ldots\}$, is a submonoid of $(Z, +)$ in (6-18).

5. Semigroups

An example of a semigroup is the set of positive integers, not including zero, together with addition. A portion of the multiplication table is shown in (6-20).

(6-20)

+	1	2	3	4	...
1	2	3	4	5	...
2	3	4	5	6	...
3	4	5	6	7	...
4	5	6	7	8	...
.	.	.	.	.	
.	.	.	.	.	
.	.	.	.	.	

This configuration is well-defined and closed in the set of positive integers and is associative, but it contains no identity element. Therefore, it is a semigroup but not a monoid. A semigroup can always be converted to a monoid by adding an identity element. It is easy to show that the resulting operation remains well-defined and closed in the new set and that it is associative. Removing the identity element from a monoid does not always give a semigroup, however. For example, if e were removed from the monoid in (6-17), the resulting configuration would not have a well-defined and closed operation in the set $\{a, b, c\}$ since $b * b = e$.

Strings

Given a set A, a *string on A* is made by juxtaposing members of A, possibly with repetitions, to form a linear array of finite length. For example, from the set $\{a, b, c\}$ the string *acbaab* can be formed. This string contains three occurrences of the symbol a, two of b, and one of c. It is distinct from the string *abcbaa*, which contains the same number of occurrences of each symbol but in a different order. Strings are thus considered as ordered from left to right with a first, i.e., leftmost, position, a second position, etc., up to an nth position, where n is an integer specifying the *length* of the string. A string is by definition finite in length, although in some branches of mathematics sequences of infinite length are also included. We allow strings of length 1, which are distinct from a single symbol not considered as a string. The unique string of length 0, the null string, is denoted by e.

It is of some importance to observe how strings differ from totally ordered sets. In the latter, each member occurs only once, and it occupies a unique position in the ordering, e.g., the linear ordering of the set $\{a, b, c\}$ represented by $b \to a \to c$. A string is a linear ordering of *occurrences* or *tokens* of the members of a set, and a string may contain any number of occurrences of the same symbol, e.g., the three tokens of the symbol a in the string *acbaab*.

To give a formal definition of a string we first assume that the positive integers are given in their "natural" linear ordering $1 < 2 < 3 < 4 \cdots$. Then for a given finite set A, a *string on A of length n* is a function from the set of integers $\{1, 2, 3, \ldots, n\}$ into A. For example, if $A = \{a, b, c\}$, a possible string on A of length 5 is $\{(1, a), (2, b), (3, a), (4, c), (5, b)\}$, which is the string ordinarily denoted as *abacb*. Each integer in the domain of the function marks the position in the string, and the value is the symbol that appears in that position. The function is in general into, since it is not necessary that every member of A occur in a string on A; e.g., $\{(1, a), (2, a), (3, a)\} = aaa$. Defining strings in this way guarantees that strings that we would intuitively regard as different are represented by different functions. In general, two strings are nonidentical under this definition if they are of different length or if they differ in at least one position.

From two strings one can form a new string by juxtaposing them. For example, juxtaposing the string *abca* to the left end of *bbac* produces the string *abcabbac*. This operation of juxtaposing strings is known formally as *concatenation*. It is defined as follows:

> **DEFINITION:** Given a string φ of length n and a string ψ of length m, where $\varphi = \{(1, x_1), (2, x_2), \ldots, (n, x_n)\}$ and
>
> $$\psi = \{(1, y_1), (2, y_2), \ldots, (m, y_m)\},$$
>
> the *concatenation of* φ *with* ψ, denoted $\varphi \frown \psi$, is the string of length $m + n$ given by the function $\{(1, x_1), (2, x_2), \ldots, (n, x_n), (n + 1, y_1), (n + 2, y_2), \ldots, (n + m, y_m)\}$.

Concatenation is thus a binary operation on strings giving a string as result. It is associative, since for any strings φ, ψ, and ω, $\varphi \frown (\psi \frown \omega) = (\varphi \frown \psi) \frown \omega$; i.e., in forming $\varphi\psi\omega$ it is immaterial whether φ is first concatenated with ψ or ψ with ω. Concatenation is not commutative, since, in general, $\varphi \frown \psi$ and $\psi \frown \varphi$ are different strings. The null string is the two-sided identity for concatenation. Juxtaposing it to either the left or the right of any string leaves that string unchanged; i.e., for all strings φ, $e \frown \varphi = \varphi \frown e = \varphi$. It is general practice to omit the concatenation symbol in most contexts and write, for example, $\varphi\psi$ for $\varphi \frown \psi$.

Consider now the set $A = \{a, b\}$ and the set A^* consisting of all strings on A; i.e., $A^* = \{e, a, b, aa, ab, ba, bb, aaa, aab, \ldots\}$. Observe that the null string e is included as a string on A. We form the configuration $(A^*, \frown)$ from A^* and the operation of concatenation. A portion of the multiplication table is shown in (6-21):

(6-21)

$\frown$	e	a	b	aa	ab	$\cdots$
e	e	a	b	aa	ab	$\cdots$
a	a	aa	ab	aaa	aab	$\cdots$
b	b	ba	bb	baa	bab	$\cdots$
aa	aa	aaa	aab	$aaaa$	$aaab$	$\cdots$
ab	ab	aba	abb	$abaa$	$abab$	$\cdots$
.	.	.	.	.	.	
.	.	.	.	.	.	
.	.	.	.	.	.	

Concatenation is well-defined and closed in A^* since any two strings in A^* can be juxtaposed to give a string in A^*. As we have already seen, concatenation is associative and has e as its two-sided identity element. No string in A^* has an inverse except e, which is its own inverse. Therefore, $(A^*, \frown)$ is a monoid. Because concatenation is not commutative, it is not an Abelian monoid.

Problem: Find a simple rule for determining how many times any given string φ appears as a value in the multiplication table (6-21).

The configuration $(A^*, \frown)$ is called *the free monoid on A*. It is very often denoted by A^*, although technically it is not the set A^* but the configuration $(A^*, \frown)$ that is a monoid. In this usage, the operation is, so to speak, understood from the context. The members of A, i.e., a and b, are known as the *generators* of the monoid. A monoid is called *free* if there are no restrictions on allowed occurrences of the generators in forming a string. An example of a monoid that is not free is $(B, \frown)$, where B is the set of all strings on $\{a, b\}$ that do not begin with an a; i.e., $B = \{e, b, ba, bb, baa, bab, \ldots\}$.

Problem: Verify that $(B, \frown)$ is a monoid.

The notion of a string is fundamental to many approaches toward formalization in linguistics. A sentence, for example, can be considered at one level of description as a string of words or a string of morphemes, while a morpheme can be considered as a string of phonemes, and so on. Most of the studies that comprise the field of mathematical linguistics are concerned with a language as a set of strings on some finite set. In this context the finite set is called the *vocabulary* or *alphabet*, and strings made from these elements are called *words* or *sentences*. A *language*, in the formal sense of mathematical linguistics, is some specified set of sentences, i.e., a subset of the free monoid on the vocabulary. A precise specification of this subset of sentences—the *grammatical* sentences of the language—constitutes a *grammar*. There are many ways in which this formal conception of languages and grammars is inadequate as a reflection of the languages and grammars of the real world, the most notable of which is that it ignores the fact that sentences have a much more complex internal structure than that described by the simple concatenation of symbols. Consequently, treating a sentence as a string is only a first approximation, albeit a sometimes useful one, to a representation of its structure.

Isomorphisms

Two mathematical configurations constructed from different sets and different relations may turn out to have remarkably similar structures.

Isomorphisms

Instances of this sort are of interest since they indicate that there is a common abstract structure underlying what would otherwise have been considered two quite distinct configurations.

As a simple example, take the configurations composed of the set $A = \{1, 2, 3, 4, 5\}$ together with the relation $<$, 'less than,' and the configuration (B, P), where $B = \{a, b, c, d, e\}$ and P is the relation of 'preceding in alphabetical order.' The relation $<$ is a strict linear order in $A \times A$, and likewise P is a strict linear order in $B \times B$, since both are irreflexive, asymmetric, and transitive. Immediate predecessor diagrams of these configurations are shown in Fig. 6-15.

$$1 \to 2 \to 3 \to 4 \to 5 \qquad a \to b \to c \to d \to e$$
$$(A, <) \qquad\qquad\qquad (B, P)$$

Figure 6-15

Immediate predecessor diagrams of two isomorphic configurations

From the diagrams it is clear that the two structures are identical except for the names of the elements. The totally ordered set $(A, <)$ could be converted into (B, P) by uniformly replacing 1 by a, 2 by b, 3 by c, 4 by d, and 5 by e. Conversely, (B, P) is convertible into $(A, <)$ by making these name changes in the reverse direction. We can represent this correspondence of names by a function $f = \{(1, a), (2, b), (3, c), (4, d), (5, e)\}$, which is a one-to-one correspondence from A to B, and its inverse f^{-1}, a function that is a one-to-one correspondence from B to A. When we say that the structure of $(A, <)$ is "preserved" in the mapping into (B, P) by the function f, what we mean is this: f maps A onto B in such a way that whenever there is an ordered pair (x, y) in $<$, the ordered pair $(f(x), f(y))$ is in the relation P and, further, that *all* the ordered pairs in P are images of pairs in $<$ under the mapping f. In other words, there is a one-to-one correspondence between the ordered pairs of the two relations such that $(x, y) \in <$ if and only if $(f(x), f(y)) \in P$. The function f is said to define (or, simply, to be) an *isomorphism* from $(A, <)$ to (B, P). Since the "structures" that are preserved by the mapping are the ordering relations $<$ and P, the function f could be further specified as a *relation-preserving* isomorphism or, even more specifically, as an *order-preserving* isomorphism.

DEFINITION: Given a set A and a relation R_A in A and a set B and a relation R_B in B, a function f from A to B is an *(relation-preserving) isomorphism* if and only if f is a one-to-one correspondence such that for all x, y,

$$(x, y) \in R_A \leftrightarrow (f(x), f(y)) \in R_B$$

For example, the relations $<$ and P of Fig. 6-15 are given by the following sets of ordered pairs:

(6-22) $\quad < = \{(1, 2), (1, 3), (1, 4), (1, 5), (2, 3), (2, 4), (2, 5), (3, 4),$
$(3, 5), (4, 5)\}$

(6-23) $\quad P = \{(a, b), (a, c), (a, d), (a, e), (b, c), (b, d), (b, e), (c, d),$
$(c, e), (d, e)\}$

and the isomorphism f is

(6-24) $\quad f = \{(1, a), (2, b), (3, c), (4, d), (5, e)\}$

It is easy to see that f defines a one-to-one correspondence of the required sort between the pairs of $<$ and those of P. It is important to observe, however, that f itself is *not* a one-to-one correspondence from $<$ to P but rather a one-to-one correspondence from A to B that defines a one-to-one correspondence from $<$ to P of a very special sort, viz., one that preserves the relation. There are many one-to-one correspondences from $<$ to P that do not have this property, just as there are many one-to-one correspondences from A to B that are not relation-preserving isomorphisms with respect to $<$ and P.

Since f is a one-to-one correspondence, the inverse mapping f^{-1} is necessarily also a one-to-one correspondence (Corollary 5-4), and thus it defines an isomorphism from (B, P) to $(A, <)$. In general, for any two configurations (A, R_A) and (B, R_B), if there is an isomorphism from A to B, its inverse is an isomorphism from B to A. In other words, the relation of 'being isomorphic to' defined on configurations is symmetric. This relation is also reflexive since the identity function constitutes an isomorphism from any configuration to itself, and it is transitive, as shown by the following.

Let f be an isomorphism from (A, R_A) to (B, R_B) and let g be an isomorphism from (B, R_B) to (C, R_C). We want to prove that (A, R_A) is isomorphic to (C, R_C), and we do this by showing that the required function from A to C is given by $g \circ f$. First, it is straightforward to prove that if f and g are both one-to-one correspondences, then $g \circ f$ is also (where $f: A \to B$ and $g: B \to C$ so that the composite is defined). To show that $g \circ f$ is relation preserving, we use an indirect proof. Assume that $g \circ f$ is not an isomorphism from (A, R_A) to (C, R_C), i.e., that for some x and y in A, $(x, y) \in R_A$ but $((g \circ f)(x), (g \circ f)(y)) \notin R_C$. Since g is an isomorphism from (B, R_B) to (C, R_C), however, its inverse g^{-1} is an isomorphism in the reverse direction. Thus, if $((g \circ f)(x), (g \circ f)(y)) \notin R_C$, then the image of this ordered pair under the mapping g^{-1} is not in R_B; i.e., $((g^{-1} \circ (g \circ f))(x), (g^{-1} \circ (g \circ f))(y)) \notin R_B$. By the associativity of composition of functions the last expression can be rewritten as $(((g^{-1} \circ g) \circ f)(x), ((g^{-1} \circ g) \circ f)(y)) \notin R_B$, and since $(g^{-1} \circ g)$ is just the identity function in B, i_B, and $i_B \circ f = f$, this reduces to $(f(x),$

$f(y)) \notin R_B$. $(x, y) \in R_A$, however, and f is an isomorphism from (A, R_A) to (B, R_B), so $(f(x), f(y)) \in R_B$. Therefore, $(g \circ f)$ is an isomorphism from (A, R_A) to (C, R_C), and the relation of 'being isomorphic to' is transitive. We have already seen that it is reflexive and symmetric, and thus it is an equivalence relation. The set of all configurations is partitioned by it into equivalence classes, each of which contains all the configurations that are isomorphic to each other. In this sense configurations isomorphic to each other can be regarded as "the same" although the particular sets and relations comprising each one may be quite different.

These remarks about isomorphism apply generally to configurations regardless of the special properties the relation may have, that is, whether R_A in (A, R_A) is a function, an order, an operation, etc. Thus, one can speak not only of isomorphic partially ordered sets but also of isomorphic semigroups, monoids, groups, and other configurations of arbitrarily great complexity. The definition of isomorphism may have to be modified correspondingly. For example, if the configuration consists of a set and a binary operation, then $(A, *_A)$ is isomorphic to $(B, *_B)$ if and only if there is a one-to-one correspondence f from A to B such that for all x, y, and z, $x *_A y = z \leftrightarrow f(x) *_B f(y) = f(z)$.

The following example points up the possibility that more than one isomorphism may exist between two configurations. Consider the set $A = \{a, b, c, d\}$ with the relation $\leq_1 = \{(d, c), (d, a), (d, b), (c, a), (c, b),$ $(d, d), (c, c), (b, b), (a, a)\}$, which is a weak partial order in A, and the set $B = \{1, 2, 6, 8\}$ with the relation $\leq_2$, specified by the predicate 'x divides y without remainder.' The relation $\leq_2$ consists of the set of ordered pairs, $\{(1, 2), (1, 6), (1, 8), (2, 6), (2, 8), (1, 1), (2, 2), (6, 6), (8, 8)\}$, also a weak partial order. We may diagram $(A, \leq_1)$ and $(B, \leq_2)$ as in Fig. 6-16.

Figure 6-16

Two isomorphic partially ordered sets

It is clear from inspection of the diagrams that the two structures are isomorphic. The one-to-one correspondence $f = \{(d, 1), (c, 2), (a, 6), (b, 8)\}$ is an order-preserving isomorphism from $(A, \leq_1)$ to $(B, \leq_2)$, which can be verified by referring to the ordered pairs in $\leq_1$ and $\leq_2$ and noting that $(x, y) \in \leq_1$ if and only if $(f(x), f(y)) \in \leq_2$. There is another order-preserving isomorphism from $(A, \leq_1)$ to $(B, \leq_2)$, however; namely, $g = \{(d, 1), (c, 2), (a, 8), (b, 6)\}$. This can again be verified by matching every ordered pair (x, y) in $\leq_1$ with an ordered pair $(g(x), g(y))$ in $\leq_2$. Since f and g are different functions, we must say that in this case there are two distinct isomorphisms from $(A, \leq_1)$ to $(B, \leq_2)$. Of course it is still true to say simply that the configurations are isomorphic since the existence of *at least one* relation-preserving one-to-one correspondence is both a necessary and sufficient condition for isomorphism.

Problem: How many distinct one-to-one correspondences are there between $(A, \leq_1)$ and $(B, \leq_2)$ in Fig. 6-16? Between A and B? Are any of the latter, besides the two already noted, isomorphisms?

To construct an example of a group that is isomorphic to the one given in Fig. 6-13, we introduce the operation of *addition modulo* 3, denoted $+_3$, which is defined on the positive integers and zero. Addition modulo 3 works in the following way: Two integers are added in the normal fashion and then the sum is divided by 3; the *remainder* after division is the *sum modulo* 3 of the two integers. For example, $4 + 7 = 11$; 11 divided by 3 leaves a remainder of 2; therefore, $4 +_3 7 = 2$. Further examples are given in (6-25):

(6-25)
$$0 +_3 1 = 1 \quad 5 +_3 1 = 0$$
$$2 +_3 1 = 0 \quad 2 +_3 2 = 1$$
$$3 +_3 2 = 2 \quad 5 +_3 6 = 2$$

The only possible sums modulo 3 are 0, 1, and 2, so addition modulo 3 is an operation defined from $Z \times Z$ onto B where $Z = \{0, 1, 2, 3, 4, \ldots\}$ and $B = \{0, 1, 2\}$.

Now let us consider this operation defined on the set B itself. The multiplication table for $(B, +_3)$ is shown in Fig. 6-17.

$+_3$	0	1	2
0	0	1	2
1	1	2	0
2	2	0	1

Figure 6-17

Group multiplication table for $(B, +_3)$

It is easy to verify that $(B, +_3)$ is an Abelian group with 0 as its identity element. The elements 1 and 2 are inverses of each other, and 0 is its own inverse.

Comparison of this group multiplication table with that in Fig. 6-13 shows that the two are isomorphic. Specifically, the function $f = \{(a, 0), (b, 1), (c, 2)\}$ is an isomorphism since for all x, y, z, $x * y = z$ iff $f(x) +_3 f(y) = f(z)$. It happens that in this case also there is a second operation-preserving isomorphism from $(A, *)$ to $(B, +_3)$; namely, $g = \{(a, 0), (b, 2), (c, 1)\}$. This can be seen more clearly by writing the multiplication table for $+_3$ as shown in Fig. 6-18 and comparing it with Fig. 6-13.

$+_3$	0	2	1
0	0	2	1
2	2	1	0
1	1	0	2

Figure 6-18

Group multiplication table for $(B, +_3)$

It is important to recognize that Fig. 6-17 and 6-18 represent the same multiplication table. Even though the rows and columns are listed in different orders, exactly the same set of ordered triples is specified in both.

There is a useful theorem of group theory, which we shall not prove here, stating that every isomorphism from a group G_1 to a group G_2 maps the (unique) identity element of G_1 into the identity element of G_2. In the examples of Fig. 6-13 and 6-17, of the six possible one-to-one correspondences from A to B, only two map a into 0, and both of these happen to be operation-preserving isomorphisms. The theorem just referred to assures us that none of the other four one-to-one correspondences is an operation-preserving isomorphism from $(A, *)$ to $(B, +_3)$ since the identity elements do not correspond under these mappings.

Another group that is isomorphic to $(A, *)$ and $(B, +_3)$ can be constructed as follows. Consider the set $A = \{a, b, c\}$ and the three functions, $f_1, f_2,$ and f_3, each from A onto A, as shown in (6-26). Now form the configuration

(6-26)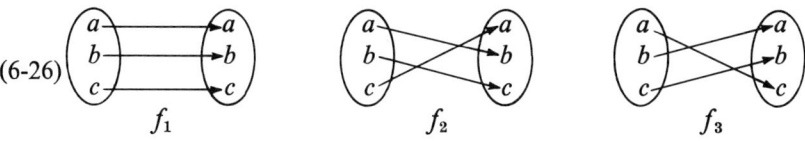

composed of the set $F = \{f_1, f_2, f_3\}$ and the operation of composition of functions. Since f_1 is the identity function in A, we have that $f_1 \circ f_2 = f_2 \circ f_1 = f_2$; $f_1 \circ f_3 = f_3 \circ f_1 = f_3$; and $f_1 \circ f_1 = f_1$. When we construct the composites $f_2 \circ f_2$, $f_2 \circ f_3$, $f_3 \circ f_2$, and $f_3 \circ f_3$, we see that $f_2 \circ f_2 = f_3 = \{(a, c), (b, a), (c, b)\}$; $f_3 \circ f_3 = f_2 = \{(a, b), (b, c), (c, a)\}$; and $f_2 \circ f_3 = f_3 \circ f_2 = f_1$. These results are represented in a multiplication table for the operation $\circ$, defined on the set F, shown in Fig. 6-19:

$\circ$	f_1	f_2	f_3
f_1	f_1	f_2	f_3
f_2	f_2	f_3	f_1
f_3	f_3	f_1	f_2

Figure 6-19

Group multiplication table for $(F, \circ)$

$(F, \circ)$ forms a group since it is well-defined and closed in F; it is associative by Theorem 5-11; it has an identity element, namely f_1; and each element has an inverse. This group is isomorphic to $(A, *)$ and to $(B, +_3)$ as shown by comparison of the respective multiplication tables.

Problem: How many isomorphisms are there from $(B, +_3)$ to $(F, \circ)$?

EXERCISES

1. Let $A = \{1, 2, 3, 5, 6, 10, 15, 30\}$, and let R be a relation in A defined as follows:

    $(x, y) \in R$ iff x divides y without remainder

    (a) List the members of R, and show that it is a weak partial order but not a total order.
    (b) Construct an immediate predecessor diagram for the partially ordered set (A, R) and identify any maximal, minimal, greatest, and least elements.
    (c) Show that (A, R) is isomorphic to the partially ordered set $(\mathscr{P}(B), \subseteq)$, where $B = \{a, b, c\}$. How many distinct one-to-one correspondences are there from A to $\mathscr{P}(B)$? How many of these are isomorphisms from (A, R) to $(\mathscr{P}(B), \subseteq)$?

2. Let (A, R_1) and (B, R_2) be isomorphic partially ordered sets. Prove that any isomorphism f from (A, R_1) to (B, R_2) maps maximal and minimal elements, if any, in R_1 into maximal and minimal elements, respectively, in R_2.

3. Prove that if a relation R is a partial order in a set A, the inverse relation R^{-1} is also a partial order in A. Prove also that maximal elements, if any, in R are minimal elements in R^{-1}, and conversely.

4. Klima (1964, p. 297) defines the relation 'in construction with' on pairs of nodes in a tree in the following way: x is in construction with y iff for some node z, z immediately dominates y and z dominates x. Is x necessarily in construction with y if y commands x? if x and y are clause mates? Investigate the properties of reflexivity, symmetry, and transitivity of the relations 'clause mates,' 'commands,' and 'in construction with.'

5. Determine whether the operation 'symmetric difference' (Chapter 4, Exercise 4) is commutative, associative, and idempotent. Is there an identity element for this operation? What sets, if any, have inverses? Given the set $A = \{a, b\}$, what sort of mathematical configuration is $(\mathcal{P}(A), +)$, where $+$ denotes symmetric difference?

6. Do union and intersection distribute over symmetric difference? Does symmetric difference distribute over union and intersection?

7. Let $A = \{a, b\}$. Show that $(\mathcal{P}(A), \cup)$ and $(\mathcal{P}(A), \cap)$ are both semigroups but not groups. Find an operation-preserving isomorphism between them.

8. Let $A = \{a, b, c\}$. Find all the distinct one-to-one correspondences from A onto A. Construct composites of all pairs of these one-to-one correspondences, and express your results in the form of a multiplication table. What sort of mathematical configuration is represented by this multiplication table?

9. Let A^* be the free monoid on some finite set A. For all strings x and y in A^*, x is said to be a *conjugate* of y iff there are strings u and v such that $x = uv$ and $y = vu$.

   (a) Show that conjugacy is an equivalence relation, and describe the partition it induces in A^*. For a string x_n of length n, what are the maximum and minimum number of strings in the equivalence class containing x_n?
   (b) Prove: If x is a conjugate of y, there is a string z such that $xz = zy$.
   (c) Let $T = \{T_1, T_2, T_3, T_4\}$ be the set of functions each of which maps a string in A of length 4 into one of its conjugates. That is, T_1 maps $a_1a_2a_3a_4$ into $a_1a_2a_3a_4$; T_2 maps $a_1a_2a_3a_4$ into $a_2a_3a_4a_1$; etc., where the a_i's are variables ranging over elements of A. Show that the mathematical configuration consisting of T and the operation of composition of functions is an Abelian group.

7

Infinite Sets

In the preceding chapters we have occasionally dealt with sets, such as the set of positive integers or the set of all strings on some fixed alphabet, which we intuitively regard as infinite. Since mathematical linguistics, like linguistics generally, treats a language as an infinite set of sentences, at least at one level of description, it is important to examine the concept of infiniteness in more detail.

Some initially plausible approaches to the problem of characterizing infiniteness are not satisfactory. A definition employing the terms 'never-ending' or 'impossible, in principle, to list exhaustively,' for example, would be defective since these expressions are themselves no clearer than the term 'infinite' that is to be explicated. What is needed is a definition that makes use only of set-theoretic predicates already at hand and that accords with our intuitions about what sets should be regarded as infinite. Since an infinite set is in some sense "larger" than any finite set, we start by defining what it means for two sets to be of equal or unequal size.

Equivalent Sets and Cardinality

We say that two sets A and B have the same number of members, or are *equivalent*, if and only if there exists a one-to-one correspondence between them. Since a one-to-one correspondence is a function that is one-to-one and onto, every member of A is paired with exactly one member of B, and vice versa. In such a situation it would certainly be reasonable to say that the sets are of equal size. We denote the equivalence of A and B by $A \sim B$.

The terms *equal* and *equivalent* must not be confused. Equal sets have *the same members*, while equivalent sets have *the same number of members*. Equal sets are, therefore, necessarily equivalent but the converse is, in general, not true. Further, nothing is said in the definition of equivalence about the exact nature of the one-to-one correspondence between the sets—only that one exists.

For the case of finite sets this definition of equivalence leads to the expected conclusion. A set with just four distinct members, for example, can be put into one-to-one correspondence with any other set having exactly four distinct members, but not with any set with more or fewer members. The relation of equivalence of sets is, as the name implies, an equivalence relation with the property that all the sets in a particular equivalence class have the same number of members. To each equivalence class we can assign a number, called the *cardinal number*, denoting the size of each set in the class. For finite sets, the cardinal numbers correspond exactly to the integers. Thus, a set A with just four members is said to have a *cardinality* of 4, written $\#(A) = 4$ or card $(A) = 4$.

In the case of infinite sets something rather surprising happens. Consider, for example, the set of positive integers N, the set of positive even integers E, and the function f from N to E that maps every integer x into $2x$ as indicated in Fig. 7-1.

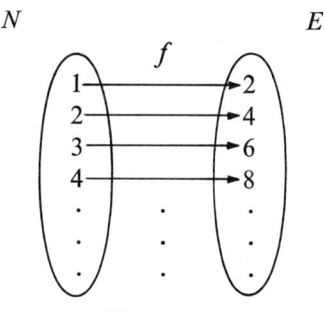

Figure 7-1

A one-to-one mapping from the positive integers to the positive even integers

Every positive integer can be multiplied by 2 to give as a unique value a positive even integer. This shows that f is a function whose range is in E. The function f is one-to-one because for any integers x and y, if $2x = 2y$, then $x = y$. Further, f is onto, since every positive even integer can be represented as $2x$, for some positive integer x. Thus, f is a one-to-one correspondence, and N and E, being equivalent sets, have the same number of members. This result is surprising in view of the fact that E is a proper subset of N (3, for example, is in N but not in E). We are accustomed to thinking of a set as being "larger" than any of its proper subsets, but if we adopt the notion of equivalence as the criterion for equal size of sets, then we are inescapably led to conclude that sometimes a set and a proper subset of that set may have the same number of members. On the other hand, if we were to agree that a set is always "larger" than a proper subset of itself, we would have to accept the puzzling consequence that sets of different size can be put into one-to-one correspondence. Either way the situation seems paradoxical. When we examine the sets that exhibit this unusual behavior, however, we find that they are just the ones that we would intuitively call infinite. Accordingly, we define an infinite set in the following way:

DEFINITION: A set is *infinite* iff it is equivalent to a proper subset of itself.

Example 7-1: The set of positive integers and zero, $Z = \{0, 1, 2, 3, \ldots\}$ is infinite. Consider the set $N = \{1, 2, 3, 4, \ldots\}$, which is a proper subset of Z, and establish the mapping g indicated in Fig. 7-2 in which each integer n is carried into $n + 1$. To each member of Z there corresponds a unique member of N, and vice versa. Therefore, g is a one-to-one correspondence, and $Z \sim N$.

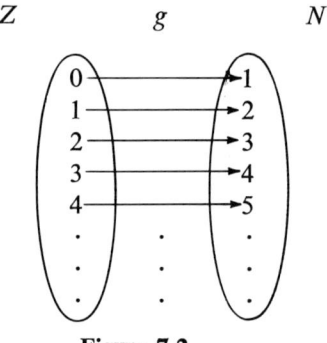

Figure 7-2

Mapping showing that the set Z is equivalent to a proper subset of itself

Example 7-2: The free monoid A^* on the set $A = \{a, b\}$ is infinite. Take as a proper subset of A^* the set $B = \{b, ba, bb, baa, bab, bba, \ldots\}$, i.e., all strings in A^* beginning with b. The mapping h shown in Fig. 7-3 is a one-to-one correspondence because for every string x in A^* there is a unique string bx in B, and vice versa.

It should be easy to see that no finite set can be equivalent to one of its proper subsets (take, for example, the set $\{a, b, c\}$ and any of its proper

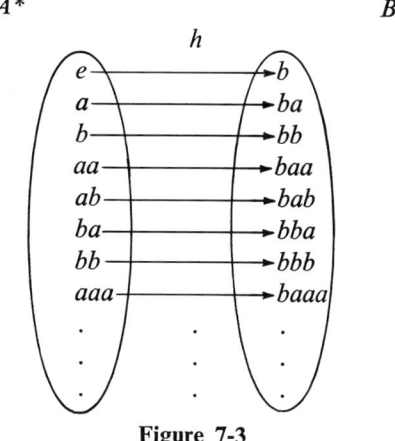

Figure 7-3

A one-to-one mapping of $\{a, b\}^*$ onto a proper subset of itself

subsets). One point about the definition of infinite sets sometimes causes confusion: Only the *existence* of at least one equivalent proper subset is required. The definition does not say that an infinite set is equivalent to *every* proper subset of itself, a condition that in fact could never be met. In Fig. 7-3, for example, A^* is not equivalent to its proper subset $\{b, ab\}$.

Denumerability of Sets

We have seen that we can associate with each finite set (more precisely, with the equivalence class to which that set belongs) a positive integer that represents its cardinality. Equivalent infinite sets can also be grouped into equivalence classes, all members of which have the same cardinality, but there is no positive integer that can be associated uniquely with such an equivalence class as its cardinal number. This follows from the fact that every integer is the cardinal number of a class of finite sets, and no infinite set can be equivalent to a finite set, since no one-to-one correspondence between them is possible. Nonetheless, it is convenient to have symbols denoting the cardinality of infinite sets; the one conventionally adopted as the cardinal number of the set of positive integers and zero and all sets equivalent to it is $\aleph_0$, read 'aleph null' or 'aleph zero.' It must be emphasized that $\aleph_0$ is *not an integer*, i.e., not a member of the set $Z = \{0, 1, 2, 3, \ldots\}$. Each integer has a corresponding cardinal number, but there are cardinal numbers, e.g., $\aleph_0$, that correspond to no integer. A cardinal number is an answer to a question about the number of members in a set. If we ask

"How many positive integers are there?" or "How many distinct finite strings on $\{a, b\}$ are there?", the answer is the cardinal number $\aleph_0$.

By definition, a set with cardinality $\aleph_0$, i.e., one that is equivalent to the set of positive integers and zero, is called *denumerable* or *denumerably infinite*. We have already seen that the set of positive even integers (E in Fig. 7-1) is denumerable. Here are some other examples:

Example 7-3: The set of positive and negative integers and zero, $Q = \{0, +1, -1, +2, -2, +3, -3, \ldots\}$, is denumerably infinite. One possible one-to-one correspondence with Z is

$$Q = \{0, +1, -1, +2, -2, +3, -3, \ldots\}$$
$$f \downarrow \downarrow \downarrow \downarrow \downarrow \downarrow \downarrow$$
$$Z = \{0, 1, 2, 3, 4, 5, 6, \ldots\}$$

The function $f: Q \to Z$ is defined by

$$f(x) = \begin{cases} 0 & \text{when } x = 0 \\ 2x - 1 & \text{when } x \text{ is positive} \\ -2x & \text{when } x \text{ is negative} \end{cases}$$

That f is indeed a one-to-one correspondence can be seen by noting that positive numbers in Q correspond to odd numbers in Z, and negative numbers in Q correspond to even numbers in Z.

Example 7-4: The set of reciprocals $S = \{\frac{1}{1}, \frac{1}{2}, \frac{1}{3}, \frac{1}{4}, \frac{1}{5}, \frac{1}{6}, \ldots\}$ is denumerably infinite, as shown by the following one-to-one correspondence with Z:

$$S = \{\tfrac{1}{1}, \tfrac{1}{2}, \tfrac{1}{3}, \tfrac{1}{4}, \tfrac{1}{5}, \tfrac{1}{6}, \ldots\}$$
$$g \downarrow \downarrow \downarrow \downarrow \downarrow \downarrow \qquad g(x) = \frac{1}{x} - 1$$
$$Z = \{0, 1, 2, 3, 4, 5, \ldots\}$$

Example 7-5: The set of odd integers $F = \{1, 3, 5, 7, 9, \ldots\}$ is denumerably infinite. One possible one-to-one correspondence with Z is

$$F = \{1, 3, 5, 7, 9, \ldots\}$$
$$h \downarrow \downarrow \downarrow \downarrow \downarrow \qquad h(x) = \frac{x-1}{2}$$
$$Z = \{0, 1, 2, 3, 4, \ldots\}$$

We have seen that the set of positive integers, the set of even integers, and the set of odd integers all have the same cardinality. Since N is equal to the union of the sets of odd and even integers, one might have supposed that N would have more members than either of these, but this is not the case. Thus, the union of two infinite sets is not necessarily a set with greater cardinality.

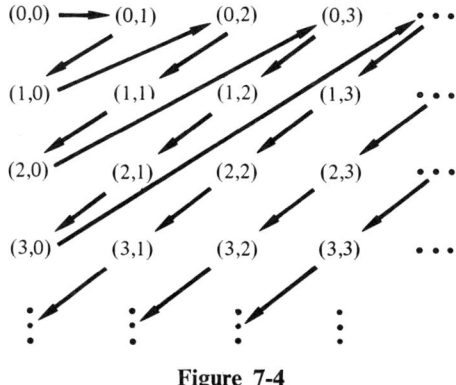

Figure 7-4

An enumeration of the members of $Z \times Z$

Are there sets larger than the set of positive integers? One that might intuitively seem so is the set of ordered pairs in the Cartesian product $Z \times Z$. When the pairs are listed in the order indicated by the arrows in Fig. 7-4, however, we find that the following one-to-one correspondence between $Z \times Z$ and Z can be established:

$$Z \times Z = \{(0,0), (0,1), (1,0), (0,2), (1,1), (2,0), (0,3), (1,2), (2,1), \ldots\}$$

f

$$Z = \{\ 0,\quad 1,\quad 2,\quad 3,\quad 4,\quad 5,\quad 6,\quad 7,\quad 8,\ \ldots\}$$

Figure 7-5

A one-to-one correspondence between $Z \times Z$ and Z

Although it is rather difficult in this case to prove that f is one-to-one, we can argue informally as follows: Consider the sum of the first and second coordinates of each ordered pair in the listing:

$$Z \times Z = \{(0,0), (0,1), (1,0), (0,2), (1,1), (2,0), (0,3), \ldots\}$$

Sum of coordinates: 0　1　1　2　2　2　3　…

First comes the ordered pair with sum 0, then the two pairs with sum 1, then the three pairs with sum 2, etc. In general, there are $n + 1$ distinct ordered pairs whose coordinate sum is n. If we agree that the pairs with coordinate sum n are listed in the order $(0, n), (1, n-1), \ldots, (n-1, 1), (n, 0)$, then there is a definite way of associating an integer with each ordered pair. Take any pair (x, y); the sum of the coordinates is $x + y$. There are $1 + 2 + 3 + 4 + \cdots + (x + y)$ pairs in the list before the first pair with sum $x + y$ appears. The sum of any sequence of integers of the form $1 + 2 + 3 \cdots + (n - 1) + n$ is given by $[n(n + 1)]/2$. Thus, the sum of $1 + 2 + \cdots + (x + y)$ is $[(x + y)(x + y + 1)]/2$. This would be the integer associated with the *last* ordered pair with coordinate sum $x + y - 1$ if we had started the counting process at 1. Since the counting was started at 0, we must subtract 1 to give $([(x + y)(x + y + 1)]/2) - 1$ as its position in the enumeration. To find the integer associated with (x, y) we count off $x + 1$ more as follows:

$$\ldots, (x+y-1,0), (0,x+y), (1,x+y-1), \ldots, (x-1,y+1), (x,y), \ldots$$
$$ 1 \qquad\quad 2 \qquad\quad \ldots \quad x \qquad\quad x+1$$

Last pair with sum $x+y-1$ First pair with sum $x+y$

Therefore, the integer associated with any pair (x, y) is given by

$$f(x, y) = \frac{(x + y)(x + y + 1)}{2} - 1 + (x + 1) = \frac{(x + y)(x + y + 1)}{2} + x$$

For example, the ordered pair $(2, 1)$ is mapped into

$$\frac{(2 + 1)(2 + 1 + 1)}{2} + 2 = \frac{3 \cdot 4}{2} + 2 = 8$$

as shown in Fig. 7-5.

This indicates that each ordered pair is mapped uniquely into a positive integer (or zero). To show the converse, that each integer corresponds to a unique ordered pair, requires some rather elaborate algebraic manipulations. We state here only that it can be done and refer the reader to Davis (1958; pp. 43–45) for details. Because there is a one-to-one correspondence between Z and $Z \times Z$, the set of all ordered pairs of positive integers and zero is denumerable.

This result can in fact be extended to any set for which it is possible to specify an enumeration of its members in a linear sequence $a_1, a_2, a_3, \ldots, a_n, \ldots$. If such a sequence is possible, the numbers $0, 1, 2$, etc., can be associated one-to-one with successive items in the list. We have just considered such an enumeration of the ordered pairs of positive integers and zero. As another example, the strings in A^*, where $A = \{a, b\}$, can be enumerated by grouping together all strings of length 0, length 1, length 2, etc., putting the groups in order of increasing length, and then arranging the strings within each group in alphabetical order as they would be found in a dictionary. The first elements of this sequence would then be as follows:

(7-1) $e, a, b, aa, ab, ba, bb, aaa, aab, aba, abb, baa, \ldots$

This sequence can be put into one-to-one correspondence with Z by letting the nth member of the sequence correspond to $n - 1$ (since we begin with 0 rather than 1). Given any integer n, we can start at the beginning and produce the items successively until we arrive at the nth item.

Problem: What string immediately follows *aabbb* in the sequence (7-1)? Can you determine the integer corresponding to this string without writing out the sequence from *e* to *aabbb* and counting?

Nondenumerable Sets

Just as there is a procedure for listing the ordered pairs of integers, so is there a procedure for the ordered triples, quadruples—in fact, for the set of n-tuples of integers for any given n.

Problem: Give a systematic method for listing the ordered triples of positive integers as a linear sequence.

Thus, a set with cardinal number greater than $\aleph_0$ will not be found by taking successive Cartesian products of Z. At one time it was supposed that there were no sets with cardinality greater than $\aleph_0$, but Georg Cantor (1845–1918), the mathematician who developed a large part of the theory of sets, proved that for any set A the power set of A always has greater cardinality than A.

Before proving Cantor's Theorem, we must state explicitly the conditions in which one set has greater cardinality than another.

DEFINITION: For any sets A and B, $\#(A) \geq \#(B)$ iff there is a function f from A to B that is onto.

$\#(A) \geq \#(B)$ is read 'the cardinality of A is greater than or equal to the cardinality of B.' This definition is constructed along the same lines as the definition of equivalence of sets. The fundamental idea is that one can compare the relative sizes of two sets by attempting to pair the members of one with the members of the other. If this pairing can be done in a one-to-one and onto fashion, the sets are of equal size. The definition of ≥ states that if the members of A can be paired with the members of B so that

1. Every member of A is paired with exactly one member of B (f is a function).
2. Every member of B is paired with at least one member of A (f is onto B).

then A has at least as many members as B.

Figure 7-6 illustrates the relation of ≥ between pairs of finite sets. Note that function g is not only onto [yielding $\#(C) \geq \#(D)$] but one-to-one as well [yielding $\#(C) = \#(D)$, i.e., $C \sim D$ as a special case].

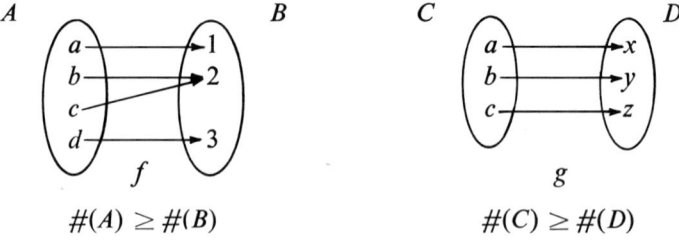

Figure 7-6

Onto mappings illustrating the relation 'greater than or equal to' between cardinal numbers

The definition also gives the expected result when an infinite set is compared with a finite set. For example, an onto function from $N = \{0, 1, 2, 3, \ldots\}$ to $Q = \{0, 1\}$ is given by

$$f(x) = \begin{cases} 0 & \text{when } x \text{ is even} \\ 1 & \text{when } x \text{ is odd} \end{cases}$$

Thus, $\#(N) \geq \#(Q)$; specifically, $\aleph_0 \geq 2$. This argument could be repeated with any finite set in place of Q, allowing us to conclude that $\aleph_0 \geq n$ for any finite cardinal number n.

Extending the definition in a straightforward way, we say that $\#(A) > \#(B)$ whenever $\#(A) \geq \#(B)$ but $\#(A) \neq \#(B)$, i.e., whenever there is a function from A to B that is onto but not one-to-one. We also remark that the notations $\#(A) \geq \#(B)$ and $\#(B) \leq \#(A)$ are equivalent, as are $\#(A) > \#(B)$ and $\#(B) < \#(A)$.

THEOREM 7-1: (Cantor) For any set A, $\#(A) < \#(\mathscr{P}(A))$.

Proof: There is a function from $\mathscr{P}(A)$ to A that maps every set containing just one element into that element in A (e.g., $\{2\} \rightarrow 2$)

and maps all the other sets into some fixed element in A. This function is onto because every member of A has at least one correspondent in $\mathscr{P}(A)$. Thus, $\#(A) \leq \#(\mathscr{P}(A))$.

We show that there is no one-to-one and onto function from A to $\mathscr{P}(A)$, and thus the sets cannot be equivalent. Assume that f is such a function. Then f maps every member of A onto some subset of A. For example, if A is the set of integers, a portion of f might appear as in Fig. 7-7:

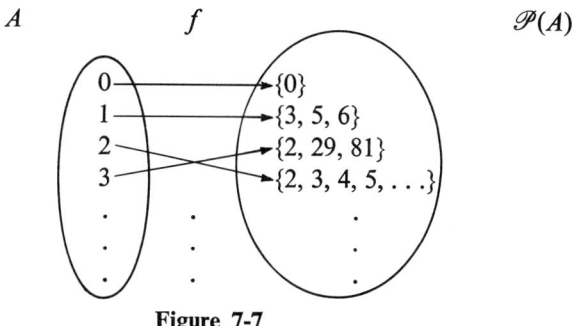

Figure 7-7

Illustration of an alleged one-to-one correspondence between a set and its power set

In general, some members of A will be mapped into a subset of which they are also members, e.g., 0 and 2 in Fig. 7-7, and some will not, e.g., 1 and 3. Now form the set B by taking every member of A that is mapped into a subset not containing that member. That is,

$$B = \{x \in A \mid x \notin f(x)\}$$

B is some subset of A and is therefore one of the members of $\mathscr{P}(A)$. By hypothesis, f is onto, so there is at least one member of A that is mapped into B. Call this member y. We now ask whether y is in B.

1. If $y \in B$, then it is not a member of the set it is mapped into, namely, B. Thus, $y \in B \to y \notin B$.

2. If $y \notin B$, then it is one of those elements not in the set it is mapped into and so by definition must be in the set B. Thus, $y \notin B \to y \in B$.

This contradiction (which is reminiscent of Russell's Paradox) indicates that the assumption that f is a one-to-one and onto function is false. Therefore, it cannot be the case that $\#(A) = \#(\mathscr{P}(A))$, and we conclude that $\#(A) < \#(\mathscr{P}(A))$.

COROLLARY 7-1: There is a cardinal number greater than $\aleph_0$.

Proof: Let $Z = \{0, 1, 2, 3, \ldots\}$ be the set A in the previous theorem. Since $\#(Z) = \aleph_0$, $\#(\mathscr{P}(Z)) > \aleph_0$.

The cardinal number of $\mathscr{P}(Z)$ is commonly denoted $2^{\aleph_0}$ by analogy with the finite cardinals where the power set of a set with n members has 2^n members. $2^{\aleph_0}$ does not denote an integer or any other real number, however, since raising 2 to the power $\aleph_0$ is not a meaningful arithmetic operation.

Forming the power set of $\mathscr{P}(Z)$ leads to a cardinal number $2^{2^{\aleph_0}}$ that is larger than $2^{\aleph_0}$; $\mathscr{P}(\mathscr{P}(\mathscr{P}(Z)))$ has cardinality $2^{2^{2^{\aleph_0}}}$, and so on. Cantor's Theorem thus yields an infinite sequence of ever greater infinite cardinal numbers: $\aleph_0 < 2^{\aleph_0} < 2^{2^{\aleph_0}} < \cdots$.

Another example of a nondenumerable set is the set of all real numbers between 0 and 1, which we denote [0, 1]. The real numbers consist of the integers, the other rational numbers (which can be expressed as the ratio of two integers, e.g., $\frac{1}{3}$, $\frac{22}{7}$, $\frac{5}{8}$), and the irrational numbers such as $\sqrt{5}$, π, $\frac{1}{3}\sqrt[3]{2}$, etc., which are not expressible as the ratio of two integers. In number theory it is proved that all real numbers, whether rational or irrational, can be written as an integer (possibly 0) followed by an infinitely long decimal fraction to the right of the decimal point. The fraction $\frac{1}{3}$, for example, can be written as 0.3333333..., where the dots indicate that the sequence of 3's is infinite. Fractions such as $\frac{1}{2}$ can be represented as 0.5 or 0.50, or 0.500, etc., or else as the infinite repeating decimal 0.499999.... Proof of this last statement would require an excursus into geometric series, but it can be made at least more plausible by considering the following: $\frac{1}{9} = 0.11111\ldots$; $1 = 9(\frac{1}{9}) = 9(0.11111\ldots) = 0.99999\ldots$. The decimal fraction of an irrational number is also infinitely long but unlike a rational number it does not have repeating digit sequences.

Cantor's proof of the nondenumerability of [0, 1] begins with the assumption that every number in this set is uniquely represented by a sequence composed of 0 and an infinitely long decimal fraction. To assure that this representation is unique for each member of the set, we also take every rational number that might be written with an infinite string of 0's, e.g., 0.5000..., in the form having an infinite string of 9's, e.g., 0.4999.... We now make the assumption that is to be proved false, namely, that the set [0, 1] is denumerable. If so, then its members can be put into a linear sequence with a first member, a second member, etc., and this sequence will contain every member of [0, 1]. In Fig. 7-8, this sequence $x_1, x_2, x_3, \ldots, x_n, \ldots$, is indicated as running vertically down the page with the decimal representation of each x_1 to the right of the equals sign. The a's are the individual digits in each decimal fraction; a_{13}, for example, is the third digit in the decimal part of the first number in the sequence. We now show

$$x_1 = 0.a_{11}a_{12}a_{13} \cdots a_{1n} \cdots$$
$$x_2 = 0.a_{21}a_{22}a_{23} \cdots a_{2n} \cdots$$
$$x_3 = 0.a_{31}a_{32}a_{33} \cdots a_{3n} \cdots$$
$$\vdots \qquad \vdots$$
$$x_n = 0.a_{n1}a_{n2}a_{n3} \cdots a_{nn} \cdots$$
$$\vdots \qquad \vdots$$

Figure 7-8

Putative enumeration of [0, 1]

that there is a number y in the set [0, 1] that is not in the sequence $x_1, x_2, x_3, \ldots, x_n, \ldots$. This number has the following characteristics: the integer part is 0; the first decimal digit, a_{y1}, is different from a_{11}; its second decimal digit, a_{y2}, is different from a_{22}; and in general the nth decimal digit a_{yn} is different from a_{nn}. Therefore, y cannot be equal to x_1 because they differ in the first decimal place (and we have agreed that each number has a unique representation in the array); likewise, y cannot be equal to x_2 because they differ in the second decimal place; and in general, y cannot equal any number x_n in the array because they differ in (at least) the nth decimal place. Yet y is a number between 0 and 1 because it is of the form $y = 0.a_{y1}a_{y2}a_{y3} \cdots a_{yn} \cdots$. Thus, our assumption that the elements of [0, 1] can be put into a linear sequence cannot be maintained, and the set is nondenumerable. This particular form of *reductio ad absurdum*, the so-called *diagonal argument* (y is constructed to be distinct from the integer $0.a_{11}a_{22}a_{33} \cdots a_{nn} \cdots$ on the diagonal of the square array), is encountered frequently in proofs involving infinite sets.

This proves that the cardinality of the set [0, 1] is greater than $\aleph_0$ but does not determine just what it is. Cantor was able to show (by a proof we shall not reproduce here) that [0, 1] is equivalent to the power set of the integers, and thus its cardinal number is $2^{\aleph_0}$.

A problem that remained unsolved for many years was whether there are any infinite cardinal numbers other than $\aleph_0$, $2^{\aleph_0}$, $2^{2^{\aleph_0}}$, etc. Is there, for example, a cardinal number β such that $\aleph_0 < \beta < 2^{\aleph_0}$ or, to put it another way, is there a set intermediate in size between Z and $\mathscr{P}(Z)$? The conjecture that the answer to this question was in the negative is known as the *Continuum Hypothesis*. It was not until 1963 that the matter was finally resolved (an event sufficiently newsworthy that it was reported in the *New York Times* (Nov. 14, 1963, p. 37)), when P. J. Cohen showed that the Continuum

Hypothesis can be neither proved nor disproved on the basis of the usual axioms of set theory. The Continuum Hypothesis is therefore *independent* of these axioms, and it or its negation could be added to set theory without being redundant or creating a contradiction.

EXERCISES

1. Prove that the relation of equivalence of sets is an equivalence relation.

2. Show that the set of integral powers of 10 {10, 100, 1000, 10,000, 100,000, ...} is denumerably infinite.

3. Let A and B be disjoint sets, finite or infinite, and let $\alpha = \#(A)$ and $\beta = \#(B)$. We can define the operations of cardinal addition, denoted by $\oplus$, and cardinal multiplication, denoted by $\otimes$, as follows:

$$\alpha \oplus \beta = \#(A \cup B)$$
$$\alpha \otimes \beta = \#(A \times B)$$

When A and B are both finite sets, cardinal addition and multiplication produce the same results as the corresponding arithmetic operations on integers. When at least one is finite, however, the operations are no longer parallel in all respects. Find examples of sets A and B for which the following hold:

(a) $\aleph_0 \oplus 1 = \aleph_0$
(b) $\aleph_0 \otimes 2 = \aleph_0$
(c) $\aleph_0 \oplus \aleph_0 = \aleph_0$
(d) $\aleph_0 \otimes \aleph_0 = \aleph_0$

Do the operations $\oplus$ and $\otimes$ appear to be commutative? associative?

4. Prove for any sets A, B, and C, if $\#(A) \geq \#(B)$ and $\#(B) \geq \#(C)$, then $\#(A) \geq \#(C)$.

5. It can be proved that $\aleph_0$ is the smallest infinite cardinal number. Consider the following putative counter-example to this claim. Choose a cardinal number x such that $2^x = \aleph_0$. x cannot be finite since 2 raised to any finite power is finite; but x cannot be equal to $\aleph_0$ either, since $2^{\aleph_0} > \aleph_0$ by Cantor's Theorem. Therefore, x is an infinite cardinal number less than $\aleph_0$. What is wrong with this argument?

References and Supplementary Reading

Much of the material in Chapters 4, 5, 6, and 7 can also be found in the references cited at the end of Chapter 1. See also, Gleason (1966; Chapters

1-7) and Birkhoff and MacLane (1953). McFadden, Moore, and Smith (1963) uses the programmed instruction approach to sets, relations, and functions and contains many problems and examples.

The proof of the independence of the Continuum Hypothesis is given in Cohen (1966). Kamke (1950) contains considerable discussion of the properties of infinite sets.

8

Recursion

We have seen that infinite sets can be formally distinguished from finite sets, and we now want to examine in more detail how the membership of an infinite set can be specified. Of the two methods we know for defining sets—exhibiting all the members as a list or giving a predicate that is true of just the members of the set—the former is clearly out of the question for infinite sets. Expressions such as $\{0, 1, 2, 3, \ldots\}$ and $\{e, a, b, aa, ab, \ldots\}$ may resemble the list notation, but they contain as an essential part the final ellipsis, which signifies something such as 'and so forth for all the other members.' Thus, this notation is formally inadequate as a set specification since in reality it constitutes an appeal to the reader to supply the specification for himself. That is, he is asked to perceive the general pattern formed by the few members given and to recognize how this pattern is continued throughout the set. (Tasks of this kind are often included on intelligence tests, where one might be asked, for example, to supply the next number in the sequence $1, 2, 3, 5, 8, 13, \ldots$). In this chapter we examine the notion of recursive definition as a means of specifying a predicate with an infinite extension, and we also look at the closely related notions of *inductive proof* and *axiomatic system*. The grammars of formal languages that are to be taken up in the next chapter will be seen to comprise a special type of axiomatic system.

Recursive Definition

Consider the set M of all mirror-image strings on $\{a, b\}$. A mirror-image string is one that can be divided into halves, the right half consisting of the same sequence of symbols as the left half but in the reverse order. For example, *aaaa*, *abba*, *babbab*, and *bbabbabb* are mirror-image strings, but *babb*, *aaab*, and *bab* are not. The following is a possible recursive definition of M.

(8-1)
1. $aa \in M \land bb \in M$
2. $(\forall x)(x \in M \rightarrow (a \frown x \frown a \in M \land b \frown x \frown b \in M))$
3. M contains nothing but those members it has by virtue of lines 1 and 2

Line 1, which is called the *base* of the recursive definition, asserts that $x \in M$ is true of the specific strings *aa* and *bb*. Line 2, called the *recursion step* or simply the *recursion*, says that for any string x if $x \in M$ is true, then it is also true of the strings formed from x by concatenating an a at both ends or a b at both ends. Line 3, the *restriction*, rules out any true instances of $x \in M$ other than those covered by lines 1 and 2. Without the restriction, the definition would specify a class of sets meeting the conditions of lines 1 and 2 but possibly containing other members as well.

The recursion step of a recursive definition is characteristically a conditional in which what is being defined occurs in both the antecedent and the consequent. This makes recursive definitions look like alleged definitions that are circular and, consequently, not really definitions at all. For example, the putative definition of 'subset' in (8-2)

(8-2) For any sets A and B, A is a *subset* of B iff every subset of A is also a subset of B.

contains a vicious circularity in which the notion 'subset' is characterized by appealing to that notion itself. That is, one could not know what a subset is until one had already determined what a subset is. If 'subset' had already been adequately defined in the customary way in terms of the predicate $\in$, then (8-2) would be a perfectly sensible, in fact, true statement; but as a statement introducing the term 'subset' for the first time (8-2) is defectively circular.

In a recursive definition this circularity is avoided by the presence of the base, which makes a nonconditional statement about the thing being defined. Given the base, one can take an appropriate substitution instance of the recursion step and by *Modus Ponens* derive the consequent of that substitution instance. From the base and the recursion of (8-1) for example, the following inference can be carried out:

(8-3)
1. $aa \in M \land bb \in M$
2. $(\forall x)(x \in M \rightarrow (axa \in M \land bxb \in M))$
3. $aa \in M$ — 1, Simp.
4. $aa \in M \rightarrow (aaaa \in M \land baab \in M)$ — 2, U.I.
5. $aaaa \in M \land baab \in M$ — 3, 4, M.P.
6. $baab \in M$ — 5, Simp.

From this line and another substitution instance of the recursion step
     7. $baab \in M \rightarrow (abaaba \in M \wedge bbaabb \in M)$ 2, U.I.
we can derive
     8. $abaaba \in M \wedge bbaabb \in M$ 6, 7, M.P.

Such a series of steps constitutes a proof that certain strings are in M, given the base and recursion of the recursive definition (8-1) as premises. The fact that such a proof is possible for every string asserted to be in M by the definition serves to convince us that this recursive definition really does define something and is not circular. Without the base, however, no such proofs are possible. From the recursion step alone one can derive only a series of conditionals.

(8-4)
1. $(\forall x)(x \in M \rightarrow (axa \in M \wedge bxb \in M))$
2. $aa \in M \rightarrow (aaaa \in M \wedge baab \in M)$ 1, U.I.
3. $(aa \in M \rightarrow aaaa \in M) \wedge (aa \in M \rightarrow baab \in M)$ 2, Log. Equiv.
4. $aa \in M \rightarrow aaaa \in M$ 3, Simp.
5. $aaaa \in M \rightarrow (aaaaaa \in M \wedge baaaab \in M)$ 1, U.I.
6. $aa \in M \rightarrow (aaaaaa \in M \wedge baaaab \in M)$ 4, 5, H.S.

The conclusions that can be derived are statements that *if* certain strings are in M, then so are certain others. Lacking the base, the definition would not assert that M contains any strings at all.

We also note that the close connection between sets and predicates allows us to regard a recursive definition either as defining a predicate, e.g., the predicate 'is a member of M' in the preceding example, or, equivalently, as defining a set that is the extension of that predicate, e.g., the set M.

A slightly more complex example is the recursive definition of the set of well-formed formulas (*wff*'s) in the propositional calculus. The following definition divides those strings constructed from the alphabet

$$C = \{p, q, r, \wedge, \vee, \sim, \rightarrow, \leftrightarrow, (,)\}$$

that are legitimate expressions in this system of logic, e.g., $((p \wedge q) \vee r) \rightarrow s$, from those, e.g., $)p \wedge \rightarrow (r$, which are not.

1. p is a *wff*; q is a *wff*; r is a *wff*

(8-5)   2. For all α and β, if α and β are *wff*'s then so is
$$\begin{cases} (a) \ (\alpha \wedge \beta) \\ (b) \ (\alpha \vee \beta) \\ (c) \ (\alpha \rightarrow \beta) \\ (d) \ (\alpha \leftrightarrow \beta) \\ (e) \ \sim(\alpha) \end{cases}$$

3. Nothing is a *wff* except as a consequence of lines 1 and 2

Using this definition we can prove that some particular expression, say $((p \wedge q) \vee r)$, is a *wff*.

(8-6)
1. p is a *wff* $\wedge$ q is a *wff* (1), Simp.
2. (p is a *wff* $\wedge$ q is a *wff*) $\rightarrow$ ($p \wedge q$) is a *wff* (2a), U.I.
3. $(p \wedge q)$ is a *wff* 1, 2, M.P.
4. r is a *wff* (1), Simp.
5. $((p \wedge q)$ is a *wff* $\wedge$ r is a *wff*) $\rightarrow$ $((p \wedge q) \vee r)$ is a *wff* (2b), U.I.
6. $(p \wedge q)$ is a *wff* $\wedge$ r is a *wff* 3, 4, Conj.
7. $((p \wedge q) \vee r)$ is a *wff* 5, 6, M.P.

The definition in (8-5) does not characterize all the *wff*'s of the propositional calculus since it allows no more than three distinguishable elementary propositions p, q, and r. Of course more symbols could be added to the alphabet and the base of the recursive definition could be appropriately expanded, but for any given finite number of symbols for elementary propositions there is some *wff* in the propositional calculus containing more than this number of distinct elementary propositions. Thus, it would appear that there must be an infinite number of symbols for elementary propositions in the alphabet and that the base of the definition must consist of an infinite conjunction of the form p is a *wff* $\wedge$ q is a *wff* $\wedge$ $\cdots$. This raises anew the problem of specifying the members of an infinite set—here, the set of conjuncts in the base of the recursive definition. The solution is to precede the recursive definition of *wff* by a recursive definition of 'elementary proposition' (more precisely, the set of symbols denoting elementary propositions). One symbol, say p, is chosen and other symbols are created by adding primes successively: p, p', p'', p''', etc. Each such symbol is considered distinct, designating an elementary proposition potentially distinct from all others. The recursive definition is as follows:

(8-7)
1. p is (or denotes) an elementary proposition
2. For all x, if x is an elementary proposition, then so is x'
3. Nothing else is an elementary proposition

The recursive definition of *wff* is now as in (8-5) except that the base is replaced by

(8-8)   Every elementary proposition is a *wff*

It is also understood, of course, that the definition of *wff* now applies to strings on the finite alphabet $C' = \{p, ', \wedge, \vee, \sim, \rightarrow, \leftrightarrow, (,)\}$.

Nothing essentially new is involved in framing one recursive definition in terms of another. We have already seen many examples of definitions in which previously defined concepts appear; for example, the definition of 'power set' in terms of 'subset' in Chapter 1. If recursive definition is a legitimate mode of definition, then there can be no objection to using one recursively defined predicate in the recursive definition of another.

As a final example of recursive definition, we consider the following definition of a very interesting set, which we denote by ω.

(8-9)
1. $\varnothing \in \omega$
2. For all X, if $X \in \omega$, then $X \cup \{X\} \in \omega$
3. Nothing else is in ω

For any given set A, the set $A \cup \{A\}$ is called the *successor of A*, and is denoted A^+. The set ω, then, contains $\varnothing$, the successor of $\varnothing$, the successor of the successor of $\varnothing$, etc. Some of these members are exhibited in (8-10):

(8-10)
1. $\varnothing^+ = \varnothing \cup \{\varnothing\} = \{\varnothing\}$
2. $(\varnothing^+)^+ = \{\varnothing\} \cup \{\{\varnothing\}\} = \{\varnothing, \{\varnothing\}\}$
3. $((\varnothing^+)^+)^+ = \{\varnothing, \{\varnothing\}\} \cup \{\{\varnothing, \{\varnothing\}\}\} = \{\varnothing, \{\varnothing\}, \{\varnothing, \{\varnothing\}\}\}$
4. $(((\varnothing^+)^+)^+)^+ = \{\varnothing, \{\varnothing\}, \{\varnothing, \{\varnothing\}\}\} \cup \{\{\varnothing, \{\varnothing\}, \{\varnothing, \{\varnothing\}\}\}\}$
$= \{\varnothing, \{\varnothing\}, \{\varnothing, \{\varnothing\}\}, \{\varnothing, \{\varnothing\}, \{\varnothing, \{\varnothing\}\}\}\}$

The set ω defined in this way has some very useful properties. There is just one set in the collection that has no members, namely $\varnothing$, and there is one set in ω with exactly one member, namely the set $\{\varnothing\}$. In general, the successor of any set X contains one member more than X does. In formal treatments of set theory these properties are exploited by using (8-9) as a definition of the set of positive integers and zero. Zero is identified with $\varnothing$, 1 with $\{\varnothing\}$, 2 with $\{\varnothing, \{\varnothing\}\}$, and so on, each integer n being identified with the unique member of ω having n members. Using the ordinary notation for the integers, we can rewrite the expressions in (8-10) as follows:

(8-11)
1. $0^+ = \{0\} = 1$
2. $(0^+)^+ = 1^+ = \{0, 1\} = 2$
3. $((0^+)^+)^+ = (1^+)^+ = 2^+ = \{0, 1, 2\} = 3$
4. $(((0^+)^+)^+)^+ = ((1^+)^+)^+ = (2^+)^+ = 3^+ = \{0, 1, 2, 3\} = 4$

In general, for any integer n the successor of n is a set consisting of all the integers 0 through n, i.e., $\{0, 1, 2, 3, \ldots, n-1, n\}$. Defining the integers in this way has some surprising consequences, e.g., $3 \subseteq 4$ and $3 \in 4$, which fortunately turn out to be harmless. The definition does, however, endow the integers with all the essential properties that we intuitively expect them to have. The Italian mathematician G. Peano at the end of the 19th century proposed a set of five propositions, which have come to be known as Peano's Axioms, setting forth some essential properties of the integers from which all their other properties were presumed to be derivable. The first four of these are shown in (8-12).

(8-12)
1. 0 is an integer
2. $(\forall x)(x$ is an integer $\to x^+$ is an integer$)$
3. $(\forall x)(x^+ \neq 0)$
4. $(\forall x, y)(x^+ = y^+ \to x = y)$

Axioms 1 and 2 follow immediately from the definition of ω and the agreement to call any member of ω an integer. Axiom 3 states that 0 is not the successor of any integer, which can easily be deduced from the definition of ω by noting that for no set X is $X \cup \{X\} = \varnothing$. Axiom 4, which is rather more difficult to prove, guarantees that the successor of any given integer is unique. Thus, within the context of set theory no additional axioms are required for the integers since they can be introduced by the recursive definition of the set ω. This is an important step in the construction of other branches of mathematics from set theory since on the basis of the positive integers and zero the other numbers—the rationals, the reals, and the imaginary numbers—can be defined, and these, in turn, are the foundation for number theory, the calculus, analysis, etc.

Induction

The fifth of Peano's Axioms, which is also known as the Principle of Mathematical Induction, is as follows:

For any predicate $P(x)$, if the following two statements are true

(8-13)
1. $P(0)$ (P is true of 0)
2. $(\forall x)(P(x) \to P(x^+))$ (for every integer, if P is true of that integer, P is true of its successor)

then the following statement can be deduced:

3. $(\forall x)P(x)$ (P is true of every integer)

The similarity between (8-13) 1 and 2 and the base and recursion step, respectively, of a recursive definition is readily apparent. The Principle of Mathematical Induction is not a definition, however, but a rule of inference to be applied to propositions about the integers. A proof that employs this rule of inference is known as a *proof by induction* or an *inductive proof*.

Let us examine the structure of such a proof in more detail. Suppose we have been given a predicate $P(x)$ such that (8-13) 1 and 2 hold. These form the premises of the argument.

(8-14)
1. $P(0)$
2. $(\forall x)(P(x) \to P(x^+))$

From $P(0)$ and a substitution instance of line 2

    3. $P(0) \rightarrow P(1)$ 2, U.I.

we can derive

    4. $P(1)$ 1, 3, M.P.

and from this and another substitution instance of line 2

    5. $P(1) \rightarrow P(2)$ 2, U.I.

we can derive

    6. $P(2)$ 4, 5, M.P.

and so on.

To prove the statement $(\forall x)P(x)$ would require an infinite number of steps, and we would ordinarily not want to consider an infinitely long sequence of lines a proof, if for no other reason than that it would be impossible to examine it in order to verify its correctness. Thus, there is no proof of $(\forall x)P(x)$ that can be constructed by using only the rules of inference we have considered up to now. Nevertheless, (8-13) 3 is intuitively a valid conclusion to draw from the premises (8-13) 1 and 2, and the Principle of Mathematical Induction is a formal assertion that this inference is legitimate. It should be noted that the Principle of Mathematical Induction itself is not susceptible of proof but only acceptance or rejection on the grounds of its effectiveness in separating intuitively valid from intuitively invalid arguments. With this additional rule of inference, the proof of $(\forall x)P(x)$ is simply as follows:

(8-15)
1. $P(0)$
2. $(\forall x)(P(x) \rightarrow P(x^+))$
3. $(\forall x)P(x)$ 1, 2, Math. Ind.

As an example we prove by induction that for every integer n the sum of the series $0 + 1 + 2 + \cdots + (n - 1) + n$ equals $[n(n + 1)]/2$.

The premises of the argument are the propositions stating all the usual arithmetic properties of the integers (the commutativity of addition, etc.), which can be deduced as theorems from Peano's Axioms or, equivalently, from the definition of ω in (8-9). As is usual in inductive proofs almost all the work comes in establishing the truth of the statements corresponding to (8-13) 1 and 2, known as the *base* and the *induction step*, respectively. Once these have been derived, the remainder of the proof consists of just one inferential step justified by the Principle of Mathematical Induction. We begin by demonstrating the truth of the base, i.e., that $0 + 1 + \cdots + n = [n(n + 1)]/2$ is true for $n = 0$. In this case the sequence to the left of the equals sign consists of just 0, and the expression to the right becomes $[0(0 + 1)]/2$, which is equal to 0.

The induction step to be established is

(8-16) $$(\forall n)\left(0 + 1 + \cdots + n = \frac{n(n+1)}{2} \to 0 + 1 + \cdots + n + (n+1)\right.$$
$$\left. = \frac{(n+1)(n+1+1)}{2}\right)$$

that is, if the equation is true for any integer n, it is also true for $n + 1$, the successor of n. To prove (8-16) we use a conditional proof in which we assume the antecedent of the conditional in (8-16) for an arbitrary integer k.

1. $0 + 1 + \cdots + k = \dfrac{k(k+1)}{2}$ C.P.

2. $0 + 1 + \cdots + k + (k+1) = \dfrac{k(k+1)}{2} + (k+1)$

     1, adding $(k+1)$ to both sides

3. $0 + 1 + \cdots + k + (k+1) = \dfrac{k(k+1) + 2(k+1)}{2}$

     2, converting to common denominator

(8-17)   4. $0 + 1 + \cdots + k + (k+1) = \dfrac{(k+1)(k+2)}{2}$

     3, factoring $(k+1)$ in numerator

5. $0 + 1 + \cdots + k + (k+1) = \dfrac{(k+1)((k+1)+1)}{2}$

     4, expressing $k+2$ as $(k+1)+1$

6. $0 + 1 + \cdots + k = \dfrac{k(k+1)}{2} \to 0 + 1 + \cdots + k + (k+1) = \dfrac{(k+1)((k+1)+1)}{2}$

Since k was chosen arbitrarily, line 6 can be universally generalized to (8-16). Having now established the truth of the base and the induction step, the Principle of Mathematical Induction allows us to conclude

(8-18) $\quad (\forall n)\left(0 + 1 + \cdots + n = \dfrac{n(n+1)}{2}\right)$

Proof by induction can be applied not only to theorems about the set of integers but to theorems about any set that can be put into one-to-one correspondence with the integers, i.e., the denumerably infinite sets. As an example of this sort we prove a generalized form of the Distributive Law for union and intersection of sets.

(8-19) $\quad A \cup (B_1 \cap B_2 \cap \cdots \cap B_n) = (A \cup B_1) \cap (A \cup B_2) \cap \cdots \cap (A \cup B_n)$

The form in which the Distributive Law was given in Chapter 2 is a special case of (8-19) in which $n = 2$; that is,

(8-20) $\quad A \cup (B_1 \cap B_2) = (A \cup B_1) \cap (A \cup B_2)$

Equation (8-19) is meaningless for $n = 0$ and trivial for $n = 1$. We take as the base of the inductive proof that (8-19) holds for $n = 2$, i.e., that (8-20) is true. This is easily shown by expressing the sets in terms of predicates and applying the Distributive Law of disjunction over conjunction in the propositional calculus.

To prove the induction step we assume that (8-19) holds for an arbitrarily chosen integer k:

(8-21) $\quad A \cup (B_1 \cap B_2 \cap \cdots \cap B_k) = (A \cup B_1) \cap (A \cup B_2) \cap \cdots \cap (A \cup B_k)$

We wish to show that (8-21) implies (8-22).

(8-22) $\quad A \cup (B_1 \cap B_2 \cap \cdots \cap B_{k+1}) = (A \cup B_1) \cap (A \cup B_2) \cap \cdots \cap (A \cup B_k) \cap (A \cup B_{k+1})$

The left side of (8-22) can be rewritten by the Associative Law as

(8-23) $\quad A \cup ((B_1 \cap B_2 \cap \cdots \cap B_k) \cap B_{k+1})$

which is equal to

(8-24) $\quad (A \cup (B_1 \cap B_2 \cap \cdots \cap B_k)) \cap (A \cup B_{k+1})$

by an application of the Distributive Law for the case $n = 2$, which has already been proved. By the induction hypothesis (8-21), equation (8-24) is equal to

(8-25) $\quad ((A \cup B_1) \cap (A \cup B_2) \cap \cdots \cap (A \cup B_k)) \cap (A \cup B_{k+1})$

By the Associative Law we can omit one set of parentheses to obtain the right side of (8-22). This shows that (8-22) holds if (8-21) does. From this and the base by the Principle of Mathematical Induction the generalized form of the Distributive Law is shown to be true for all n equal to or greater than 2 (or greater than 1 if we include this trivial case).

In this last example induction is used to prove a theorem about a class of equations of the form given in (8-19), which can be put into one-to-one correspondence with the integers. The mapping is between an equation and an integer n representing its length—specifically, the number of terms in the expression $B_1 \cap B_2 \cap \cdots \cap B_n$. Proof by induction on the length of a string is the commonest use of this method of proof in mathematical linguistics.

Problem: Prove by induction the following generalized form of one of DeMorgan's Laws:

$$(A_1 \cap A_2 \cap \cdots \cap A_n)' = A_1' \cup \cdots \cup A_n'$$

Axiomatic Systems

Recursive definition and inductive proof have a similar logical structure. From a finite number of propositions given initially an infinite number of additional propositions are derivable by repeated application of a specified set of rules. This logical structure is also common to the so-called *axiomatic method* in mathematics. The propositions assumed at the outset are the *axioms*, and additional statements, called *theorems*, are derived from the axioms and previously derived theorems by iterated applications of the *rules of inference*. The set of axioms, the set of rules of inference, and the alphabet in which all these are written constitute an *axiomatic system*. Viewed in this way, a recursive definition is like an axiomatic system in which the base states the axioms and the recursion step constitutes the rules of inference. The members of the set specified by the recursive definition, aside from those given by the base, comprise the theorems of the system.

DEFINITION: An *axiomatic system* is an ordered triple (A, S, P) in which

1. A is a finite set of symbols, called the *alphabet*.
2. S is a set of strings on A, called the *axioms*.
3. P is a set of n-place relations on strings of A^*, where $n \geq 2$ (i.e., the n-tuples in P must be at least ordered pairs). The members of P are called *productions* or *rules* (*of inference*).

We now indicate how the productions are to be employed in deriving additional strings.

DEFINITION: Given an axiomatic system (A, S, P), if

$$(x_1, x_2, \ldots, x_{n-1}, x_n)$$

is a production in P, we say that x_n *follows from* $(x_1, x_2, \ldots, x_{n-1})$. We also use $x_1, x_2, \ldots, x_{n-1} \to x_n$ as an equivalent notation for $(x_1, x_2, \ldots, x_{n-1}, x_n)$.

DEFINITION: Given an axiomatic system (A, S, P), a linearly ordered sequence of strings $y_1, y_2, \ldots, y_m$ is called a *derivation* (or *proof*) of y_m if and only if every string in the sequence is either (1) an axiom, or (2) follows by one of the productions in P from one or more strings preceding it in the sequence. If there is a derivation of y in a given axiomatic system, y is called a *theorem* of that system.

We can illustrate these definitions by reinterpreting the recursive definition in (8-1) of mirror-image strings on $\{a, b\}$ as an axiomatic system.

(8-26)
$$A = \{a, b\}$$
$$S = \{aa, bb\}$$
$$P = \{(x, y) \in A^* \times A^* \mid y = axa \lor y = bxb\}$$

The productions are thus the infinite set of ordered pairs

(8-27)
$$\{(e, aa), (e, bb), (a, aaa), (a, bab), (b, aba), (b, bbb), (aa, aaaa), \ldots\}$$

In the alternative notation, this set could be written as

(8-28)
$$\{e \to aa, e \to bb, a \to aaa, a \to aba, b \to aba, b \to bbb, aa \to aaaa, \ldots\}$$

In this axiomatic system, we see that the sequence of lines

(8-29)   *bb, abba, aabbaa*

is a derivation of *aabbaa* since the last string follows from preceding strings (in fact, from just the one immediately preceding) by the production $abba \to aabbaa$; similarly, *abba* follows from *bb* by the production $bb \to abba$; and *bb* is an axiom. Therefore, *aabbaa* is a theorem of this axiomatic system. The sequence

(8-30)   *bb, baab*

is not a derivation since *baab* does not follow from *bb* by the rules of P. This does not necessarily mean that the string *baab* is not a theorem since there may exist some derivation in the system in which *baab* is the last line. It happens in this case that there is, viz.,

(8-31)   *aa, baab*

and thus *baab* is a theorem.

One consequence of the definitions is that the first line of a derivation must be an axiom since there are no lines preceding the first from which it could follow. Thus, a sequence such as

(8-32) $ab, aaba, baabab$

is not a derivation because ab is not an axiom. A derivation may, however, consist of only one line and, if so, that line must necessarily be an axiom.

The set of productions P in (8-26) is an infinite set of all ordered pairs of the form (x, axa) and (x, bxb), where x is a variable whose values are all the strings in A^*. P, therefore, contains productions such as (a, aaa) and $(ab, babb)$ that will never actually be used in the derivation of any theorems in this system from the given set of axioms. Further, because x is a variable symbol and not a member of the alphabet A, the expressions (x, axa) and (x, bxb) are not themselves productions but rather *production schemata* or formulas for constructing productions. This finite set of schemata specifies an infinite set of productions in which the variable symbol x is replaced by any constant string on A^*. To be completely formal, we could, of course, give a recursive definition of the set of productions, thus embedding one recursive specification within another as we did in (8-7) and (8-8).

The axioms may also be specified by schemata containing variable symbols (or by recursive definition). For example, in the axiomatic system given in (8-33), whose theorems are all the *wff*'s of the propositional calculus, S is an axiom schema specifying as an axiom any string consisting of the symbol p followed by any number of primes [cf. (8-7)]. P is also a schema for the infinite set of productions of this system.

$$A = \{\wedge, \vee, \sim, \rightarrow, \leftrightarrow, (,), p, '\}$$
(8-33) $S = \{px \mid x \in \{'\}^*\}$
$P = \{(x, \sim(x)), (x, y, (x \wedge y)), (x, y, (x \vee y)), (x, y, (x \rightarrow y)),$
$(x, y, (x \leftrightarrow y))\}$ where x and y are strings in A^*

Problem: Which of the following sequences are derivations in the axiomatic system of (8-33)?

1. $p, \sim(p), \sim(\sim(p))$
2. $p, p', (p \vee p'), ((p \vee p') \wedge p'')$
3. $(p \vee p), p', (p' \rightarrow (p \vee p))$
4. $p, \sim(p), p'$

Extended Axiomatic Systems

It is common to extend the definition of an axiomatic system somewhat to allow two kinds of symbols in the alphabet. Specifically, we have a *basic alphabet* and an *auxiliary alphabet*, which are disjoint sets. Symbols from both sets may appear in the lines of a derivation, *but the theorems contain only symbols from the basic alphabet.* An axiomatic system with two disjoint alphabets of this sort will be called an *extended axiomatic system* (e.a.s.).

> **DEFINITION:** An *extended axiomatic system* is an ordered quadruple (A, B, S, P) where
> 1. A is a finite set of symbols, the *auxiliary alphabet*.
> 2. B is a finite set of symbols, the *basic alphabet*; A and B are disjoint.
> 3. S is a set of strings on $(A \cup B)^*$, the *axioms*. S may be specified by a finite set of axiom schemata.
> 4. P is a set of n-place relations on strings of $(A \cup B)^*$ ($n \geq 2$) called *productions* or *rules (of inference)*. P may be specified by a finite set of production schemata. If $(x_1, x_2, \ldots, x_{n-1}, x_n)$ is a production in P, we say that x_n *follows from* $x_1, x_2, \ldots, x_{n-1}$, which can also be denoted by $x_1, x_2, \ldots, x_{n-1} \to x_n$.

In an e.a.s. we distinguish between a derivation and a proof, since not every derivation ends in a theorem. The definition of derivation is just as before.

> **DEFINITION:** Given an e.a.s. (A, B, S, P), a linearly ordered sequence of strings $y_1, y_2, \ldots, y_m$ is called a *derivation* of y_m if every string in the sequence (1) is an axiom, or (2) follows by one of the productions in P from one or more strings preceding it in the sequence.

> **DEFINITION:** Given an e.a.s. (A, B, S, P), a string y is a *theorem* if (1) there is a derivation of y in (A, B, S, P), *and* (2) $y \in B^*$. When y is a theorem, a derivation of y is called a *proof* of y.

We note that as we have defined them every axiomatic system is also an e.a.s. with the null set as the auxiliary alphabet, but not every e.a.s. is an axiomatic system. An e.a.s. with a nonnull auxiliary alphabet is a *proper* e.a.s.

An example of a proper e.a.s., whose theorems are the mirror-image strings on $\{a, b\}$, is the following:

(8-34)
$$A = \{M\}$$
$$B = \{a,b\}$$
$$S = \{M\}$$

$$P = \begin{cases} \alpha M \beta \to \alpha a M a \beta \\ \alpha M \beta \to \alpha b M b \beta \\ \alpha M \beta \to \alpha a a \beta \\ \alpha M \beta \to \alpha b b \beta \end{cases}$$
where α and β are any strings on $(A \cup B)^*$

The following sequence of lines

(8-35) $M, aMa, aaMaa, aabMbaa$

is a derivation of *aabMbaa* but not a proof in this system, since *aabMbaa* contains a symbol of the auxiliary alphabet and therefore cannot be a theorem. The following is a proof of *aabbaa*.

(8-36) $M, aMa, aaMaa, aabbaa$

Two systems having the same set of theorems are said to be *equivalent*. Thus, the e.a.s. of (8-34) is equivalent to the axiomatic system of (8-26).

The following e.a.s. is equivalent to the axiomatic system (8-33), which generates the *wff*'s of the propositional calculus.

(8-37)
$$A = \{E, F\}$$
$$B = \{\wedge, \vee, \sim, \rightarrow, \leftrightarrow, (,), p, '\}$$
$$S = \{F\}$$

$$P = \begin{cases} \alpha F \beta \rightarrow \alpha \sim (F)\beta \\ \alpha F \beta \rightarrow \alpha(F \wedge F)\beta \\ \alpha F \beta \rightarrow \alpha(F \vee F)\beta \\ \alpha F \beta \rightarrow \alpha(F \rightarrow F)\beta \\ \alpha F \beta \rightarrow \alpha(F \leftrightarrow F)\beta \\ \alpha F \beta \rightarrow \alpha E \beta \\ \alpha E \beta \rightarrow \alpha E' \beta \\ \alpha E \beta \rightarrow \alpha p \beta \end{cases}$$ where α and β are any strings of $(A \cup B)^*$

(The symbol $\rightarrow$, unfortunately, is used for two different purposes in this system: to signify 'follows from' in the production schemata and in the fourth schema as a symbol in the alphabet of the propositional calculus.)

The following sequence is a proof of $((p' \wedge p'') \vee p)$ in this system:

1. F
2. $(F \vee F)$
3. $((F \wedge F) \vee F)$
4. $((E \wedge F) \vee F)$
5. $((E \wedge E) \vee F)$
6. $((E \wedge E) \vee E)$
7. $((E' \wedge E) \vee E)$
8. $((E' \wedge E') \vee E)$
9. $((E' \wedge E'') \vee E)$
10. $((p' \wedge E'') \vee E)$
11. $((p' \wedge p'') \vee E)$
12. $((p' \wedge p'') \vee p)$

The axiom set of the e.a.s. in (8-37) contains only the single symbol F, not an infinite set of strings specified by axiom schemata. Rather, the last two production schemata in the list generate the symbols for elementary propositions, p, p', p'', p''', etc. Note that a rather natural interpretation of this system is possible in which F is a 'well-formed formula' and E is an 'elementary proposition.' The production schemata could then be interpreted as statements such as 'if F is a well-formed formula, then so is its negation,' 'an elementary proposition is a well-formed formula,' 'p is an elementary proposition,' etc.

Problem: Describe the theorems of the following e.a.s.

(8-39)
$$A = \{Q\}$$
$$B = \{a\}$$
$$S = \{aQa\}$$
$$P = \begin{Bmatrix} \alpha Q\beta \to \alpha aQ\alpha\alpha a\beta \\ \alpha Q\beta \to \beta \end{Bmatrix} \quad \text{where } \alpha, \beta \text{ are strings in } (A \cup B)^*$$

Semi-Thue Systems

One way in which axiomatic systems can be classified is according to some property of their production schemata. One could, for example, distinguish systems with only binary productions, i.e., of the form $\varphi \to \psi$, where φ and ψ are strings, or one could consider the class of systems in which for every production $x_1, x_2, \ldots, x_{n-1} \to x_n$ the number of symbols in x_n is greater than or equal to the sum of the number of symbols in $x_1, x_2, \ldots, x_{n-1}$. Any formal property of the productions could, in principle, serve as a basis for such a classification. The systems to which we now direct our attention are the semi-Thue systems (after the Norwegian mathematician Axel Thue who first studied them). These are extended axiomatic systems whose productions are restricted in a manner specified by the following definition.

DEFINITION: A *semi-Thue* system is an e.a.s. (A, B, S, P) in which every production schema is binary and of the form

$$\alpha x \beta \to \alpha y \beta,$$

where x and y are strings on $(A \cup B)^*$ and α and β are variables taking as values strings on $(A \cup B)^*$.

Thus, the change effected by any production is restricted to the replacement of some fixed string of symbols by another fixed string. Of the axiomatic systems we have examined thus far, (8-26), (8-34), and (8-37) are semi-Thue systems [in (8-26) each production is of the form $x \to y$, where both α and β are the null string]. The system given in (8-33) is not semi-Thue since some of its productions are ternary and not binary. The e.a.s. in (8-39) fails the definition because in neither of its production schemata is a fixed string replaced by a fixed string. In $\alpha Q\beta \to \beta$, the variable string αQ is replaced by e, and in $\alpha Q\beta \to \alpha a Q\alpha\alpha\beta$, the fixed string Q is replaced by the variable string $aQ\alpha\alpha a$.

The fact that all productions in a semi-Thue system are binary allows us to narrow the definition of 'derivation' somewhat.

> **DEFINITION:** Given a semi-Thue system (A, B, S, P), a linearly ordered sequence of strings $y_1, y_2, \ldots, y_m$ is called a *derivation of* y_m iff (1) y_1 is an axiom, and (2) each string except y_1 follows from the immediately preceding string by one of the productions in P.

The definitions of 'theorem' and 'proof' remain as in an e.a.s.

A *Thue system* differs from a semi-Thue system in that for every production schema $\alpha x\beta \to \alpha y\beta$ in P, a Thue system also contains the inverse schema $\alpha y\beta \to \alpha x\beta$. We shall not be concerned with such systems here.

Although it may appear that the restrictions on the productions of a semi-Thue system are rather severe, in fact these systems can generate any set of theorems that can be generated by an arbitrary e.a.s. In other words, there is no loss in generality in restricting e.a.s.'s in the manner of semi-Thue systems because for any e.a.s. there is an equivalent semi-Thue system. (The converse is of course trivially true since every semi-Thue system is an e.a.s.) However, a semi-Thue system may be rather more complex than a nonsemi-Thue e.a.s. to which it is equivalent. To illustrate, we exhibit a semi-Thue system that is equivalent to the e.a.s. in (8-39). Since all semi-Thue production schemata are of the same form, it is generally accepted practice to omit the variables α and β in writing them; thus, we write $x \to y$ instead of $\alpha x\beta \to \alpha y\beta$.

(8-40)
$$A = \{C, D, E, F, G, H\}$$
$$B = \{a\}$$
$$S = \{HFGa\}$$

The schemata in P are numbered for convenience in referring to them.

$$P = \begin{cases} 1. & FG \to DGaa \\ 2. & FD \to DF \\ 3. & HD \to HC \\ 4. & CD \to FC \\ 5. & CG \to FFGa \\ 6. & HF \to E \\ 7. & EF \to E \\ 8. & EG \to E \\ 9. & Ea \to a \end{cases}$$

(8-41) and (8-42) show the derivations of *a* and *aaaa*, respectively.

(8-41)
HFGa	Axiom
EGa	by 6.
Ea	by 8.
a	by 9.

(8-42)
HFGa	Axiom
HDGaaa	by 1.
HCGaaa	by 3.
HFFGaaaa	by 5.
EFGaaaa	by 6.
EGaaaa	by 7.
Eaaaa	by 8.
aaaa	by 9.

Problem: Give a derivation of *aaaaaaaa* by this semi-Thue system.

EXERCISES

1. Give a recursive definition of the well-formed strings in the propositional calculus in Polish parenthesis-free notation (Chapter 2, Exercise 6). Give a proof that CENA*pppp* is a well-formed string using your definition.

2. Let f be a function that maps each x in $Z = \{0, 1, 2, 3, \ldots\}$ into 2^{2^n}; e.g. $f(1) = 2^{2^1} = 2^2 = 4$. Give a recursive definition of f, and use it to compute the value of $f(4)$.

3. Suppose we were to take the successor of any positive number x as being $x + 2$. Show that the four Peano Axioms [(8-12)] would then specify the set of "integers" as the set of even numbers $\{0, 2, 4, 6, 8, \ldots\}$. Would the Principle of Mathematical Induction still be a reasonable rule of inference when defined over this set?

4. Prove by induction that the power set of a set with n members has 2^n members, for any finite positive integer n.

5. Prove by induction the generalized distributive law of multiplication over addition; i.e., for all n, $a \cdot (b_1 + b_2 + \cdots + b_n) = a \cdot b_1 + a \cdot b_2 + \cdots + a \cdot b_n$.

6. What is wrong with the following inductive proof that all horses are of the same color? For a set containing only one horse, the base clearly holds, since that horse has only one color. Now assume that all sets of n horses contain only horses of the same color. We show that it follows that the same is true of all sets of $n + 1$ horses. Choose a set of $n + 1$ horses and select any n of them, disregarding the extra horse for the moment. By assumption, these n horses are all of the same color. Now replace one of the n horses by the extra horse, forming a new set of n horses. These again, by assumption, are all of the same color, and so the extra horse is the same color as all the others. Therefore, all horses are of the same color.

7. Consider the following axiomatic system. The "alphabet" consists of all well-formed formulas in the propositional calculus plus the symbols $\rightarrow$, (, and). There are three axioms:

(A1) $p \rightarrow (q \rightarrow p)$
(A2) $(p \rightarrow (q \rightarrow r)) \rightarrow ((p \rightarrow q) \rightarrow (p \rightarrow r))$
(A3) $(\sim p \rightarrow \sim q) \rightarrow (q \rightarrow p)$

and two rule schemata:

(R1) From any two expressions of the form $A \rightarrow B$ and A, we can derive B (A and B are variables ranging over the *wff*'s of the propositional calculus).
(R2) From A we can derive B, where B is the result of substituting a *wff* x for every instance of some elementary propositional variable, i.e., p, q, r, etc., in A.

The following is a proof of $p \rightarrow p$ in this system:

1. $(p \rightarrow (q \rightarrow r)) \rightarrow ((p \rightarrow q) \rightarrow (p \rightarrow r))$
    (A2)
2. $(p \rightarrow ((q \rightarrow p) \rightarrow r)) \rightarrow ((p \rightarrow (q \rightarrow p)) \rightarrow (p \rightarrow r))$
    1, (R2) (Substituting $(q \rightarrow p)$ for q)
3. $(p \rightarrow ((q \rightarrow p) \rightarrow p)) \rightarrow ((p \rightarrow (q \rightarrow p)) \rightarrow (p \rightarrow p))$
    2, (R2) (Substituting p for r)
4. $p \rightarrow (q \rightarrow p)$ (A1)
5. $p \rightarrow ((q \rightarrow p) \rightarrow p)$ 4, (R2) (Substituting $(q \rightarrow p)$ for q)
6. $(p \rightarrow (q \rightarrow p)) \rightarrow (p \rightarrow p)$ 3, 5, (R1)
7. $p \rightarrow p$ 4, 6, (R1)

Construct a proof of $\sim p \to (p \to q)$ in this system. *Hint:* Begin by substituting $(\sim q \to \sim p) \to (p \to q)$ for p and $\sim p$ for q in A1. It can be shown that the theorems of this system are all and only the tautologous *wff*'s of the propositional calculus [see, for example, Massey (1970, pp. 125–159)]. The connectives $\wedge$ and $\vee$, which do not appear in this system, can be defined in terms of $\sim$ and $\to$.

8. Reformulate the recursive definition in Exercise 1 as an axiomatic system having the *wff*'s in Polish notation as its theorems. Find an equivalent semi-Thue system.

9. Construct an extended axiomatic system whose theorems are all strings in $\{a\}^*$ of length divisible by 2 or by 3. For example, *aa, aaa, aaaa, aaaaaa, aaaaaaaa* are theorems, but *a, aaaaa, aaaaaaa* are not. Can you see why there is no equivalent axiomatic system without an auxiliary alphabet?

References and Supplementary Reading

Further reading on axiomatic systems can be found in Wilder (1952; Chapters 1 and 2), Nelson (1968; Chapter 3), Lightstone (1964), Stoll (1961, Chapter 3), and in any of the standard works on mathematical logic, such as Church (1956), Hilbert and Ackerman (1950), Kleene (1967), Mendelson (1964), Quine (1957), Rosenbloom (1950), and Shoenfield (1967).

9

Grammars of Formal Languages

As we remarked in Chapter 6, a natural language, at one very simple level of description, can be regarded as a set of strings on some finite alphabet—say, a set of phonemes or morphemes. The strings in the language (the grammatical strings) in general form some proper subset of the free monoid over this alphabet. Further, since there is no longest grammatical sentence in a language, this subset is an infinite one. A grammar of a natural language must (at least) specify in some precise fashion the set of strings in the language. It is natural, therefore, to look to axiomatic systems, as devices that characterize infinite sets of strings, for possible models of natural language grammars.

Formal Grammars

The theory of formal grammars derives directly from that of semi-Thue systems with a few, mostly terminological, modifications. The basic and auxiliary alphabets of the semi-Thue system are called, respectively, the *terminal* and *nonterminal vocabularies* of the grammar. We denote these by V_T and V_N. As in a semi-Thue system, V_T and V_N are disjoint. We call V, the union of V_T and V_N, the *vocabulary*. The productions of a grammar are called (*grammatical*) *rules* and consist of a finite set of schemata of the form $\alpha\varphi\beta \to \alpha\psi\beta$, where φ and ψ are strings of symbols in V and α and β are variables ranging over strings in V^*. In writing such schemata we abbreviate by omitting the variable symbols α and β, writing simply $\varphi \to \psi$, which can be read 'φ is rewritten as ψ.' A grammar has only one axiom; namely, the string consisting of the single symbol S (for 'sentence').

Throughout this chapter we adhere to certain notational conventions regarding symbols and strings. These are taken from Chomsky (1959) and are shown in Table 9-1.

	Single symbols (represented by early letters in the alphabet)	Strings (represented by late letters in the alphabet)
Nonterminal	$A, B, C, \ldots$	$\ldots, X, Y, Z$
Terminal	$a, b, c, \ldots$	$\ldots, x, y, z$
Unspecified	$\alpha, \beta, \gamma, \ldots$	$\ldots, \varphi, \chi, \psi, \omega$

Table 9-1

Notational conventions for symbols and strings

The following definitions apply to formal grammars.

DEFINITION: Given a grammar $G = (V_N, V_T, \{S\}, P)$, ψ *follows from* φ *(by G)* iff there are strings $\psi_1, \psi_2, \chi, \omega$ such that $\varphi = \psi_1 \chi \psi_2$ and $\psi = \psi_1 \omega \psi_2$, and there is a rule $\chi \to \omega$ in P. Equivalently, we say that φ *immediately dominates* ψ *(by G)* and denote this by $\varphi \underset{G}{\Rightarrow} \psi$. The symbol for the grammar may be omitted from this notation when it is clear from the context.

DEFINITION: A sequence of strings $\varphi_1, \varphi_2, \ldots, \varphi_n$ is a *derivation (of φ_n from φ_1)* iff $\varphi_i \underset{G}{\Rightarrow} \varphi_{i+1}$, for all $1 \leq i < n$.

Note that by this definition a derivation is not required to begin with the axiom.

DEFINITION: If there is a derivation $\varphi, \ldots, \psi$ by G, we say that φ *dominates* ψ and denote this by $\varphi \underset{G}{\overset{*}{\Rightarrow}} \psi$, or by $\varphi \overset{*}{\Rightarrow} \psi$ if the grammar is clear from the context.

Domination is a transitive relation in V^* because if in some grammar G there is a derivation $\varphi_1, \ldots, \varphi_n$ and a derivation $\varphi_n, \ldots, \varphi_p$, then there is also a derivation $\varphi_1, \ldots, \varphi_n, \ldots, \varphi_p$; thus $\varphi_1 \overset{*}{\Rightarrow} \varphi_n$ and $\varphi_n \overset{*}{\Rightarrow} \varphi_p$ imply $\varphi_1 \overset{*}{\Rightarrow} \varphi_p$. By convention the relation of domination is taken to be reflexive, which is equivalent to saying that any string φ_i is a one-line derivation of φ_i from φ_i.

DEFINITION: A derivation $\varphi_1, \ldots, \varphi_n$ by G is *terminated* iff there is no longer derivation by G $\varphi_1, \ldots, \varphi_n, \ldots, \varphi_p$ such that $\varphi_p \neq \varphi_n$.

Thus, the last line of a terminated derivation is a string that cannot be rewritten by any of the rules of the grammar.

DEFINITION: x is a *terminal string* generated by the grammar G iff (1) there is a terminated derivation of x beginning with the axiom S, and (2) $x \in V_T^*$, i.e., x is a string of terminal symbols.

The terminal strings of a grammar are therefore like the theorems of a semi-Thue system except that terminal strings cannot be further rewritten. In a semi-Thue system any string of symbols on the basic alphabet that is derivable from the axioms is a theorem, and the possibility is not excluded that some production can be applied to a theorem to give another string.

DEFINITION: Given a grammar G, the set of terminal strings of G is called the *language generated by* G, denoted $L(G)$.

DEFINITION: Two grammars G and G' are (*weakly*) *equivalent* iff $L(G) = L(G')$; i.e., they generate the same language.

To illustrate these definitions, we consider the following grammar:

(9-1)
$$G = (V_N, V_T, \{S\}, P)$$
$$V_N = \{S, A, B, C\}$$
$$V_T = \{a, b, c\}$$
$$P = \begin{cases} 1.\ S \to ABC \\ 2.\ A \to aA \\ 3.\ A \to a \\ 4.\ B \to Bb \\ 5.\ B \to b \\ 6.\ BC \to Bcc \\ 7.\ ab \to ba \end{cases}$$

Note: The productions are numbered only for convenience in referring to them; there is no implication that they are an ordered set.

In (9-1) all the conditions on a grammar are satisfied: V_T and V_N are disjoint sets; S is the only axiom; and all the rules are semi-Thue productions.

The following sequence is a derivation by G

(9-2) $BCA, BccA, BbccA, BbccaA$

since $BCA \Rightarrow BccA$ by rule 6, $BccA \Rightarrow BbccA$ by rule 4, and $BbccA \Rightarrow BbccaA$ by rule 2. Thus, we may write $BCA \stackrel{*}{\Rightarrow} BccA$, $BCA \stackrel{*}{\Rightarrow} BbccA$, $BccA \stackrel{*}{\Rightarrow} BbccaA$, etc. Note that (9-2) is a derivation despite the fact that there is no derivation of BCA from the axiom in this grammar. By the definition a derivation is any sequence of strings such that each string (except the last) immediately dominates the following one by the rules of the grammar. The derivation in (9-2) is not a terminated derivation since the last line, $BbccaA$, can be further rewritten (by rules 2, 3, 4, or 5). Application of rules 3 and 5 would produce the terminated derivation in (9-3):

(9-3) $BCA, BccA, BbccA, BbccaA, Bbccaa, bbccaa$

Here the last entry, $bbccaa$, consists entirely of terminal symbols and it cannot be further rewritten; thus, the derivation is terminated. It does not follow from this, however, that $bbccaa$ is a terminal string generated by G because (9-3) is not a derivation beginning with the axiom S. Neither can one conclude from (9-3) that $bbccaa$ is not a terminal string of G, since this depends on whether there exists some derivation of $bbccaa$ beginning with S. (It happens in this particular case that no such derivation does exist.)

The following derivation shows that $bacc$ is a terminal string of G:

(9-4) $S, ABC, aBC, aBcc, abcc, bacc$

This derivation is terminated, it begins with S, and $bacc$ consists entirely of terminal symbols. Observe that although $S \stackrel{*}{\Rightarrow} abcc$, $abcc$ is not a terminal string of G, because it can be rewritten by rule 7.

The derivation in (9-5)

(9-5) S, ABC, aBC, abC

is terminated since rule 6 rewrites C only when it is immediately preceded by B, but abC is not a terminal string because it contains the nonterminal symbol C.

To summarize, given a grammar G, a string x is a terminal string of G if and only if all three of the following are true:

(9-6)
1. x consists entirely of terminal symbols
2. x cannot be rewritten by the rules of G
3. x is the last line of some derivation by G beginning with S

The string $BbccaA$ in (9-2) fails all three conditions; $bbccaa$ in (9-3) meets conditions 1 and 2 but fails condition 3. The next to last line of (9-4), $abcc$, meets conditions 1 and 3 but fails condition 2. The string abC in (9-5) fails only condition 1. The final line of (9-4), $bacc$, meets all three conditions and is thus a terminal string of G.

Problem: Using the grammar in (9-1), construct examples in which a string meets one of the conditions in (9-6) and fails the other two.

By examining a few terminated derivations the reader should be able to convince himself that the terminal strings of G all consist of one or more b's followed by one or more a's followed by two c's. We adopt an abbreviatory notation for strings in which a symbol with positive integer n as superscript stands for n consecutive occurrences of that symbol; e.g., $a^3 = aaa$, $a^2b^3 = aabbb$. To denote sets of strings we use variables as superscripts; thus, a^n $(1 \leq n \leq 3) = \{a, aa, aaa\}$; a^n $(n \geq 0) = \{e, a, aa, aaa, \ldots\} = \{a\}^*$. In this notation the set of terminal strings of G can be represented by $b^n a^m cc$ $(n \geq 1, m \geq 1)$.

The grammar given in (9-7) generates exactly the same set of terminal strings and is therefore weakly equivalent to the grammar in (9-1).

(9-7)
$$G' = \{V_N, V_T, \{S\}, P'\}$$
$$V_N = \{S, A, B, C\}$$
$$V_T = \{a, b, c\}$$
$$P' = \begin{cases} 1.\ S \rightarrow bA \\ 2.\ A \rightarrow bA \\ 3.\ A \rightarrow aB \\ 4.\ B \rightarrow aB \\ 5.\ B \rightarrow cC \\ 6.\ C \rightarrow c \end{cases}$$

Problems:

1. For the grammar G' of (9-7), give examples of (a) a terminated derivation, (b) a sequence of lines beginning with S that is not a derivation, and (c) a derivation beginning with S that is not terminated. Are there any terminated derivations beginning with S that do not end in a terminal string?
2. Must equivalent grammars have the same nonterminal vocabularies? the same terminal vocabularies?

Types of Grammars

By restricting further the form of the rules in a grammar, one can establish a hierarchy of such systems with properties of more linguistic interest than those of the full class allowed by the definitions. The following subclasses of formal grammars, called *constituent-structure grammars* are the ones that have been most studied.

Type 1: Every production is of the form $\varphi A \psi \to \varphi \omega \psi$, where φ and ψ, but not ω, may be the null string. Thus, a single nonterminal symbol is rewritten as a nonnull string by each rule.

Type 2: Every production is of the form $A \to \omega$, where $\omega \neq e$. Thus, a type 2 grammar is a type 1 grammar with the additional condition that both φ and ψ are the null string.

Type 3: Every production is of the form $A \to xB$ or $A \to x$, where $x \neq e$. Thus, a type 3 grammar is a type 2 grammar with the additional restriction that in every rule the right side is a string of terminal symbols followed by at most one nonterminal.

Types 1 and 2 are called *context-sensitive* and *context-free* grammars, respectively; abbreviated csg and cfg. Type 3 grammars are known variously as *right-linear, regular,* or *finite-state*. Formal grammars with none of these restrictions on their rules, i.e., essentially the semi-Thue systems, are called *type* 0 and also by the name *unrestricted rewriting systems* (urs). Since each restriction specifying a grammar of type n is added to restrictions for type $n - 1$, type $n - 2$, etc., it follows that every type 3 grammar is also a type 2, a type 1, and a type 0 grammar, every type 2 grammar is also type 1 and type 0, etc. However, there are grammars of type 1 that are not type 2, grammars of type 2 that are not type 3; that is, in general, there are grammars of type n that are not of type $n + 1$. Symbolizing by $\mathscr{G}_n$ the set of all grammars of type n, we can represent these facts as follows:

(9-8) $\qquad \mathscr{G}_0 \supset \mathscr{G}_1 \supset \mathscr{G}_2 \supset \mathscr{G}_3$

The grammars given in (9-1) and (9-7) are type 0 and type 3, respectively. Grammar (9-1) is not type 1 (and *a fortiori* not type 2 or 3) because in rule 7 two terminal symbols are rewritten. If rule 7 were omitted, the resulting grammar would be type 1. If both rules 6 and 7 were omitted, the grammar would be of type 2, but it would not be type 3 since rules 1 and 4 are not of that form. Grammar (9-7) is type 3 because only single nonterminals appear on the left sides of the rules, and the right sides contain only terminals followed by at most one nonterminal symbol.

The grammar G'' shown in (9-9) is type 2 but not type 3. It generates the language $a^n b^n$ $(n \geq 1)$.

(9-9)
$$G'' = \{V_N, V_T, \{S\}, P\}$$
$$V_N = \{S\}$$
$$V_T = \{a, b\}$$
$$P = \begin{Bmatrix} S \to aSb \\ S \to ab \end{Bmatrix}$$

Types of Languages

DEFINITION: A language is a *type n language* ($n = 0, 1, 2,$ or 3) iff there is some type n grammar that generates it.

For example, $b^n a^m cc$ is a type 0 language since the type 0 grammar in (9-1) generates it. It is also a type 3 language, however, because it is generated by the type 3 grammar in (9-7). A type 3 grammar is necessarily also type 2, type 1, and type 0, so it follows that every type 3 language is also a type 2, type 1, and type 0 language. Denoting by $\mathscr{L}_n$ the set of all languages of type n, we have

(9-10) $\quad \mathscr{L}_0 \supseteq \mathscr{L}_1 \supseteq \mathscr{L}_2 \supseteq \mathscr{L}_3$

It is important to recognize the fact that it does not follow from the definitions of types of grammars and languages that the inclusions in (9-10) are proper inclusions. For example, it is true that $\mathscr{L}_2 \supseteq \mathscr{L}_3$ because every type 3 language is generated by a type 3 grammar, which is necessarily also type 2. It might happen that every language generated by a type 2 grammar could also be generated by some type 3 grammar, however, and this would not be incompatible with the fact that $\mathscr{G}_2 \supset \mathscr{G}_3$. To verify that a grammar is of type n, one need only inspect the rules and determine what formal conditions they meet. Thus, it is a simple matter to classify a grammar by type. In contrast, it is often very difficult to classify a language. One cannot determine merely from inspection of the language $a^n b^n$, for example, that it is of type 2. One must either exhibit a type 2 grammar that generates it [(9-9) is one such] or else in some way prove such a grammar exists without necessarily exhibiting it. To prove that $a^n b^n$ is not also a type 3 language is not at all a trivial task, since one must prove that it cannot be generated *by any type 3 grammar whatever*. Among the earliest results to be achieved in the study of these formal grammars were proofs that the inclusions in (9-10) are, in fact, proper; that is,

(9-11) $\quad \mathscr{L}_0 \supset \mathscr{L}_1 \supset \mathscr{L}_2 \supset \mathscr{L}_3$

Some of these proofs are given in later sections.

Corresponding to the terminology for grammars, type 1 languages are called *context-sensitive languages* (csl); type 2, *context-free languages* (cfl); and type 3, *regular languages*, *regular sets*, or *finite-state languages* (fsl). Languages of type 0 are called *recursively enumerable* (r.e.) sets, the term used in the theory of automata and recursive functions where these sets were first studied. The names 'context-sensitive' and 'context-free' refer to the conditions under which a symbol can be rewritten. In a csg a rule $\varphi A \psi \to \varphi \omega \psi$ specifies that an A may be rewritten as ω when that A occurs in a string with φ immediately to the left and ψ immediately to the right. Linguists frequently use the notation $A \to \omega/\varphi\_\!\_\psi$ for such a rule, where the slanting line is read as 'in the environment.' By contrast, in a cfg all rules are of the form $A \to \omega$, which indicates that an A can be rewritten as ω regardless of the context in which it occurs.

Grammars and Constituent-Structure Trees

The restriction of grammar rules to those that rewrite only a single symbol leads to a rather natural proposal for associating a constituent-structure tree with a derivation. The basic idea is that if a rule rewrites A as aBc, for example, we can associate with this the subtree

(9-12)

```
        A
       /|\
      a B c
```

and if B is subsequently rewritten as ba, the corresponding subtree is appended to the previous one as follows:

(9-13)

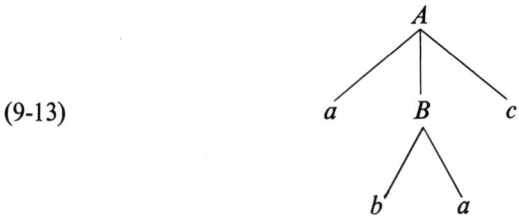

In a type 0 grammar, which allows rules such as $AB \to CDE$ and $AB \to C$ where more than a single symbol is rewritten, there is no nonarbitrary way to make such correspondences. For example, when the rule $AB \to CDE$ applies, should we consider C and D as immediately dominated by A or D and E as immediately dominated by B? Difficulties such as these are the principal motivations for focusing attention on grammars that meet at least the restrictions for type 1.

To consider the process of associating a tree with a derivation in more detail, let us take as an example the grammar given in (9-14). Henceforth, we do not list V_T and V_N explicitly but allow them to be inferred from the symbols occurring in the rules.

(9-14)
$$S \to AcB$$
$$Ac \to aAc$$
$$A \to a$$
$$B \to Bb$$
$$B \to b$$

A derivation of the terminal string *aacbb* is shown in (9-15), and the phrase-structure tree associated with this derivation is given in (9-16):

(9-15)
$$S$$
$$AcB$$
$$aAcB$$
$$aacB$$
$$aacBb$$
$$aacbb$$

(9-16)
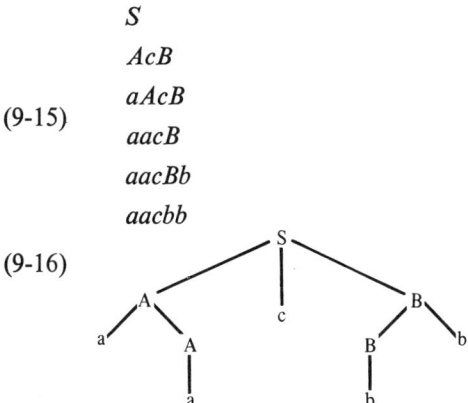

The procedure for constructing the tree is as follows. Start with a node labeled S as the root of the tree. If $\alpha_1\alpha_2\cdots\alpha_n$ is the second line of the derivation, add the symbols $\alpha_1, \alpha_2, \ldots, \alpha_n$ to the tree in this left-to-right order, each immediately dominated by S. For each subsequent pair of lines φ_i and φ_{i+1} in the derivation, find segmentations of φ_i and φ_{i+1} such that $\varphi_i = \psi_1\psi_2 A\psi_3\psi_4$, $\varphi_{i+1} = \psi_1\psi_2\beta_1\beta_2\cdots\beta_m\psi_3\psi_4$, and $\psi_2 A\psi_3 \to \psi_2\beta_1\beta_2\cdots\beta_m\psi_3$ is a rule of the grammar. On the tree constructed to this point, find a leaf node labeled A such that $\psi_1\psi_2$ is the sequence of leaves on the left of A and $\psi_3\psi_4$ is the sequence of leaves to the right of A. Add the nodes $\beta_1, \beta_2, \ldots, \beta_m$ in this left-to-right order, all immediately dominated by A.

The tree constructed after the second line of the derivation in (9-15) is as shown in (9-17):

(9-17)
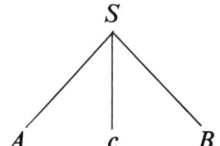

We segment the second and third lines of the derivation as follows:

(9-18)
$$AcB = A \,|c|\, B$$
$$aAcB = aA \,|c|\, B$$

where ψ_1 and ψ_2 are the null string, $\psi_3 = c$, and $\psi_4 = B$. As required, $\psi_2 A \psi_3 \rightarrow \psi_2 aA\psi_3$, i.e., $Ac \rightarrow aAc$, is a rule of the grammar. Accordingly, we add to the tree the sequence aA immediately dominated by A to produce the tree shown in (9-19):

(9-19)

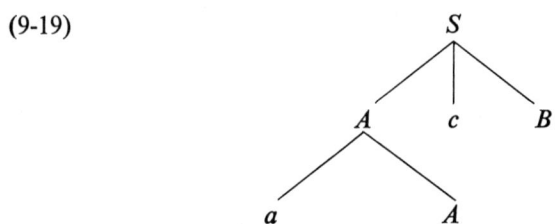

It should now be easy for the reader to follow the remaining steps in the construction of the tree in (9-16).

This procedure will fail to lead from a derivation to a unique constituent-structure tree in the following situation. If there is a pair of lines φ_i and φ_{i+1} in the derivation such that $\varphi_i = \chi AB\psi$ and $\varphi_{i+1} = \chi A\alpha_1 \cdots \alpha_n B\psi$, then there are two segmentations that correspond to the rewriting of a single symbol: A rewritten as $A\alpha_1 \cdots \alpha_n$ or B rewritten as $\alpha_1 \cdots \alpha_n B$. If both $A \rightarrow A\alpha_1 \cdots \alpha_n$ and $B \rightarrow \alpha_1 \cdots \alpha_n B$ also happened to be among the rules of the grammar, then we could not tell whether to construct the corresponding portion of the tree as in (9-20) or (9-21).

(9-20)

(9-21)

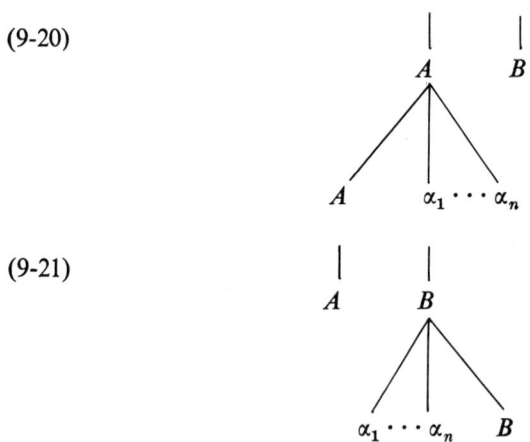

It is clear that in order to resolve the ambiguity we would need not only the derivation and the rules of the grammar but we would also have to know exactly which rule had been applied at this point in the derivation.

This suggests that the definition of 'derivation' in a constituent-structure grammar should perhaps be reformulated as an alternating sequence of strings and rules,

(9-22) $\varphi_1, R_{i_1}, \varphi_2, R_{i_2}, \ldots, \varphi_{n-1}, R_{i_{n-1}}, \varphi_n$, where each φ_j ($j > 1$) follows from φ_{j-1} by application of rule $R_{i_{j-1}}$

While this is a perfectly feasible proposal, it does not entirely solve the problem. Suppose, for example, that the context-sensitive rule $AB \to ACB$ were applied to a string of the form $\psi_1 AB \psi_2$. Even given the rule that connects two such lines in the derivation, we still cannot determine whether A dominates AC or B dominates CB in the corresponding tree. To remove this uncertainty, the rule must be given either as $A \to AC/\_\_B$ or as $B \to CB/A\_\_$, in which the contexts are explicitly marked. Thus, the notations $\varphi A \psi \to \varphi \omega \psi$ and $A \to \omega/\varphi\_\_\psi$ for context-sensitive rules, which are equivalent when we consider only the derivation of one string from another, may not be equivalent when we consider how to construct the corresponding trees from these strings. With the added stipulation that context-sensitive rules are to be written in the unambiguous "environment notation," it becomes possible to associate a tree uniquely with every derivation of the form given in (9-22).

The proposal just outlined is equivalent to allowing the rules of a grammar to generate trees directly rather than through the intermediary of a derivation consisting of strings. That is, we may regard a derivation as a sequence of trees $T_1, T_2, \ldots, T_n$ such that each T_j ($j > 1$) follows from T_{j-1} by one of the rules of the grammar. Tree T_j follows from T_{j-1} iff

1. The sequence of leaf nodes of T_{j-1} is a string $\psi_1 \psi_2 A \psi_3 \psi_4$.
2. The sequence of leaf nodes of T_j is a string $\psi_1 \psi_2 \omega \psi_3 \psi_4$ such that each element of ω is immediately dominated by A.
3. $A \to \omega/\psi_2\_\_\psi_3$ is a rule of the grammar.

For example, in this formulation the tree in (9-19) follows from that in (9-17) by the rules of the grammar in (9-14) (with the second rule replaced by $A \to aA/\_\_c$). We would then call the tree in (9-16) a *terminal tree* generated by this grammar since no tree follows from it by the rules, all its leaves are terminal symbols, and there is a sequence of trees beginning with the tree having only the node labeled S and ending with (9-16) such that each tree except the first follows from the preceding one.

Viewed in this way, a terminal string generated by a grammar consists of the entire left-to-right sequence of (labels of) leaf nodes on some terminal tree.

Henceforth, we shall assume that some such proposal has been adopted, although for convenience we shall continue to write derivations as sequences of strings, without explicit reference to the rules applied at each step, when no ambiguity can result. We shall also write context-sensitive rules in the form $\varphi A \psi \to \varphi \omega \psi$ when there is no danger of confusion.

McCawley (1968) has advanced an alternative proposal for connecting grammar rules and constituent-structure trees. He suggests that each rule be interpreted as a *node admissibility condition*, specifying which subtrees are considered well-formed. For example, the rule $A \to BC$ allows the well-formed subtree

(9-23)

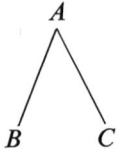

A tree is then said to be generated by the grammar if and only if the root is labeled S, each leaf is labeled by a terminal symbol, and each of its subtrees is allowed by the node admissibility conditions. When all the rules of a grammar are context-free, it is immaterial whether they are regarded as node admissibility conditions or as rules specifying allowed derivations consisting of sequences of trees. A context-sensitive rule, however, can be given a nonequivalent interpretation as a node admissibility condition. The rule $A \to BC/D\_E$, for example, is most naturally construed as a node admissibility condition in the following way: The subtree with A immediately dominating the sequence BC is well-formed provided that elsewhere in the tree a node D immediately precedes A and A immediately precedes a node E. ('Precedes,' of course, refers to the precedence relation on tree nodes defined in Chapter 6.) The tree in (9-24) is one that would meet this node admissibility condition.

(9-24)

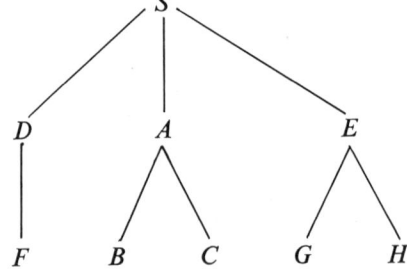

The rules given in (9-25) will not generate this tree if they are interpreted as string-derivation rules or as tree-derivation rules in the manner previously

described but will generate it if they are interpreted as node admissibility conditions.

(9-25)
$$S \to DAE$$
$$D \to F/\_B$$
$$E \to GH/C\_$$
$$A \to BC/F\_G$$

Thus, the particular constituent-structure trees generated by a grammar depend on how the rules are interpreted. McCawley states that most of the constituent-structure grammars written within the American structuralist tradition should be regarded as sets of node admissibility conditions, and he further argues that the constituent-structure component of a transformational grammar as outlined in *Aspects of the Theory of Syntax* (Chomsky, 1965) should also be reformulated in this way. The reader is referred to McCawley's article for details of this proposal and some of its consequences for the theory of grammar.

Returning once again to the question of constructing a tree from the sequence of lines in a derivation, we note that the derivation given in (9-15) is only one of six derivations of *aacbb* by the grammar in (9-14) that are associated with the tree in (9-16). The other five are

(9-26)

S	S	S	S	S
AcB	AcB	AcB	AcB	AcB
$aAcB$	$aAcB$	$AcBb$	$AcBb$	$AcBb$
$aAcBb$	$aAcBb$	$aAcBb$	$aAcBb$	$Acbb$
$aacBb$	$aAcbb$	$aacBb$	$aAcbb$	$aAcbb$
$aacbb$	$aacbb$	$aacbb$	$aacbb$	$aacbb$

These derivations and the one in (9-15) differ only in the order in which the nonterminal symbols are rewritten. They are all distinct derivations in that they are composed of different ordered sequences of strings. Thus, the information contained in the derivation concerning the order of rewriting nonterminals is not contained in the tree diagram. We shall refer to derivations that give rise to the same tree as *equivalent derivations*.

It is also possible for derivations of the same terminal string to be nonequivalent. For example, the grammar shown in (9-27) produces two nonequivalent derivations of *acb*,

(9-27)
$$S \to AB$$
$$A \to a$$
$$A \to ac$$
$$B \to b$$
$$B \to cb$$

220 Grammars of Formal Languages

given in (9-28) and (9-29), which are associated with

(9-28)
$$\begin{array}{c} S \\ AB \\ acB \\ acb \end{array}$$

(9-29)
$$\begin{array}{c} S \\ AB \\ aB \\ acb \end{array}$$

the trees in (9-30) and (9-31), respectively.

(9-30)
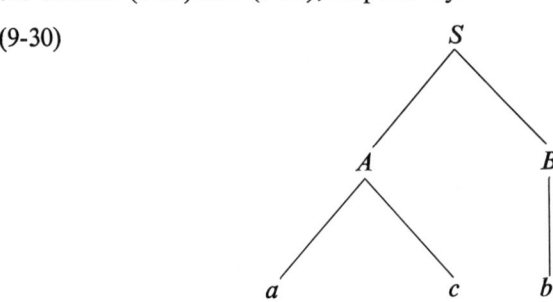

(9-31)
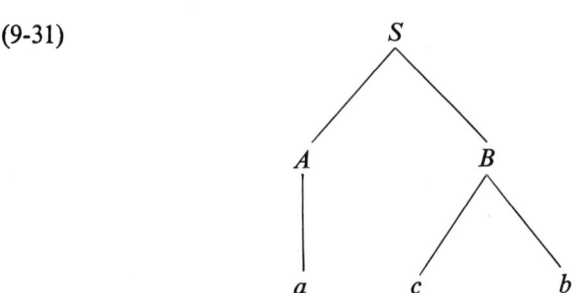

A grammar that generates nonequivalent derivations of at least one terminal string is said to be *ambiguous*.

Problems:

1. Prove that the relation 'is associated with the same phrase-structure tree' defined on pairs of derivations is an equivalence relation.
2. Show that all the lines in the derivations (9-15) and (9-26) together with the relation 'dominates' is a partially ordered set. Diagram this

Right-Linear Grammars and Languages   221

partially ordered set by connecting strings to their immediate successors by arrows.

3. For the grammar given in (9-7), how many equivalent derivations of *bbacc* are there? Is this grammar ambiguous?

Right-Linear Grammars and Languages

In a right-linear grammar every rule is of the form $A \to xB$ or $A \to x$. Therefore, in a derivation of a terminal string by such a grammar each line except the last will have a nonterminal as its rightmost symbol, with all other symbols being terminals. The tree corresponding to such a derivation contains a path of terminals extending from S along the rightmost branches. This is illustrated by the type 3 grammar in (9-32), a derivation by this grammar in (9-33), and the corresponding tree in (9-34).

(9-32)
$S \to aA$
$A \to aA$
$A \to bbB$
$B \to bB$
$B \to b$

(9-33)
S
aA
aaA
$aabbB$
$aabbbB$
$aabbbb$

(9-34)
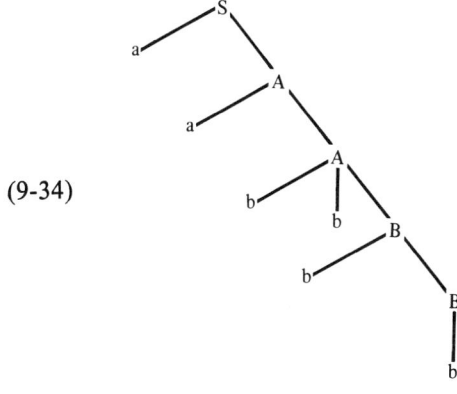

There is a corresponding class of *left-linear grammars* in which every rule is of the form $A \rightarrow Bx$ or $A \rightarrow x$. Everything we shall have to say about right-linear grammars is also valid, with trivial modifications, for left-linear grammars. Right-linear and left-linear grammars are each special cases of a class called *one-sided linear grammars*.

The term 'linear' is used to refer to a subclass of type 2 grammars in which every rule is of the form $A \rightarrow xBy$ or $A \rightarrow z$ (where x or y or both may possibly be null). In a derivation of a terminal string by a linear grammar each line except the last contains exactly one nonterminal symbol, but unlike a derivation by a right-linear grammar, this nonterminal need not be at the right end of the string. (9-36) shows a derivation by the linear grammar in (9-35).

(9-35)
$$S \rightarrow aAb$$
$$A \rightarrow bbA$$
$$A \rightarrow Bc$$
$$B \rightarrow bAc$$
$$A \rightarrow ab$$

(9-36)
S
aAb
abbAb
abbBcb
abbbAccb
abbbabccb

The corresponding constituent-structure tree in (9-37) shows a single path of nonterminal symbols, which is the motivation for the name 'linear.'

(9-37)
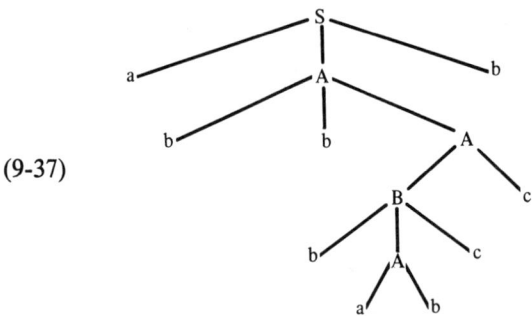

Thus, a right-linear grammar is a restricted variety of linear grammar in which every rule of the form $A \rightarrow xBy$ has $y = e$. In a left-linear grammar, $x = e$.

1. An Equivalent Formulation of Right-Linear Grammars

In the discussion following the definition of the various types of languages we pointed out that proper inclusion of one class of grammars by another does not necessarily imply a proper inclusion relation between the corresponding languages. That is, $\mathscr{G}_i \supset \mathscr{G}_j$ does not necessarily imply $\mathscr{L}_i \supset \mathscr{L}_j$ (although it does imply $\mathscr{L}_i \supseteq \mathscr{L}_j$). As a case in point, we define a class of grammars that is properly included in the type 3 grammars and show that the same languages are generated by both.

DEFINITION: A **type 3.1 grammar** is a constituent structure grammar in which every rule is of the form $A \to aB$ or $A \to a$.

Here the right side of each rule contains only a single terminal symbol followed by at most one nonterminal, and thus type 3.1 grammars are a proper subclass of type 3 grammars.

(9-38) $\quad \mathscr{G}_3 \supset \mathscr{G}_{3.1}$

As before, we call a language type 3.1 iff there is some type 3.1 grammar that generates it, and we denote the class of all type 3.1 languages by $\mathscr{L}_{3.1}$. It follows that every type 3.1 language is a type 3 language; i.e.,

(9-39) $\quad \mathscr{L}_3 \supseteq \mathscr{L}_{3.1}$

Thus, to show that $\mathscr{L}_3 = \mathscr{L}_{3.1}$ we need only show that $\mathscr{L}_{3.1} \supseteq \mathscr{L}_3$, that is, that every type 3 language is generated by some type 3.1 grammar.

THEOREM 9-1: For every type 3 grammar there is an equivalent type 3.1 grammar.

Proof: We give a procedure that converts any given type 3 grammar into an equivalent type 3.1 grammar. Let $G = (V_N, V_T, \{S\}, P)$ be a type 3 grammar. For each rule of the form $A \to xB$, where x is a string of terminal symbols $a_1 a_2 \cdots a_n$ ($n \geq 2$) (i.e., x is more than one symbol long), we add new nonterminal symbols $A_1, A_2, \ldots, A_{n-1}$, which are not already in V_N. We then replace the rule $A \to xB$ by the type 3.1 rules:

$$A \to a_1 A_1$$
$$A_1 \to a_2 A_2$$
$$\vdots$$
$$A_{n-2} \to a_{n-1} A_{n-1}$$
$$A_{n-1} \to a_n B$$

Clearly, for any step in a derivation by G involving the rule $A \to xB$, there is a corresponding set of steps in a derivation by the new grammar with the same outcome. That is, rather than

.

.

.

yA

$ya_1a_2 \cdots a_nB$

in one step by G, we have

yA

ya_1A_1

$ya_1a_2A_2$

.

.

.

$ya_1a_2 \cdots a_{n-1}A_{n-1}$

$ya_1a_2 \cdots a_{n-1}a_nB$

in n steps by the new grammar.

We continue in this fashion, replacing every rule of the form $A \to a_1a_2 \cdots a_nB$ ($n \geq 2$) that remains, choosing nonterminal symbols not already used and adding them to the nonterminal vocabulary. Similarly, we replace every rule of the form $B \to b_1b_2 \cdots b_n$ ($n \geq 2$) by the type 3.1 rules:

$B \to b_1B_1$

$B_1 \to b_2B_2$

.

.

.

$B_n \to b_n$

The result is a type 3.1 grammar $G' = (V'_N, V_T, \{S\}, P')$ that generates the same language as G.

Example 9-1: Convert the type 3 rule $A \to bcdB$ to an equivalent set of type 3.1 rules. We choose new nonterminals A_1 and A_2 and form the rules $A \to bA_1$, $A_1 \to cA_2$, $A_2 \to dB$.

Example 9-2: Convert the following type 3 grammar to an equivalent type 3.1 grammar.

$$(9\text{-}40) \quad \begin{aligned} S &\to abA \\ A &\to bA \\ A &\to cc \\ A &\to a \end{aligned}$$

Only the first and third rules are not already of type 3.1. We replace the first by the rules $S \to aA_1$ and $A_1 \to bA$. The third is replaced by $A \to cA_2$ and $A_2 \to c$. The resulting type 3.1 grammar is

$$(9\text{-}41) \quad \begin{aligned} S &\to aA_1 \\ A_1 &\to bA \\ A &\to bA \\ A &\to cA_2 \\ A_2 &\to c \\ A &\to a \end{aligned}$$

2. Type 3 Languages and Regular Sets

We noted earlier that it is easy to classify a grammar as type 0, 1, 2, or 3 by inspection of its rules but that it is generally not a simple matter to so classify a language. It is therefore of some interest to find a formal characteristic that is shared by all languages of a given type, since it is then possible to prove a language to be of this type without actually exhibiting a grammar that generates it and, probably more important, to show that a language is *not* of the given type by proving that it lacks the necessary formal property.

In this section we shall show that the type 3 languages include a class called *regular sets*. The remainder of the proof—that the regular sets also include the type 3 languages and therefore they are equal—must wait until finite-state automata have been introduced in the next chapter.

Before giving the definition of a regular set, we must introduce the binary operation of *set product*.

DEFINITION: The product of two sets A and B, denoted $A \cdot B$, is the set of strings $\{x \frown y \mid x \in A \land y \in B\}$.

For example, if $A = \{a, b\}$ and $B = \{cc, d\}$, $A \cdot B = \{acc, ad, bcc, bd\}$. Note that the set product of two sets is a set of strings in contrast to the Cartesian product, which is a set of ordered pairs.

We now define 'regular set' recursively:

DEFINITION:
1. Every finite set is a regular set.
2. (a) If A and B are regular sets, then so is $A \cup B$.
   (b) If A and B are regular sets, then so is $A \cdot B$.
   (c) If A is a regular set, then so is A^*.
3. Nothing else is a regular set.

For example, $\{a, b\}$ and $\{c\}$, being finite sets, are regular sets by part 1 of the definition. Since these are regular sets, so is their union, $\{a, b, c\}$, by part 2(a), their product $\{ac, bc\}$, by part 2(b), and the free monoids on each, $\{a, b\}^*$ and $\{c\}^*$, by part 2(c). Further, since the definition is recursive, $\{a, b, c\} \cup \{ac, bc\}$ is also a regular set, and similarly for $\{a, b, c\}^*$, $\{ac, bc\}^*$, $\{a, b\}^* \cdot \{c\}^*$, $\{a, b\} \cup \{c\}^*$, etc. The restriction of the recursive definition, part 3, states that *all* regular sets are formed from finite sets by repeated applications of the operations of union, product, and formation of the free monoid (the "star" operation). An equivalent statement of the definition is as follows:

DEFINITION: The *regular sets* are the smallest class that contains all finite sets and is closed under the operations of union, product, and star.

"Smallest" in the preceding definition does not refer to cardinality but means only that the class contains no other members.

To show that the regular sets are included in the type 3 languages we prove that every finite set is a type 3 language and then that the type 3 languages are closed under union, product, and star.

LEMMA 9-1: Every finite set is a type 3 language.

Proof: For any finite set $\{x_1, x_2, \ldots, x_n\}$, the grammar containing just the rules $S \to x_1, S \to x_2, \ldots, S \to x_n$ is type 3 and generates the language $\{x_1, x_2, \ldots, x_n\}$.

LEMMA 9-2: The union of any two type 3 languages is also type 3.

Proof: Let L_1 and L_2 be type 3 languages generated by the grammars $G_1 = (V_{N_1}, V_{T_1}, \{S\}, P_1)$ and $G_2 = (V_{N_2}, V_{T_2}, \{S\}, P_2)$, respectively. Replace the symbol S everywhere it occurs in G_1 by the symbol S_1, and similarly substitute S_2 for S in G_2. If necessary, rename the other nonterminals of G_2 so that $V_{N_1} \cap V_{N_2} = \emptyset$. Call the resulting grammars G_1' and G_2', respectively. Now form grammar G_3 in the following way:

1. Put all rules of G_1' and G_2' into G_3.
2. For every rule of the form $S_1 \to xA$ in G_1', and $S_2 \to yB$ in G_2', put the rules $S \to xA$ and $S \to yB$ in G_3.
3. For every rule of the form $S_1 \to x$ in G_1' and $S_2 \to y$ in G_2', put the rules $S \to x$ and $S \to y$ in G_3.

The resulting grammar generates the set of all strings that are in $L(G_1)$ or $L(G_2)$; that is, $L(G_3) = L(G_1) \cup L(G_2)$, and G_3 is a type 3 grammar.

Example 9-3:

G_1: $S \to aaA$ G_2: $S \to aaA$
        $S \to a$ $S \to aa$
        $A \to aaA$ $A \to aaA$
        $A \to a$ $A \to aa$

$L(G_1) = a^{2n+1}$ $(n \geq 0)$ and $L(G_2) = a^{2n}$ $(n \geq 1)$. We replace S in G_1 and G_2 by S_1 and S_2, respectively, and change the symbol A in G_2 to B so that the grammars have no nonterminals in common.

G_1': $S_1 \to aaA$ G_2': $S_2 \to aaB$
        $S_1 \to a$ $S_2 \to aa$
        $A \to aaA$ $B \to aaB$
        $A \to a$ $B \to aa$

To form G_3, we take all the rules of G_1' and G_2' plus the rules $S \to aaA$, $S \to a$, $S \to aaB$, and $S \to aa$.

G_3: $S \to aaA$ $S_1 \to aaA$
        $S \to aaB$ $S_1 \to a$
        $S \to a$ $S_2 \to aaB$
        $S \to aa$ $S_2 \to aa$
        $A \to aaA$
        $B \to aaB$
        $A \to a$
        $B \to aa$

G_3 generates a^n $(n \geq 1)$, which is the union of $L(G_1)$ and $L(G_2)$.

LEMMA 9-3: The product of any two type 3 languages is also type 3.

Proof: Let L_1 and L_2 be languages generated by the type 3 grammars $G_1 = (V_{N_1}, V_{T_1}, \{S\}, P_1)$ and $G_2 = (V_{N_2}, V_{T_2}, \{S\}, P_2)$, respectively. Replace the initial symbol S in G_2 by S_2 and if necessary rename the other nonterminals of G_2 so that $V_{N_1} \cap V_{N_2} = \emptyset$. The resulting grammar is G_2'. Form G_3 in the following way:

1. For every rule of the form $A \to x$ in G_1, put the rule $A \to xS_2$ in G_3.

2. Put all rules of G_2' in G_3 and also all rules of G_1, except those mentioned in part 1.

Now where G_1 generates the terminal string x, G_3 generates the nonterminal string xS_2 and then rewrites S_2 in the manner of G_2. The resulting strings are all of the form xy where $x \in L(G_1)$ and $y \in L(G_2)$.

Example 9-4:

G_1: $S \to aS$ G_2: $S \to bS$
         $S \to a$ $S \to b$

$L(G_1) = a^n$ $(n \geq 1)$, and $L(G_2) = b^m$ $(m \geq 1)$.

G_2': $S_2 \to bS_2$
        $S_2 \to b$

Because $S \to a$ is a rule of G_1 having a terminal string as its right side, we put the rule $S \to aS_2$ in G_3. All rules of G_2' are put in G_3 and also the remaining rule of G_1, $S \to aS$.

G_3: $S \to aS$
       $S \to aS_2$
       $S_2 \to bS_2$
       $S_2 \to b$

$L(G_3) = a^n b^m$ $(n, m \geq 1)$, which is the product of $L(G_1)$ and $L(G_2)$.

Before proving that type 3 languages are closed under star we must rid ourselves of a slight technical difficulty. We intend to show that from a type 3 grammar generating a language L we can construct another type 3 grammar generating L^*. The difficulty is that L^*, being the free monoid on the set L, contains the null string, e, and by the definitions of the various types of grammars it is not possible to generate a language containing e. If we simply modified the definitions to allow the rule $S \to e$ to appear, other problems would arise, among which is that of associating a tree with a derivation in which this rule had been applied. If it were the case that the symbol S never appeared on the right side of any rule, however, then we could add the rule $S \to e$ and be sure that it would never be used except in generating the null string as a member of the language. Accordingly, we add the following condition to the definitions of type 1, 2, and 3 grammars:

CONDITION 9-1: A grammar of type 1, 2, or 3 may contain the rule $S \to e$ where S is the initial symbol, only if S does not appear on the right side of any rule.

Fortunately, we can easily adjust a grammar to meet the requirement that its initial symbol never appears on the right side of any rule without affecting the language generated.

LEMMA 9-4: For any type 3 grammar there is an equivalent type 3 grammar that has no occurrences of its initial symbol on the right side of any rule.

Proof: Given a type 3 grammar $G = (V_N, V_T, \{S\}, P)$, let S_1 be a new nonterminal symbol not in V_N or V_T. Construct a new grammar G' having S_1 as its initial symbol and containing all the rules of G. For every rule of the form $S \to \psi$ in G, add the rule $S_1 \to \psi$ to G'. Since S_1 does not occur in the rules of G, it cannot, by this construction, appear on the right side of any rules of G'. The productions of G' are of the same form as the productions of G, so G' is also type 3. Furthermore, for every derivation of a terminal string x by G, $S, \varphi_1, \ldots, \varphi_n, x$, there is a corresponding derivation $S_1, \varphi_1, \ldots, \varphi_n, x$, by G', and vice versa. Thus, the grammars are equivalent. The corresponding lemmas for type 1 and type 2 grammars can be proved in the same way.

Example 9-5:

$G: \quad S \to aS$

$\quad\quad\; S \to a$

An equivalent type 3 grammar with no occurrences of its initial symbol S_1 on the right side of any rule is

$G': \quad S_1 \to aS$

$\quad\quad\;\; S_1 \to a$

$\quad\quad\;\; S \to aS$

$\quad\quad\;\; S \to a$

$L(G) = L(G') = a^n$ $(n \geq 1)$. G' can be converted to a type 3 grammar G'' generating a^n $(n \geq 0)$ by adding the rule $S_1 \rightarrow e$. G'' meets Condition 9-1.

We are now prepared to prove the following lemma.

LEMMA 9-5: If L is a type 3 language, then so is L^*.

Proof: Let L be a language generated by the type 3 grammar $G = (V_N, V_T, \{S\}, P)$. Form a new grammar G' in the following way. If G contains the rule $S \rightarrow e$, disregard it, and put all the other rules in G'. For every rule in G of the form $A \rightarrow x$ (except $S \rightarrow e$), put an additional rule $A \rightarrow xS$ in G'. Thus, in every case in which G generates the last symbol of a terminal string, G' can either generate this string and stop or else generate another instance of the initial symbol S, which has the effect of concatenating another nonnull string of L to the right of the one already generated. This can be repeated an arbitrary number of times, so G' generates the language composed of the concatenation of any number of nonnull strings of L, that is, $L^* - \{e\}$. Now convert G' to an equivalent type 3 grammar G'' having no occurrences of its initial symbol on the right side of any rule by the procedure given in the proof of Lemma 9-4. Finally, add the rule $S_1 \rightarrow e$ to G'' (where S_1 in the initial symbol of G'') forming the grammar G''', which generates L^*.

Example 9-6:

G: $S \rightarrow e$ $L(G) = \{e, a\}$
        $S \rightarrow a$

G': $S \rightarrow a$ $L(G') = a^n$ $(n \geq 1)$
        $S \rightarrow aS$

G'': $S \rightarrow a$ $L(G'') = a^n$ $(n \geq 1)$
        $S \rightarrow aS$
        $S_1 \rightarrow a$
        $S_1 \rightarrow aS$

G''': $S_1 \rightarrow e$ $L(G''') = a^n$ $(n \geq 0) = \{a\}^*$
        $S \rightarrow a$
        $S \rightarrow aS$
        $S_1 \rightarrow a$
        $S_1 \rightarrow aS$

THEOREM 9-2: Every regular set is a type 3 language.

Proof: Every finite set is a regular set, by definition, and by Lemma 9-1, every finite set is a type 3 language. Let A and B be arbitrarily given finite sets. Then $A \cup B$, $A \cdot B$, and A^* are regular sets, by definition, and are type 3 languages by Lemmas 9-2, 9-3, and 9-5, respectively, and similarly for sets constructed from such sets by the repeated application of the operators, $\cup$, $\cdot$, and $*$. Every regular set is constructed in this way, and thus every regular set is also a type 3 language.

This theorem guarantees that any well-formed expression composed of a finite number of representations of finite sets and a finite number of occurrences of $\cup$, $\cdot$, and $*$ denotes a set that is a type 3 language. We shall call such an expression a *representing expression*. For example, $(\{a, b\}^* \cdot a) \cup (a \cdot \{a, b\}^*)$ is a representing expression, and therefore the set it represents must be generated by some type 3 grammar. This set consists of all strings on the alphabet $\{a, b\}$ that either end or begin with an a, and it is generated by the following type 3 grammar:

(9-42)
$$
\begin{array}{ll}
S \to aA & S \to bB \\
A \to bA & B \to aB \\
A \to aA & B \to bB \\
A \to b & B \to a \\
A \to a & \\
S \to a &
\end{array}
$$

There is, in fact, a general procedure for constructing a type 3 grammar that generates the set represented by any given representing expression. We shall not give this procedure here, but the interested reader should be able to discover it for himself by referring to the proofs of Lemmas 9-2, 9-3, and 9-5. On the other hand, given a specification of a type 3 language in some other form (e.g., 'all strings on $\{a, b\}$ containing an even number of a's and an even number of b's'), it often requires considerable ingenuity to find an equivalent representing expression. Nonetheless, the converse of Theorem 9-2, which is proved in the next chapter, assures that for every type 3 language such a representing expression exists.

3. *Inadequacy of Right-Linear Grammars for Natural Languages*

A right-linear grammar is probably the simplest sort of grammar one could conceive of that still generates an infinite language. Because these grammars are so severely restricted in the form of their rules, it is perhaps not surprising that there are type 2 languages that they cannot generate. One of the first to be pointed out (Chomsky, 1956) was the mirror-image language xx^{-1}, where x is a string in $\{a, b\}^*$ and x^{-1} is the reflection of x, i.e., with the symbols in the reverse order. The following type 2 grammar generates xx^{-1}.

(9-43)
$$\begin{aligned} S &\to aSa \\ S &\to bSb \\ S &\to aa \\ S &\to bb \end{aligned}$$

We prove in the next chapter (Theorem 10-4) that no type 3 grammar can generate exactly the language xx^{-1}. For the moment, we shall argue informally that it is impossible to construct such a grammar. The problem one runs into is that strings in xx^{-1} have nested pairwise correspondences of symbols of the sort illustrated in Fig. 9-1. For every i, the ith symbol from

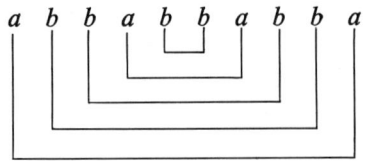

Figure 9-1

Correspondences of symbols in a string of xx^{-1}

the left and the ith symbol from the right must match. A type 3 grammar generates terminal symbols strictly from left to right, and at any point in the derivation (up to the last step) there is only one nonterminal symbol in each string, this being at the right end. Consider now an attempted derivation of a string of xx^{-1} at the stage at which the left half has been produced and the generation of its mirror image is beginning. The one nonterminal symbol, since it is rewritten without regard to context, must somehow carry in itself all the information about the existing left half so that its one correct mirror image, and no other string, will be generated. By introducing into the grammar a larger and larger number of different nonterminals we could encode more and more of this information (e.g., we could use A_1 to generate a, A_2 to generate b, A_3 to generate aa, etc.), but because xx^{-1} is an infinite language, there is no limit to the number of different left halves that would have to be encoded in this way. By definition, a grammar has a finite number of nonterminals in its vocabulary. Therefore, for any given type 3 grammar, there is some string in xx^{-1} whose left side is too long to be uniquely encoded by any of the nonterminals of the grammar. To put the matter another way, n different nonterminals can be used in a type 3 derivation to distinguish at most n different derivational histories (left halves), and the number of such histories that must be distinguished to generate xx^{-1} is always larger than any finite n.

Chomsky has argued (Chomsky, 1956; 1957, Chapter 3) that English exhibits arbitrarily large sets of correspondences like those of xx^{-1}, and thus it cannot be generated by a type 3 grammar. This argument illustrates one sort of practical result that can be obtained from the study of formal grammars and languages. Suppose a linguistic theory is proposed that claims that the grammar of every natural language is drawn from some infinite class $\mathscr{G}$ of generative devices. Like all theories, this one would be supported (but not of course proved true) by each instance of a successful prediction, i.e., whenever we can show that there is an adequate type 3 grammar for some natural language. On the other hand, no number of failures in attempting to construct a type 3 grammar for, say, Swahili would suffice to prove the theory wrong. Since $\mathscr{G}$ is an infinite set, our lack of success after any finite number of tries may be the result only of ineptness or bad luck. The next attempt might be the one that succeeds.

Therefore, to prove that a proposed linguistic theory is incorrect, it does not suffice to say that for some particular natural language we have not yet been able to find a grammar of the prescribed form. We must show that *no* adequate grammar of the prescribed form exists, and to do this we must construct an argument involving the properties of the languages that can be generated by the given class of grammars and about the properties of one or more natural languages. The form of the argument is this: The sentences of natural language L have property P; no grammar from class $\mathscr{G}$ can generate a language with property P; therefore, $\mathscr{G}$ cannot contain a grammar of L, and a linguistic theory that claims otherwise must be false. In Chomsky's argument, $\mathscr{G}$ is the class of type 3 grammars, L is English, and P is the property of having an arbitrarily large number of nested symbol correspondences of the sort illustrated in Fig. 9-1. Those who wish to escape the conclusion of this argument have attacked the premise that English has property P (see, for example, Reich, 1969). This reduces to a dispute over which strings are to be considered grammatical in English and which are not, and clearly this is a linguistic rather than a mathematical question. There can be no doubt, however, of the other premise because it can be shown by a mathematical proof.

Another example of this form of argument is given in Postal (1964a), where the language is Mohawk, $\mathscr{G}$ is the class of type 2 grammars, and P is the property of having an arbitrarily large number of intercalated symbol correspondences of the type shown in Fig. 9-2. Once again, it is possible to prove mathematically that type 2 languages cannot have this property; the

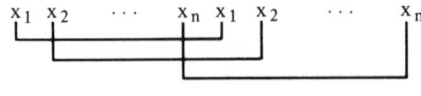

Figure 9-2

Type of intercalated symbol correspondence claimed to be found in Mohawk (Postal, 1964a)

linguistic question is whether Mohawk (or some other natural language) does have it.

We next consider the type 1 grammars and languages, deferring further discussion of type 2 until later.

Context-Sensitive Grammars and Languages

1. Existence of a Decision Procedure for Membership in a Type 1 Language

We first show that for any given type 1 grammar G (and therefore necessarily also for any type 2 or type 3 grammar) and for any given string of terminal symbols x, it is always possible to find the answer to the question 'Does G generate x?' What makes this possible is the fact that the right side of a rule in a type 1 grammar is at least as long as its left side (in $\varphi A \psi \to \varphi \omega \psi$, ω cannot be null). The only exception is the single rule $S \to e$, which is present only if the grammar generates the null string, and if so, the rule is used only for that purpose. Thus, all derivations by a type 1 grammar (except for the derivation of the null string) are "nonshrinking," in the sense that no line is shorter than the one immediately preceding it. We use this property in the proof of the following theorem.

> **THEOREM 9-3:** For any type 1 grammar $G = (V_N, V_T, \{S\}, P)$ and any string $x \in V_T^*$, one need examine only a finite number of sequences of strings in order to determine whether or not $x \in L(G)$.

> *Proof:* If x is the null string, then $x \in L(G)$ iff $S \to e$ is a rule of G and G meets Condition 9-1. If x is nonnull, it contains some finite number k of symbols. If there is a derivation of x from S,
>
> $$S \Rightarrow \varphi_1 \Rightarrow \cdots \Rightarrow \varphi_n \Rightarrow x$$
>
> then none of the lines preceding x can contain more than k symbols. This is true because each rule of G used in the derivation of a nonnull string has at least as many symbols on the right as on the left.

Further, we can disregard any derivations in which a line occurs more than once. That is, if

$$S \Rightarrow \varphi_1 \Rightarrow \cdots \Rightarrow \varphi_i \Rightarrow \cdots \Rightarrow \varphi_j \Rightarrow \cdots \Rightarrow x$$

is a derivation, where $\varphi_i = \varphi_j$, then

$$S \Rightarrow \varphi_1 \Rightarrow \cdots \Rightarrow \varphi_{i-1} \Rightarrow \varphi_j \Rightarrow \cdots \Rightarrow x$$

is also a derivation without the repetition. Thus, if there is any derivation of x from S, there is one with no repeated lines. Because V_T and V_N are finite sets, there are only a finite number of strings of length k or less. That is, if n is the cardinality of $V_T \cup V_N$, then there are n distinct strings of length 1, n^2 strings of length 2, n^3 strings of length 3, etc. Thus, there are $n + n^2 + \cdots + n^k$ strings of length k or less, which is a finite number. The longest possible sequence of lines that could be a derivation of x from S without repeating any lines would contain each string of length k or less exactly once, and this sequence would be $n + n^2 + \cdots + n^k$ strings long. There are a finite number of sequences at most $n + n^2 + \cdots + n^k$ strings long in which each string is at most k symbols long. Thus, there are only a finite number of candidates to be examined to determine whether any is a derivation of x from S.

When this situation obtains, we say that there exists a *decision procedure* for membership in the set $L(G)$ or, equivalently, that the membership question for $L(G)$ is *decidable*. A set for which there exists a decision procedure for membership is called a *recursive set*. (This use of the term 'recursive' turns out to be related to its use in connection with recursive definitions and axiomatic systems, although the connection is not obvious in this context.) We have not yet said just what constitutes a decision procedure—this is one of the topics in the next chapter—but intuitively speaking we mean a well-defined set of instructions which can be carried out mechanically in stepwise fashion and which is always guaranteed to lead us to a definite answer after some finite number of steps. The examination of a finite number of sequences to determine whether one is a derivation of some given string x from S according to the rules of some given type 1 grammar would surely qualify as a decision procedure in this sense. It might in reality take a person or a computing machine a long time to check a very large number of such sequences, but this is a practical and not a theoretical consideration; since the number is finite, the process must eventually come to an end and give us the answer.

This decision procedure will not work for derivations in type 0 grammars, where the right side of a rule may in general be shorter than the left. The reason is that a string of length k might be derived from strings that are longer than k, and therefore we could not fix an upper bound on the length of sequences we would have to investigate in order to check whether one of them is a derivation of the given string. This reasoning does not prove that there is no decision procedure for membership in type 0 languages (although in fact there is none), only that the one we used for type 1 languages will not work here.

It is important to recognize that the lack of a decision procedure for membership in a *class* of languages does not preclude the existence of a decision procedure for *particular members* of the class. In other words, the following two statements are not mutually contradictory:

(9-44) There is no procedure for determining for an arbitrary type 0 grammar G and an arbitrary string x whether or not $x \in L(G)$.

(9-45) For some type 0 grammar G_0 there is a decision procedure for determining for an arbitrary string x whether or not $x \in L(G_0)$.

The latter possibility is illustrated by the fact that it is relatively easy to prove that the type 0 grammar in (9-1) generates just the strings $b^n a^m cc$ ($n, m \geq 1$). Thus, there is a decision procedure for membership in the language generated by this grammar, and it is simply this: Given an arbitrary string x, is it of the form $b^n a^m cc$ ($n, m \geq 1$)? If so, $x \in L(G)$; if not, $x \notin L(G)$.

Most linguists would probably agree that every natural language is a recursive set. It is reasonable to suppose, for example, that for any arbitrarily given string of phones, morphemes, words, or whatever, a person who commands a natural language grammar G can determine, if he is given enough time and memory aids, whether or not the string is grammatical. This amounts to saying that the speaker-hearer has available to him a decision procedure for membership in $L(G)$ and, if so, the language is a recursive set (cf. Chomsky, 1965, pp. 31–32 and footnote 18, p. 202).

2. *Type 1 Languages and Recursive Sets*

In the following theorem we use the intuitively based notion of a decision procedure in proving that there are recursive sets that are not generated by any type 1 grammar. The technique is similar to the diagonal argument used in Chapter 7 to show the nondenumerability of [0, 1].

THEOREM 9-4: There is a recursive set that is not the language generated by any type 1 grammar.

Proof: Every grammar consists of a finite set of production schemata, each composed of a finite number of symbols. We can assume these symbols are drawn from some fixed finite alphabet since we can always

Context-Sensitive Grammars and Languages 237

create new symbols, if necessary, by adding 'primes' to old ones. Let each type 1 grammar be given in a "standard" representation in which its productions are listed in increasing length and all productions of the same length are arranged in some previously determined "alphabetical" order. Each grammar now has a unique representation.

Let the grammars themselves be ordered according to the number of productions in each one, and let grammars with the same number of productions be ordered "alphabetically." Thus, the grammars are ordered such that there is a first grammar, a second grammar, and in general an nth grammar in the ordering for any integer n. The procedure just described is said to give an *enumeration* of the infinite class of type 1 grammars.

In a similar fashion, we can give an enumeration of all the strings on some fixed alphabet $\bar{V}_T$, which we can take to the finite set of terminal symbols for the type 1 grammars. Let words on $\bar{V}_T^*$ be arranged in increasing length with all words of the same length listed in some fixed "alphabetical" order.

The result is an enumeration of type 1 grammars:

$$G_1, G_2, \ldots, G_n, \ldots$$

and an enumeration of strings in $\bar{V}_T^*$:

$$x_1, x_2, \ldots, x_n, \ldots$$

We now construct a new language M in the following way. Take the first string x_1 in $\bar{V}_T^*$ and see whether it is in the language generated by G_1, the first grammar in the enumeration. Since G_1 is a type 1 grammar, we are guaranteed by Theorem 9-3 that the answer to this question can always be determined. If x_1 is not in $L(G_1)$, then we put x_1 in M; if x_1 is in $L(G_1)$, we do not put x_1 in M. Similarly we put x_2, the second string in the enumeration of $\bar{V}_T^*$, in M if and only if it is not in the language generated by G_2, the second grammar in the enumeration, etc. In general

(9-46) $\qquad M = \{x_i \in \bar{V}_T^* \mid x_i \notin L(G_i)\}$

The language M is not generated by any of the type 1 grammars in the enumeration. To see this, select any grammar G_i. M cannot be equal to $L(G_i)$ since there is some string, namely x_i, contained in one but not the other. If x_i is in M, then it is not in $L(G_i)$, and if x_i is not in M, then it is in $L(G_i)$. M is a recursive set, however, because there is a decision procedure for determining for any arbitrarily given string x whether $x \in M$. The procedure is this: Find x in the enumeration of $\bar{V}_T^*$ (this can always be done since the strings are ordered by increasing length), and determine its place in the order by counting from the front. Now find the corresponding grammar in the enumeration of grammars and determine whether the grammar generates x. This is always possible by Theorem 9-3. If the grammar generates x, then by the definition of M, $x \notin M$, and if the grammar does not generate x, then $x \in M$. Thus M is a recursive set, but it is not generated by any type 1 grammar.

3. Some Undecidable Questions Concerning Type 1 Grammars and Languages

Although there is a decision procedure for membership in a type 1 language, there are several related questions pertaining to these languages for which no decision procedure exists. Some of these are stated in the following theorem.

> **THEOREM 9-5:** For an arbitrary type 1 grammar G there is no decision procedure for determining whether
> (a) $L(G)$ is empty,
> (b) $L(G)$ is finite, or
> (c) some particular string $a_1 a_2 \cdots a_n$ occurs as a proper subpart of some terminal string of G.
> For any two arbitrary type 1 grammars G_1 and G_2 there is no decision procedure for determining whether $L(G_1) = L(G_2)$.

We omit the proofs, which are given in Chomsky (1963, pp. 361–362). We note, however, that a decision procedure constructed along the lines of that in Theorem 9-3 fails in these cases. For example, given some arbitrary type 1 grammar G, if we have examined a finite number of sequences and found none that is a derivation of a terminal string, we cannot on this basis conclude that $L(G)$ is empty because there might be some sequence we have not yet examined that does yield a terminal string. Since there is no upper bound on the length of a derivation that produces a terminal string, no finite number of cases of failure to produce one will suffice to prove that none exists. Similar arguments can be made for other parts of Theorem 9-5.

Context-Free Grammars and Languages

In the following sections we sketch briefly four kinds of results obtained in the study of these systems:

1. Existence of a decision procedure for the emptiness question, i.e., the question whether an arbitrary type 2 grammar generates any terminal strings.

2. Reductions of type 2 grammars by removal of superfluous rules and terminal symbols while the language generated is left unchanged.
3. A characterization theorem for type 2 languages.
4. Closure properties of context-free languages under the operations of union, intersection, and complementation.

1. Decidability of the Emptiness Question for Context-Free Grammars

We noted in the previous section that there is no general procedure for determining whether an arbitrary type 1 grammar generates any terminal strings. There is such a procedure for arbitrary type 2 grammars and it is made possible by the fact that for any given type 2 grammar the number of generated trees that must be examined in order to discover the answer to the question of emptiness is finite. To illustrate, consider the following type 2 grammar:

(9-47)
$$S \to AB$$
$$A \to aAa$$
$$A \to a$$
$$B \to ABb$$
$$B \to b$$

The following is one of the constituent-structure trees that can be generated. (We have numbered the B's only for convenience of reference; they are all to be considered instances of the same symbol.)

(9-48)
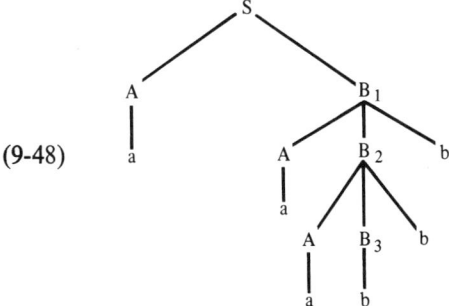

This tree has as its leaves the terminal string $aaabbb$, and this in itself suffices to establish that the language of the grammar in (9-47) is nonempty. What we want to show now, however, is that if the grammar generates this tree, then it also generates a terminal string whose associated constituent-structure tree has no occurrences of the same symbol along any path. (By a *path* we mean a continuously descending sequence of branches.) The tree in (9-48) has repeated occurrences of B along the path S——B_1——B_2——B_3——b. Because B_1 could have been rewritten as B_3 was, i.e., as b rather than as ABb, the grammar also generates a tree like (9-48) except that the subtree with B_1 as root is replaced by the subtree with B_3 as root; thus:

(9-49)
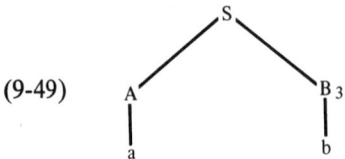

Since the B_3-rooted tree has a string of terminal symbols as leaves (in this case just the string b), the tree formed by replacing the B_1-rooted subtree by the B_3-rooted subtree necessarily also has leaves that are terminal symbols. Repeated occurrences of symbols can be eliminated from all paths in this way, and if the original tree had a terminal string as leaves, then so will the resulting tree.

The nonterminal vocabulary of a grammar contains a finite number n of symbols, and therefore the longest path that can be formed from these without repetitions is of length n. (The length of a path is the number of nodes on it.) For a given grammar, there are a finite number k of trees that can be generated with maximum path length n. As we have just seen, if the grammar generates any terminal strings at all, it will generate at least one whose associated tree has no path with a repeated symbol. Therefore, such a tree, if it exists, will be found among the k trees with maximum path length n. In other words, to determine whether some given type 2 grammar generates any terminal strings, one need look at no more than a finite number of trees—those with path length no greater than the size of the nonterminal alphabet of the grammar. If no tree in this finite set has leaves composed entirely of terminal symbols, we can conclude that the grammar generates no terminal strings.

As an example, the grammar in (9-50) generates the empty language, as can be verified by constructing all generated trees of maximum path length 3

(9-50)
$$S \rightarrow AB$$
$$B \rightarrow ABa$$
$$A \rightarrow a$$

and noting that none has a terminal string as its leaves.

This sort of procedure is not possible in the case of context-sensitive grammars, since the replacement of a node such as B_1 in (9-48) by the tree rooted by B_3 does not necessarily yield a tree that can be generated by the grammar. The environment in which B_1 was rewritten during the course of the derivation might not have allowed rewriting B in the manner of B_3, and therefore the tree with B_1 in place of B_3 might not correspond to any derivation by the grammar. There is no such problem with cfg's because the environment in which a symbol appears in a line of a derivation does not restrict the ways in which it can be rewritten. Therefore, the substitution of the B_3 tree for the B_1 tree as above always produces another tree generable by the grammar. Thus, we have the following theorem:

THEOREM 9-6: There is a procedure for determining whether the language generated by an arbitrary context-free grammar is empty.

2. Reductions of Context-Free Grammars

Suppose that a cfg $G = (V_N, V_T, \{S\}, P)$ contains a nonterminal symbol A such that no terminal strings are dominated by A; i.e., there are no derivations $A \Rightarrow \varphi_1 \Rightarrow \cdots \Rightarrow \varphi_n \Rightarrow x$ by G, where $x \in V_T^*$. Now if A appears in any line of a derivation by G, that derivation cannot possibly result in a terminal string. This is clear if we think of the tree associated with such a derivation; for the entire tree to have terminal symbols as its leaves, it is necessary, in particular, that the subtree rooted by A have terminal symbols as its leaves, and this is possible only if $A \stackrel{*}{\Rightarrow} x$ for some $x \in V_T^*$.

Since A can never be involved in the derivation of a terminal string, it can be eliminated from G without affecting the language generated. That is, A can be removed from V_N, and every rule containing at least one occurrence of A can be removed from P. How can we locate such superfluous nonterminals? We do so by the same technique used to determine whether a cfg generates any terminal strings.

Given any cfg $G = (V_N, V_T, \{S\}, P)$, for each A_i in V_N we form the grammar $G_i = (V_N, V_T, \{A_i\}, P)$ with A_i as initial symbol and determine, by the procedure outlined above, whether $L(G_i)$ is empty. If so, one can remove A_i from V_N and remove from P all rules containing A_i to produce a grammar G' that is equivalent to G.

Example 9-7:

$$G = (\{S, A, B, C\}, \{a, b\}, \{S\}, P)$$

$$P = \begin{cases} S \to AB \\ S \to CA \\ A \to CAAa \\ A \to Bb \\ B \to a \\ C \to aCA \end{cases}$$

The terminal symbols S, A, and B all dominate terminal strings, as shown in the following trees generated by G:

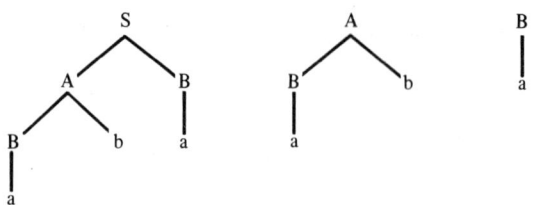

Examining all trees with C as root and of maximum path length 4 fails to turn up a tree with a terminal string as leaves. All C-rooted trees are of the form

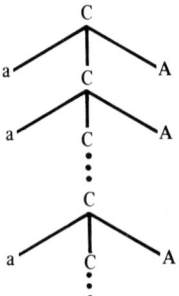

in which the path of C's never terminates. Thus, G can be simplified by omitting C and all rules in which it occurs to give the equivalent grammar G':

$$G' = (\{S, A, B\}, \{a, b\}, \{S\}, P')$$

$$P' = \begin{Bmatrix} S \rightarrow AB \\ A \rightarrow Bb \\ B \rightarrow a \end{Bmatrix}$$

Although a nonterminal symbol A dominates a terminal string, it still might not be involved in the *derivation* of a terminal string if it happens that A is not "reachable" from S, i.e., if no string containing A ever appears in a derivation beginning with S. The procedure for determining whether a particular cfg contains any such symbols is again to examine a finite number of generated constituent-structure trees with S as root. By an argument similar to that for Theorem 9-6 we can show that if a particular nonterminal symbol ever appears in any S-rooted tree, it will appear in one whose maximum path length is n, where n is the cardinality of V_N. Since there are a finite number of trees that a given grammar can generate with maximum path length n, failure to find any occurrence of a particular nonterminal in this finite number of trees is sufficient grounds for concluding that that symbol is never involved in the generation of a terminal string of the grammar.

Example 9-8:

$$G = (\{S, A, B\}, \{a, b, c\}, \{S\}, P)$$

$$P = \begin{Bmatrix} S \to AS \\ A \to aS \\ S \to b \\ B \to bS \end{Bmatrix}$$

The following phrase-structure trees with S as root and a maximum path length of 3 contain no occurrences of B. Therefore, this symbol

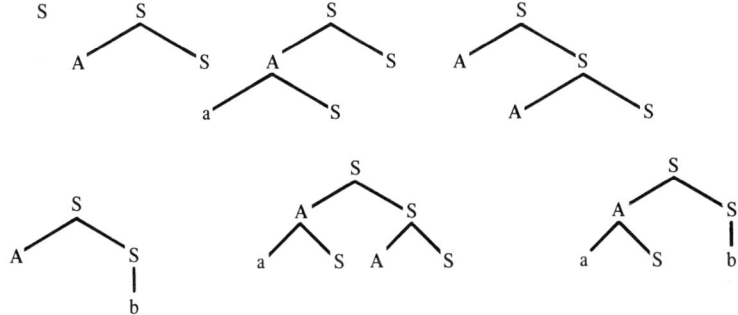

never occurs in any derivation from S, and so B and the single rule involving it, $B \to bS$, can be eliminated from G without affecting $L(G)$.

In this way, nonterminal symbols that are superfluous, in the sense that they are not used in the generation of any terminal strings, can be found and eliminated from a cfg. We can also eliminate any nonterminal symbols that dominate only a *finite number* of terminal strings. If some nonterminal A dominates a finite number of strings of terminal symbols $x_1, x_2, \ldots, x_n$, then every rule $B \to \varphi A \psi$ in which A appears on the right side can be replaced by the rules $B \to \varphi x_1 \psi$, $B \to \varphi x_2 \psi$, ..., $B \to \varphi x_n \psi$, without affecting the language generated. Now if A is not S, the initial symbol, we can eliminate all rules with A on the left side since they will never be used in any derivation beginning with S. Of course, in the case where A is S, rules with S on the left cannot be eliminated or there would be no way to generate any terminal strings at all.

The existence of a procedure for locating such nonterminals again depends on the fact that only a finite number of trees need be examined. Given any cfg $G = (V_N, V_T, \{S\}, P)$, we first reduce it to an equivalent grammar $G' = (V'_N, V_T, \{S\}, P')$ by removing superfluous nonterminal symbols and rules in the manner described previously. We are then guaranteed that every symbol in V'_N can be used in the derivation of a terminal string. For each nonterminal symbol A_i in V'_N of G' we form all derivation trees with A_i as root and maximum path length $n + 1$, where n in the cardinality of V'_N. If any tree with root A_i has some path with repeated occurrences of some symbol A_j (possibly identical to A_i), then we can conclude that A_j and, therefore, also A_i dominate an infinite number of terminal strings. Our reasoning is as follows:

Since A_j repeats on a path, there must be terminal strings x and y such that

(9-51) $\quad A_j \overset{*}{\Rightarrow} x A_j y$

If A_j repeats, it may repeat any number of times; therefore

(9-52) $\quad A_j \overset{*}{\Rightarrow} x A_j y \overset{*}{\Rightarrow} xx A_j yy \overset{*}{\Rightarrow} \cdots \overset{*}{\Rightarrow} x^n A_j y^n$

for any integer n.

All nonterminals dominate terminal strings, so there is some $z \in V_T^*$ such that $A_j \overset{*}{\Rightarrow} z$. Thus,

(9-53) $\quad A_j \overset{*}{\Rightarrow} x^n A_j y^n \overset{*}{\Rightarrow} x^n z y^n$

for any integer n.

Finally, since A_j is on a path leading from A_i, and A_i must also dominate some terminal string, there exist terminal strings v and w such that

(9-54) $\quad A_i \overset{*}{\Rightarrow} v A_j w \overset{*}{\Rightarrow} v x^n z y^n w$

for any integer n. Therefore, A_i dominates an infinite number of terminal strings.

By a similar argument we can also show the converse: If a symbol A_i dominates an infinite number of terminal strings, then there is a derivation tree with A_i as root that contains a path with repeated occurrences of some symbol A_j. Thus, this condition is both necessary and sufficient.

To identify just those symbols that dominate an infinite number of terminal strings, we examine for each nonterminal A_i the finite number of trees allowed by the grammar with root A_i and maximum path length $n + 1$. If any symbol is going to repeat, it must do so on a path no longer than $n + 1$. Then, we can select those symbols that dominate a finite number of terminal strings, find all the terminal strings that each symbol dominates (these can be found from the finite number of trees examined) and then replace each rule with an occurrence of such a symbol on the right side by the appropriate finite set of rules, as indicated previously. The result is a grammar in which each nonterminal dominates an infinite number of terminal strings or else it is a grammar generating only a finite language in which the only nonterminal is S and each rule is of the form $S \to x$, for $x \in V_T^*$.

There is one difficulty with the argument above, which we must now deal with. We claimed that a nonterminal symbol A_j that can repeat along a path dominates an infinite number of strings because

(9-55) $\qquad A_j \overset{*}{\Rightarrow} xA_j y \overset{*}{\Rightarrow} \cdots \overset{*}{\Rightarrow} x^n A_j y^n \overset{*}{\Rightarrow} x^n z y^n$

for all integers n. $x^n z y^n$ represents an infinite set of strings only if either x or y is nonnull, however; if both are null, then A_j could repeat any number of times without dominating any strings other than z. This can happen just when there is a path from A_j to a second occurrence of A_j through single nonterminal symbols only; i.e., $A_j \Rightarrow A_k \Rightarrow \cdots \Rightarrow A_l \Rightarrow A_j$. In this case, no terminals are generated in going from A_j to A_j and thus x and y in $vx^n z y^n w$ are null.

We can avoid this difficulty by removing from the grammar all rules of the form $A \to B$ with single nonterminals on both sides. Since every nonterminal, including S, dominates a terminal string (we assume the grammar to be so reduced), then there must be some nonterminal C and some rule $C \to \varphi$ in the grammar such that φ is not a string consisting of just one nonterminal symbol. In other words, some nonterminal reachable from A_j must either branch into two or more symbols or else be rewritten as a terminal symbol. Therefore, there is a derivation of the form

(9-56) $\qquad A_j \Rightarrow A_k \Rightarrow \cdots \Rightarrow A_l \Rightarrow A_m \Rightarrow \varphi$

and, further, there is such a derivation with no repetitions of a single nonterminal (if $A_j \overset{*}{\Rightarrow} \varphi$ with repetitions, $A_j \overset{*}{\Rightarrow} \varphi$ also without repetitions). We can find all such derivations since they are at most $n + 1$ lines long. We then replace all the rules $A_j \to A_k, \ldots, A_l \to A_m, A_m \to \varphi$ that produced such a derivation by the single rule $A_j \to \varphi$. The resulting grammar generates the same set of terminal strings but has no rules of the form $A \to B$. With this reduction, all remaining nonterminals that dominate a tree with repeating symbols on a path necessarily dominate infinitely many terminal strings.

Example 9-9:

$\qquad S \to aAb$

$\qquad A \to BCD$

$\qquad B \to bb$

$\qquad C \to Ab$

$\qquad D \to Ea$

$\qquad E \to F$

$\qquad F \to ab$

$\qquad A \to b$

This grammar contains the rules $E \to F$, and $F \to ab$, which allow the following derivation:

(9-57) $E \Rightarrow F \Rightarrow ab$

We can therefore replace these rules by the single rule $E \to ab$ and remove F from the nonterminal vocabulary (since it occurs nowhere else).

The following constituent-structure trees, which contain repetitions along a path, show that S, A, and C dominate an infinite set of terminal strings. The symbols B, D, and E dominate only the terminal strings

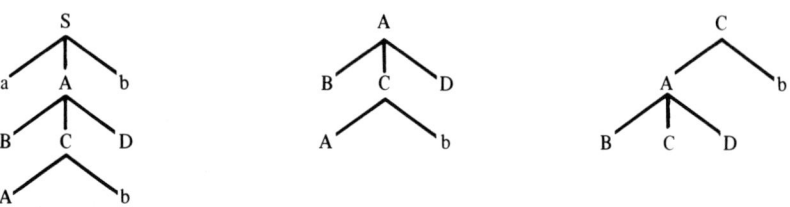

shown in the following trees:

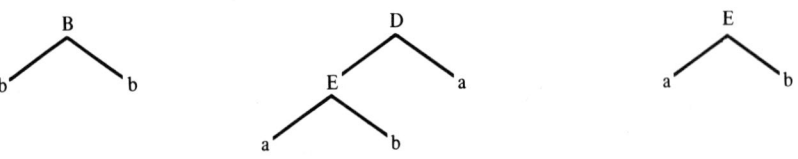

Thus, every occurrence of B on the right side of a rule can be replaced by bb; similarly, aba replaces D, and ab replaces E. All rules with B, D, or E in the left side are deleted. The resulting grammar is

$S \to aAb$
$A \to bbCaba$
$C \to Ab$
$A \to b$

The possibility of effecting all these reductions on cfg's is stated in the following theorem:

THEOREM 9-7: For every cfg $G = (V_N, V_T, \{S\}, P)$ there is an equivalent *reduced* grammar $G' = (V'_N, V_T, \{S\}, P')$ such that
1. Every nonterminal symbol appears in the derivation of some terminal string.

2. P' contains no rules of the form $A \to B$ $(A, B \in V'_N)$.
3. Either the grammar generates only a finite number of terminal strings $x_1, x_2, \ldots, x_n$ and contains only the nonterminal symbol S and the rules $S \to x_1, S \to x_2, \ldots, S \to x_n$ or the grammar generates an infinite set of terminal strings, and every nonterminal symbol dominates an infinite set of terminal strings.

3. A Characterization Theorem for Context-Free Languages

The following theorem gives a formal characteristic by which infinite context-free languages can be recognized. As we have already observed, any finite language $\{x_1, \ldots, x_n\}$ is necessarily context-free since it can be generated by a cfg with just the rules $S \to x_1, \ldots, S \to x_n$.

THEOREM 9-8: If a cfg $G = (V_N, V_T, \{S\}, P)$ generates an infinite set of terminal strings, then there are strings u, v, w, x, y in V_T^* (w not null; v and x not both null) such that G generates $uv^n w x^n y$ for all $n \geq 0$.

Proof: From G, form the equivalent reduced grammar G' by the procedure given above. If G' generates an infinite language, then there must be some nonterminal symbol A which can occur repeatedly on a path of an S-rooted tree which dominates a terminal string. If there were no such symbol, only a finite number of trees and, hence, a finite number of terminal strings would be generated. Therefore, there must be derivations by G' of the form

$$S \overset{*}{\Rightarrow} uAy \overset{*}{\Rightarrow} uvAxy \overset{*}{\Rightarrow} uv^2Ax^2y \overset{*}{\Rightarrow} \cdots \overset{*}{\Rightarrow} uv^nAx^ny$$
$$\overset{*}{\Rightarrow} uv^n w x^n y$$

for arbitrarily large n. Since there are no rules of the form $A \to B$ in G', the strings v and x cannot both be null.

Example 9-10: The following reduced cfg generates an infinite language:

$$S \to Cb$$
$$C \to cbCac$$
$$C \to bSa$$
$$C \to cc$$

Since $C \overset{*}{\Rightarrow} cbCac$, it follows that $C \overset{*}{\Rightarrow} (cb)^n C(ac)^n$ for all $n \geq 0$. This together with $S \overset{*}{\Rightarrow} Cb$ and $C \overset{*}{\Rightarrow} cc$ implies that $S \overset{*}{\Rightarrow} (cb)^n cc(ac)^n b$ for all $n \geq 0$, as required by Theorem 9-8 (u is null here). Note that the set of terminal strings $(cb)^n cc(ac)^n b$ is only a proper subset of the whole language generated. The language also contains $b^n cc(ba)^n b$ $(n \geq 0)$, as can be seen from $S \stackrel{*}{\Rightarrow} Cb$; $C \stackrel{*}{\Rightarrow} bSa \stackrel{*}{\Rightarrow} bCba$; and $C \stackrel{*}{\Rightarrow} cc$; it contains other strings as well.

Example 9-11: We show that the infinite language $a^i b^i a^i (i \geq 1)$ cannot be generated by any cfg. If $a^i b^i a^i$ were a cfl, it would contain an infinite set of strings of the form $uv^n wx^n y$, where u, v, w, x, and y are strings on the alphabet $\{a, b\}$. For $a^i b^i a^i$ to be represented as $uv^n wx^n y$, v and x must be strings consisting entirely of a's or entirely of b's. Otherwise, if v, for example, consisted of ab, then the substrings v^n in $uv^n wx^n y$ would be $ab, abab, \ldots, (ab)^n$, which cannot be substrings of $a^i b^i a^i$. A similar argument applies to x. Thus, there are four possible cases: $v \in \{a\}^*$ or $\{b\}^*$, and $x \in \{a\}^*$ or $\{b\}^*$. We show that in each case it is impossible to analyze $a^i b^i a^i$ into $uv^n wx^n y$ and maintain the assumption that the grammar generates *only* the strings $a^i b^i a^i$.

Case 1. $v \in \{a\}^*$ and $x \in \{a\}^*$

If $a^i b^i a^i$ is to be analyzed as $u(a^p)^n w(a^q)^n y$, then both u and y must consist entirely of a's, and w must be of the form $a^r b^s a^t$; that is, $a^i b^i a^i$ must be analyzable as

(9-58) $\quad \underbrace{a^{n_1}}_{u} \quad \underbrace{a^{n_2}}_{v} \quad \underbrace{a^{n_3} b^{n_4} a^{n_5}}_{w} \quad \underbrace{a^{n_6}}_{x} \quad \underbrace{a^{n_7}}_{y}$

and since the number of b's must be equal to the number of a's on either side,

$$(n_1 + n_2 + n_3) = n_4 = (n_5 + n_6 + n_7)$$

However, this analysis of $a^i b^i a^i$ implies that all strings of the form

(9-59) $\quad a^{n_1}(a^{n_2})^n a^{n_3} b^{n_4} a^{n_5} (a^{n_6})^n a^{n_7}$

for $n \geq 0$ are also generated by the grammar. Thus, strings in which the number of b's is not matched by the number of a's on at least one side would be produced as well, and the language could not be $a^i b^i a^i$.

Case 2. $v \in \{a\}^*$ and $x \in \{b\}^*$

$a^i b^i a^i$ must be analyzed as

(9-60) $\quad \underbrace{a^{n_1}}_{u} \quad \underbrace{a^{n_2}}_{v} \quad \underbrace{a^{n_3} b^{n_4}}_{w} \quad \underbrace{b^{n_5}}_{x} \quad \underbrace{b^{n_6} a^{n_7}}_{y}$

where

$$(n_1 + n_2 + n_3) = (n_4 + n_5 + n_6) = n_7$$

but this implies that all strings

(9-61) $\quad a^{n_1}(a^{n_2})^n a^{n_3} b^{n_4} (b^{n_5})^n b^{n_6} a^{n_7}$

Context-Free Grammars and Languages 249

for $n \geq 0$ are also produced, in which $n_4 + (n \cdot n_5) + n_6$ exceeds n_7 or $n_1 + (n \cdot n_2) + n_3$ exceeds n_7.

Case 3. $v \in \{b\}^*$ and $x \in \{a\}^*$
Symmetrical with Case 2.

Case 4. $v \in \{b\}^*$ and $x \in \{b\}^*$
$a^i b^i a^i$ must be analyzed as

(9-62) $\quad \underbrace{a^{n_1} b^{n_2}}_{u} \; \underbrace{b^{n_3}}_{v} \; \underbrace{b^{n_4}}_{w} \; \underbrace{b^{n_5}}_{x} \; \underbrace{b^{n_6} a^{n_7}}_{y}$

where
$$n_1 = (n_2 + n_3 + n_4 + n_5 + n_6) = n_7$$

but this implies that all strings

(9-63) $\quad a^{n_1} b^{n_2} (b^{n_3})^n b^{n_4} (b^{n_5})^n b^{n_6} a^{n_7}$

for $n \geq 0$ are also produced, in which $n_2 + (n \cdot n_3) + n_4 + (n \cdot n_5) + n_6$ exceeds both n_1 and n_7.

Thus, $a^i b^i a^i$ cannot be a context-free language. It is, however, a context-sensitive language since it is generated by the following csg:

(9-64)
$$S \to aSBA$$
$$S \to abA$$
$$AB \to CB$$
$$CB \to CA$$
$$CA \to BA$$
$$bB \to bb$$
$$bA \to ba$$
$$aA \to aa$$

These facts suffice to establish the following theorem:

THEOREM 9-9: The class of context-sensitive languages properly includes the class of context-free languages, i.e., $\mathscr{L}_1 \supset \mathscr{L}_2$.

4. Closure Properties of Context-Free Languages

In proving Theorem 9-2, we first showed that the type 3 languages are closed under the operations of union, product, and star. In this section we show that the union of any two type 2 languages is also a type 2 language, but that this is not necessarily true of the intersection of two such languages. Further, if we assume all type 2 languages to be constructed from some fixed alphabet $\bar{V}_T$, then we can meaningfully ask whether the complement of a type 2 language L, i.e., $L' = \bar{V}_T^* - L$, is necessarily also type 2. We shall show that it is not.

THEOREM 9-10: *The class of context-free languages is closed under union.*

Proof: Given any two cfg's $G_1 = (V_{N_1}, V_{T_1}, \{S\}, P_1)$ and $G_2 = (V_{N_2}, V_{T_2}, \{S\}, P_2)$, form the grammar G_3 in the following way. Replace S everywhere it occurs in G_1 by the new nonterminal S_1, and similarly replace S in G_2 by the new symbol S_2. If necessary, rename the other nonterminals in one of the grammars so that $V_{N_1} \cap V_{N_2} = \emptyset$. Call the resulting grammars G_1' and G_2'. The rules of G_3 are just the rules of G_1' and G_2' together with the additional rules

$$S \to S_1$$
$$S \to S_2$$

G_3 generates every terminal string generated by either G_1 or G_2 and only these strings, i.e., $L(G_3) = L(G_1) \cup L(G_2)$. Since G_3 is a cfg, $L(G_3)$ is a cfl.

THEOREM 9-11: *The class of context-free languages is not closed under intersection.*

Proof: The languages $L_1 = a^n b^n a^m$ $(m, n \geq 1)$ and $L_2 = a^m b^n a^n$ $(m, n \geq 1)$ are context-free, being generated by the cfg's (9-65) and (9-66), respectively.

(9-65)
$$S \to BA$$
$$B \to aBb$$
$$B \to ab$$
$$A \to aA$$
$$A \to a$$

(9-66)
$$S \to AB$$
$$A \to aA$$
$$A \to a$$
$$B \to bBa$$
$$B \to ba$$

The intersection of L_1 and L_2 is $a^n b^n a^n$ $(n \geq 1)$, which is not context-free, as seen in Example 9-11. Thus, in general, the intersection of two cfl's need not be context-free.

THEOREM 9-12: **The class of context-free languages is not closed under complementation.**

Proof: Assume a common alphabet $\bar{V}_T$ for all context-free languages. Choose two arbitrary cfl's L_1 and L_2. If the cfl's were closed under complementation, then L_1' and L_2' would also be context-free, and by Theorem 9-10 so would the union $L_1' \cup L_2'$. The complement of the latter, $(L_1' \cup L_2')'$, would also be context-free, but by DeMorgan's Laws $(L_1' \cup L_2')' = L_1 \cap L_2$, which by Theorem 9-11 is not necessarily context-free. Therefore, the cfl's cannot be closed under complementation.

The closure properties of type 0, 1, 2, and 3 languages under union, intersection, and complementation are summarized in Table 9-2. It is not known whether the context-sensitive languages are closed under complementation; indeed, this question has remained open for several years despite the efforts of many very able people to find the answer.

Language type	Closed under		
	Union	Intersection	Complementation
0 (r.e. sets)	Yes	Yes	No
1 (csl)	Yes	Yes	?
2 (cfl)	Yes	No	No
3 (fsl)	Yes	Yes	Yes

Table 9-2

Closure properties of type 0, 1, 2, and 3 languages

EXERCISES

1. Construct type 3 grammars that generate each of the following languages. Assume a fixed terminal vocabulary $V_T = \{a, b\}$.
   (a) $L_1 = \{aa, ab, ba, bb\}$
   (b) $L_2 = \{x \mid x \text{ contains any number of occurrences of } a \text{ and } b \text{ in any order}\}$
   (c) $L_3 = \{x \mid x \text{ contains exactly two occurrences of } a, \text{ not necessarily contiguous}\}$

(d) $L_4 = \{x \mid x$ contains exactly one occurrence of a, or exactly one occurrence of b, or both$\}$

(e) $L_5 = \{x \mid x$ contains an even number of a's and an even number of b's$\}$ (Zero counts as even.)

(f) $L_6 = L_3 \cap L_5$

2. Give a representing expression for each of the languages in (a), (b), (c), and (d) of Exercise 1.

3. Construct type 1 grammars for each of the following languages.
   (a) $a^n b^n c^n$ $(n \geq 1)$
   (b) $\{x \in \{a, b, c\}^* \mid x$ consists of an equal number of a's, b's, and c's$\}$
   (c) $\{xx \mid x \in \{a, b\}^*\}$ (i.e., all strings in $\{a, b\}^*$ with identical left and right halves.)

4. Construct type 2 grammars generating each of the following languages.
   (a) $L_1 = a^n b^m a^n$ $(n, m \geq 1)$
   (b) $L_2 = a^n b^n a^m b^m$ $(n, m \geq 1)$
   (c) $L_3 = \{x \mid x \in \{a, b\}^*$ and x contains twice as many b's as a's$\}$

5. Show that for every type 2 grammar there is an equivalent grammar in which all productions are of the form $A \rightarrow BC$ or $A \rightarrow a$ (A, B, C in V_N, a in V_T). Such a grammar is said to be in *Chomsky Normal Form* (Chomsky, 1959).

6. Show by means of Theorem 9-8 that the following languages are not type 2.
   (a) a^{n^2} $(n \geq 1)$
   (b) a^n (n is prime, i.e., divisible only by 1 and by itself.)

7. Show that the type 2 languages are closed under the operation of set product.

8. Prove that set product distributes over union and intersection.

References and Supplementary Reading

Chomsky (1963) is a thorough survey of the field of formal languages and their corresponding automata up to that time. Two recent textbooks, Gross and Lentin (1970) and Hopcroft and Ullman (1969), include newer material as well. The former has an annotated bibliography, and the latter has references at the end of each chapter to guide the reader to the original sources. See also Nelson (1968, Chapters 7 and 8). Wood (1970) is an exhaustive bibliography of formal language and automata theory. Ginsburg (1966) is a treatise on context-free languages covering many topics such as behavior under various mappings, decidability, and inherent ambiguity.

The basic notion of a formal grammar and many of the associated definitions (derivation, terminal string, etc.) first appear in Chomsky (1956). A more detailed formulation and the classification of grammars and languages into types 0, 1, 2, and 3 are found in Chomsky (1959) and, with some further refinements, in Chomsky and Miller (1963) and Chomsky (1963).

The association of derivations with phrase-structure trees is outlined in Chomsky (1956). The difficulties raised by rules of the form $AB \to A\psi B$ are pointed out in Chomsky (1959) and discussed in more detail in Postal (1964b, Chapter 3) and McCawley (1968). McCawley also presents an explicit formulation of the proposal for interpreting phrase-structure rules as tree formation rules.

Right-linear grammars as defined in Chomsky (1963, p. 369) are our type 3; what is called type 3 in Chomsky (1959) corresponds to our type 3.1. Many of the basic results concerning type 3 languages (e.g., Lemmas 9-2, 9-3, and 9-5) were first proved for the equivalent finite-state languages. See, for example, Kleene (1956), Chomsky and Miller (1958), and Rabin and Scott (1959). The notions of regular set and representing expression are from Kleene (1956), both in slightly different form. Representing expressions also appear in Chomsky and Miller (1958) (cf. Chomsky, 1963, Theorem 2).

Theorems 9-3 and 9-4 are from Chomsky (1959).

The fundamental papers on context-free languages are Chomsky (1956), Chomsky (1959), and Bar-Hillel, Perles, and Shamir (1961). The last contains a proof of the decidability of the emptiness question (Theorem 9-6), the reductions leading up to Theorem 9-7, the characterization of infinite cfl's (Theorem 9-8), and the closure properties (Theorems 9-10, 9-11, and 9-12). In Chomsky (1959) there is a proof of Theorem 9-9, in which reference is made to the sort of reductions allowed by Theorem 9-7 and which makes use of what is in essence Theorem 9-8, although these results are not proved in detail.

Of the closure properties of languages in Table 9-2 not already mentioned, those for type 0 are well-known results in Turing machine theory (see, for example, Davis, 1958), and those for type 1 are from Landweber (1963).

10

Automata

Mathematicians have long been interested in procedures for performing some operation or solving some problem. Two examples from ancient times are the Euclidian algorithm for finding the greatest common divisor of two integers and the procedure known as the "sieve of Eratosthenes" for determining whether a given integer n is prime. Attempts to determine what is involved essentially in this notion of a "procedure" have, among other things, given rise to a branch of mathematics devoted to the study of automata. An automaton is an abstract device that receives an input on which it performs certain elementary operations in stepwise fashion according to a set of instructions given it initially. It is a basic premise of automata theory that every procedure, no matter how complex, can be decomposed into a series of these elementary operations. Thus, an automaton works in a recursive fashion, in that the result of performing one step becomes the input to the next.

The theory of automata and the theory of formal grammars are isomorphic in most important respects, and this is the motivation for including a chapter on automata in a work on mathematical linguistics. In the following sections we introduce four classes of automata—finite, pushdown, and linear bounded automata and Turing machines—and investigate their relationships with the four types of grammars described in the preceding chapter.

Finite Automata

A finite automaton (fa) is an abstract device that receives a string of symbols as input, computes for a finite number of steps, and halts in some configuration signifying either that the input has been accepted or else that it has been rejected. We can visualize an fa as composed of a control box, a tape-reading head, and an input tape. The tape is blocked off into squares and is infinitely long in both directions. The input string is written on the tape, one symbol to a square, from left to right. All squares that do not contain an input symbol contain instead a special blank symbol $\#$. At any given moment the automaton is allowed to be in one of a finite number of internal arrangements, or *states*, and one of these, the *initial state*, is the state in which the automaton always begins its processing of an input string. Initially, the tape-reading head is on the leftmost nonblank symbol of the input tape (Fig. 10-1).

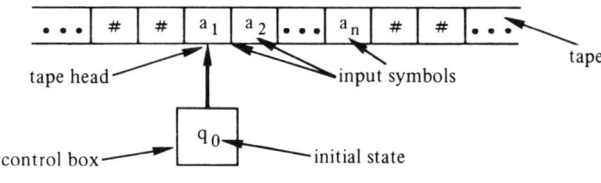

Figure 10-1

A finite automaton at the beginning of a computation

The computations of an fa are directed by a "program," which constitutes part of the definition of that automaton. The program consists of a finite number of triples of the form (a_i, q_j, q_k), where q_j and q_k are states of the automaton and a_i is an input symbol. An instruction (a_i, q_j, q_k) is interpreted in the following way. If the automaton is in state q_j and the tape head is reading the symbol a_i on the input tape, then the state can be switched to q_k (possibly identical with q_j) while the tape head is moved one square to the right. The instruction, if there is one, for this new state-symbol combination is then carried out, and the computation continues in this way until the automaton is forced to halt by arriving at a combination of internal state and input symbol for which there is no instruction. This could occur while the tape head is scanning any one of the input symbols, but in any event the automaton necessarily halts when it moves off the rightmost symbol of the input string and onto a blank. The blank is not considered to be a symbol of the input alphabet, and thus there are no instructions of the form $(\#, q_i, q_j)$. If the computation halts before the end of the tape is reached, the automaton is said to have *blocked*, and this signifies that the input tape is rejected. If the automaton reads the entire input string and halts on the first blank symbol to the right, then acceptance or rejection of the input string depends on the state in which the automaton has halted. If it is one of a designated set of "final" or "accepting" states, the input is accepted; otherwise, it is rejected.

Example 10-1: Input strings are over the alphabet $\{a, b\}$; the states of the automaton are q_0, q_1, and q_2; the initial state is q_0; and the final states are q_0 and q_2. The instructions, which are numbered only for convenience of reference, are the following:

1. (a, q_0, q_1)
2. (b, q_1, q_2)
3. (a, q_2, q_2)
4. (b, q_2, q_2)

Computation 1:

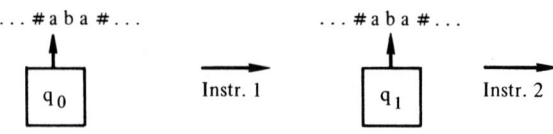

Initial configuration

Halt. All symbols have been read, and q_2 is a final state; therefore, the input tape *aba* is accepted.

Computation 2:

Initial configuration

Halt. There is no instruction beginning with a and q_1. Not all the tape has been read, so it is rejected.

Computation 3:

Initial configuration

Halt. All symbols have been read, but since q_1 is not a final state, the input is rejected.

Problem: Determine whether the automaton of Example 10-1 accepts or rejects each of the following input strings: *aa, ba, abaa, abab.* Can you describe the set of all input strings that this automaton accepts?

1. State Diagrams of Finite Automata

A revealing representation for an fa, called a *state diagram*, can be constructed in the following way. Each state of the automaton is represented by a circle labeled with the name of the state. For each instruction (a_i, q_j, q_k) an arrow is drawn from q_j to q_k and labeled with the symbol a_i. The final

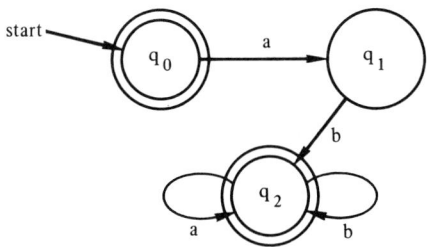

Figure 10-2

State diagram for the fa of Example 10-1

states are enclosed by an additional circle, and the initial state is marked by an arrow labeled with the word "start." The state diagram corresponding to the fa of Example 10-1 is shown in Fig. 10-2.

It is easy to trace the steps of a computation by an fa with such a diagram. For example, to follow the moves of the automaton of Example 10-1 in the first computation, we start in state q_0 and then pass to state q_1 reading an *a*. The next move is from q_1 to q_2, reading a *b*; and when the final *a* is read, the automation returns to state q_2. Since there are no more symbols in the input string, the automaton halts, and since q_2 is a final state, the string is accepted.

In tracing the second computation of Example 10-1 by means of the diagram, we note that there is no exit from state q_1 when *a* is the input symbol. Therefore, the computation blocks at this point, and the input is rejected. In the third computation, the entire tape, which consists of the single symbol *a*, is read, and the automaton halts in state q_1. Since this is not a final state, the tape is rejected.

2. Deterministic versus Nondeterministic Finite Automata

At any given point in a computation the next move is determined by the input symbol being read, the current state, and the instruction, if any, that applies. If for every state-symbol pair there is at most one next move, the fa is said to be *deterministic*. That is, an fa is deterministic if and only if for all input symbols a_i and all states q_j, q_k, q_l, if (a_i, q_j, q_k) and (a_i, q_j, q_l) are instructions of the automaton, then $q_k = q_l$. In a nondeterministic fa the next move from a state-symbol pair is in general to any one of a set of states; i.e., for some a_i and q_j there may be a number of instructions (a_i, q_j, q_k), $(a_i, q_j, q_l), \ldots, (a_i, q_j, q_r)$, where $q_k, q_l, \ldots, q_r$ are all distinct. In a deterministic fa each such set has either one member or it is empty; thus, the deterministic finite automata are a proper subclass of the nondeterministic finite automata.

The fa represented by the state diagram in Fig. 10-3 is nondeterministic since in state q_1, reading input symbol b, the automaton can enter either q_1 or q_2.

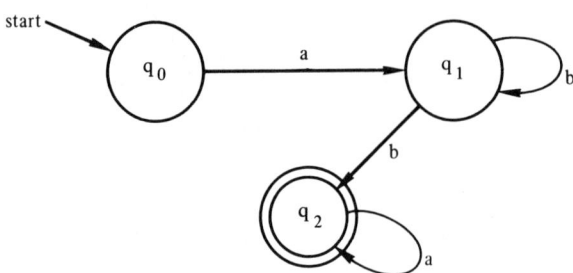

Figure 10-3

A nondeterministic fa

The notion of accepting an input tape must be modified in the case of nondeterministic automata. The automaton of Fig. 10-3, for example, allows two distinct computational paths for the input tape ab, one ending in q_1, a nonaccepting state, and the other ending in q_2, an accepting state. By our previous formulation the tape would be accepted on one path and rejected on the other. To avoid such a contradiction, we say that an fa (deterministic or nondeterministic) accepts a given input string iff there is at least one computational path beginning in state q_0 such that the entire string is read and the automaton halts in an accepting state. By this definition, the automaton of Fig. 10-3 accepts the input string ab because of the existence of the computational path ending in state q_2.

Nondeterministic fa are neither more nor less powerful than deterministic fa in terms of the sets of strings they are able to accept. For every nondeterministic fa there is a deterministic fa that accepts exactly the same set of strings. Such automata are said to be *equivalent*. We omit the proof of this equivalence; it can be found, for example, in Hopcroft and Ullman (1969, pp. 31–32). The theorem is originally from Rabin and Scott (1959) and Chomsky and Miller (1958).

The state diagram of a deterministic fa that is equivalent to the nondeterministic automaton of Fig. 10-3 is shown in Fig. 10-4. The language accepted by each is $\{a\} \cdot \{b\} \cdot \{b\}^* \cdot \{a\}^*$.

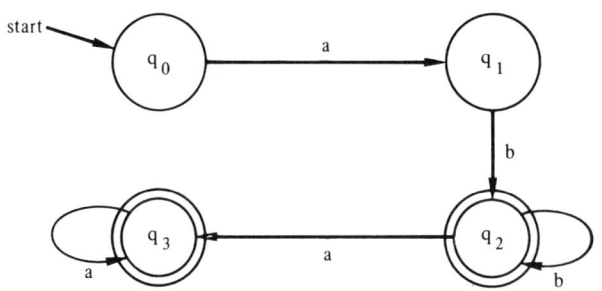

Figure 10-4

Deterministic fa equivalent to the nondeterministic fa of Fig. 10-3

3. Formal Definition of Deterministic Finite Automata

DEFINITION: A *deterministic finite automaton* is a configuration $(K, \Sigma, \delta, q_0, F)$, where

K is a finite, nonempty set of states

Σ is a finite, nonempty set, the input alphabet

δ is a partial function from $\Sigma^* \times K$ into K as given in (10-3) below

q_0 is a designated member of K, the initial state

F is a subset of K, the set of final states.

The partial function δ takes as its arguments a pair consisting of a string on the input alphabet and a state. Given such a pair, if δ is defined at this argument, the value is a state in K. In terms of our intuitive conception of an fa, the value of δ at argument (x, q_i) is the state the automaton ultimately reaches when it begins in state q_i, scanning the leftmost symbol of the string x, and computes according to its instructions until it has successfully scanned all the symbols of x. If the automaton blocks before reading all the input string, then δ is not defined at the argument (x, q_i). (This is why δ was said to be a partial function.)

The function δ is specified by a recursive definition, and accordingly it is called a *recursive function*. Recall that to define a function is to give a specification of how it pairs arguments and values. In a recursive function a finite number of argument-value pairs are stated in the base of the recursive definition, and in the recursion step the value at the nth argument is given in terms of the value of the function at the $(n-1)$st argument. As an example, consider the function f which maps a positive integer n into $n!$ (read 'n factorial') which is the product of the positive integers 1 through n. For example, $5! = 1 \cdot 2 \cdot 3 \cdot 4 \cdot 5 = 120$. This function can be defined recursively as follows:

(10-1)
$$\text{Base: } f(1) = 1$$
$$\text{Recursion: } f(n+1) = f(n) \cdot (n+1)$$

That is, the value of f at argument 1 is 1, and the value of f at argument $(n+1)$ is the product of $(n+1)$ and the value of the function at argument n. The value of $f(5)$ can be computed as follows:

(10-2)
$$f(1) = 1$$
$$f(2) = f(1) \cdot 2 = 1 \cdot 2 = 2$$
$$f(3) = f(2) \cdot 3 = 2 \cdot 3 = 6$$
$$f(4) = f(3) \cdot 4 = 6 \cdot 4 = 24$$
$$f(5) = f(4) \cdot 5 = 24 \cdot 5 = 120$$

The recursive definition of the function δ specifies the value for strings of length n in terms of the value of δ for strings of length $(n-1)$. Specifically, given an input string $a_1 a_2 \cdots a_{n-1} a_n$ and state q_i as arguments, the value of δ is given by

(10-3) $\qquad \delta(a_1 a_2 \cdots a_{n-1} a_n, q_i) = \delta(a_n, \delta(a_1 a_2 \cdots a_{n-1}, q_i))$

The value of $\delta(a_1 a_2 \cdots a_{n-1} a_n, q_i)$ is equal to $\delta(a_n, q_j)$, where q_j is the state that results from reading $a_1 a_2 \cdots a_{n-1}$ starting in state q_i. That is, $\delta(a_n, q_j)$ is just $\delta(a_n, \delta(a_1 a_2 \cdots a_{n-1}, q_i))$. The value of $\delta(a_1 a_2 \cdots a_{n-1}, q_i)$ can, in turn, be found from the value of $\delta(a_1 a_2 \cdots a_{n-2}, q_i)$, and so on, until finally the string in the argument consists of a single symbol, i.e., $\delta(a_1, q_i)$. The values of δ at these arguments form the base of the recursive definition of δ. In specifying anfsa one gives just these base values. The remainder of δ is then determined by the recursion step (10-3).

To illustrate, let us consider the fa of Example 10-1 and compute the value of δ at argument (abb, q_0). We first analyze $\delta(abb, q_0)$ as $\delta(b, \delta(ab, q_0))$, and this, in turn, as $\delta(b, \delta(b, \delta(a, q_0)))$. Thus,

(10-4) $\quad \delta(abb, q_0) = \delta(b, \delta(b, \delta(a, q_0)))$

From the instructions of the fa in Example 10-1 we find that $\delta(a, q_0) = q_1$. Substituting this value into (10-4), we have

(10-5) $\quad \delta(abb, q_0) = \delta(b, \delta(b, q_1))$

From instruction 4, $\delta(b, q_1) = q_2$. We substitute this in (10-5):

(10-6) $\quad \delta(abb, q_0) = \delta(b, q_2)$

Finally, by instruction 3,

(10-7) $\quad \delta(abb, q_0) = q_2$

The reader will observe that determining the value of $\delta(x, q_i)$ in this way is tantamount to tracing the steps of a computation symbol by symbol starting in state q_i. If the computation blocks before all the input symbols have been read, then there must be some argument (a_i, q_j) for which δ is undefined. Since this enters recursively into the specification of the value of δ for the entire input string, all subsequent values of δ will likewise be undefined.

We now give a formal statement of the notions of acceptance and rejection of input strings by a deterministic fa.

DEFINITION: *A deterministic fa* $M = (K, \Sigma, \delta, q_0, F)$ *accepts* **an input string** x **in** Σ^* **if and only if** $\delta(x, q_0) \in F$; *it rejects* x **if and only if** $\delta(x, q_0)$ **is not in** F **or is undefined.**

The formal definition of a nondeterministic fa is somewhat more complex since $\delta(a_i, q_j)$ in general has as a value not a single state but a set of states. To extend the definition of δ to strings of arbitrary length, we would then have to allow it to take as arguments pairs consisting of a string and a set of states. The details can be found in Hopcroft and Ullman (1969, p. 30).

4. *Finite Automata and Type 3 Grammars*

We are now ready to demonstrate the equivalence of finite automata and type 3 grammars. It is more convenient here to use the equivalent formulation for type 3 grammars—type 3.1 grammars—given in the preceding chapter. Recall that every rule of a type 3.1 grammar is of the form $A \to aB$ or $A \to a$, where a is a terminal symbol.

Suppose we are given a type 3.1 grammar $G = (V_N, V_T, \{S\}, P)$ generating $L(G)$. We proceed to construct an fa M that accepts exactly the strings in $L(G)$ as follows:

1. The input alphabet of M is V_T.

2. The states of M are the members of V_N plus a new symbol Q not in V_N.
3. For every rule of the form $A \to aB$ in G, we put the corresponding instruction (a, A, B) in M. For every rule of the form $A \to a$ in G, we put the corresponding instruction (a, A, Q) in M. M has no other instructions. (Note that M may, in general, be nondeterministic.)
4. S is the initial state of M.
5. Q is the only final state of M.

We now show that if $x \in L(G)$, x is accepted by M. Let $a_1 a_2 \cdots a_n$ be a terminal string generated by G. Then, since G is a type 3.1 grammar, there is a derivation beginning with S and ending with $a_1 a_2 \cdots a_n$ of the form

(10-8) $\quad S \Rightarrow a_1 A_1 \Rightarrow a_1 a_2 A_2 \Rightarrow \cdots \Rightarrow a_1 a_2 \cdots a_{n-1} A_{n-1} \Rightarrow a_1 a_2 \cdots a_{n-1} a_n$

for some nonterminal symbols $A_1, A_2, \ldots, A_{n-1}$ in V_N (not necessarily distinct). As required, there is one nonterminal at the right end of each line

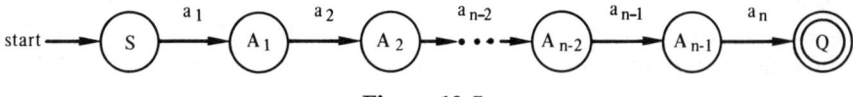

Figure 10-5

Portion of the state diagram of the fa M constructed from G corresponding to the derivation in (10-8)

of the derivation except the last one. For there to be such a derivation by G, G must contain the rules $S \to a_1 A_1$, $A_1 \to a_2 A_2, \ldots, A_{n-2} \to a_{n-1} A_{n-1}$, and $A_{n-1} \to a_n$. In the fa M constructed from G there will therefore appear the corresponding instructions (a_1, S, A_1), $(a_2, A_1, A_2), \ldots, (a_{n-1}, A_{n-2}, A_{n-1})$, and (a_n, A_{n-1}, Q). These are represented schematically in the state diagram in Fig. 10-5.

From the diagram it is readily apparent that M accepts the string $a_1 a_2 \cdots a_n$ by a computation that starts in state S and passes through the indicated sequence of states, ending in the final state Q. Thus, if x is generated by G, it is accepted by M.

To prove the converse we take the steps of this argument in reverse. Let $x = a_1 a_2 \cdots a_n$ be a string accepted by M. Then there is a sequence of states $S, A_1, \ldots, A_{n-1}$ (not necessarily distinct) such that (a_1, S, A_1), (a_2, A_1, A_2), $\ldots, (a_{n-1}, A_{n-2}, A_{n-1})$, (a_n, A_{n-1}, Q) are instructions of M. From the manner in which M was constructed we know that the corresponding rules $S \to a_1 A_1$, $A_1 \to a_2 A_2, \ldots, A_{n-2} \to a_{n-1} A_{n-1}$, $A_{n-1} \to a_n$ are in G. Thus, there is a derivation of $a_1 a_2 \cdots a_n$ beginning with S by the rules of G. Therefore, every string accepted by M is generated by G.

We shall say that an automaton and a grammar are *equivalent* just in case the automaton accepts exactly the set of terminal string generated by the latter. What we have just shown is that for every type 3.1 grammar there is an equivalent (nondeterministic) fa. To demonstrate the complete equivalence of these devices we must also prove the converse: For every nondeterministic fa there is an equivalent type 3.1 grammar. The method of proof is similar. Let $M = (K, \Sigma, \delta, q_0, F)$ be a nondeterministic fa. We construct the grammar G as follows:

1. $V_T = \Sigma$
2. $V_N = K$
3. For every instruction (a, q_i, q_j) in M, G contains the rule $q_i \to aq_j$. If q_j is a final state, G contains the rule $q_i \to a$ as well. G has no other rules.
4. The initial symbol of G is q_0.

If $a_1 a_2 \cdots a_n$ is accepted by M, there is some sequence of states $q_0, q_1, \ldots, q_n$ such that q_n is a final state and the instructions $(a_1, q_0, q_1), (a_2, q_1, q_2), \ldots, (a_n, q_{n-1}, q_n)$ are in M. G, therefore, contains the corresponding rules $q_0 \to a_1 q_1, q_1 \to a_2 q_2, \ldots, q_{n-2} \to a_{n-1} q_{n-1}, q_{n-1} \to a_n$, and hence there is a derivation of the terminal string $a_1 a_2 \cdots a_n$ by the rules of G. Conversely, if $a_1 a_2 \cdots a_n$ is generated by G, then corresponding to each of the rules involved in the derivation there is an instruction in M such that the sequence of instructions leads to acceptance of $a_1 a_2 \cdots a_n$. Thus, we have

THEOREM 10-1: The type 3.1 languages are exactly the sets accepted by the nondeterministic finite automata.

In view of the aforementioned equivalence of deterministic and nondeterministic fa's and Theorem 9-1 establishing the equivalence of type 3 and type 3.1 languages, we can state

COROLLARY 10-1: The type 3 languages are exactly the sets accepted by the deterministic finite automata.

Example 10-2:

G: $S \to aA$
$A \to bS$
$A \to aB$
$B \to c$

The equivalent fa contains the productions

(a, S, A)
(b, A, S)
(a, A, B)
(c, B, Q)

The state diagram of M is the following:

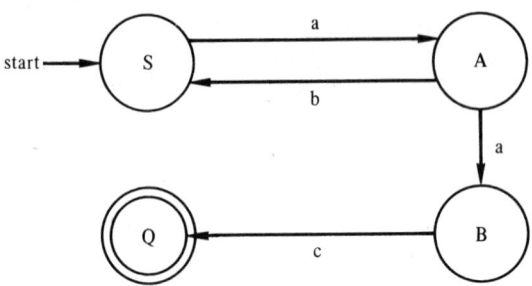

G generates and M accepts the language $\{a\} \cdot \{ba\}^* \cdot \{ac\}$.

Example 10-3: Let M be the fa of Example 10-1. The equivalent type 3 grammar G contains the productions

$q_0 \to aq_1$

$q_2 \to aq_2$

$q_2 \to bq_2$

$q_1 \to bq_2$

$q_2 \to a$

$q_2 \to b$

$q_1 \to b$

M accepts, for example, the string *abab*. This is generated by G by the derivation $q_0 \Rightarrow aq_1 \Rightarrow abq_2 \Rightarrow abaq_2 \Rightarrow abab$.

5. *Finite Automata as Generators*

We have described finite automata as devices that accept or reject input strings. It would do just as well to regard an fa as a device that starts in the initial state q_0 with a blank tape and moves from state to state printing a symbol on successive squares of the tape with each transition. To do this, we can reinterpret each triple (a_i, q_j, q_k) as an instruction for the automaton to change from state q_j to state q_k while printing the symbol a_i on the tape and then move the printing head one square to the right. When the fa is in a final state, it is permitted to halt or it may continue to another state that is allowed by the instructions. An fa interpreted in this way prints a string and halts in a final state just in case that string would have been accepted by the fa interpreted as an acceptor. This is easily seen by tracing the computation of an fa on its state diagram. If there is a sequence of state transitions beginning with the initial state and ending in a final state that accepts a string x, then the same sequence of transitions corresponds to the generation of x when the fa is interpreted as a generator. For every computation by an acceptor that blocks or ends in a nonfinal state, there is a corresponding computation in the generator in which a string may be printed on the output tape but which is not, technically speaking, "generated" by this computation.

6. Finite Automata and Regular Sets

In the preceding chapter we proved (Theorem 9-2) that the regular sets are included in the type 3 languages, and we showed in Sec. 4 above that the type 3 languages and the sets accepted by finite automata are identical. We next prove that the sets accepted by finite automata are included in the regular sets. It will follow then that the regular sets, the type 3 languages, and the languages accepted by finite automata are all identical.

THEOREM 10-2: The class of languages accepted by the finite automata is included in the smallest class that contains all finite sets and is closed under union, product, and star (i.e., the regular sets).

Proof: It will be helpful in following the proof to refer to the fa in Fig. 10-6 as an example.

Let $M = (K, \Sigma, \delta, q_1, F)$ be an fa (either deterministic or nondeterministic) with states $q_1, q_2, \ldots, q_n$ and initial state q_1. We assume that M is represented in the form of a state diagram. We denote by R_{ij}^k the set of all strings the automaton can read in passing from state q_i to state q_j in such a way that the path goes *through* (i.e., enters and subsequently leaves) no state whose subscript is greater than k. For the automaton in Fig. 10-6, for example, R_{12}^1 is the set consisting of the single string a, which is the string read in passing from state q_1 to state

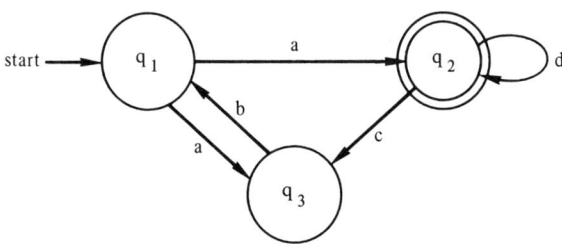

Figure 10-6

Example to illustrate the proof of Theorem 10-2

q_2. All other paths from q_1 to q_2 require entering and leaving states q_2 or q_3, and these are ruled out by the superscript of R^1_{12}, which restricts the paths to those that enter and leave no state q_n for $n > 1$. R^2_{12} allows all paths from q_1 to q_2 that do not enter and leave q_3. Thus, R^2_{12} is the set $\{a\} \cdot \{d\}^*$. In this notation, R^0_{ij} denotes the set of strings that correspond to the direct passage from q_i to q_j in one step. For example, in Fig. 10-6 $R^0_{23} = \{c\}$. In general, R^k_{ij} is allowed to be the null set, e.g., R^0_{32} in Fig. 10-6.

R^k_{ij} can be defined recursively as follows:

For all i and j,

(10-9)   Base: $R^0_{ij} = \{a \mid \delta(a, q_i) = q_j\}$

Recursion: $R^k_{ij} = R^{k-1}_{ij} \cup (R^{k-1}_{ik} \cdot (R^{k-1}_{kk})^* \cdot R^{k-1}_{kj})$

The recursion can be interpreted in the following way. The set of strings which take the fa from q_i to q_j without passing through a state higher than q_k consists of (1) those which don't pass through q_k at all, i.e., which pass through no state higher than q_{k-1} (this set is represented by R^{k-1}_{ij}) and (2) those which do pass through state q_k but through no state with subscript higher than k. The latter set can be analyzed as the product of three sets: (1) those strings that take M from q_i to state q_k for the first time (R^{k-1}_{ik}); (2) all paths that take M from q_k to a first return to q_k, repeated any number of times $[(R^{k-1}_{kk})^*]$; and (3) all strings that take M from its last exit from q_k up to q_j(R^{k-1}_{kj}). For example, in Fig. 10-6, R^2_{13} is given by

(10-10) $R^2_{13} = R^1_{13} \cup (R^1_{12} \cdot (R^1_{22})^* \cdot R^1_{23})$

R^1_{13}, the set of all strings read by the automaton in going from q_1 to q_3 without entering and leaving a state numbered higher than q_1, is the set $\{a\}$. Next, R^1_{12} is $\{a\}$; R^1_{22} is $\{d\}$; and R^1_{23} is $\{c\}$.

The set of strings $L(M)$ accepted by M is given by the union of all the R^n_{1p} such that q_p is a final state. We show that $L(M)$, the set of strings accepted by M, is a regular set by showing that every R^k_{ij} is. Then $L(M)$, being the union of some of these, must also be a regular set since the regular sets are closed under union.

We prove that for all i, j, and k, R^k_{ij} is a regular set by induction on the value of k. First, for all i and j, R^0_{ij} is regular since it is finite. This establishes the base. Next, by the recursive definition of R^k_{ij}, it can be expressed in terms of four sets, R^{k-1}_{ij}, R^{k-1}_{ik}, R^{k-1}_{kk}, and R^{k-1}_{kj}, all with superscript $k - 1$, combined by the operations of union, product, and star. Since the class of regular sets is closed under these operations, if all the R^{k-1}_{ij} are regular, then so are all the R^k_{ij}. This completes the induction step. The conclusion is that R^k_{ij} is regular for all i, j, and k. Therefore, R^n_{1p}, in particular, is regular for given n, where q_p is a final state, and the union of all such R_{1p}^n, which is the language accepted by M, is also regular. This completes the proof.

To illustrate once again with Fig. 10-6, the language accepted by this automaton is R_{12}^3. (There is only one final state, so there is only one set with which to form the union of all R_{1p}^3.) When all the computations are carried out, we have

(10-11) $\quad R_{12}^3 = (\{a\} \cup (\{a\} \cdot \{d\}^* \cdot \{d\})) \cup ((\{a\} \cup (\{a\} \cdot \{d\}^* \cdot \{c\}))$
$\cdot (\{ba\} \cup (\{ba\} \cdot \{d\}^* \cdot \{c\}))^* \cdot (\{ba\} \cup (\{ba\} \cdot \{d\}^* \cdot \{d\})))$

which is a set composed of finite sets combined by the operations of union, product, and star. Thus, R_{12}^3 is a regular set.

7. Finite Automata and Equivalence Relations

We conclude this section on finite automata by proving a very useful theorem in which an fa is viewed as effecting a partition of the set of all input strings into equivalence classes. The essential point of the theorem is that the number of these equivalence classes is always finite—in fact, no greater than the number of states in the automaton. With this general result it is simple to prove that certain languages, for example the mirror image language on $\{a, b\}^*$, are not type 3.

The theorem is much easier to state and to prove if we stipulate that every fa is first converted to an equivalent fa that is both deterministic and *complete*. In a complete fa, no matter what the current state and the current input symbol, there is always a next move available to it. Formally, for all a_i in Σ and q_j in K, there is some q_k in K such that $\delta(a_i, q_j) = q_k$. Thus, a complete fa never blocks before the entire input tape has been read.

If a given fa is not complete, it is easy to turn it into an equivalent one that is. We simply add a new "absorbing" state (call it q_a) and let all previously blocking symbol-state pairs now lead directly to q_a. We must also allow transitions *from* q_a, and these we construct as "self loops" leading immediately back to q_a for any input symbol. q_a is taken to be a nonfinal state, and thus any string that formerly would have been rejected because the fa blocked before reaching the end of the tape will also be rejected in the new automaton, but now because the automaton reads the whole tape and ends in a nonfinal state. The set of accepted strings is unchanged, however, since the computational paths through a whole tape ending in one of the final states are just as they were before. Therefore, the new complete fa is equivalent to the original.

Figure 10-7 shows how the fa of Fig. 10-2 has been made complete by the addition of the new state q_a and the transitions $(b, q_0, q_a), (a, q_1, q_a), (a, q_a, q_a),$

and (b, q_a, q_a). With input tape *aab*, for example, the fa of Fig. 10-2 blocks (cf. Computation 2 of Example 10-1), while the fa of Fig. 10-7 rejects by ending in q_a.

For every symbol-state pair a complete fa has at least one next move, and a deterministic fa has at most one. Thus, if an fa is both deterministic and complete, it has for every symbol-state pair *exactly one* next move. The advantage of arranging the fa in this way is that every input string on Σ^* is

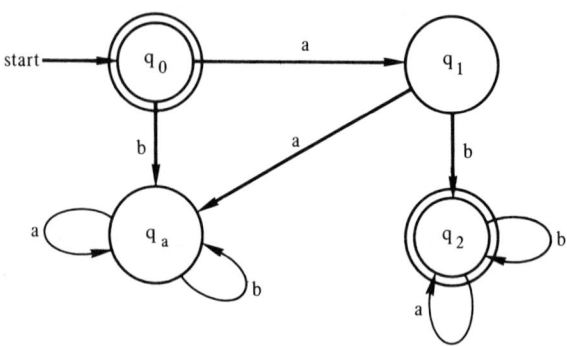

Figure 10-7

Complete fa equivalent to the fa of Fig. 10-2

sure to be read to the end, and, furthermore, the input string determines uniquely the state in which the fa ultimately halts. That is, for every x in Σ^*, $\delta(x, q_0)$ is defined and has a unique value.

For any given deterministic complete fa $M = (K, \Sigma, \delta, q_0, F)$, we define the following important relation R_M on pairs of strings in Σ^*.

(10-12) $\quad R_M = \{(x, y) \in \Sigma^* \times \Sigma^* \mid \delta(x, q_0) = \delta(y, q_0)\}$

That is, x stands in relation R_M to y just in case both x and y take M from q_0 to the same state. For example, if M is the fa of Fig. 10-7, $(abb, ab) \in R_M$ since both *abb* and *ab* take M from q_0 to q_2.

By the definition of R_M, $(x, x) \in R_M$ for all x in Σ^*, and if $(x, y) \in R_M$, then $(y, x) \in R_M$ for all x and y in Σ^*. Further, for all x, y, and z in Σ^*, if $(x, y) \in R_M$ and $(y, z) \in R_M$, then $(x, z) \in R_M$. Thus, R_M is an equivalence relation. Because M is complete, every string in Σ^* is a member of one of the equivalence classes; thus, R_M effects a partitioning of Σ^*. The number of cells in the partition is at most the number of states of the fa—at most, because there may be states of M that are inaccessible from q_0 (in the definition of an fa we have not excluded the possibility that there are states that are never used in any computation). If there are such states, there would be no strings in Σ^* that take M there ultimately and thus no corresponding equivalence class. In any event, since the number of states in M is finite, the number of equivalence classes in the partition induced by R_M is also finite. An equivalence relation that induces a partition composed of a finite number of equivalence classes is said to be of *finite index*.

For example, if M is the fa of Fig. 10-7, R_M induces the partition $\Pi = \{P_0, P_1, P_2, P_3\}$ in $\{a, b\}^*$ where

$P_0 = \{e\}$

$P_1 = \{a\}$

$P_2 = \{x \mid x \text{ is a string beginning with } ab\}$

$P_3 = \{x \mid x \text{ is a string beginning with } aa \text{ or } b\}$

P_0 is the set of strings that take M from q_0 to q_0; P_1, those that take M from q_0 to q_1, etc. Since Π is a finite set, R_M is of finite index. Observe that we are here concerned only with the *number of equivalence classes in the partition*, not with the finiteness or infiniteness of the equivalence classes themselves. P_0 and P_1 are finite sets, while P_2 and P_3 are infinite. The only connection with the finite index of R_M is this: If an infinite set is partitioned into a finite number of equivalence classes, then at least one of the equivalence classes must necessarily be infinite.

The relation R_M also has the property of *right invariance*. This means that if $(x, y) \in R_M$, the strings formed by concatenating any string z in Σ^* to the right of x and y, i.e., xz and yz, also stand in relation R_M. This is apparent if we consider that $(x, y) \in R_M$ means that both x and y take M from q_0 to the same state (call it q_i). Now because M is deterministic and complete, for any string z in Σ^* there is a unique computational path beginning in q_i and ending in some state q_j (possibly identical to q_i, of course). Therefore, xz takes M from q_0 to q_j and likewise yz takes M from q_0 to q_j; i.e., $(xz, yz) \in R_M$. In the fa of Fig. 10-7, for example, we note that $(b, aa) \in R_M$. Because R_M is right invariant, (ba, aaa), (bb, aab), $(baa, aaaa)$, ... are also in R_M.

We now shift the focus somewhat to define a new relation R_L. We assume that we are given some language L in Σ^* (whether or not L is finite state doesn't matter at this point), and we define R_L as follows:

(10-13) $\quad R_L = \{(x, y) \in \Sigma^* \times \Sigma^* \mid (\forall z \in \Sigma^*)(xz \in L \leftrightarrow yz \in L)\}$

In words, x and y stand in relation R_L just in case every string z in Σ^* when concatenated to the right of both x and y produces a new pair of strings xz and yz that are either both in L or else both outside L. The reason for defining such a strange-looking relation will hopefully become clear as we proceed. We first want to show, however, that R_L as defined is an equivalence relation.

(Reflexivity) For all x in Σ^*, $(x, x) \in R_L$ because in this case $(\forall z \in \Sigma^*)(xz \in L \leftrightarrow xz \in L)$ is trivially true. (Symmetry) If $(x, y) \in R_L$, then by definition $(\forall z \in \Sigma^*)(xz \in L \leftrightarrow yz \in L)$. The latter is logically equivalent to $(\forall z \in \Sigma^*)(yz \in L \leftrightarrow xz \in L)$, i.e., $(y, x) \in R_L$. (Transitivity) If $(x, y) \in R_L$ and $(y, w) \in R_L$, then, by definition, for all z in Σ^*, $(xz \in L \leftrightarrow yz \in L)$ and $(yz \in L \leftrightarrow wz \in L)$. Thus, $(xz \in L \leftrightarrow wz \in L)$, i.e., $(x, w) \in R_L$. Note that this proof proceeds independently of the exact nature of L.

The character of the equivalence classes induced by R_L is difficult to describe succinctly, but we might try something like the following: Given L, the members of each equivalence class that R_L partitions Σ^* into are equivalent with respect to their potentiality for being turned into members of L by further concatenation of strings to the right. R_L equivalent strings might be called equivalent "left beginnings," which under every possible right continuation share the same fate with respect to whether or not they become strings in L.

To illustrate, suppose L is the set of all strings in $\{a, b\}^*$ that contain exactly two (not necessarily contiguous) occurrences of a. The strings abb and bab, for example, are R_L equivalent. Right continuations such as a, ba, ab, abb, bab, etc. (containing exactly one occurrence of a) convert both into strings of L, while all other continuations convert both into strings which are not in L. On the other hand, abb and baa are not R_L equivalent since the continuation a, for example, converts the former into $abba$, which is in L, but converts the latter into $baaa$, which is not.

To take another example, let $L = xcx$ ($x \in \{a, b\}^*$), i.e., the language composed of any string in $\{a, b\}^*$ followed by one c followed by an identical copy of the first string. Now take any string $y \in \{a, b\}^*$ and let us ask if there are any other strings that are R_L equivalent to it. There are none, since for any $z \in \{a, b, c\}^*$ distinct from y there are right continuations of y, e.g., cy, that turn it into a string of L, while zcy cannot be in L since $z \neq y$. There are an infinite number of such strings y in $\{a, b, c\}^*$, each occupying an equivalence class of its own. Thus, in this case R_L induces a partition of Σ^* that is of infinite index.

When we take L to be the language accepted by the fa in Fig. 10-7, we discover that R_L induces exactly the same partition as R_M. The crux of the theorem we are about to prove is that there is always a certain close relationship between R_M and R_L whenever L is a finite-state language (and M is an fa which accepts L). The fact that R_M and R_L happen to be identical in this instance is a result of a special feature of the fa in Fig. 10-7, viz., that it is a *minimum-state* automaton in the sense that there is no deterministic complete fa with fewer states which accepts L. In the more general case—where L is a finite-state language and M is not necessarily minimum state—R_M induces a partition which is a "refinement" of the partition induced by R_L. That is, the R_M equivalence classes are just further subdivisions of the R_L equivalence classes. This is the situation represented schematically in Fig. 10-8.

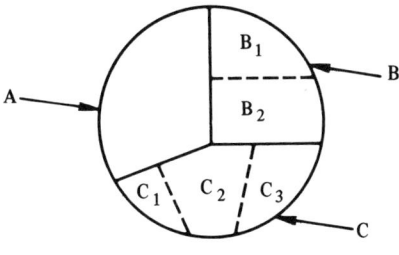

Figure 10-8

Schematic representation of a partition induced by R_L (solid lines) and a refinement of this partition (broken lines) induced by R_M

The circle represents Σ^*. The solid lines within the circle represent a partitioning by R_L into three equivalence classes (here labeled A, B, and C). The broken lines represent the "refined" partitioning effected by R_M, which contains six equivalence classes $(A, B_1, B_2, C_1, C_2, C_3)$ rather than three. Formally, if Π and Θ are partitions of a set A, Π is a *refinement* of Θ iff every cell of Π is a subset of some cell of Θ. There is of course the trivial case of refinement in which the partitions are identical—the case just encountered with the fa of Fig. 10-7. We are now ready to state the following theorem.

THEOREM 10-3: Given a finite set Σ and a set of strings L in Σ^*, L is a finite-state language if and only if R_L (as defined in (10-13)) is of finite index.

Proof: We first show that if L is finite state, the partition induced in Σ^* by R_M is a refinement of that induced by R_L. If L is finite state, it is accepted by some deterministic complete fa $M = (K, \Sigma, \delta, q_0, F)$. Let R_M be defined for this automaton as in (10-12). Recall that R_M partitions Σ^* into one equivalence class for each state of M that can be reached from q_0. L is just the set of all those strings that take M from q_0 to some final state, and thus L is the union of all the equivalence classes induced by R_M that correspond to the final states of M. Now suppose (x, y) is in R_M. Since R_M is right invariant, for all $z \in \Sigma^*$, $(xz, yz) \in R_M$; i.e., xz and yz take M from q_0 to the same state. If this happens to be a final state, then both xz and yz are in L; otherwise, neither is in L. Thus, if $(x, y) \in R_M$, then for all z in Σ^*, $xz \in L \leftrightarrow yz \in L$; that is, (x, y) is also in R_L. Thus, if x and y are in the same equivalence class of R_M they are in the same equivalence class of R_L. Hence, each equivalence class of R_M is a subset of an equivalence class of R_L, and the partition induced by R_M is a refinement of that induced by R_L. Since R_M is of finite index (there being a finite number of states in M) and since R_L is of index no greater than the index of R_M, R_L is also of finite index. This establishes the "only if" part of the theorem.

We must now prove the "if" part: If R_L is of finite index, L is a finite-state language. We do this by showing how to convert the partitioning effected by R_L into an fa that accepts L. Let each of the finite number of equivalence classes induced by R_L be denoted in the usual way; i.e., '$[x]$' denotes the equivalence class that contains the string x. Let each of these equivalence classes be a state of an fa M'. The initial state is $[e]$, the equivalence class that contains the empty string (there must be such a class since R_L partitions the entire set Σ^*). M' is to be constructed so that any string x in Σ^* takes M' from the initial state to state $[x]$. To get M' to accept just the strings of L, then, we take as the final states of M' all those equivalence classes $[x]$ such that $x \in L$. One might wonder whether this is a legitimate stipulation. What if some class $[x]$ such that $x \in L$ also contained another string y such that $y \notin L$? Would $[x]$ then become a final state or not? The answer is that such a situation can never arise. By definition, $(x, y) \in R_L$ if and only if $(\forall z \in \Sigma^*)(xz \in L \leftrightarrow yz \in L)$. In particular, z can be the null string, and thus if $(x, y) \in R_L$, then $x \in L \leftrightarrow y \in L$. This means that for any equivalence class induced by R_L either all the members are in L or else all of them are outside L. Therefore, we can select as final states of M' all those equivalence classes having all their members in L, and each of the other equivalence classes, which is guaranteed to contain no string of L, becomes a nonfinal state.

It remains to be shown that the next-move function δ' can be defined so that M' works in the desired fashion. The crucial step here is to show that R_L, like R_M, is right invariant. By the definition of R_L, $(x, y) \in R_L$ iff $(xz \in L \leftrightarrow yz \in L)$ for any string z in Σ^* whatever. We can, therefore, suppose that z consists of two parts, i.e., $z = vw$, and write equivalently

(10-14) $\quad (x, y) \in R_L \quad$ iff $\quad (\forall v \in \Sigma^*)(\forall w \in \Sigma^*)(xvw \in L \leftrightarrow yvw \in L)$.

But by the definition of R_L the right side of (10-14) is equivalent to $(\forall v \in \Sigma^*)(xv, yv) \in R_L$. Thus, we have

(10-15) $\quad (x, y) \in R_L \quad$ iff $\quad (\forall v \in \Sigma^*)(xv, yv) \in R_L$

and R_L is right invariant. This means, in particular, that if all the members of some equivalence class $[x]$ induced by R_L were to have a single symbol, say a, concatenated on the right, the resulting strings would all fall together in the same equivalence class, namely, the class

[xa]. Therefore we can, without contradiction, construct δ' to map any pair consisting of the symbol a and the state $[x]$ into state $[xa]$; i.e., $\delta'(a, [x]) = [xa]$, for all $a \in \Sigma$ and all $[x]$ in the partition induced by R_L. The fa M' now accepts just the intended strings since for all x in Σ^*, $\delta'(x, [e]) = [xe] = [x]$; i.e., x takes M' from the initial state to state $[x]$. x is accepted iff $[x]$ is a final state, that is, just in case x is in L. This completes the proof.

Since this theorem is a rather complex and subtle one, it may help to try to clarify the intuitive picture of the relationship among an fa, the language it accepts, and the relations R_L and R_M.

At any point in a computation an fa "sees" only the current state and the current input symbol. Whatever has gone before—the string that took the fa from the initial state to the current state—is past history to the automaton and has no effect on its subsequent operations. In this sense all the strings that might have brought the fa from q_0 to the current state are equivalent—equivalent, that is, with respect to the next step of the computation. Clearly, every state of the fa that can be "current," i.e., that can be reached from q_0, has associated with it some such set of strings that "look" equivalent to it. This is the partitioning induced by R_M. (Cf. the discussion in Chapter 9 of the inadequacy of right-linear grammars to generate xx^{-1}.)

Now let us focus attention on some state q_i as the current state during some computation, and let x and y be strings that look equivalent to q_i. Imagine any string z added to the right of both x and y. The fa processes z in a fixed way (the fa is assumed to be deterministic and complete) and ends in either a final or a nonfinal state. Therefore, the fa either accepts both xz and yz as being in the language L or else it rejects both as being outside L. The same sort of argument can be given for every accessible state of the fa and the sets of strings that look equivalent to each of those states. This gives us the result that when strings stand in relation R_M to each other (they look equivalent to some state of the fa), they also stand in relation R_L to each other (right continuations either put all of them in L or all of them outside L). That is, the R_M equivalence classes are subsets of the R_L equivalence classes.

If an R_L equivalence class contains more than one R_M equivalence class, this means that the fa happens to have more distinct classes of equivalent-looking strings than are actually required to separate strings in L from those not in L. In other words, in such a case the fa unnecessarily keeps separate two or more states and their associated equivalence classes of strings which are in fact equivalent with respect to right continuations. It is the R_L equivalence classes, then, that correspond to the states of the minimum-state automaton accepting L.

With Theorem 10-3 we can now prove that the language $L = xx^{-1}$ ($x \in \{a, b\}^*$; x^{-1} the mirror image of x) is not finite state. As an assumption to be proved false, suppose L is type 3. Then there is an fa accepting L and by Theorem 10-3 the equivalence relation R_L defined as in (10-13) is of finite index. Now in $\{a, b\}^*$ there are an infinite number of strings of the form $a^i bb$, for $i \geq 1$, and since R_L induces a partitioning of the entire set Σ^*, each of these strings is in some equivalence class. But if R_L is of finite index, there must be at least two strings $a^j bb$ and $a^k bb$, where $j \neq k$, in the same equivalence class; i.e., $(a^j bb, a^k bb) \in R_L$. By the definition of R_L it follows that, for all $z \in \{a, b\}^*$, $a^j bbz \in L \leftrightarrow a^k bbz \in L$. But this is false when $z = a^j$, because $a^j bba^j \in L$ but $a^k bba^j \notin L$. Therefore, L cannot be a type 3 language. On the other hand, L is type 2 since it is generated by the cfg in (9-43). Thus, we have proved that the class of type 3 languages is properly included in the type 2 languages.

THEOREM 10-4: There are type 2 languages that are not type 3.

Turing Machines

The finite automaton is perhaps the most restricted variety of automaton capable of accepting an infinite set of strings. At the other end of the scale is the Turing machine, an automaton that can carry out any set of operations that could reasonably be called a computation. A Turing machine (named for the English mathematician A. M. Turing) can also be visualized as having a control box, a tape marked off into squares, and a tape head that scans one square of the tape at a time. The Turing machine, however, can write on the tape as well as read from it, and it can move its reading head either left or right. As before, a computation begins in a distinguished initial state q_0 with the reading head over the leftmost nonblank symbol on the tape. We also assume that the tape is infinitely long to the left and right, that the initial string is composed of a finite number of symbols from the alphabet, and that all other squares are inscribed with a special blank symbol $\#$.

The moves of a Turing machine are directed by a finite set of quintuples of the form (a_i, q_j, q_k, a_l, X) where a_i and a_l are (possibly identical) symbols of the alphabet, q_j and q_k are (possibly identical) states, and X has either the value L (left) or R (right). Such a quintuple is interpreted in the following way: If the tape head is scanning a_i and the machine is in state q_j, then the state is changed to q_k, the symbol a_i is replaced by the symbol a_l, and the reading head is moved either one square to the left or one square to the right, depending on the value of X. The symbols being read and replaced may, in particular, be blanks, and the machine is therefore able to reach any portion of the tape beyond that on which the input string was written initially.

The machine halts only when it reaches a combination of symbol and state for which there is no quintuple allowing it to continue. A subset of the states of the machine is designated as final states, and if the machine halts in one of these, it accepts the input string given it originally. If it halts in a nonfinal state, the input string is, of course, rejected, but there is another possible situation in which inputs are said to be rejected. Since a Turing machine is not necessarily stopped by the blank symbols on the tape as an fa is, there is no guarantee that a given computation will ever halt. If the machine never halts for a given input string, that string is also rejected.

Example 10-4: The alphabet for input strings is $\{a, b\}$; the machine can read and write the blank $\#$ as well. The states are q_0, q_1, and q_2, where q_0 is the initial state and the set of final states is $\{q_0, q_2\}$. The instructions are

1. (a, q_0, q_1, a, R)
2. (a, q_1, q_2, b, L)
3. (a, q_2, q_0, b, R)
4. (b, q_0, q_0, b, R)
5. $(\#, q_1, q_1, a, R)$
6. $(\#, q_0, q_2, \#, R)$

Computation 1:

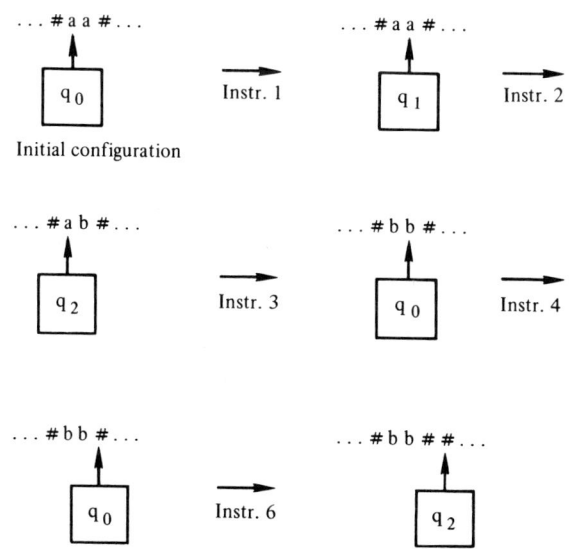

No instruction is now applicable. The machine halts, and since q_2 is a final state, the input tape aa is accepted.

276 *Automata*

Computation 2:

Initial configuration

No instruction is now applicable. The machine halts, and since q_1 is not a final state, the input tape is rejected.

Computation 3:

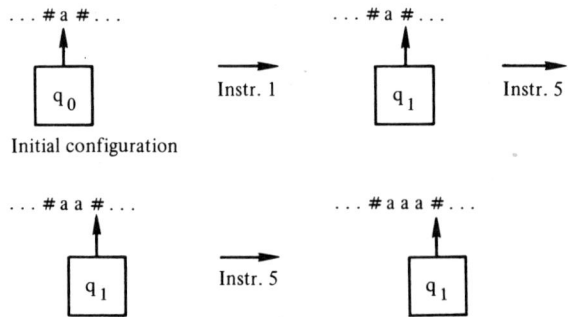

Initial configuration

The machine does not halt, but keeps moving right replacing blanks by a's. Therefore, the input tape is rejected.

1. Formal Definition of Turing Machines

DEFINITION:
A *Turing machine* is a sextuple $(K, \Sigma, \#, \delta, q_0, F)$, where
K is a finite set of states
Σ is a finite set, the input alphabet
$\#$, the blank symbol, is a symbol not in Σ
δ, the next-move function, is a partial function from

$$(\Sigma \cup \{\#\}) \times K \quad \text{to} \quad K \times (\Sigma \cup \{\#\}) \times \{L, R\}$$

q_0, the initial state, is a designated member of K
F, the set of final states, is a subset of K.

The function δ maps a pair consisting of a symbol and a state into a triple composed of a state, a symbol, and an indicator of the direction in which the tape head is to move. This more elaborate specification of the values of δ was unnecessary in the case of a finite automaton since it could not write on the tape and could move in only one direction. Turing machines are usually defined to be deterministic. Thus, for each pair (a_i, q_j) there is at most one triple in $K \times (\Sigma \cup \{\#\}) \times \{L, R\}$ that is its value. In general, δ may be undefined at some arguments.

In order to extend the definition of δ to arguments containing strings of input symbols, we define a *situation* of a Turing machine. This is a description of the entire tape and the internal state of the machine at any particular moment in the course of a computation. We denote a situation by a string of the form:

(10-16) $\quad a_1 a_2 \cdots a_{i-1} q_j a_i a_{i+1} \cdots a_n$

where the a's are tape symbols and q_j is a state in K. By convention, the state symbol is immediately to the left of the tape symbol currently being scanned by the reading head. Thus, in (10-16) the Turing machine is in state q_j, has the string $a_1 a_2 \cdots a_{i-1} a_i a_{i+1} \cdots a_n$ on its tape, and is scanning symbol a_i. Some of the a's at the far left or the far right may be blanks if the

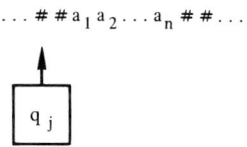

Figure 10-9

A Turing machine scanning the blank portion of its tape

reading head is currently scanning a blank. In order to keep the description of a situation finite, we include as a part of the tape at any moment only those blanks occurring between the reading head and the furthest nonblank symbol away from the reading head. For example, if a Turing machine is in the situation shown in Fig. 10-9, we would denote it by $q_j \#\# a_1 a_2 \cdots a_n$, and the tape would be said to consist of $\#\# a_1 a_2 \cdots a_n$.

A *move* of a Turing machine is the transition from one situation to another by means of applying one of its instructions. If the machine is in situation $a_1 a_2 \cdots a_{i-1} q_j a_i a_{i+1} \cdots a_n$ and it executes the instruction (a_i, q_j, q_k, a_l, R), then the resulting situation is $a_1 a_2 \cdots a_{i-1} a_l q_k a_{i+1} \cdots a_n$. We write

(10-17) $\quad a_1 a_2 \cdots a_{i-1} q_j a_i a_{i+1} \cdots a_n \mid_{\overline{T}} a_1 a_2 \cdots a_{i-1} a_l q_k a_{i+1} \cdots a_n$

to denote that Turing machine T goes from the situation on the left to that on the right in a single move. If the Turing machine is in situation $a_1 a_2 \cdots a_{i-1} q_j a_i a_{i+1} \cdots a_n$ and it executes a left-moving instruction (a_i, q_j, q_k, a_l, L), the resulting situation would be $a_1 a_2 \cdots q_k a_{i-1} a_l a_{i+1} \cdots a_n$, and we would write accordingly

(10-18) $\quad a_1 a_2 \cdots a_{i-1} q_j a_i a_{i+1} \cdots a_n \left|\overline{T}\right. a_1 a_2 \cdots q_k a_{i-1} a_l a_{i+1} \cdots a_n$

If situation $b_1 b_2 \cdots q_j b_l \cdots b_n$ results from situation $a_1 a_2 \cdots q_i a_k \cdots a_m$ by some finite number of moves (including zero moves), we write

(10-19) $\quad a_1 a_2 \cdots q_i a_k \cdots a_m \left|\overline{T}^*\right. b_1 b_2 \cdots q_j b_l \cdots b_n$

Given a Turing machine $T = (K, \Sigma, \#, \delta, q_0, F)$, the set of strings accepted by T is the set of all strings $a_1 a_2 \cdots a_n$ in Σ^* such that (1) $q_0 a_1 a_2 \cdots a_n \left|\overline{T}^*\right. b_1 b_2 \cdots q_i b_j \cdots b_m$ for some $b_1, b_2, \ldots, b_m$ in $\Sigma \cup \{\#\}$ and q_i in F; that is, the computation from the initial situation reaches a situation in which T is in a final state and (2) there is no instruction applicable; i.e., δ is undefined at the argument (b_j, q_i), and thus T has halted.

2. *Equivalent Formulations of Turing Machines*

There are many equivalent ways in which Turing machines can be defined. One can, for example, stipulate that the tape is infinite on the right but not on the left (or vice versa); or the machine can be endowed with any finite number of tapes that are infinite in one or both directions; or the machine can have a single multiple-track tape. It is also inessential that a Turing machine be deterministic since for every nondeterministic Turing machine there is an equivalent deterministic one.

We have formulated Turing machines, as we did originally the finite automata, as recognizers, i.e., as devices that accept or reject input strings. A Turing machine can also be regarded as generating a set A of strings if we modify its definition in the following way. Let T be a Turing machine that takes as input a tape on which there is some suitable encoding of a positive integer. This could be done, for example, by letting a tape consisting of n a's, surrounded by blanks, stand for the integer n. Given such a tape as input, T, when it halts in a final state, has on its tape some member of the set A. If T halts in a nonfinal state, the output tape is not a member of A, and, of course, if T never halts, there is no output tape as such. If T behaves in this fashion, it is said to *recursively enumerate* the set A, and A is said to be a *recursively enumerable* (r.e.) set. It is fairly straightforward to show that if A is recursively enumerated by some Turing machine T, then there is a Turing machine T' acting as a recognition device in the manner originally stated that accepts just the members of A. Conversely, if A is accepted by some Turing machine, then there is another Turing machine that recursively enumerates A. Thus, the r.e. sets are just those that are accepted by some Turing machine.

A Turing machine that recursively enumerates a set A can also be regarded as computing the values of a function f whose arguments are positive integers and whose values are strings in A. Since f may be undefined for some arguments, it is, in general, a partial function. A function having the property that its value can be computed by some Turing machine whenever it is defined but for which the Turing machine might not halt when the function is undefined is called a *partial recursive function*. The range of a partial recursive function is the recursively enumerable set generated by the Turing machine that computes the value of the function. Thus, the r.e. sets are just those sets that are the range of some partial recursive function.

3. *Recursive versus Recursively Enumerable Sets*

A Turing machine T that accepts a set A must eventually halt in a final state whenever it is given a member of A as its input. If T is given an input that is not in A, T might not halt. If T does halt for *every* input however—in a final state if the input is in A and in a nonfinal state otherwise—then A is said to be a *recursive* set (cf. the discussion following Theorem 9-3). In other words, A is a recursive set if and only if there is some Turing machine which accepts A and which eventually halts given any input whatever. In particular, it will halt given any string in Σ^*. This amounts to saying that both A and its complement with respect to Σ^*, i.e., $\Sigma^* - A$, are recursively enumerable sets. For if A is accepted by T and T halts for all inputs, then by interchanging final and nonfinal states of T and removing all transitions that involve a symbol not in Σ^*, we get a Turing machine T' that accepts all strings in Σ^* that T rejects and vice versa. On the other hand, given that A and $\Sigma^* - A$ are both r.e. sets accepted by Turing machines T_1 and T_2, respectively, it is a simple matter to merge T_1 and T_2 to form a new Turing machine T_3 which accepts any member of A and which halts in a nonfinal state when the input is in $\Sigma^* - A$. Accordingly, we have the following theorem:

THEOREM 10-5: A set of strings A on the alphabet Σ is recursive if and only if both A and $\Sigma^* - A$ are recursively enumerable.

If A is recognized (or generated) by some Turing machine T, we also say that T defines a *procedure* for recognizing (or generating) the members of A. In the everyday sense of the word we think of a "procedure" as a finite set of instructions that can be executed in a completely mechanical fashion, i.e., without the use of judgment, intuition, or other capacities that humans, but not computing machines, are generally considered to possess. A Turing machine is certainly an example of a device that carries out instructions in a completely mechanical fashion, and so every Turing machine represents a procedure. The question then arises whether everything that would intuitively be called a procedure can be carried out by some Turing machine. Most mathematicians believe that the answer is yes, but it is impossible either to prove or to disprove this since the question ultimately turns on what the imprecise term "procedure" will be taken to include. All we can say is that thus far every example of what most people would agree is a "procedure" can be represented by a Turing machine. The hypothesis that this will continue to be the case in the face of new examples is known as Church's Thesis (after the logician A. Church who proposed it).

If we accept this formulation of procedures in terms of Turing machines, then it follows that there may be cases in which a procedure, acting on some input, never terminates. This happens when the Turing machine that embodies the procedure fails to halt, given the same input. A procedure that is guaranteed to terminate after some finite number of steps, regardless of its input, is known as an *algorithm*. Accordingly, the statements of (10-20) are all equivalent:

(10-20)
1. A is accepted (generated) by some Turing machine.
2. A is a recursively enumerable set.
3. There is a procedure for recognizing (generating) the members of A.

and the statements of (10-21) are all equivalent:

(10-21)
1. Both A and its complement are recursively enumerable sets.
2. A is a recursive set.
3. There is an algorithm for recognizing (generating) the members of A.

Nothing that we have said here necessarily commits us to the view that there exist procedures that are not also algorithms or, equivalently, that there are recursively enumerable sets that are not recursive. An important result in Turing machine theory that we state here without proof is that such procedures and sets do exist (cf. Nelson, 1968, pp. 125–128; Hopcroft and Ullman, 1969, pp. 109–110).

THEOREM 10-6: **There exist recursively enumerable sets that are not recursive.**

4. *Equivalence of Turing Machines and Type 0 Grammars*

If L is accepted by some Turing machine, there is a type 0 grammar that generates L and, conversely, every type 0 language is accepted by some

Turing machine. Thus, the type 0 languages are identical with the recursively enumerable sets.

To show this, we let $G = (V_N, V_T, \{S\}, P)$ be a type 0 grammar generating $L \subseteq V_T^*$. We construct a nondeterministic Turing machine T that accepts a string x just in case $S \overset{*}{\underset{G}{\Rightarrow}} x$. Essentially, T works by reversing the steps in the derivation, so that if $\alpha_1\alpha_2 \cdots \alpha_n \to \beta_1\beta_2 \cdots \beta_m$ is a rule of G, T is designed to replace the sequence $\beta_1\beta_2 \cdots \beta_m$ on its tape by the sequence $\alpha_1\alpha_2 \cdots \alpha_n$. T must do this one symbol at a time, of course, and so it will in general take several moves to do the reverse of what is done in one step in the derivation in G. If the strings $\alpha_1\alpha_2 \cdots \alpha_n$ and $\beta_1\beta_2 \cdots \beta_m$ are not of the same length, T will have to shift whole sequences to the right or to the left in order to make room for additional symbols or to fill in space after symbols have been erased. This is not difficult to arrange by supplying T with additional states and extra marking symbols; the details, however, are tedious and not too instructive. As T continues to simulate the derivation in reverse, it finally reaches a situation in which the tape contains S as its only nonblank symbol. T then halts and accepts the input x. Thus, if there is a derivation from S to x by the rules of G, T will convert an initial string x on its input tape to S and halt in an accepting state.

The demonstration of the equivalence in the reverse direction proceeds similarly. Let T be a Turing machine accepting a set of strings $L(T)$. We modify T in the following way to obtain a new machine T'. T' has the same productions as T except that whenever T enters an accepting state, T' erases all nonblank symbols on the tape, replacing them with blanks, and finally prints an S and halts in a final state q_f. Therefore, T' accepts the same strings as T but it does so in such a way that when a string is accepted the final situation is $q_f S$. Also, by adding new states, we can construct T' so that it leaves its initial state q_0 on the first move and never returns to it. We now construct a type 0 grammar G whose derivations simulate the moves of T' in reverse. G has initial symbol S' and the rules $S' \to q_f S$ and $q_0 \to e$. In addition, if (a_i, q_j, q_k, a_l, R) is an instruction of T', the rule $a_l q_k \to q_j a_i$ is added to G; and if (a_i, q_j, q_k, a_l, L) is an instruction of T', the set of rules $q_k \alpha a_l \to \alpha q_j a_i$ for each α in Σ is added to G. If T' accepts x, there is a sequence of situations:

(10-22) $\quad q_0 x \vdash_{T'} \cdots \vdash_{T'} a_1 a_2 \cdots q_j a_i \cdots a_n \vdash_{T'} \cdots \vdash_{T'} q_f S$

and, correspondingly, there is a derivation in G:

(10-23) $\quad S' \Rightarrow q_f S \Rightarrow \cdots \Rightarrow a_1 a_2 \cdots q_j a_i \cdots a_n \Rightarrow \cdots \Rightarrow q_0 x \Rightarrow x$

generating x as a terminal string. G is a type 0 grammar.

In view of the equivalence of type 0 languages and r.e. sets and the fact that type 1 languages are properly included in the recursive sets (Theorems 9-3 and 9-4), which are, in turn, properly included in the r.e. sets (Theorem 10-6), we can state the following theorem:

THEOREM 10-7: There are type 0 languages that are not type 1.

This is the final result needed to establish the sequence of proper inclusions in (9-11). The others were given as Theorems 9-9 and 10-4.

Pushdown Automata

Intermediate in power between the Turing machines and the finite automata there is, among many others that have been defined, a class called *pushdown automata* (pda). A pda reads its input tape one symbol at a time from left to right; it also has a "scratch" tape of a special form on which it can write, read, and erase symbols during a computation. This scratch tape, or pushdown store, has an end or "bottom" and is infinite in the other direction. The move the pda makes at any point depends on (1) its internal state, (2) the symbol being scanned on the input tape, and (3) the topmost symbol in

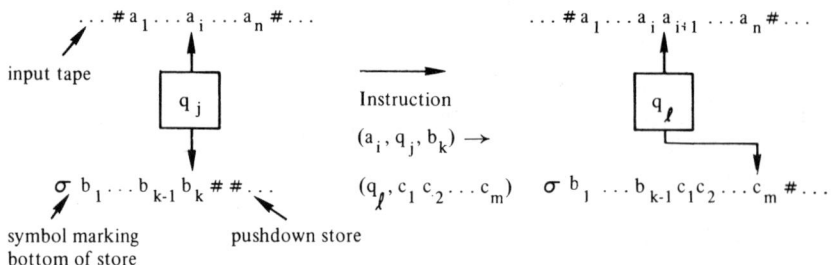

Figure 10-10

A move of a pushdown automaton

the pushdown store. If this state-symbol-symbol combination occurs among its instructions, the pda enters another (possibly identical) state, moves its reading head one square to the right on the input tape, and erases the topmost symbol of the pushdown store, replacing it with some string of symbols (possibly the empty string) specified by the instruction. The reading head on the pushdown store is then positioned to read the topmost nonblank symbol in the store. A move of a pda is illustrated in Fig. 10-10.

Thus, the pushdown store works on the principle of "last in—first out." The only position at which a change can occur on any given move is at the top of the list, and the latest symbol added is the one scanned to determine the next move of the automaton. A symbol below the top one is effectively hidden until the symbols above it have been erased. The pushdown store thus behaves like a device for stacking plates that is often seen in cafeterias. A spring supports the weight of the plates so that only the topmost one is visible; if it is removed, the stack rises to expose the next plate down, and if more plates are added at the top, the whole stack sinks so that only the last plate added is visible.

A special symbol σ marks the bottom of the pushdown store, and it is the only symbol in the store at the beginning of a computation. An input tape is accepted by a pda just in case it halts in a final state after the entire input tape has been read. (An equivalent formulation is that a pda accepts an input just in case it reads the entire input and halts with an empty pushdown store; we shall use the notion of acceptance by final state in order to preserve the parallels with Turing machines and finite automata.) A pda, like the other automata we have considered, may be deterministic or nondeterministic. It is deterministic just in case there is at most one move possible for every combination of state, input symbol, and pushdown symbol; if no such stipulation is made, the pda is nondeterministic. Thus, deterministic pda's are a proper subclass of the nondeterministic pda's.

Example 10-5: The following pda accepts all and only strings of the form xcx^{-1}, where x is any string in $\{a, b\}^*$ and x^{-1} is the mirror image of x. The input alphabet is $\{a, b, c\}$; the set of states is $\{q_0, q_1, q_2\}$; the set of symbols that can appear on the pushdown tape is $\{\sigma, A, B\}$; the initial state is q_0; and the only final state is q_2. The next-move function δ is given by

1. $(a, q_0, \sigma) \to (q_0, \sigma A)$
2. $(a, q_0, A) \to (q_0, AA)$
3. $(a, q_0, B) \to (q_0, BA)$
4. $(b, q_0, \sigma) \to (q_0, \sigma B)$
5. $(b, q_0, A) \to (q_0, AB)$
6. $(b, q_0, B) \to (q_0, BB)$
7. $(c, q_0, \sigma) \to (q_2, \sigma)$
8. $(c, q_0, A) \to (q_1, A)$
9. $(c, q_0, B) \to (q_1, B)$
10. $(a, q_1, A) \to (q_1, e)$
11. $(b, q_1, B) \to (q_1, e)$
12. $(\#, q_1, \sigma) \to (q_2, \sigma)$

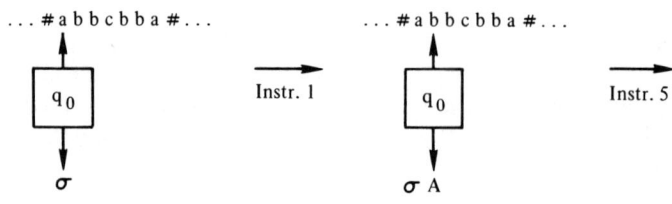

Initial configuration

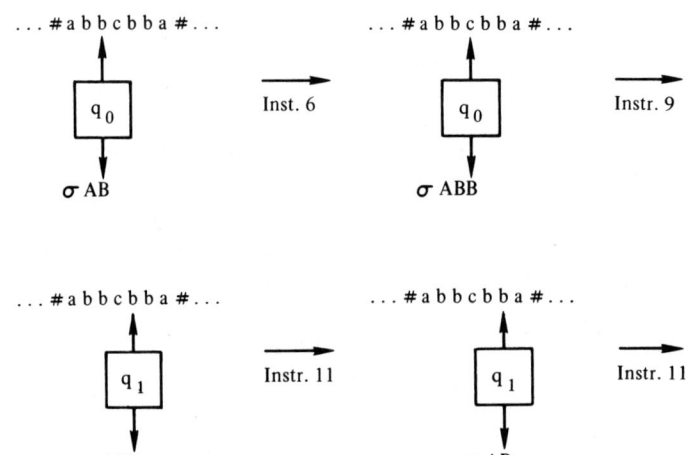

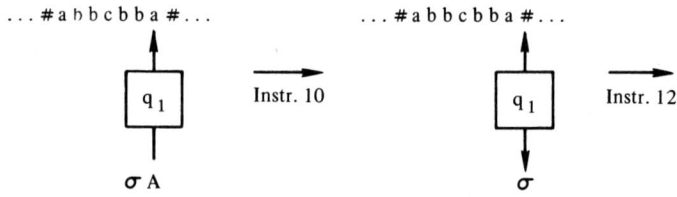

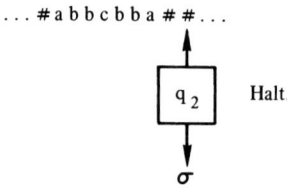

This pda works by writing an image of the left half of the input string on its pushdown tape. When it encounters the symbol c, signifying the middle of the input string, it switches to a new state and then checks each subsequent input symbol against the topmost symbol of the pushdown store. If these agree, then the symbol being read on the input tape is a right-hand mate to a symbol in the left half in the corresponding position, and the computation continues. Should the input symbol and the topmost pushdown symbol not agree, the right half of the input is not the mirror image of the left half, and the pda blocks rejecting the input. If the pushdown store contains only σ after the entire input has been read, this means that every left-half symbol has been successfully matched with a right-half symbol, and the pda moves to a final state and accepts the input.

This pda is deterministic. If we were to construct a pda to recognize the language xx^{-1}, $x \in \{a, b\}^*$, where the middle of the string is not specially marked, it could not be deterministic. Since there is no overt mark in the input string to tell the pda to shift from the left-half "recording" state to the right-half "checking" state, the automaton can only proceed by guessing nondeterministically when the middle of the string has been reached. If it guesses correctly, that computation will result in acceptance (provided the input is in xx^{-1}), but if it guesses incorrectly, the computation will eventually block without accepting. Since there is *some* computation that leads to a final state whenever the input is in xx^{-1}, however, the nondeterministic pda accepts this language. As we have seen, xx^{-1} is a context-free language. Thus, here is a case of a cfl that is accepted by a nondeterministic pda but not by any deterministic pda. The nondeterministic pushdown automata, in fact, accept exactly the class of context-free languages. A proof of this is somewhat too involved to be presented here; proofs can be found in Hopcroft and Ullman (1969; pp. 74–78), Chomsky (1962), and Evey (1963).

Linear Bounded Automata

A pda is able to accept languages, viz., the context-free languages, that are beyond the discriminative powers of a finite automaton. In doing so, it relies on the additional "memory" provided by its pushdown store. With this tape, the pda is able to "remember" a much greater amount of the information already encountered on the input tape than can an fa, and subsequent steps in the computation can be controlled in part by the information contained in the pushdown store. A pda has less flexibility, however, than a Turing machine in the ways this memory can be used. A Turing machine can return to any part of its tape to read a symbol or string of symbols written there previously, while a pda can read only the topmost symbol on its pushdown store at any particular moment. In order to have access to a symbol lower in the store, it must erase all the symbols above it, thereby destroying part of its "memory."

Another difference between a pda and a Turing machine is that the maximum amount of tape a given pda will use in the course of a computation is determinable from the length of the input string, whereas there is, in general, no way to ascertain how much tape a given Turing machine will inscribe with nonblank symbols in computing a given input tape. For every pda we can, by examining its instructions, find the number m that is the maximum number of symbols written on the pushdown tape by a single instruction. Thus, in one move the length of the string in the pushdown store can be increased by at most $m - 1$ symbols (since the top symbol is erased before the new string is written). In reading an input tape of length n, the automaton makes $n + 1$ moves (as we have formulated it, the extra move is to detect the blank at the right end of the input), and thus if nothing were ever erased from the pushdown tape, there could be at most $((n + 1)(m - 1)) + 1$ symbols on it during the computation ('+1' is for the initial symbol σ). This equals $(m - 1)n + m$, and thus for every additional square of input tape the pda can use at most another $m - 1$ squares on the pushdown store. As we have seen, m is a constant whose value depends on the particular pda being considered; the expression $(m - 1)n + m$ is therefore of the form $an + b$, where a and b are constants, and this is said to be a *linear function* of n. (The values of $an + b$ for each value of n when plotted on graph paper lie on a straight line, whereas plots of $an^2 + b$, $an^3 + b$, etc., give curves.) The amount of additional memory, in the form of the pushdown store, that can be used by a pda is accordingly said to be *linearly bounded*.

The general class of automata whose memory capacity is limited in this way is the class of *linear bounded automata* (lba). An lba can be described in one way as a Turing machine that cannot move its tape head beyond the squares on which the input string was originally inscribed. Otherwise, it can read and write and move its tape head right or left just as any other Turing machine can. Equivalently, an lba can be characterized as a pda which can move its tape head either left or right on the input tape, provided that it doesn't leave the nonblank squares, and which uses its second tape not in the fashion of a pushdown store but rather as a general "scratch" tape on which it can read, write, and erase symbols in the manner of a Turing machine. The amount of scratch tape available, however, is directly proportional to the length of the input tape.

The nondeterministic linear bounded automata accept exactly the context-sensitive languages (Kuroda, 1964). The languages accepted by the deterministic linear bounded automata are included in the context-sensitive languages (Landweber, 1963), but it is not known at present whether this inclusion is proper or whether every csl is accepted by some deterministic lba. This unsolved problem is equivalent to the question mentioned in the

Automata	Grammars
Turing machines (deterministic or nondeterministic)	Type 0
Linear bounded automata	
nondeterministic	Type 1
deterministic	(Proper?) subset of type 1
Pushdown automata	
nondeterministic	Type 2
deterministic	Proper subset of type 2
Finite automata (deterministic or nondeterministic)	Type 3

Table 10-1

Equivalences of automata and formal grammars

preceding chapter about whether the complement of a csl is also context-sensitive.

The equivalences of grammars and automata mentioned in this chapter are summarized in Table 10-1.

An important consequence of these equivalences for the study of formal languages is that results that have been established for the automata can be transferred directly to the corresponding grammars. For example, an important theorem in Turing machine theory states that there is no procedure for determining for an arbitrary Turing machine T and arbitrary input tape x whether T will ever halt given x. (This is usually stated by saying that the halting problem for Turing machines is recursively unsolvable.) In particular, there is no procedure for determining whether T will halt in a final state and accept x. Because of the one-to-one correspondence between Turing machines and type 0 grammars, it follows at once that there is no procedure for determining for an arbitrary type 0 grammar G and arbitrary string x whether G generates x. Similarly, it is known that there is no procedure to determine whether an arbitrary Turing machine accepts any strings at all, and hence there can be no procedure to determine whether an arbitrary type 0 grammar generates the empty language.

Another advantageous by-product of these equivalences is that some proofs are much easier to construct for a particular class of automata than for the corresponding class of grammars directly. For instance, many proofs involving context-sensitive grammars are simplified if done in terms of the equivalent nondeterministic lba.

EXERCISES

1. Construct finite automata accepting each of the type 3 languages in Chapter 9, Exercise 1.

2. Given a finite automaton M accepting a set L in Σ^*, show that there is also a finite automaton M' accepting the complement of L, i.e., $\Sigma^* - L$. *Hint:* First convert M to an equivalent complete fa.

3. Use the result in Exercise 2 to show that the type 3 languages are closed under intersection.

4. Prove by means of Theorem 10-3 that $a^n b^n$ ($n \geq 1$) is not a type 3 language.

5. Construct a Turing machine that accepts any tape written on the vocabulary $\{0, 1\}$ and converts every contiguous string of two or more 1's to 0's. Everything else is left unchanged. For example, the input tape $\cdots \# 01011011101 \# \cdots$ should end up as $\cdots \# 01000000001 \# \cdots$.

6. Construct a Turing machine with three states $\{q_0, q_1, q_2\}$, initial state q_0, and final state q_2, that begins with an input tape consisting entirely of blanks and halts with exactly four contiguous 1's on the tape.

7. Construct deterministic pushdown automata that accept
   (a) $a^n b^m a^n$ ($m, n \geq 1$)
   (b) $a^n b^n a^m b^m$ ($m, n \geq 1$)
   (c) $\{x \mid x \in \{a, b\}^*$ and x contains an equal number of a's and b's$\}$

References and Supplementary Reading

For further reading on automata and their correspondences with formal grammars, see Hopcroft and Ullman (1969), Nelson (1968), Booth (1967), Salomaa (1969), Arbib (1969), and Harrison (1965, Chapter 15). Minsky (1967) is an exceptionally readable introduction to finite-state automata and Turing machines, which explores their connections with neural nets and digital computers. Other useful introductions to the basic notions of automata theory may be found in Trakhtenbrot (1963) and Korfhage (1966, Chapter 5). Davis (1958), Hermes (1965), and Rogers (1967) are more advanced works covering computability, decidability, recursive functions, etc.

Finite automata appear in various formulations in Moore (1956), Kleene (1956), and Chomsky and Miller (1958). Much of the formalism adopted here is from Rabin and Scott (1959). The equivalence of deterministic and nondeterministic finite automata is proved there and also in Bar-Hillel and Shamir (1960). The equivalence of finite-state and type 3 languages is proved in a somewhat different form in Chomsky and Miller (1958). Theorem 10-2 is from Kleene (1956), and the formulation of the proof presented here follows Minsky (1967). Theorem 10-3 is from Nerode (1958).

The original conception of a Turing machine is in Turing (1936). A discussion of Church's Thesis as well as many other fundamental results of Turing machine theory can be found in Davis (1958). The equivalence of r.e. sets and type 0 languages is stated in Chomsky (1959), where the reader is referred for proof to Davis (1958, Chapter 6, §2). The proof we have sketched is essentially that from Chomsky (1963).*

Pushdown automata are characterized in Newell, Shaw, and Simon (1959), Oettinger (1961), and Chomsky (1962), although the fundamental notion is traceable at least as far back as Burks, Warren, and Wright (1954).

Deterministic linear bounded automata were first defined in Myhill (1960).

* Copyright © 1963 by John Wiley & Sons, Inc. Reprinted by permission.

11

Mathematical Characterization of Transformational Grammars

The results on formal languages and grammars we have cited in the two preceding chapters are rather limited insofar as their immediate applicability to current linguistic theory is concerned. First of all, they are models of constituent-structure grammars, and such devices are now almost universally regarded as inadequate as grammars of natural languages. We shall not recount the arguments for this position here since they have been widely discussed in the linguistic literature (see, for example, Chomsky, 1957; Postal, 1964b). Worse still, however, is the fact that nearly all the work on formal grammars deals exclusively with the sets of strings they generate (called the *weak generative capacity* of the grammar) and has little to say about the kinds of structural descriptions (constituent-structure trees) assigned to the grammatical strings (*strong generative capacity*). A natural language grammar must, of course, not only generate the correct set of strings but it must also specify correct structural descriptions—"correct" in the sense that they agree with the speakers' intuitions in marking a sentence as n-ways ambiguous, marking two sentences as paraphrases of each other, specifying the grammatical relations that hold between parts of a sentence, etc. A few results in mathematical linguistics concerning weak generative capacity have been of direct linguistic significance (for example, the argument that English is not a finite-state language cited in Chapter 9), but, by and large, they permit very few inferences about grammars of natural languages.

Why, then, did anyone bother to study these systems at all? In part, the answer lies in their applicability to computer programming languages and, by virtue of the correspondences between these formal grammars and automata, to the theory of abstract computing devices. A sizable branch of mathematics has now emerged that is based on these notions (see, for example, Hopcroft and Ullman, 1969, for a recent textbook and Wood, 1970, for an extensive bibliography). From a linguistic point of view, constituent-structure grammars characterized at least certain important aspects of sentence structure, and they were also sufficiently simple to permit precise mathematical formulation. Moreover, since a transformational grammar (Chomsky, 1957, 1965) contains a set of constituent-structure rules as a part of its apparatus, it was hoped that the formal study of constituent-structure systems might one day form the basis for mathematical characterization of this linguistically more interesting class of grammars. Until recently, this program was only a hope for the future, but there have now appeared two mathematical formulations (Ginsburg and Partee, 1969; Peters and Ritchie, forthcoming) of the theory of transformational grammar as outlined in Chomsky, 1965. We give in this chapter a brief synopsis of some of the results of Peters and Ritchie since the consequences of their model have been more thoroughly explored. The two formulations are alike in most important respects, however.

The syntactic component of a transformational grammar consists of two parts: (1) a base component, which is a constituent-structure grammar, and (2) a transformational component, composed of an ordered set of transformational rules. The base generates constituent-structure trees (phrase markers) in some fashion as outlined in Chapter 9, and because the initial symbol S appears on the right side of certain rules, the class of trees generated is infinite. Each such tree serves as an input to the transformational rules, each of which defines a mapping of a set of phrase markers into a set of phrase markers. The transformational rules are assumed to be linearly ordered, the output of one forming the input to the next. If a given transformational rule cannot apply to a particular tree, the tree is left unchanged and the next rule in the sequence is considered.

In the version of transformational grammar here being considered, the transformational rules are assumed to apply in accordance with the principle of the *transformational cycle*. This specifies that the entire sequence of transformational rules applies first to the lowest S-rooted subtrees (those that properly contain no S-rooted subtrees). A single pass through all the transformational rules is said to constitute a *cycle*. Subsequent cycles take as their domains successively larger S-rooted subtrees, until finally on the last cycle the domain of application of the rules is the entire tree.

For example, in the tree diagram represented schematically in (11-1), all transformations apply first to the S_4-rooted subtree, then two independent cycles apply to the S_2 and S_3 subtrees, respectively, and finally the last cycle takes the entire tree as its domain.

The tree that is the final output of the transformational rules is called a *surface structure*.

(11-1)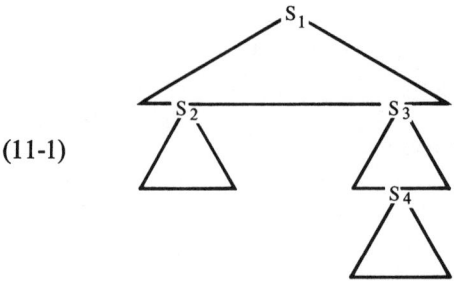

Not every phrase marker generated by the base need be mapped into a well-formed surface structure by the transformational component. For example, a special boundary symbol #, which is placed on both sides of every S by the rules of the base, may be erased by the application of certain transformational rules. If a phrase marker that is the final output of the transformational component contains any instance of #, it is not a well-formed surface structure, and the phrase marker that formed the original input is said to have been *filtered out* by the transformational rules.

A transformational grammar with this property is called a transformational grammar *with filtering*. On this view, then, a transformational grammar is a device for pairing base phrase markers with well-formed surface structures. The language generated by the grammar is the set of all strings that appear as the sequence of leaves of some well-formed surface structure tree.

Each transformational rule consists of a *structural condition* and a *structural change*. The former is a finite sequence of terms indicating (1) certain formal properties a tree must have in order for the rule to be applied to it, and (2) if it has these properties, how the tree is to be broken up into the parts that enter into the structural change. The structural change consists of a finite sequence of so-called *elementary transformations*. These are of three types: (1) deletion, (2) substitution, and (3) adjunction (either to the left or the right), and they apply to the parts of the tree specified by the structural condition.

As an example, let us consider a common formulation of the passive transformation T_p. The structural condition is given by

(11-2) $$(W, NP, Aux, V, X, NP, Y, Pass, Z)$$
$$1 2 3 4 5 6 7 8 9$$

where NP, Aux, V, and $Pass$ are nonterminal symbols and W, X, Y, and Z are variables that range over arbitrary (possibly null) subtrees. (11-2) is to be interpreted as follows. T_p is applicable to a tree only if its leaves can be partitioned into nine contiguous strings such that the first substring is anything at all (possibly null), the second string forms the leaves of a subtree rooted by *NP* (briefly, the second string *is an NP*), the third string is an *Aux*, etc. The tree shown in Fig. 11-1 meets these conditions. The strings of leaves are marked with the numbers of the terms in (11-2) to which they correspond. The values of the variables W and X are both the null string in this case.

The structural change of T_p is composed of four elementary transformations:

1. Substitution of the sixth term for the second.
2. Substitution of the second term for the eighth.
3. Adjunction of the string *be en* to the left of the fourth term.
4. Deletion of the sixth term.

The operations are intended to be carried out "simultaneously" rather than in sequence. A "term" refers to the largest subtree having the designated string as its leaves. The result is shown in Fig. 11-2.

There are many details concerning the operation of the elementary transformations that we shall leave aside here. However, the theory of transformational grammar formalized by Peters and Ritchie specifies that the deletion elementary can operate only if at least one of the following conditions is met:

1. There is a duplicate of the deleted subtree at a specified location elsewhere in the tree.
2. The deleted term is one of a finite set of constant strings and is mentioned specifically in the structural condition of the transformation.

An example of a transformation in which the deletion elementary meets the former condition is Conjunction Reduction, which transforms a structure

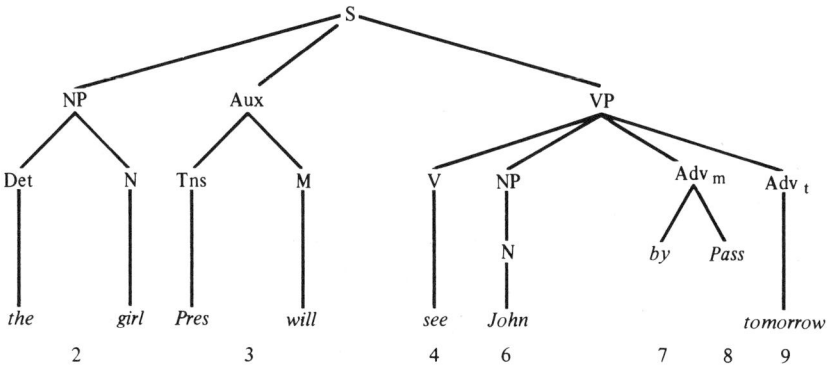

Figure 11-1

Tree meeting the structural condition in (11-2)

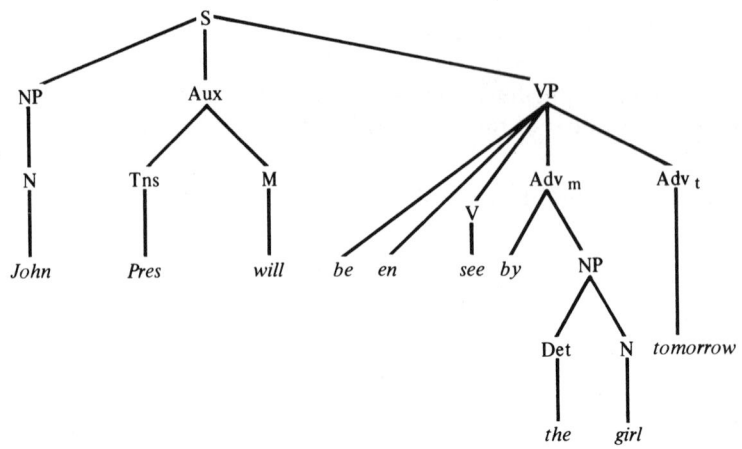

Figure 11-2

Tree resulting from the operation of the passive transformation to the tree in Fig. 11-1

corresponding to 'The boy saw the dog and the girl saw the dog' into one corresponding to 'The boy and the girl saw the dog' by deletion of one of the identical verb phrases. The second condition is exemplified by a transformation that putatively derives imperatives of the form 'Close the door' from an underlying structure corresponding to 'You will close the door' by deleting the constant terms 'you' and 'will' (Katz and Postal, 1964, pp. 74–79). Taken together, statements 1 and 2 are known as the *condition on recoverability of deletion*.

Peters and Ritchie showed that a transformational grammar formalized in this way with a context-sensitive grammar as its base has the same weak generative capacity as the type 0 grammars. That is, the languages generated by context-sensitive based transformational grammars are just the recursively enumerable sets.

The proof, which we only outline here, proceeds by showing first, for any given context-sensitive based transformational grammar G, how to construct a Turing machine that accepts all and only the terminal strings in $L(G)$. Thus, every transformational language is an r.e. set. The converse is proved in the following way. If L is an r.e. set, then there is some type 0 grammar G_0 generating L. Next, a type 1 grammar G_1 is constructed from G_0 such that for every x if $x \in L(G_0)$, $xb^m \in L(G_1)$ for some integer m, and conversely. Thus G_1 generates all the strings in $L(G_0)$ (equal to L) followed by some number of occurrences of the special terminal symbol b. From G_1 it is possible by using some results of Kuroda (1964) to construct an equivalent type 1 grammar G_1' in which every string xb^m generated is assigned the sort of tree structure shown in (11-3), where $x = \alpha_1 \cdots \alpha_{n-1}\alpha_n$, and A, A', A'', A''',

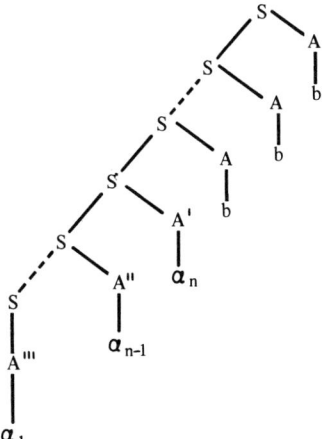

Figure 11-3

etc., are nonterminals distinct from S. G_1' is then taken as the base of a transformational grammar whose only transformational rule is to delete an occurrence of b if it is the rightmost terminal symbol of the sentence being processed on that cycle. Since this is the deletion of a fixed terminal symbol in a fixed position, it meets the condition on recoverability of deletions. Thus, the transformational component takes as input a tree of the form given in (11-3) and deletes all occurrences of b (together with the nonterminals dominating each b) to produce a tree having $x = \alpha_1 \cdots \alpha_{n-1}\alpha_n$ as its leaves. This transformational grammar, therefore, generates all and only the strings of the recursively enumerable set L.

Peters and Ritchie (1971) were able to show that transformational grammars still generate all r.e. sets even if the base is made context-free rather than context-sensitive. With a context-free base, however, the filtering effect of the transformational component must be used extensively; this feature is not needed at all for context-sensitive based transformational grammars to generate the r.e. sets.

These results raise certain difficulties for the theory of transformational grammar as it appears in Chomsky (1965). Since it is commonly supposed that natural languages are properly included in the recursive sets (cf. the discussion following the proof of Theorem 9-3), which are, in turn, properly included in the r.e. sets, transformational grammars, by this formulation, are capable of generating sets of strings that are not possible natural languages. One of the goals of linguistic theory is to give a precise characterization of the notion 'possible grammar of a natural language,' and thus this version of the theory of transformational grammar is shown to fail to meet this goal by virtue of being too broad, i.e., allowing too large a class of grammars.

The nonrecursiveness of transformational languages was shown by Peters and Ritchie (1971) to arise solely from the fact that for any arbitrarily given string of terminal symbols x and for any arbitrarily given transformational grammar G, there is no upper bound on the number of S-rooted subtrees that can occur in the base phrase marker underlying x. This is a consequence of the fact that the theory allows the transformational rules to pare down base phrase markers containing a large number of component S trees to produce very short strings without violating the condition on recoverability of deletion. In order for transformational grammars to generate only recursive sets they would have to be restricted in such a way that for any given grammar and any given sentence there is a procedure for determining the maximum number of cycles that could be involved in the derivation of the sentence by the grammar. Whether this can be done by restricting the class of transformational rules, by tightening up the condition on recoverability of deletions, or in some other entirely different way are possibilities still to be explored. We should note that the results just cited concern only the weak generative capacity of transformational grammars, and it may be that when the requirements on strong generative capacity of natural language grammars are better understood, we shall be able to discover suitable ways of narrowing the theory along those lines.

In its current insufficiently restricted state the theory allows even the following disturbing conclusion to be drawn: Given the sort of data that linguists ordinarily consider relevant, the Universal Base Hypothesis (the conjecture that the grammars of all natural languages have the same base rules) cannot be proved false (cf. Peters and Ritchie, 1969; Peters, 1970). The essential part of the argument comes in showing that even the trivial base component consisting of just two right-linear rules,

(11-4)
1. $S \rightarrow S\#$
2. $S \rightarrow a_1 a_2 \cdots a_n b \#$

together with a small number of transformational rules, suffices to generate any recursively enumerable language on the alphabet $\{a_1, a_2, \ldots, a_n\}$. From this it is relatively straightforward to show that there are an infinite number of such trivial 'universal bases.' This result still holds when the grammar is constrained to be 'descriptively adequate,' in the sense that it gives the intuitively correct results with respect to grammaticality, ambiguity, and paraphrase. Thus, given the powerful nature of the current theory, certain propositions such as the Universal Base Hypothesis, whose truth value ought to depend on the facts of natural language, turn out to be trivially true.

Results such as these provide a particularly convincing demonstration of the importance of finding precise mathematical formulations of the grammars allowed by a linguistic theory, for it is only with the aid of such formulations that the consequences of the theory can be carefully investigated. Without them, we have little hope of being able to prove a theory wrong, much less of seeing wherein it fails and how it might possibly be corrected.

References and Supplementary Reading

In addition to those papers referred to in the text, Kimball (1967) is a study of transformational grammar as formalized by Peters and Ritchie (forthcoming), and Salomaa (1971) is based on the system of Ginsburg and Partee (1969).

Bibliography

Ambrose, Alice, and Morris Lazerowitz, *Logic: The Theory of Formal Inference.* New York: Holt, Rinehart & Winston, Inc., 1961.

Arbib, Michael A., *Theories of Abstract Automata.* Englewood Cliffs, N.J.: Prentice-Hall, Inc., 1969.

Austin, John L., *How to Do Things with Words.* New York: Oxford University Press, 1962.

Bar-Hillel, Y., M. Perles, and E. Shamir, "On Formal Properties of Simple Phrase Structure Grammars," *Zeitschrift für Phonetik, Sprachwissenschaft, and Kommunikationsforschung,* **14** (1961) 143–172. Reprinted in Luce, Bush, and Galanter (1965).

Bar-Hillel, Y., and E. Shamir, "Finite-State Languages: Formal Representation and Adequacy Problems," *Bulletin of the Research Council of Israel* 8F (1960), 155–166.

Birkhoff, Garrett, and Saunders MacLane, *A Survey of Modern Algebra* (rev. ed.). New York: The Macmillan Company, 1953.

Booth, Taylor L., *Sequential Machines and Automata Theory.* New York: John Wiley & Sons, Inc., 1967.

Breuer, Joseph, *Introduction to the Theory of Sets.* Englewood Cliffs, N.J.: Prentice-Hall, Inc., 1958.

Burks, A. W., D. W. Warren, and J. B. Wright, "An Analysis of a Logical Machine Using Parenthesis-Free Notation," *Mathematical Tables and Other Aids to Computation,* **8** (1954), 53–57.

Carnap, Rudolph, *Introduction to Symbolic Logic and Its Applications.* New York: Dover Publications, Inc., 1958.

Chomsky, Noam, "Three Models for the Description of Language," *IRE Trans. Inform. Theory,* Vol. IT-2 (1956), 113–124. A corrected version appears in Luce, Bush, and Galanter (1965).

Chomsky, Noam, *Syntactic Structures*. The Hague: Mouton and Co., 1957.

———, "On Certain Formal Properties of Grammars," *Information and Control*, **2** (1959), 137–167. Reprinted in Luce, Bush, and Galanter (1965).

———, "Context-Free Grammars and Pushdown Storage," *Quart. Prog. Rept. No. 65*. M.I.T. Res. Lab. Elect. (1962), 187–194.

———, "Formal Properties of Grammars," in Luce, Bush, and Galanter (1963), pp. 323–418.

———, *Aspects of the Theory of Syntax*. Cambridge, Mass.: M.I.T. Press, 1965.

Chomsky, Noam, and G. A. Miller, "Finite-State Languages," *Information and Control*, **1** (1958), 91–112. Reprinted in Luce, Bush, and Galanter (1965).

———, "Introduction to the Formal Analysis of Natural Languages," in Luce, Bush, and Galanter (1963), pp. 269–321.

Christian, Robert, *Introduction to Logic and Sets*. Boston: Ginn and Company, 1958.

Church, Alonzo, *Introduction to Mathematical Logic*, Vol. I. Princeton, N.J.: Princeton University Press, 1956.

Cohen, Paul J., *Set Theory and the Continuum Hypothesis*. New York: W. A. Benjamin, Inc., 1966.

Cooper, William S., *Set Theory and Linguistic Description*. The Hague: Mouton and Co., 1964.

Copi, Irving M., *Symbolic Logic* (3rd ed.). New York: The Macmillan Company, 1967.

Davis, Martin, *Computability and Unsolvability*. New York: McGraw-Hill Book Company, 1958.

Dodgson, Charles Lutwidge, *Symbolic Logic*. London and New York: Macmillan and Co., 1896.

Evey, R. James, *The Theory and Applications of Pushdown Store Machines*. Doctoral Dissertation, Harvard University, Cambridge, Mass., 1963. Also published as Harvard University Computation Lab Report NSF-10, May, 1963.

Fisk, Milton, *A Modern Formal Logic*. Englewood Cliffs, N.J.: Prentice-Hall, Inc., 1964.

Fitch, Frederic B., *Symbolic Logic*. New York: Ronald Press Co., 1952.

Fraenkel, Abraham, *Abstract Set Theory*. Amsterdam: North-Holland Publishing Co., 1961.

Ginsburg, Seymour, *The Mathematical Theory of Context-Free Languages*. New York: McGraw-Hill Book Company, 1966.

Ginsburg, Seymour, and Barbara Hall Partee, "A Mathematical Model of Transformational Grammar," *Information and Control*, **15** (1969), 297–334.

Gleason, Andrew M., *Fundamentals of Abstract Analysis*. Reading, Mass.: Addison-Wesley Publishing Co., 1966.

Gross, M., and A. Lentin, *Introduction to Formal Grammars*. New York, Heidelberg, and Berlin: Springer-Verlag, 1970. Translation of *Notions sur les Grammaires Formelles*. Paris: Gauthier-Villars, 1967.

Halberstadt, William H., *An Introduction to Modern Logic*. New York: Harper & Row, Publishers, Inc., 1960.

Halmos, Paul R., *Naive Set Theory*. Princeton, N.J.: D. Van Nostrand Co., Inc., 1960.

Harary, Frank, and Herbert H. Paper, "Toward a General Calculus of Phonemic Distribution," *Language*, **33** (1957), 143–169.

Harrison, Michael A., *Introduction to Switching and Automata Theory*. New York: McGraw-Hill Book Company, 1965.

Hermes, Hans, *Enumerability, Decidability, Computability*. New York: Academic Press Inc.; Berlin, Heidelberg, New York: Springer-Verlag, 1965.

Hilbert, D. and W. Ackerman, trans., *Principles of Mathematical Logic*. New York: Chelsea Publishing Co., 1950.

Hockett, Charles F., *Language, Mathematics and Linguistics*. The Hague: Mouton and Co., 1967.

Hopcroft, John E., and Jeffrey D. Ullman, *Formal Languages and Their Relation to Automata*. Reading, Mass.: Addison-Wesley Publishing Co., 1969.

Hughes, G. E., and M. J. Cresswell, *An Introduction to Modal Logic*. London: Methuen & Co. Ltd., 1968.

Kalish, Donald, and Richard Montague, *Logic: Techniques of Formal Reasoning*. New York: Harcourt Brace Jovanovich, Inc., 1964.

Kamke, E., *Theory of Sets*. New York: Dover Publications, Inc., 1950.

Katz, Jerrold J., and Paul Postal, *An Integrated Theory of Linguistic Description*. Cambridge, Mass.: M.I.T. Press, 1964.

Kimball, John P., "Predicates Definable Over Transformational Derivations by Intersection with Regular Languages," *Information and Control*, **11** (1967), 177–195.

Kleene, Stephen Cole, "Representation of Events in Nerve Nets and Finite Automata," in C. E. Shannon and J. McCarty (eds.), *Automata Studies*. Princeton, N.J.: Princeton University Press, 1956, pp. 3–41.

———, *Mathematical Logic*. New York: John Wiley & Sons, Inc., 1967.

Klima, Edward S., "Negation in English," in Jerry A. Fodor and Jerrold J. Katz (eds.), *The Structure of Language: Readings in the Philosophy of Language*. Englewood Cliffs, N.J.: Prentice-Hall, Inc., 1964, pp. 246–323.

Kneale, William, and Martha Kneale, *The Development of Logic*. Oxford: Clarendon Press of Oxford University Press, 1962.

Korfhage, Robert R., *Logic and Algorithms*. New York: John Wiley & Sons, Inc., 1966.

Kuroda, S. Y., "Classes of Languages and Linear Bounded Automata," *Information and Control*, **7** (1964), 207–223.

Landweber, P. S., "Three Theorems on Phrase Structure Grammars of Type 1," *Information and Control*, **6** (1963), 131–136.

Langacker, Ronald W., "On Pronominalization and the Chain of Command," in David A. Reibel and Sanford A. Schane (eds.), *Modern Studies in English: Readings in Transformational Grammar*. Englewood Cliffs, N.J.: Prentice-Hall, Inc., 1969, pp. 160–186.

Langer, Susanne K., *An Introduction to Symbolic Logic* (2nd ed.). New York: Dover Publications, Inc., 1953.

Leblanc, Hughes, *Techniques of Deductive Inference*. Englewood Cliffs, N.J.: Prentice-Hall, Inc., 1966.

Lee, Harold N., *Symbolic Logic: An Introductory Textbook for Non-Mathematicians*. New York: Random House, Inc., 1961.

Lewis, C. I., and C. H. Langford, *Symbolic Logic* (2nd ed.). New York: Dover Publications, Inc., 1959.

Lightstone, A. H., *The Axiomatic Method: An Introduction to Mathematical Logic*. Englewood Cliffs, N.J.: Prentice-Hall, Inc., 1964.

Lipschutz, Seymour, *Set Theory and Related Topics*. New York: Schaum Publishing Co., 1964.

Luce, R. Duncan, Robert R. Bush, and Eugene Galanter (eds.), *Handbook of Mathematical Psychology*, Vol. II. New York: John Wiley & Sons, 1963.

———, *Readings in Mathematical Psychology*, Vol. II. New York: John Wiley & Sons, 1965.

McCawley, James D., "Concerning the Base Component of a Transformational Grammar," *Foundations of Language*, **4** (1968), 243–269.

McFadden, Myra, J. William Moore, and Wendell I. Smith, *Sets, Relations, and Functions: A Programmed Unit in Modern Mathematics*. New York: McGraw-Hill Book Company, 1963.

Massey, Gerald J., *Understanding Symbolic Logic*. New York, Evanston, and London: Harper & Row, Publishers, 1970.

Mates, Benson, *Elementary Logic*. New York: Oxford University Press, 1965.

Mendelson, Elliott, *Introduction to Mathematical Logic*. Princeton, N.J.: D. Van Nostrand Co., 1964.

Minsky, Marvin L., *Computation: Finite and Infinite Machines*. Englewood Cliffs, N.J.: Prentice-Hall, Inc., 1967.

Moore, E. F., "Gedanken Experiments on Sequential Machines," *Automata Studies*, Princeton, N.J.: Princeton University Press, 1956, pp. 129–153.

Myhill, J., "Linear Bounded Automata," WADD Technical Note 60-165. Wright Air Development Division, Wright-Patterson Air Force Base, Ohio, 1960.

Nelson, R. J., *Introduction to Automata*. New York: John Wiley & Sons, Inc., 1968.

Nerode, A., "Linear Automaton Transformations," *Proc. Amer. Math. Soc.*, **9** (1958), 541–544.

Newell, A., J. C. Shaw, and H. A. Simon, "Report on a General Problem-Solving Program," *Information Processing. Proc. International Conference on Information Processing*, UNESCO, Paris, June, 1959, pp. 256–264. Reprinted in Luce, Bush, and Galanter (1965).

Oettinger, A. G., "Automatic Syntactic Analysis and the Pushdown Store," in R. Jakobson (ed.), *Structure of Language and Its Mathematical Aspects, Proc. 12th Symp. in Applied Math.* Providence, R.I.: American Mathematical Society, 1961, pp. 104–129.

Ortiz, Alejandro, and Ernesto Zierer, *Set Theory and Linguistics*. The Hague: Mouton and Co., 1968.

Peters, P. Stanley, "Why There Are Many 'Universal' Bases," *Papers in Linguistics*, Vol. 1, No. 2 (1970), 27–43.

Peters, P. Stanley and R. W. Ritchie, "A Note on the Universal Base Hypothesis," *Journal of Linguistics*, **5** (1969), 150–152.

———, "On Restricting the Base Component of Transformational Grammars," *Information and Control*, **18** (1971), 483–501.

——— (forthcoming), "On the Generative Power of Transformational Grammars," Technical Report CSci 69-2-3, Dept. of Computer Sciences, University of Washington, Seattle, n.d.; to appear in *Information Sciences*.

Postal, Paul, "Limitations of Phrase Structure Grammars," in Jerry A. Fodor and Jerrold J. Katz (eds.), *The Structure of Language: Readings in the Philosophy of Language*. Englewood Cliffs, N.J.: Prentice-Hall, Inc., 1964a, pp. 137–154.

———, *Constituent Structure: A Study of Contemporary Models of Syntactic Description*. Supplement to *International Journal of American Linguistics*, **30**, No. 1, 1964b.

Quine, Willard Van Orman, *Mathematical Logic* (2nd ed.). Cambridge, Mass.: Harvard University Press, 1957.

———, *Methods of Logic*. New York: Holt, Rinehart & Winston, Inc., 1959.

———, *Elementary Logic*. New York: Harper & Row, Publishers, 1965.

———, *Set Theory and Its Logic*. Cambridge, Mass.: Belknap Press of Harvard University Press, 1969.

Rabin, M. O., and D. Scott, "Finite Automata and Their Decision Problems," *IBM J. Res. Develop.* **3**, No. 2 (1959), 114–125.

Reich, Peter A., "The Finiteness of Natural Language," *Language*, **45** (1959), 831–843.

Reichenbach, Hans, *Elements of Symbolic Logic*. New York: The Macmillan Company, 1947.

Rogers, Hartley, Jr., *Theory of Recursive Functions and Effective Computability*. New York: McGraw-Hill Book Company, 1965.

Rosenbloom, Paul C., *The Elements of Mathematical Logic*. New York: Dover Publications, Inc., 1950.

Rosser, J. Barkley, *Logic for Mathematicians*. New York: McGraw-Hill Book Company, 1953.

Salomaa, Arto, *Theory of Automata*. Oxford: Pergamon Press, 1969.

———, "The Generative Capacity of Transformational Grammars of Ginsburg and Partee," *Information and Control*, **18** (1971), 227–232.

Scheinberg, S., "A Note on the Boolean Properties of Context-Free Languages," *Information and Control*, **3** (1960), 372–375.

Shoenfield, Joseph R., *Mathematical Logic*. Reading, Mass.: Addison-Wesley Publishing Co., 1967.

Stoll, Robert R., *Sets, Logic, and Axiomatic Theories*. San Francisco: W. H. Freeman and Co., 1961.

———, *Set Theory and Logic*. San Francisco: W. H. Freeman and Co., 1963.

Suppes, Patrick, *Introduction to Logic*. Princeton, N.J.: D. Van Nostrand Co., Inc., 1957.

———, *Axiomatic Set Theory*. Princeton, N.J.: D. Van Nostrand Co., Inc., 1960.

Tarski, Alfred, *Introduction to Logic* (2nd ed.). New York: Oxford University Press, 1946.

Trakhtenbrot, B. A., *Algorithms and Automatic Computing Machines*. Boston: D. C. Heath & Company, 1963.

Whitehead, A. N., and B. Russell, *Principia Mathematica*, 3 vol. Cambridge: Cambridge University Press, 1910. First ed. 1910–1913; second ed. 1923–1927; paperback, to *56. 1961.

Wilder, Raymond L., *The Foundations of Mathematics*. New York: John Wiley & Sons, Inc., 1952.

Wood, D., "Bibliography of Formal Language Theory and Automata Theory," *Computing Reviews*. **11,** No. 7 (1970), 417–430.

Zehna, Peter W., and Robert L. Johnson, *Elements of Set Theory*. Boston: Allyn & Bacon, Inc., 1962.

Answers to Selected Exercises

Chapter 1: pp. 9–10

1. (a) t, (b) f, (c) f, (d) t, (e) f, (f) t, (g) t, (h) f, (i) f, (j) t, (k) f, (l) t, (m) f, (n) t, (o) f, (p) f, (q) f, (r) t

3. (b) {a}, ∅ ; (c) ∅ ; (d) {∅}, ∅ ; (e) ∅, {{a}}, {{b}}, {{a, b}}, {∅}, {∅, {a}}, {∅, {b}}, {∅, {a, b}}, {{a}, {b}}, {{a}, {a, b}}, {{b}, {a, b}}, {∅, {a}, {b}}, {∅, {a}, {a, b}}, {∅, {b}, {a, b}}, {{a}, {b}, {a, b}}, {∅, {a}, {b}, {a, b}}

4. $31 = (2^5 - 1)$

5. (a) {5, 6, 7, 8, 9}, (b) {b, a, n}, (c) ∅, (d) ∅, (e) {∅, {c}, {a}, {r}, {c, a}, {c, r}, {a, r}, {c, a, r}}, (f) {∅, {c}, {a}, {r}, {c, a}, {c, r}, {a, r}}

6. (a) $\{x \mid x$ is an even number greater than 1 and less than 11$\}$, (b) $\{x \mid x$ is a prime number (divisible only by itself and 1) less than 14$\}$, (c) $\{x \mid x$ is a number greater than itself$\}$, or $\{x \mid x$ is a set which is not a subset of itself$\}$, or $\{x \mid x$ is a round square$\}$, etc., (d) $\{x \mid x$ is a set with no members$\}$

Chapter 2: pp. 45–50

1. (b) $C \to R$; C = Clarence can be considered well educated, R = Clarence can read Chuvash, (c) $C \vee I$, or equivalently $\sim C \to I$; C = this cat goes, I = I go. (The statement might also be taken to mean $\sim C \leftrightarrow I$.) (d) $M \to (B \wedge D)$; M = Marsha goes out with John, B = John shaves off his beard, D = John stops drinking. (The

Answers to Selected Exercises   305

statement might also be taken to mean $M \leftrightarrow (B \wedge D)$.) (f) $N \rightarrow B$; N = negotiations commence, B = Barataria ceases all acts of aggression against Titipu.

2. (a) and (b) are logically equivalent. Note that the truth table for (d) consists of two identical halves. One need construct only one of them since $P \wedge P$ is logically equivalent to P.

3. (b) p:t, q:f, or p:f, q:t, (d) p:t, q:f, r:f or t, s:t, (e) p:t, q:f, r:t, s:t, or p:f, q:t, r:t, s:t

4. (a) 1. $\sim p \vee (p \wedge q)$
    2. $(\sim p \vee p) \wedge (\sim p \vee q)$ Distr.
    3. $(p \vee \sim p) \wedge (\sim p \vee q)$ Comm.
    4. $T \wedge (\sim p \vee q)$ Compl.
    5. $(\sim p \vee q) \wedge T$ Comm.
    6. $\sim p \vee q$ Ident.
  (b) 1. $p \rightarrow (q \rightarrow p)$
    2. $\sim p \vee (q \rightarrow p)$ Cond.
    3. $\sim p \vee (\sim q \vee p)$ Cond.
    4. $(\sim q \vee p) \vee \sim p$ Comm.
    5. $\sim q \vee (p \vee \sim p)$ Assoc.
    6. $\sim q \vee T$ Compl.
    7. T Ident.
  (c) $\sim p$, (d) F, (e) $\sim p$, (f) T

5. No. Let p be false and q and r true, for example.

6. (a) (i) KKApqAqrAps, (ii) CKNpCNpqq, (iii) CApqKErsp
  (b) (i) $p \vee ((\sim p \wedge \sim q) \rightarrow (p \wedge (q \leftrightarrow r)))$
    (ii) $(\sim((((p \leftrightarrow q) \leftrightarrow r) \wedge s) \vee p) \wedge q) \vee r) \wedge s$
    (iii) $\sim((((p \leftrightarrow q) \wedge r) \vee s) \rightarrow t)$
  (c) NA$pq \equiv$ KNpNq, NK$pq \equiv$ ANpNq

7. (a) valid, (b) invalid, (c) valid

8. (b) Commutative Law only; no, since $p \mid T \equiv \sim p$ and $p \mid F \equiv T$
  (c) (i) $\sim p \equiv p \mid p$, (ii) $p \wedge q \equiv (p \mid q) \mid (p \mid q)$,
    (iii) $p \vee q \equiv (p \mid p) \mid (q \mid q)$

9. (a) p:f, q:t, r:f, s:f, (c) p:t, q:t, r:f, s:f, u:f, (e) p:f, q:t, r:t, s:f, u:f

10. (a) 1. $p \rightarrow q$
    2. $q \rightarrow r$
    3. $\sim r$
    4. $\sim q$ 2,3, M.T.
    5. $\sim p$ 1,4, M.T.

(d) 1. $p \to \sim q$
2. $r \to q$
3. $\sim r \to s$
4. p C.P.
5. $\sim q$ 1,4 M.P.
6. $\sim r$ 2,5, M.T.
7. s 3,6, M.P.
8. $p \to s$

(f) 1. $p \lor (q \land r)$
2. $\sim t$
3. $(p \lor q) \to (s \lor t)$
4. $\sim p$
5. $(p \lor q) \land (p \lor r)$ 1, Distr.
6. $p \lor q$ 5, Simpl.
7. $s \lor t$ 3,6, M.P.
8. s 2,7, D.S.
9. $p \lor r$ 5, Simpl.
10. r 4,9, D.S.
11. $r \land s$ 8,10, Conj.

(h) 1. $\sim p \to q$
2. $r \to (s \lor t)$
3. $s \to \sim r$
4. $p \to \sim t$
5. r C.P.
6. $s \lor t$ 2,5, M.P.
7. $\sim s$ 3,5, M.T.
8. t 6,7, D.S.
9. $\sim p$ 4,8, M.T.
10. q 1,9, M.P.
11. $r \to q$

(i) 1. $p \to (q \land r)$
2. $q \to s$
3. $r \to t$
4. $(s \land t) \to \sim u$
5. u
6. p I.P.
7. $q \land r$ 1,6, M.P.
8. q 7, Simpl.
9. s 2,8, M.P.
10. r 7, Simpl.
11. t 3,10, M.P.
12. $s \land t$ 9,11, Conj.
13. $\sim u$ 4,12, M.P.
14. $u \land \sim u$ 5,13, Conj.
15. $\sim p$

(l) 1. p
2. $(p \land q) \lor (p \land r)$
3. $(p \lor q) \to \sim r$
4. $p \lor q$ 1, Addn.
5. $\sim r$ 1,3, M.P.
6. $p \land (q \lor r)$ 2, Distr.
7. $q \lor r$ 6, Simpl.
8. q 5,7, D.S.
9. $p \land q$ 1,8, Conj.
10. $(p \land q) \lor (\sim p \land \sim q)$ 9, Addn.
11. $p \leftrightarrow q$ 10, Bicond.

11. (a) valid, $B =$ the butler killed the baron, $K =$ the cook killed the baron, $C =$ chauffeur killed the baron, $S =$ the stew was poisoned, $Q =$ there was a bomb in the car
1. $B \lor K \lor C$
2. $(K \to S) \land (C \to Q)$

3. $\sim S \wedge \sim B$
4. $\sim B$ 3, Simpl.
5. $K \vee C$ 1,4, D.S.
6. $K \rightarrow S$ 2, Simpl.
7. $\sim S$ 3, Simpl.
8. $\sim K$ 6,7, M.T.
9. C 5,8, D.S.

(b) valid, (c) invalid (recall that 'p only if q' is represented logically as $p \rightarrow q$), (d) valid, (e) invalid (let it be false that the segment is voiceless and let all the other elementary propositions be true)

12. The conjunction of the premises is a contradiction, and any conditional with a contradiction as antecedent is a tautology.

13. 1. $((P \wedge Q \wedge \ldots \wedge Z) \wedge \sim A) \rightarrow F$
   2. $\sim((P \wedge Q \wedge \ldots \wedge Z) \wedge \sim A) \vee F$ Cond.
   3. $(\sim(P \wedge Q \wedge \ldots \wedge Z) \vee \sim \sim A) \vee F$ DeM.
   4. $(\sim(P \wedge Q \wedge \ldots \wedge Z) \vee A) \vee F$ Compl.
   5. $\sim(P \wedge Q \wedge \ldots \wedge Z) \vee A$ Ident.
   6. $(P \wedge Q \wedge \ldots \wedge Z) \rightarrow A$ Cond.

Chapter 3: pp. 76–79

1. (a) first two x's bound, last x and the y free, (b) x free, y's and z's bound, (c) everything bound, (d) first two x's bound, everything else free, (e) everything bound

2. (a) Everything I touch is something that turns to gold. (This is perhaps a better rendering than 'Everything I touch turns to gold,' which suggests a temporal and causal relation between the events that is not implied by the formula.) (b) Everything I touch is something which does not turn to gold. ('Nothing I touch turns to gold' is open to the same sort of objection as in (a)). (c) I touch everything, and (also) everything turns to gold. (d) All and only those things I touch are things that turn to gold. (e) There is at least one thing such that I touch it and it (also) turns to gold.

3. (a) $T(x) = x$ is a tree, $D(x) = x$ is deciduous, $\sim(\forall x)(T(x) \rightarrow D(x))$, or equivalently $(\exists x)(T(x) \wedge \sim D(x))$, (c) $D(x) = x$ is a duck, $A(x) = x$ is amphibious, $\sim(\exists x)(D(x) \wedge A(x))$, or equivalently $(\forall x)(D(x) \rightarrow \sim A(x))$, (e) $R(x) = x$ is a Rosicrucian, $E(x) = x$ experiences complete happiness, $(\forall x)(E(x) \rightarrow R(x))$, (h) $W(x, y) = x$ is the worst enemy of y, $(\forall x)(W(x, x))$, (i) $W(x, y) = x$ wants it to be the case that y, $R(x) = x$ is rich, $(\forall x)(W(x, (\forall y)R(y)))$, (j) $(\forall x)(W(x, R(x)))$

4. (a) $\sim(\exists x)(P(x) \wedge (\forall y)(Q(y) \to A(x, y)))$,
   (b) $(\forall x)(Q(x) \to (\exists y)(P(y) \wedge A(y, x)))$,
   (d) $(\exists x)(P(x) \wedge (\forall y)(Q(y) \to \sim A(x, y)))$, although 'some people' might also be taken to mean not 'at least one person' but 'at least two persons,'
   (e) $L(x, y) = x$ likes y, $(\forall x)(P(x)(L(x, \text{Mary}) \leftrightarrow \sim E(x, \text{Mary})))$
   (g) $T(x, y) = x$ attempted y,
   $(\forall x)((P(x) \wedge (\exists y)(Q(y) \wedge A(x, y))) \to (\exists z)(Q(z) \wedge T(x, z)))$

5. (a)
   1. $\sim(\exists x)(P(x) \wedge Q(x))$
   2. $(\exists x)(P(x) \wedge R(x))$
   3. $P(w) \wedge R(w)$ 2, E.I.
   4. $(\forall x) \sim (P(x) \wedge Q(x))$ 1, Quant. Neg.
   5. $\sim(P(w) \wedge Q(w))$ 4, U.I.
   6. $\sim P(w) \vee \sim Q(w)$ 5, DeM.
   7. $P(w)$ 3, Simpl.
   8. $\sim Q(w)$ 6,7, D.S.
   9. $R(w)$ 3, Simpl.
   10. $R(w) \wedge \sim Q(w)$ 8,9, Conj.
   11. $(\exists x)(R(x) \wedge \sim Q(x))$ 10, E.G.
   (e)
   1. $(\forall x)(P(x) \to Q(x))$
   2. $R(a)$
   3. $P(a)$
   4. $P(a) \to Q(a)$ 1, U.I.
   5. $Q(a)$ 3,4, M.P.
   6. $R(a) \wedge Q(a)$ 2,5, Conj.
   7. $(\exists x)(R(x) \wedge Q(x))$ 6, E.G.
   (f)
   1. $(\forall x)((P(x) \vee Q(x)) \to R(x))$
   2. $(\forall x)((R(x) \vee S(x)) \to T(x))$
   3. $P(v)$ C.P.
   4. $(P(v) \vee Q(v)) \to R(v)$ 1, U.I.
   5. $P(v) \vee Q(v)$ 3, Addn.
   6. $R(v)$ 4,5, M.P.
   7. $(R(v) \vee S(v)) \to T(v)$ 2, U.I.
   8. $R(v) \vee S(v)$ 6, Addn.
   9. $T(v)$ 7,8, M.P.
   10. $P(v) \to T(v)$
   11. $(\forall x)(P(x) \to T(x))$ 10, U.G.

6. (d) $D(x) = x$ is a duck, $O(x) = x$ is an officer, $P(x) = x$ is (one of) my poultry, $W(x) = x$ waltzes
   1. $(\forall x)(D(x) \to \sim W(x))$
   2. $(\forall x)(O(x) \to W(x))$

Answers to Selected Exercises   309

    3. $(\forall x)(P(x) \to D(x))$
    4. $P(v) \to D(v)$ 3, U.I.
    5. $D(v) \to \sim W(v)$ 1, U.I.
    6. $P(v) \to \sim W(v)$ 4,5, H.S.
    7. $O(v) \to W(v)$ 2, U.I.
    8. $\sim W(v) \to \sim O(v)$ 7, Cond.
    9. $P(v) \to \sim O(v)$ 6,8, H.S.
  10. $(\forall x)(P(x) \to \sim O(x))$ 9, U.G.
(e) $D(x) = x$ is a cab driver, $H(x) = x$ is a head waiter, $S(x) = x$ is surly, $C(x) = x$ is churlish
    1. $(\forall x)((D(x) \lor H(x)) \to (S(x) \land C(x)))$
    2. $D(v)$ C.P.
    3. $D(v) \lor H(v)$ 2, Addn.
    4. $((D(v) \lor H(v)) \to (S(v) \land C(v))$ 1, U.I.
    5. $S(v) \land C(v)$ 3,4, M.P.
    6. $S(v)$ 5, Simpl.
    7. $D(v) \to S(v)$
    8. $(\forall x)(D(x) \to S(x))$ 7, U.G.

7. Line 5, an internal quantifier has been removed, and v has already occurred in a previous line; line 7, z has been instantiated by a symbol that has previously occurred, and $P(w)$ has been changed to $P(v)$ without justification; line 8, x has been instantiated by different symbols, w and v, either of which would be an illegal instantiation here since both have occurred previously; lines 12 and 13, this order of U.G. and E.G. is not allowed here since line 3, which is used in the derivation, has $\forall$ before $\exists$.

Chapter 4: pp. 102–103

1. (a) $\{a, b, c, 2\}$, (b) $\{a, b, c, 2, 3, 4\}$, (c) $\{a, b, c, \{c\}\}$, (d) $\{a, b, \{a, b\}, \{c, 2\}\}$, (e) $\{b, c\}$, (f) $\{a, b\}$, (g) $\{a, b\}$, (h) $\{c\}$, (i) $\varnothing$, (j) $\varnothing$, (k) $\varnothing$, (l) $\{c, 2, 3, 4\}$, (m) $\varnothing$, (n) $\{2\}$, (o) $\{a, b, \{c\}\}$, (p) $\varnothing$, (q) $\{\{a, b\}, \{c, 2\}\}$
2. (a) $\{a, b, c, 2\}$, (b) $\{a, b, c, 2\}$, (c) $\{a\}$, (d) $\{2\}$, (e) $\{2\}$, (f) $\{a, b, c, 2, 3, 4, \{c\}\}$, (g) $\{2, 3, 4, \{a, b\}, \{c, 2\}\}$, (h) $\{2, 3, 4, \{a, b\}, \{c, 2\}\}$, (i) $\varnothing$, (j) I, (k) $\{b, c, 2\}$, (l) $\{2\}$, (m) I, (n) I
4. (b) 1. $(A \cup B) - (A \cap B)$
        2. $(A \cup B) \cap (A \cap B)'$ Theorem 4-13
        3. $(A \cup B) \cap (A' \cup B')$ DeM.
        4. $((A \cup B) \cap A') \cup ((A \cup B) \cap B'$ Distr.
        5. $(A \cap A') \cup (B \cap A') \cup (A \cap B') \cup (B \cap B')$
                                                            Distr. (twice)
        6. $\varnothing \cup (B \cap A') \cup (A \cap B') \cup \varnothing$ Compl. (twice)

310   Answers to Selected Exercises

      7. $(B \cap A') \cup (A \cap B')$ Ident. (twice)
      8. $(B - A) \cup (A - B)$ Theorem 4-13 (twice)
      9. $(A - B) \cup (B - A)$ Comm.
  (c) $(X \cup Y) - (Y \cap X) = (Y \cup X) - (Y \cap X)$ by the commutativity of union and intersection.
  (d) i. $\emptyset$, ii. A', iii. A, iv. $B - A$, v. $A \cup B$

5. (a)   1. $V_1 \subseteq V_2 \wedge V_2 \subset V_3$ C.P.
         2. $V_2 \subset V_3$ 1, Simpl.
         3. $V_2 \subseteq V_3 \wedge V_2 \neq V_3$ 2, Def. of $\subseteq$
         4. $V_2 \subseteq V_3$ 3, Simpl.
         5. $V_1 \subseteq V_2$ 1, Simpl.
         6. $V_1 \subseteq V_2 \wedge V_2 \subseteq V_3$ 4,5, Conj.
         7. $V_1 \subseteq V_3$ 6, Theorem 4-2
         8. $V_1 = V_3$ I.P.
         9. $V_1 \subseteq V_3 \wedge V_3 \subseteq V_1$ 8, Theorem 4-1
        10. $V_3 \subseteq V_1$ 9, Simpl.
        11. $V_3 \subseteq V_1 \wedge V_1 \subseteq V_2$ 5,10, Conj.
        12. $V_3 \subseteq V_2$ 11, Theorem 4-2
        13. $V_2 \subseteq V_3 \wedge V_3 \subseteq V_2$ 4,12, Conj.
        14. $V_2 = V_3$ 13, Theorem 4-1
        15. $V_2 \neq V_3$ 3, Simpl.
        16. $V_2 = V_3 \wedge V_2 \neq V_3$ 14,15, Conj.
        17. $V_1 \neq V_3$
        18. $V_1 \subseteq V_3 \wedge V_1 \neq V_3$ 7,17, Conj.
        19. $V_1 \subset V_3$ 18, Def. of $\subset$
        20. $(V_1 \subseteq V_2 \wedge V_2 \subset V_3) \rightarrow V_1 \subset V_3$
        21. $(\forall X, Y, Z)((X \subseteq Y \wedge Y \subset Z) \rightarrow X \subset Z)$ 20, U.G.

6. (a) false, (b) Assume $x \in (A - B)$. Then $x \in A$ and $x \notin B$, from which it follows that $x \in A$. Therefore, if $x \in (A - B)$, then $x \in A$. Thus, $(A - B) \subseteq A$. (c) $A \cap (B - A) = A \cap (B \cap A') = A \cap A' \cap B = \emptyset \cap B = \emptyset$, (d) false, (e) false

7. (a)   1. $(A - B) + (B - A)$
         2. $((A - B) \cup (B - A)) - ((A - B) \cap (B - A))$
                                                      Def. of $A + B$
         3. $(A + B) - ((A - B) \cap (B - A))$ Def. of $A + B$
         4. $(A + B) - ((A \cap B') \cap (B \cap A'))$ Theorem 4-13
         5. $(A + B) - (A \cap A' \cap B \cap B')$ Assoc., Comm.
         6. $(A + B) - \emptyset$ Compl., Ident.
         7. $(A + B) \cap \emptyset'$ Theorem 4-13
         8. $(A + B) \cap I$ Compl.
         9. $A + B$ Ident.
  (b) If $A = B$, then $(A - A) \cup (A - A) = \emptyset \cup \emptyset = \emptyset$. If

$(A - B) \cup (B - A) = \emptyset$, then both $A - B = \emptyset$ and $B - A = \emptyset$ (otherwise the union could not equal $\emptyset$). $A - B = \emptyset$ means $\sim(\exists x)(x \in A \wedge x \notin B)$, which by Quant. Neg., DeM., and Cond. is equivalent to $(\forall x)(x \in A \rightarrow x \in B)$, i.e., $A \subseteq B$. Similarly, $B - A = \emptyset$ is equivalent to $B \subseteq A$. Thus, $A = B$.

(d) 1. $(A + B) \subseteq B$
2. $(A + B) \cup B = B$ Cons. Prin.
3. $((A \cup B) - (A \cap B)) \cup B = B$ Def. of $A + B$
4. $((A \cup B) \cap (A \cap B)') \cup B = B$ Theorem 4-13
5. $((A \cup B) \cap (A' \cup B')) \cup B = B$ DeM.
6. $((A \cup B) \cup B) \cap ((A' \cup B') \cup B) = B$ Distr.
7. $(A \cup (B \cup B)) \cap (A' \cup (B' \cup B)) = B$ Assoc. (twice)
8. $(A \cup B) \cap (A' \cup I) = B$ Idemp., Ident.
9. $(A \cup B) \cap I = B$ Ident.
10. $A \cup B = B$ Ident.
11. $A \subseteq B$ Cons. Prin.

8. (a) If $x \in \mathcal{P}(A) \cap \mathcal{P}(B)$ then $x \in \mathcal{P}(A)$ and $x \in \mathcal{P}(B)$. $x \in \mathcal{P}(A)$ iff $x \subseteq A$ and $x \in \mathcal{P}(B)$ iff $x \subseteq B$. If $x \subseteq A$ and $x \subseteq B$, then $x \subseteq A \cap B$, and thus $x \in \mathcal{P}(A \cap B)$. The converse is proved by taking these steps in the opposite order.

Chapter 5: pp. 133–136

1. (a) i. $\{(b, 2), (b, 3), (c, 2), (c, 3)\}$
   ii. $\{(2, b), (2, c), (3, b), (3, c)\}$
   iii. $\{(b, b), (b, c), (c, b), (c, c)\}$
   iv. $\{(b, 2), (b, 3), (c, 2), (c, 3), (2, 2), (2, 3), (3, 2), (3, 3)\}$
   v. $\emptyset$ (since $A \cap B = \emptyset$)
   vi. same as $A \times B$
   (b) i. true, ii. false, iii. false $[(c, c) \in (A \times A)]$, iv. true, v. true, vi. true, vii. true.

2. (a) dom $R = A$, ran $R = \{b, 2, 3\}$
   (b) $R' = \{(b, c), (b, 3), (c, b), (c, c)\}$
       $R^{-1} = \{(b, b), (2, b), (2, c), (3, c)\}$
   (c) $(b, b), (c, c), (2, 2), (3, 3)$

3. R_1 and R_1^{-1}: reflexive, antisymmetric, nontransitive, nonconnex;
   R_1': irreflexive, nonsymmetric, nontransitive, connex;
   R_2 and R_2^{-1}: irreflexive, asymmetric, transitive, connex;
   R_2': reflexive, antisymmetric, transitive, connex;
   R_3 and R_3^{-1}: nonreflexive, symmetric, nontransitive, nonconnex;
   R_3': nonreflexive, symmetric, nontransitive, nonconnex;
   R_4 and R_4^{-1}: reflexive, symmetric, transitive, nonconnex;
   R_4': irreflexive, symmetric, intransitive, nonconnex;

$R_4 (= R_4^{-1})$ is an equivalence relation. The partition induced in A is $\{\{1, 3\}, \{2, 4\}\}$.
4. $\{(1, 1), (2, 2), (3, 3), (4, 4), (2, 3), (3, 2)\}$
5. 15
6. (a) Irreflexive (no utterance forms a minimal pair with itself), symmetric, nontransitive (e.g., (cat, bat) and (bat, bag) are minimal pairs but not (cat, bag)), and nonconnex.
   (d) Irreflexive or reflexive (depending on how the term 'allophone' is interpreted), symmetric, transitive (if "phonemic overlap" is excluded, otherwise nontransitive) and nonconnex. If one takes the view that it is reflexive, symmetric, and transitive, then A is an equivalence relation that partitions the set of English phones into equivalence classes corresponding to the ("taxonomic") phonemes of English.
   (e) Reflexive, antisymmetric, transitive, and nonconnex (in general).
   (g) Reflexive, symmetric, transitive, and nonconnex (in general). Each equivalence class contains all the sets that have the same number of members.
7. Let R be asymmetric. If there is some $(x, y) \in R \cap R^{-1}$, then $(x, y) \in R$ and $(x, y) \in R^{-1}$. But $(x, y) \in R^{-1}$ implies $(y, x) \in R$, contradicting the assumption that R is asymmetric. Therefore, $R \cap R^{-1} = \emptyset$. Now assume $R \cap R^{-1} = \emptyset$. If R is not asymmetric, there are x and y such that $(x, y) \in R$ and $(y, x) \in R$. But $(x, y) \in R$ implies $(y, x) \in R^{-1}$, contradicting the assumption that $R \cap R^{-1} = \emptyset$. Therefore, R is asymmetric.
8. It fails to prove that $(x, x) \in R$ *for all x in A*. Rather, it establishes only that if R is symmetric and transitive and *if* $(x, y) \in R$, then $(x, x) \in A$. There is, of course, no necessity for (x, y) to be in R for all x in A.
9. $R_2 \circ R_1 = \{(1, 2), (1, 3), (1, 4), (2, 2), (2, 3), (2, 4), (3, 4), (4, 2), (4, 3), (4, 4)\}$
   $R_1 \circ R_2 = \{(1, 1), (1, 2), (1, 3), (1, 4), (2, 1), (2, 3), (2, 4), (3, 1), (3, 4)\}$
10. Assume $(x, y) \in R$. Because S is reflexive, $(y, y) \in S$. Thus, since $(x, y) \in R$ and $(y, y) \in S$, $(x, y) \in S \circ R$. Therefore $R \subseteq (S \circ R)$.
11. Let R be transitive. Assume $(R \circ R) \nsubseteq R$. Then there is some $(x, y) \in R \circ R$ such that $(x, y) \notin R$. $(x, y) \in R \circ R$ implies that for some z, $(x, z) \in R$ and $(z, y) \in R$, but this, together with $(x, y) \notin R$, contradicts the assumption that R is transitive. To prove the converse, let $(R \circ R) \subseteq R$. Assume R is not transitive. Then there are (x, y) and (y, z) in R such that $(x, z) \notin R$. But (x, y) and (y, z) in R implies that $(x, z) \in R \circ R$, contradicting the assumption that $(R \circ R) \subseteq R$.

13. In relations from A to B each of a, b, and c can be paired with 1, with 2, with both 1 and 2, or with neither, i.e., in four possible ways. Therefore there are $4 \times 4 \times 4 = 64$ distinct relations. In functions from A to B each of a, b, and c can be paired with 1 or with 2, i.e., in two possible ways. Therefore, there are $2 \times 2 \times 2 = 8$ distinct functions. Six of these are onto (only $\{(a, 1), (b, 1), (c, 1)\}$ and $\{(a, 2), (b, 2), (c, 2)\}$ are not onto), and none are one-to-one. Since none are one-to-one and onto, none have inverses that are functions. There are $8 \times 8 = 64$ distinct relations from B to A of which $3 \times 3 = 9$ are functions. None are onto, none are one-to-one, and therefore none have inverses that are functions.

14. For every x in Z it is possible to add 1 to get a single value. Similarly, each x in Z can be squared to produce a single value. Therefore both f and g are functions into Z. Conversely, subtracting 1 from any member of $\{1, 2, 3, 4, \ldots\}$ yields a unique element of Z, and so does taking the square root of any member of $\{0, 1, 4, 9, 16, \ldots\}$ (since Z does not contain the negative numbers). Therefore both f and g are one-to-one. Neither is an onto function since there is no x in Z such that $f(x) = 0$ nor such that $g(x) = 3$, for example. $g \circ f$ maps x into $(x + 1)^2$, i.e., $x^2 + 2x + 1$. $f \circ g$ maps x into $x^2 + 1$. Both are one-to-one functions and are into, but not onto, Z.

15. For most dialects R is irreflexive (there are no initial geminate clusters), asymmetric (with the possible exception of /st/ and the /ts/ of 'tsetse'), nontransitive, and nonconnex. Only the cluster /sr/ is lacking to make R transitive, however, and some people claim to have this in 'syringe'. (The glides /w/ and /y/ are assumed not to be in P.) T contains /spl/, /spr/, /str/, /skl/, /skr/, /sfl/, and /sfr/. Four of these are common initial clusters, /skl/ occurs in 'sclerosis' and its derivatives, and /sfr/ in the rare word 'sphragistic.' Apparently only /sfl/ does not occur in English.

Chapter 6: pp. 172–173

1. (c) One such isomorphism is $f = \{(1, \varnothing), (2, \{a\}), (3, \{b\}), (5, \{c\}), (6, \{a, b\}), (10, \{a, c\}), (15, \{b, c\}), (30, \{a, b, c\})\}$. There are $8! = 40{,}320$ distinct one-to-one correspondences from A to $\mathscr{P}(B)$, of which 6 are isomorphisms from (A, R) to $(\mathscr{P}(B), \subseteq)$.

2. Let x be minimal in R_1, and let $f(x) = x'$. Suppose x' is not minimal in R_2. Then for some $y' \in B$ such that $y' \neq x'$, $(y', x') \in R_2$. Let $f^{-1}(y') = y$. Since f is a one-to-one correspondence, $y \neq x$. But because f is an isomorphism, $(y', x') \in R_2$ implies $(y, x) \in R_1$,

contradicting the assumption that x is minimal. The proof for maximal elements is analogous.

4. No; no; clause mates: irreflexive, symmetric, nontransitive (let A and B be clause mates and also B and C, and let A dominate C); commands: irreflexive, nonsymmetric, transitive; in construction with: nonreflexive (the root node is not in construction with any other), nonsymmetric, transitive.

5. Symmetric difference can easily be shown to be commutative and associative by Venn diagrams. It is not idempotent since $A + A = \emptyset$. $\emptyset$ is the two-sided identity element, and every set is its own inverse. $(\mathscr{P}(A), +)$ is an Abelian group of order 4.

6. Intersection, but not union, distributes over symmetric difference. Symmetric difference distributes over neither union nor intersection.

8. A non-Abelian group of order 6.

9. (a) Every string is a conjugate of itself since $x = x \frown e = e \frown x$. Conjugacy is symmetric by the definition. To prove transitivity, let x and y be conjugate and also y and z. Then for some t, u, v, w, $x = t \frown u$, $y = u \frown t$, $y = v \frown w$, and $z = w \frown v$. Case 1: let $u = v$ and $t = w$. Then $x = t \frown u = w \frown v = z$; thus x and z are conjugate because they are identical. Case 2: let u be shorter than v; that is, there is some r such that $u \frown r = v$. Since $y = v \frown w = u \frown r \frown w = u \frown t$, it follows that $r \frown w = t$. Therefore, $x = t \frown u = r \frown w \frown u$, and $z = w \frown v = w \frown u \frown r$; thus x and z are conjugate. Case 3: let u be longer than v; that is, for some s, $v \frown s = u$. Since $y = u \frown t = v \frown s \frown t = v \frown w$, it follows that $w = s \frown t$. Therefore, $x = t \frown u = t \frown v \frown s$, and $z = w \frown v = s \frown t \frown v$; thus, x and z are conjugate. This exhausts the possible cases. This relation partitions A^* into equivalence classes, each class containing all the strings that are conjugates of each other. A string of length n may be the only string in its equivalence class (*aaaa*, for example, is conjugate only with itself) or there may be as many as n strings in the class (*abca* for example, is conjugate with itself and with *bcaa*, *caab*, and *aabc*).

(b) Let x and y be conjugate. Therefore, $x = uv$ and $y = vu$, for some u and v. The string u is a string such that $x \frown u = u \frown y$, since $x \frown u = u \frown v \frown u = u \frown y$.

Chapter 7: p. 186

1. There is one-to-one correspondence of every set with itself—for example, the identity function. Thus, the relation of equivalence of sets is reflexive. If f is a one-to-one correspondence from A to B, then

Answers to Selected Exercises 315

f^{-1} is a one-to-one correspondence from B to A. Therefore, the relation is symmetric. If f and g are one-to-one correspondences from A to B and from B to C, respectively, then $g \circ f$ is a one-to-one correspondence from A to C. (This can be easily shown by an indirect proof.) Thus, the relation is transitive.

2. The set can be denoted $\{10^1, 10^2, 10^3, 10^4, \ldots\}$.
3. (a) Let $A = \{1, 2, 3, \ldots\}$ and $B = \{0\}$.
   (b) Let $A = \{0, 1, 2, 3, \ldots\}$ and $B = \{a, b\}$. The set $\{(0, a), (0, b), (1, a), (1, b), (2, a), (2, b), \ldots\}$ is mapped one-to-one and onto $\{0, 1, 2, 3, \ldots\}$ by $f(n, a) = 2n$, $f(n, b) = 2n + 1$.
   (c) Let $A = \{0, 2, 4, 6, \ldots\}$ and $B = \{1, 3, 5, 7, \ldots\}$.
   (d) Let $A = \{0, 1, 2, 3, \ldots\}$ and let B be the set of "primed" integers $\{0', 1', 2', 3', \ldots\}$ disjoint from A. $A \times B$ is equivalent to $A \times A$, which has cardinality $\aleph_0$.
4. If $\#(A) \geqslant \#(B)$ and $\#(B) \geqslant \#(C)$, there are functions $f: A \to B$ and $g: B \to C$ which are onto B and C, respectively. We prove that $g \circ f$ is an onto function (from A to C). Assume that it is not onto. Then there is some $z \in C$ such that for no $x \in A$, $(g \circ f)(x) = z$, i.e., $g(f(x)) = z$. But g is onto C, and thus there is some $y \in B$ such that $g(y) = z$. Thus it must be that there is no $x \in A$ such that $f(x) = y$. But this contradicts the assumption that f is onto B. Therefore, $g \circ f$ is onto C, and $\#(A) \geqslant \#(C)$.

Chapter 8: pp. 204–206

1. Assume that elementary propositions are recursively defined as in (8-7).
   Base: Every elementary proposition is a *Pwff* (Polish well-formed formula).
   Recursion: For all α and β, if α and β are *Pwff*'s then so are

   (a) $N\alpha$, (b) $A\alpha\beta$, (c) $K\alpha\beta$, (d) $C\alpha\beta$, (e) $E\alpha\beta$

   Restriction: Nothing else is a *Pwff*.
2. $f(0) = 2, f(n) = (f(n-1))^2$;
   $f(0) = 2$
   $f(1) = (f(0))^2 = 2^2 = 4$
   $f(2) = (f(1))^2 = 4^2 = 16$
   $f(3) = (f(2))^2 = 16^2 = 256$
   $f(4) = (f(3))^2 = 256^2 = 65{,}536$
4. The power set of the set with zero members, $\varnothing$, is $\{\varnothing\}$, which has one member. Since $2^0 = 1$, this establishes the base. To prove the induction step, let A_{k+1}, a set with $k + 1$ members, be formed from

A_k, a set with k members, by the addition of some element x not in A_k; i.e., $A_{k+1} = A_k \cup \{x\}$. Let $B_1, B_2, \ldots, B_{2^k}$ be the 2^k members of $\mathscr{P}(A_k)$. $\mathscr{P}(A_{k+1})$ contains all these sets plus the sets formed by taking the union of each of these with $\{x\}$, i.e., $B_1 \cup \{x\}, B_2 \cup \{x\}, \ldots, B_{2^k} \cup \{x\}$. This makes an additional 2^k sets. Thus, $\mathscr{P}(A_{k+1})$ has $2(2^k) = 2^{k+1}$ members. The desired result now follows by Mathematical Induction.

6. The induction fails in going from 1 to 2 as the reader can verify by letting n take on the value 1 in the induction step.

7. 1. $p \to (q \to p)$ (A1)
    2. $((\sim q \to \sim p) \to (p \to q)) \to (\sim p \to ((\sim q \to \sim p) \to (p \to q)))$
           1, (R2)
       (Subst. $(\sim q \to \sim p) \to (p \to q)$ for p and $\sim p$ for q)
    3. $(\sim p \to \sim q) \to (q \to p)$ (A3)
    4. $(\sim q \to \sim p) \to (p \to q)$ 3, (R2)
       (Subst. p for q and q for p)
    5. $\sim p \to ((\sim q \to \sim p) \to (p \to q))$ 2,4, (R1)
    6. $(p \to (q \to r)) \to ((p \to q) \to (p \to r))$ A2
    7. $(\sim p \to ((\sim q \to \sim p) \to (p \to q))) \to ((\sim p \to (\sim q \to \sim p)) \to (\sim p \to (p \to q)))$ 6, (R2)
       (Subst. $\sim p$ for p, $(\sim q \to \sim p)$ for q, and $(p \to q)$ for r)
    8. $(\sim p \to (\sim q \to \sim p)) \to (\sim p \to (p \to q))$ 5,7, (R1)
    9. $\sim p \to (\sim q \to \sim p)$ 1, (R2)
       (Subst. $\sim p$ for p and $\sim q$ for q)
    10. $\sim p \to (p \to q)$ 8,9, (R1)

8. The alphabet is $\{p, ', N, A, K, C, E\}$; the axioms are the elementary propositions as defined in (8-7); the productions are:

   $x \to Nx$
   $x, y \to Axy$
   $x, y \to Kxy$
   $x, y \to Cxy$
   $x, y \to Exy$

   where x and y are any strings on the alphabet. An equivalent semi-Thue system has a basic alphabet as above, an auxiliary alphabet $\{Q, R\}$, and axiom set $\{Q\}$, and productions:

   $Q \to NQ$
   $Q \to AQQ$
   $Q \to KQQ$
   $Q \to CQQ$
   $Q \to EQQ$
   $Q \to R$
   $R \to R'$
   $R \to p$

9. $A = \{J, K\}$, $B = \{a\}$, $S = \{J, K\}$;
   P: $\alpha J\beta \to \alpha Jaa\beta$
   $\alpha J\beta \to \alpha\beta$
   $\alpha K\beta \to \alpha Kaaa\beta$
   $\alpha K\beta \to \alpha\beta$
   where α,β are any strings on $(A \cup B)^*$.

Chapter 9: pp. 251–252

1. (a) $S \to aa$
       $S \to ab$
       $S \to ba$
       $S \to bb$

   (b) $S \to e$
       $S \to aA$
       $S \to a$
       $S \to bA$
       $S \to b$
       $A \to aA$
       $A \to a$
       $A \to bA$
       $A \to b$

   (c) $S \to aA$
       $S \to bS$
       $A \to a$
       $A \to aB$
       $A \to bA$
       $B \to bB$
       $B \to b$

   (d) $S \to a$
       $S \to b$
       $S \to bA$
       $S \to aC$
       $A \to bA$
       $A \to aB$
       $A \to a$
       $B \to bB$
       $B \to b$
       $C \to aC$
       $C \to bD$
       $C \to b$
       $D \to aD$
       $D \to a$
       $S \to bD$
       $S \to aB$

   (e) $S \to e$
       $S \to aA$
       $S \to bC$
       $A \to aD$
       $A \to a$
       $A \to bB$
       $B \to bA$
       $B \to aC$
       $C \to aB$
       $C \to bD$
       $C \to b$
       $D \to aA$
       $D \to bC$

   (f) $S \to bA$
       $S \to aB$
       $A \to bS$
       $A \to aC$
       $B \to bC$
       $C \to bB$
       $B \to aD$
       $B \to a$
       $C \to aE$
       $D \to bE$
       $E \to bD$
       $E \to b$

2. (a) $\{aa, ab, ba, bb\}$
   (b) $\{a, b\}^*$
   (c) $\{b\}^* \cdot \{a\} \cdot \{b\}^* \cdot \{a\} \cdot \{b\}^*$
   (d) $(\{b\}^* \cdot \{a\} \cdot \{b\}^*) \cup (\{a\}^* \cdot \{b\} \cdot \{a\}^*)$

3. (Rules of the form $AB \to BA$ are abbreviations for a series of type 1 rules of the form $AB \to DB$, $DB \to DA$, $DA \to BA$).

(a) $S \to aSBC$ (b) $S \to ABCD$ $AC \to CA$
     $S \to aBC$ $S \to e$ $CA \to AC$
     $CB \to BC$ $AB \to BA$ $A \to a$
     $aB \to ab$ $BA \to AB$ $B \to b$
     $bB \to bb$ $BC \to CB$ $C \to c$
     $C \to c$ $CB \to BC$ $D \to ABCD$
                                                 $D \to ABC$

4. (a) $S \to aSa$ (b) $S \to AA$ (c) $S \to aBB$
       $S \to aBa$ $A \to aAb$ $S \to bAB$
       $B \to bB$ $A \to ab$ $S \to bBA$
       $B \to b$ $A \to aC$
                                                 $A \to a$
                                                 $A \to bBAA$
                                                 $A \to bABA$
                                                 $A \to bAAB$
                                                 $B \to bC$
                                                 $B \to b$
                                                 $B \to aBBB$
                                                 $C \to aBB$
                                                 $C \to bAB$
                                                 $C \to bBA$
                                                 $S \to e$

5. Any rules which are already of the form $A \to a$ or $A \to BC$ can be left unchanged. Remove all rules of the form $A \to B$ by the procedure outlined following (9-55). For each rules of the form $A \to \alpha_1 \alpha_2 \cdots \alpha_n$, where $n \geqslant 2$ and one or more of the α_i is a terminal symbol, replace each occurrence of such an α_i by a new nonterminal A_i that occurs nowhere else and add the rule $A_i \to \alpha_i$ (which is of the allowed form). The right sides of all rules now consist either of a single terminal symbol or else a string of two or more nonterminals. Each remaining rule of the form $A \to B_1 B_2 \cdots B_n$ $(n \geqslant 3)$ is now replaced by the rules $A \to B_1 C_1$, $C_1 \to B_2 C_2, \ldots, C_{n-1} \to B_{n-1} B_n$, where $C_1, C_2, \cdots, C_{n-1}$ are new nonterminals that occur nowhere else in the grammar. All rules are now of the required form. Clearly for every derivation of a terminal string in the original grammar there is a derivation of that string in the new grammar and conversely.

6. (a) If a^{n^2} $(n \geqslant 1)$ is type 2 there are $u = a^{i_1}$, $v = a^{i_2}$, $w = a^{i_3}$, $x = a^{i_4}$, $y = a^{i_5}$, where $i_3 \neq 0$ and $i_2 + i_4 \neq 0$, such that $a^{i_1}(a^{i_2})^j a^{i_3}(a^{i_4})^j a^{i_5} = a^{n^2}$ for all $j \geqslant 0$ and $n \geqslant 1$. That is, $(i_1 + i_3 + i_5) + j(i_2 + i_4) = n^2$, for all $j \geqslant 0$ and $n \geqslant 1$. Let $b = i_1 + i_3 + i_5$ and $c = i_2 + i_4$. What is required is that there be constant integers b and c such that $b + jc$ is a perfect square for every positive

integral value of j. No linear function $b + jc$ can grow so fast as the function n^2, so there will be some values of $b + jc$ which are not perfect squares. To prove this explicitly we note that $b + jc$ must be a perfect square for $j = 0$; that is, there is some integer m such that $b + 0 \cdot c = b = m^2$. Note that b (and hence m) cannot be zero since $i_3 \neq 0$. Since j takes on all integral values, it can in particular take on the value bc. Then for some integer p, $b + (bc)c = p^2$. Since $b = m^2$, $p^2 = m^2 + (m^2c)c = m^2 + m^2c^2 = m^2(1 + c^2)$. From this we have $c^2 + 1 = p^2/m^2 = (p/m)^2$. (Division by m^2 is allowed since $m \neq 0$.) Because c is an integer, $c^2 + 1$ is also an integer, and thus p/m is an integer. Let $k = p/m$. Then $c^2 + 1 = k^2$, or $k^2 - c^2 = 1$. Factoring the left side, $(k + c)(k - c) = 1$. Since both $k + c$ and $k - c$ must be integers and their product is 1, we have $k + c = 1$ and $k - c = 1$, from which it follows that $k = 1$ and $c = 0$. But this contradicts the assumption that $i_2 + i_4 \neq 0$. Therefore, a^{n^2} is not type 2.

(b) The proof begins analogously to part (a). $b + jc$ must be prime for all $j \geqslant 0$. By assumption b is not equal to zero. When $j = bc^2$, $b + jc = b + (bc^2)c = b + bc^3 = b(1 + c^3) = b(1 + c)(1 - c + c^2)$. Since $c \geqslant 1$, $(c + 1) \geqslant 2$ and thus $b + bc^3$ is divisible by 2 or some large integer. This establishes that $b + bc^3$ could not be prime unless it happened to equal 2. However, in this case $b = 1$ and $c = 1$, and it is obviously false that $1 + j \cdot 1$ is prime for all integral values of j. Therefore a^n (n prime) is not type 2.

8. $A \cdot (B \cup C) = \{x \frown y \mid x \in A \land y \in (B \cup C)\} = $
$\{x \frown y \mid x \in A \land (y \in B \lor y \in C)\} = $
$\{x \frown y \mid (x \in A \land y \in B) \lor (x \in A \land y \in C)\} = $
$\{x \frown y \mid x \in A \land y \in B\} \cup \{x \frown y \mid x \in A \land y \in C\} = $
$(A \cdot B) \cup (A \cdot C)$
The proof for intersection is similar.

Chapter 10: p. 288

1. (a) (a, q_0, q_1)
   (b, q_0, q_1)
   (a, q_1, q_2)
   (b, q_1, q_2)
   $F = \{q_2\}$

   (c) (b, q_0, q_0)
   (a, q_0, q_1)
   (a, q_1, q_2)
   (b, q_1, q_1)
   (b, q_2, q_2)
   $F = \{q_2\}$

   (e) (a, q_0, q_1)
   (a, q_1, q_0)
   (b, q_1, q_2)
   (b, q_2, q_1)
   (a, q_2, q_3)
   (a, q_3, q_2)
   (b, q_3, q_0)
   (b, q_0, q_3)
   $F = \{q_0\}$

2. Convert M to an equivalent complete fa and this, in turn, to an equivalent deterministic fa. Call this fa M_1. Now form M' from M_1 by interchanging final and nonfinal states. Thus M' accepts every string on Σ^* that M_1 rejects and rejects every string that M_1 accepts. M', therefore, accepts exactly $\Sigma^* - L$.

4. If $a^n b^n$ ($n \geq 1$) is type 3 then R_L of (10-13) is of finite index. Then there must be two strings a^i and a^j such that $i \neq j$ in the same equivalence class. Therefore, for all $z \in \{a, b\}^*$, $a^i z \in L \leftrightarrow a^j z \in L$. But this is false when $z = b^i$, for example, since $a^i b^i \in L$ but $a^j b^i \notin L$.

5. $(0, q_0, q_0, 0, R)$
$(1, q_0, q_1, 1, R)$
$(0, q_1, q_0, 0, R)$
$(1, q_1, q_2, 1, L)$
$(1, q_2, q_2, 0, R)$
$(0, q_2, q_0, 0, R)$

6. $(\#, q_0, q_1, 1, R)$
$(\#, q_1, q_1, 1, L)$
$(1, q_1, q_2, 1, L)$
$(\#, q_2, q_0, 1, L)$

7. (a) $(a, q_0, \sigma) \rightarrow (q_0, \sigma A)$
$(a, q_0, A) \rightarrow (q_0, AA)$
$(b, q_0, A) \rightarrow (q_1, A)$
$(b, q_1, A) \rightarrow (q_1, A)$
$(a, q_1, A) \rightarrow (q_2, e)$
$(a, q_2, A) \rightarrow (q_2, e)$
$(\#, q_2, \sigma) \rightarrow (q_3, \sigma)$
$F = \{q_3\}$

(c) $(a, q_0, \sigma) \rightarrow (q_0, \sigma A)$
$(b, q_0, \sigma) \rightarrow (q_0, \sigma B)$
$(a, q_0, A) \rightarrow (q_0, AA)$
$(a, q_0, B) \rightarrow (q_0, e)$
$(b, q_0, A) \rightarrow (q_0, e)$
$(b, q_0, B) \rightarrow (q_0, BB)$
$(\#, q_0, \sigma) \rightarrow (q_1, \sigma)$
$F = \{q_1\}$

Index of Symbols

$/p/$ 1
$\{,\}$ 2
$|$ (such that)   4
$\in$ 4
$\notin$ 5
$=$ 5
$\varnothing$ 6
$\subseteq, \supseteq$ 7
$\subset, \supset$ 7
$\nsubseteq, \nsupseteq$ 7
$\not\subset, \not\supset$ 7
$\mathscr{P}$ 8
2^A 9
t, f   13
$\wedge$ 15
$\vee$ 16
$\sim$ (negation)   17
$\rightarrow$ (conditional)   18
$+$ (addition)   20
$\leftrightarrow$ 21
$\equiv$ 28
T (tautology)   30
F (contradiction)   30
$\times$ (multiplication)   31
$\therefore$ 34
$\Rightarrow$ (logical implication)   36
N, A, K, C, E   46–47
$|$ (alternative denial)   48
$H(s), H(x)$ 52
$L(x, y)$ 53

$\forall$ 53
$\exists$ 53
v 66
w 68
$\cup$ 87
$\stackrel{\text{def}}{=}$ 87
$\cap$ 89
$-$ (relative complement)   91
$'$ (absolute complement)   92
I (universal set)   92
$\longrightarrow$ 99
$\longleftrightarrow$ 99
$+$ (symmetric difference)   102
(a, b) 104
$(a, b, c), (a, b, c, d)$ 106
$\times$ (Cartesian product)   106
(multiplication)   107
$<$ 108
$\geq$ 108
dom R 109
ran R 109
i_A 109
R' 109
R^{-1} 110
$>$ 115
$\not>$ 115
$[x]$ 123
$f: A \rightarrow B$ 126
$f(c)$ 126
$g \circ f$ 129

Index of Symbols

$S \circ R$ 132
$\sqrt{}$ 133
$\leq$ 142
$*$ (operation)   153
$-$ (subtraction)   154
$/$ (division)   154
e_l, e_r 155
e (two-sided identity)   156
x_l, x_r, x^{-1} 156
$0_l, 0_r$ 157
$*_B$ 160
e (null string)   164
$\varphi \frown \psi$ 165
A^* 165
$+_3$ 170
$A \sim B$ (equivalence)   174
$\#(A)$ (cardinality)   175
$\aleph_0$ 177
$[0, 1]$ 184
$\oplus$ 186
$\otimes$ 186
A^+ 192
$\rightarrow$ (follows from)   198
V_T 207

V_N 207
$\underset{G}{\Rightarrow}, \Rightarrow$ (immediate domination)   208
$\underset{G}{\overset{*}{\Rightarrow}}, \overset{*}{\Rightarrow}$ 208
$a^n b^m$ 211
$\mathscr{G}_n$ 212
$\mathscr{L}_n$ 213
$A \rightarrow \omega/\varphi \text{---} \psi$ 214
$A \cdot B$ (set product)   225
(a_i, q_j, q_k) 255
$\#$ (blank)   255
K 259
Σ 259
δ 259
q_0 259
F (final states)   259
$!$ (factorial)   260
R_{ij}^k 265
(a_i, q_j, q_k, a_l, X) 274
L, R 274
$\vdash_T$ 277
$\overset{*}{\vdash_T}$ 278
σ 283
$\#$ (boundary)   292

General Index

'Ex.' indicates that the reference is found in an exercise on the page given. 'Def.' indicates a definition.

Abelian group. *See* Group, Abelian
Abelian monoid. *See* Monoid, Abelian
Abelian semigroup. *See* Semigroup, Abelian
Absolute complementation, Ex. 102
 definition, 92
 and negation, 98
 of relations, 109-110
 and relative complementation, 92
 Venn diagram of, 93
Addition (operation):
 arithmetic, 31, 153-57, 162-63
 cardinal, Ex. 186
 modulo 3, 170-71
Addition (rule of inference), 39
Adjunction (elementary transformation), 291-92
Aleph null/Aleph zero, 177
Algorithm, 280. *See also* Procedure; Decision procedure
 Euclidian, 254
Allophone, Ex. 134
Alphabet, 166. *See also* Vocabulary
 auxiliary and basic, 199-200
 in axiomatic system, 197
 input, 259, 276
Alternation. *See* Disjunction
Alternative denial, Ex. 48

Ambiguous grammar, 219-20, Ex. 221
Analytic truth, 26. *See also* Tautology
Antecedent, 18
Antisymmetry, 112-13
 in diagram of relation, 116
 of dominance relation in tree, 145-46
 of weak order, 139
Argument. *See also* Argument form
 conclusion, 12, 34
 enthymeme, 37
 of function, 126
 with multiply quantified propositions, 73-76, Ex. 79
 premise. *See* Premise
 proof. *See* Proof
 in propositional calculus, 34-45
 quantifiers in, 65-76
 schema, 34
 from substitution in argument form, 34, 36-37
 valid. *See* Validity
Argument form, 34
 substitution in, 36-37
 substitution instance of, 34
 valid. *See* Validity
Associative Laws. *See* Associativity
Associativity. *See also* Nonassociativity
 of composition of functions, 130, 154

323

Associativity (cont.)
  of composition of relations, 132
  of concatenation, 165
  of conjunction and disjunction, 29-31, 154
  of intersection and union, 89-90, 99, 154
    proof by Venn diagram, 97
  of operation (Def.), 154
  of symmetric difference, Ex. 173
Asymmetry, Ex. 134
  definition, 112
  in diagram of relation, 116
  of precedence relation in tree, 147
  of strict order, 139
Austin, J. L., 14
Automaton. See also Finite automaton; Linear bounded automaton; Pushdown automaton; Turing machine
  equivalences with formal grammars (Table), 287
Axiom(s), 5, 197
  in axiomatic system, 197
  in extended axiomatic system, 200
  in formal grammar, 208
  Peano's, 192-94, Ex. 204
Axiomatic method, 197
Axiomatic system, 188, 197-204. See also Extended axiomatic system
  alphabet, 197
  axiom, 197
  definition, 197
  derivation (Def.), 198
  equivalence of, 201
  extended. See Extended axiomatic system
  'follows from' relation (Def.), 197-98
  generating wff's of propositional calculus, 199
  production, 197
  production schema, 199
  proof (Def.), 198
  rules of inference, 197
  theorem (Def.), 198
Axiom of Extension, 4-6, 82

Base:
  of inductive proof, 194
  of recursive definition, 189
  of recursive function, 260
Base component, 290
  Universal Base Hypothesis, 295
'Belonging to' relation, 150-52
Biconditional, 21-22
Biconditional Laws, 30-31
Blank symbol, 255, 274
Boundary symbol, 291

Bound variable. See Variable, bound vs. free
Branch, of tree, 144

Cantor, G., 181
Cantor's diagonal argument, 184-85, 236
Cantor's Theorem, 181-84, 186
Cardinality, 174-86. See also Cardinal number
  of Cartesian product, 107
Cardinal number:
  addition, Ex. 186
  greater than aleph null, 181-86, Ex. 186
  'greater than or equal to' relation, 181-82, Ex. 186
  infinite, 177-86
  multiplication, Ex. 186
Cartesian product, Ex. 133
  cardinality of, 107
  containing null set, 107
  definition, 106
  infinite, 179-81
  nonassociativity and noncommutativity of, 107
  relation as subset of, 107-108
  of three or more sets, 107
Cell. See Partition
cfg (context-free grammar). See Type 2 grammar
cfl (context-free language). See Type 2 language
Chomsky, N., 219, 232-33, 259, 285
Chomsky Normal Form, Ex. 252
Church, A., 280
Church's Thesis, 280
Class, 6. See also Set
  equivalence. See Equivalence class
Clause mates, 151-52, Ex. 173
Closure (Def.), 154
Closure properties of formal languages (Table), 251
Codomain, 126
Cohen, P. J., 185
Collection, 6. See also Set
Command, 151-52, Ex. 173
Commutative group. See Group, Abelian
Commutative Laws. See Commutativity
Commutative monoid. See Monoid, Abelian
Commutative semigroup. See Semigroup, Abelian
Commutativity. See also Noncommutativity
  of alternative denial, Ex. 48
  of conjunction and disjunction, 30-31
  definition, 154

Commutativity (*cont.*)
  of intersection and union, 89-90, 99, 154
  of symmetric difference, 103, Ex. 173
Complementary distribution, Ex. 134
Complementary relations, 109-110, Ex. 134
  properties of, 117-21
  table, 120
Complementation. *See also* Complement Laws
  absolute. *See* Absolute complementation
  relative. *See* Relative complementation
Complement Laws:
  conjunction and disjunction, 30-31
  truth tables for, 26, 28
  intersection and union, 99, 157
Composite. *See* Composition
Composition:
  of functions, 129-32, Ex. 135, Ex. 173
  associativity of, 130, 154
  as group operation, 171-72
  with identity function, 130-31, 155-56
  inverses, 130-32
  noncommutativity of, 130, 154
  nonidempotence of, Ex. 155
  of relations, 132, Ex. 135
Concatenation, 165-66
Conclusion. *See* Argument
Conditional, 18-21
  antecedent, 18
  compared with 'if . . . then', 19-20
  consequent, 18
  contrapositive form, 31
  definition, 18
  logical implication, 19
  material, 20
  'necessary condition', 21
  subjunctive, 19
  'sufficient condition', 21
  tautologous. *See* Logical implication
  truth table, 18
Conditional Laws, 30-31
Conditional proof, Ex. 49-50
  compared with direct proof, 73
  in predicate calculus, 71-73
  in propositional calculus, 41-44
  self-embedding of, 44
Configuration. *See* Mathematical configuration
Conjugate strings, Ex. 173
Conjunction (of propositions):
  compared with 'and', 15-16
  definition, 15
  and intersection of sets, 98

Conjunction (of propositions) (*cont.*)
  in logical equivalences (Table), 30
  as operation, 154-55
  truth table, 16
Conjunction reduction (transformation), 292-93
Conjunction (rule of inference), 39
Connexity:
  of complementary and inverse relations, 120-21
  definition, 114
  in diagram of relation, 117
  of linear order, 141
Consequent, 18
Consistency Principle, 99-100
Consonant cluster, Ex. 135
Constant, nonspecific or variable, 66
Constituent-structure grammar, 211-12. *See also* Formal grammar
  inadequacy for natural languages, 289
Constituent-structure tree. *See* Tree
Context-free grammar/language. *See* Type 2 grammar/language
Context-sensitive grammar/language. *See* Type 1 grammar/language
Context-sensitive rule, notations for, 213-14
Contingent proposition, 27
Continuum Hypothesis, 185-86
Contradiction, 26, Ex. 50
  and logical equivalence, 28-29
  and null set, 98-99
  in predicate calculus, 62-63
  truth table, 26
Contrapositive, 31
Corollary, 118
Correspondence, 126. *See also* Function
  one-to-one. *See* One-to-one correspondence
Counter-example, 60
csg (context-sensitive grammar). *See* Type 1 grammar
csl (context-sensitive language). *See* Type 1 language
Cycle, transformational, 290-91, 295

Daughter node, 146
Davis, M., 180
Decidability. *See* Decision procedure
Decision procedure. *See also* Procedure; Algorithm
  for emptiness of Type 2 language, 238-41
  for membership in Type 1 language, 234-36
Definition:
  biconditional in, 22

Definition (cont.)
  circularity in, 189-90
  equality of sets in, 87
  recursive. See Recursive definition
Deletion:
  elementary transformation, 291-92
  recoverability of, 292-95
DeMorgan's Laws:
  for propositions, 30-31
    generalized form, 64
    and Laws of Quantifier Negation, 64
    truth table, 28
  for sets, 98-99
    generalized form, 197
Denumerability. See Denumerably infinite set; Nondenumerability
Denumerably infinite set, 177-86, Ex. 186
  Cartesian product, 179-81
Derivation:
  in axiomatic system (Def.), 198
  equivalent, 219
  in extended axiomatic system (Def.), 200
  in formal grammar (Def.), 208
    reformulation, 217
  "nonshrinking", 234
  in semi-Thue system, 203
  terminated (Def.), 209
Descriptive adequacy, 295
Deterministic automaton. See Finite automaton; Linear bounded automaton; Pushdown automaton; Turing machine
Diagonal argument, Cantor's, 184-85, 236
Disjoint sets, 90
  Venn diagrams, 93-94
Disjunction, 16-17
  compared with 'or', 16
  definition, 16
  in logical equivalences (Table), 30
  as operation, 154-55
  truth table, 16
  and union, 98
Disjunctive Syllogism (D.S.), 39
Distributive Laws. See Distributivity
Distributivity:
  conjunction over conditional, Ex. 46
  conjunction over disjunction, and vice versa, 30-31
    truth table for, 30
  definition, 155
  intersection over union, and vice versa, 99, Ex. 102, 155
    generalized form, 196-97
  multiplication over addition, 31, 155
  set product over union and intersection, Ex. 252

Distributivity (cont.)
  symmetric difference over union and intersection, and vice versa, Ex. 173
Division, 154-57, 169, Ex. 172
Domain:
  of function, 124-25
  of relation, 108-109
Domain of discourse, 57-58, 62-65
Dominance:
  in formal grammar (Def.), 208
  immediate. See Immediate dominance
  in tree, 145-46, 149

e.a.s. See Extended axiomatic system
Elementary proposition, 22
  recursive definition of, 191
Elementary transformation, 291-92
Empty set, 2. See also Null set
Enthymeme, 37
Enumeration, 179-81, 237. See also Denumerably infinite set; Recursive enumeration
Equality (of sets):
  Axiom of Extension, 4-6
  vs. equivalence, 175
  fundamental set-theoretic equalities (Table), 99
  vs. naming sets, 5
  in Venn diagram, 93
Equivalence:
  of axiomatic systems, 201
  of derivations, 219
  of sets, 174-77
  weak, of formal grammars (Def.), 209
Equivalence class, 121. See also Equivalence relation
Equivalence relation, 121-24, Ex. 135, Ex. 220
  and finite automaton, 267-74
  finite index of, 269
  and isomorphism, 168-69
  partition induced by, 121-24
  right invariant, 269
Euclidian algorithm, 254
Every, R. J., 285
Exclusive 'or', 16
Exclusivity Condition, in tree, 147, 149
Existential Generalization (E.G.), 65, 68
  and U.G., order of application, 75-76
Existential Instantiation (E.I.), 65, 68-71
  of multiply quantified propositions, 74-76
  restriction on application, 68-70
Existential quantifier, 53-55. See also Quantifiers; Quantification

Extended axiomatic system, Ex. 206. *See also* Axiomatic system; Semi-Thue system
  auxiliary alphabet, 199-200
  axiom, 200
  basic alphabet, 199-200
  definition, 200
  derivation (Def.), 200
  equivalence of, 201
  'follows from' relation (Def.), 200
  production, 200
  proof (Def.), 200
  proper, 200
  rules of inference, 200
  and semi-Thue system, 202-203
  theorem (Def.), 200
Extension, Axiom of. *See* Axiom of Extension
Extension, of predicate, 59

fa. *See* Finite automaton
Factorial, 260
Filtering, 291
Finite automaton, 254-74, Ex. 287
  acceptance and rejection of input, 255
  blocking of, 255
  complete, 267-68
  deterministic, 258-59
    acceptance and rejection of input, 261
    definition, 259-61
    equivalence to nondeterministic, 259
    next-move function, 259-61
  and equivalence relations, 267-74
  equivalence to type 3 grammar, 261-64
  final state, 255, 259
  as generator, 264-65
  initial state, 255, 259
  input alphabet, 259
  instructions, 255
  minimum-state, 270
  nondeterministic, 258-59, 261
  and regular sets, 265-67
  state diagram of, 257
Finite-state automaton. *See* Finite automaton
Finite-state grammar/language. *See* Type 3 grammar/language
First coordinate, of ordered pair, 104-105
'Follows from' relation:
  in axiomatic system, 197-98
  in extended axiomatic system, 200
  in formal grammar, 208
Formal grammar. *See also* Formal language
  ambiguous, 219-20, Ex. 221
  axiom, 208

Formal grammar (*cont.*)
  as axiomatic system, 188
  and constituent-structure trees, 214-21
  context-free. *See* Type 2 grammar
  context-sensitive. *See* Type 1 grammar
  derivation (Def.), 208
    reformulation of, 217
    terminated (Def.), 209
  dominance (Def.), 208
  equivalences with automata (Table), 287
  finite-state. *See* Type 3 grammar
  'follows from' relation, 208
  generating null string, 228-29
  generative capacity, strong vs. weak, 289
  immediate dominance (Def.), 208
  language generated by, 166, 209
  left-linear, 222
  linear, 222
  notational conventions for, 208
  one-sided linear, 222
  regular. *See* Type 3 grammar
  right-linear. *See* Type 3 grammar
  rules, 207-208
  rule schema, 207-208
  and semi-Thue system, 207-208
  terminal string, 209-10
  terminal tree, 217
  tree-derivation, 217
  type 0. *See* Type 0 grammar
  type 1. *See* Type 1 grammar
  type 2. *See* Type 2 grammar
  type 3. *See* Type 3 grammar
  type 3.1. *See* Type 3.1 grammar
  types, defined, 211-12
  vocabulary, terminal and nonterminal, 207
  weak equivalence (Def.), 209
Formal language, 166, 174. *See also* Formal grammar
  types, defined, 213
Formative, 144, 149
Four-valued logic, 13-14
Free monoid, 166, 176, 207. *See also* Monoid
Free variable. *See* Variable, bound vs. free
Free variation, Ex. 134
fsl (finite-state language). *See* Type 3 language
Function:
  argument of, 126
  codomain, 126
  composition of. *See* Composition, of functions
  diagrams of, 125

Function (cont.)
  domain, 124-25
  from A to B, 126
  identity, 130-31, 155-56
  in A, 126
  into, 126
  inverse, 127-28, Ex. 135
    of composite, 131-32
  composition of, 130-31
  labeling, 144, 148-49
  linear, 286
  of $n - 1$ variables, 132-33
  one-to-one, 127-28, Ex. 135
  one-to-one correspondence. See One-to-one correspondence
  onto, 126, Ex. 135
  partial, 133, 259-60, 276
  partial recursive, 278-80. See also Recursive function
  propositional. See Propositional function
  range, 124-25
  recursive. See Recursive function
  restriction of, 133
  as type of relation, 124-25
  value of, 126

Grammar:
  constituent-structure, 211-12. See also Formal grammar
  of formal language. See Formal grammar
  of natural language. See Natural language, grammar
Grammatical category, 144, 149
Grammatical rule. See Rule, grammatical
Grammatical sentence, 166, 207
Greatest element, 143, Ex. 172
Grelling's Paradox, 87
Group, 157-61
  Abelian, 158, 160, 170, Ex. 173
  isomorphism of, 170-72
  multiplication table, 158-59
  order of, 161
  subgroup, 160-61

Halmos, P. R., 2
Harary, F., 135-36
Hopcroft, J. E., 259, 261, 280, 285
Hypothetical Syllogism (H.S.), 39

Idempotence. See also Nonidempotence
  of conjunction and disjunction, 29-30, 154-55
  truth table for, 28
  of intersection and union, 89-90, 99, 154

Idempotence (cont.)
  of operation (Def.), 154-55
  of symmetric difference, Ex. 173
Identical Quantifiers, Laws of (Ident. Quant.), 63-64
Identity element, 155-56
Identity function, 130-31, 155-56
Identity Laws, Ex. 48
  for conjunction and disjunction, 30-31
  for intersection and union, 87, 90, 99
Identity loop, in diagram of relation, 115, 140
Identity relation, 109, 130
  in composition, 132
  and reflexivity, 111
iff (if and only if), 22
'If . . . then', 18-20
  compared to material conditional, 20
  uses of:
    causal, 19
    definitional, 19
    logical, 19
    in subjunctive conditional, 19-20
Immediate dominance:
  in formal grammar (Def.), 208
  in tree, 146
Immediate predecessor:
  definition, 140
  diagram, 140-41, 167, Ex. 172, Ex. 220-21
Implication, logical. See Logical implication
Inclusion, 7. See also Subset
  reflexivity of, 8
  transitivity of, 8, 83-84
  Venn diagrams of, 93-94
Inclusive 'or', 16
Index, of equivalence relation, 269
Indirect proof, 7, 44-45, Ex. 49-50, Ex. 86
Induction, Mathematical, Priniciple of. See Mathematical induction
Induction step, in inductive proof, 194
Inductive proof. See Mathematical induction
Inference, rules of. See Rules of inference
Infinite set, 2, 174-86. See also Denumerably infinite set
  definition, 176
  recursive specification of, 188-204
Informal proof, 84-86
Instantiation:
  Existential. See Existential Instantiation
  in propositional functions, 52-54
  Universal. See Universal Instantiation
Instructions, of finite automaton, 255
Integers, 2, 4, 143
  recursive definition of, 192

Intersection, Ex. 102
  associativity of, 90, 99, 154
    proof by Venn diagrams, 97
  commutativity of, 90, 99, 154
  Complement Laws, 99, 157
  connections with subset, 90-91, 99
  definition, 89
  DeMorgan's Laws, 99
  Distributive Laws, 99, Ex. 102, 155, Ex. 173
  idempotence of, 90, 99, 154
  Identity Laws, 99, 156-57
  related to conjunction, 98
  as semigroup operation, Ex. 173
  in Venn diagrams, 93-94, 97
Into function, 126
Intransitivity (Def.), 114
Invalidity. *See* Validity
Inverse element, 156-57
Inverse function. *See* Function, inverse
Inverse relation. *See* Relation, inverse
Irrational number, 184
Irreflexivity:
  definition, 111
  in diagram of relation, 116
  of precedence relation in tree, 147
  of strict order, 139
Isomorphism, 166-72, Ex. 172
  and equivalence relation, 168-69
  of groups, 170-72
  inverse of, 168
  operation-preserving, 169-72, Ex. 173
  order-preserving, 169-70
  relation-preserving, 167-69

Klima, E. S., 173
Kuroda, S. Y., 286, 293

Label (Labeling function), in tree, 144, 148-49
Landweber, P. S., 286
Langacker, R. W., 151
Language:
  formal. *See* Formal language
  natural. *See* Natural language
lba. *See* Linear bounded automaton
Leaf node, 146, 150
Least element, 142, Ex. 172
Left identity element, 155-56
Left inverse element, 156-57
Left-linear grammar, 222. *See also* Type 3 grammar
Left zero element, 157
Lexical category, 149
Linear bounded automaton, 285-86
  deterministic, 286
  nondeterministic, acceptance of type 1 languages, 286

Linear function, 286
Linear grammar, 222. *See also* Type 3 grammar
Linear order, 141
Linguistic theory, 233, 294-96
List notation for sets, 2-3, Ex. 10, 188
Logical connectives, 15-22, Ex. 45-46, Ex. 48. *See also* Alternative denial; Biconditional; Conditional; Conjunction; Disjunction
  truth functionality of, 15
Logical equivalence:
  of contradictions, 28-29
  and logical implication, 37-38
  in predicate calculus, 55, 62-64
    table, 63
  in propositional calculus, 27-34, Ex. 46, Ex 48
    table, 30
  use of in manipulating formulas, 33-34
  and set theoretic equalities, 98-99
  shown by truth table, 28-30
  substitution in proof, 41
  and tautology, 28-29, 31-32
Logical form, 27
Logical implication:
  expressed by 'if . . . then', 19
  and logical equivalence, 37-38
  in predicate calculus (Table), 63
  and validity, 36
Logical meaning, 16
Logical truth, 26. *See also* Tautology

McCawley, J., 218
Map/Mapping, 126. *See also* Function
Material conditional, 20. *See also* Conditional
Mathematical configuration, 141-42, 157-64. *See also* Group; Isomorphism; Monoid; Semigroup; Tree
Mathematical induction:
  base, 194
  induction step, 194
  principle of, 193-97, Ex. 204-205
Maximal element, 143, Ex. 172-73
Membership of set:
  vs. inclusion, 7-8
  irreflexivity of, 8
  mathematical vs. ordinary usage, 1-2
Miller, G. A., 259
Minimal element, 142, Ex. 172-73
Minimal pair, Ex. 134
Minimum-state finite automaton, 270
Mirror-image language/strings:
  accepted by nondeterministic pushdown automaton, 285
  in English, 232-33

Mirror-image langauge/strings (*cont.*)
  generated by axiomatic system, 198-99
  generated by extended axiomatic system, 200-201
  not type 3, 232-33, 273-74
recursive definition of, 188-90
Modulo 3 addition, 170-71
Modus Ponens, 39
Modus Tollens, 39
Monoid, 162-63
  Abelian, 158, 162, 166
  with concatenation operation, 165-66
  free, 166, 176, 207
  submonoid, 163
Multiplication:
  arithmetic, 31, 153-57, Ex. 163
  cardinal, 186
Multiplication table, for group, 158-59

Natural language:
  arguments in, 12, 34, 36-37, Ex. 49-50, Ex. 78-79. *See also* Argument
  constituent-structure trees, 144, 149-52, Ex. 173
  DeMorgan's Laws, 31
  English not type 3, 233
  grammar of:
    inadequacy of constituent-structure grammar, 289-90
    specifying infinite set, 207
    specifying structural descriptions, 289, 295
    transformational. *See* Transformational grammar
  initial consonant clusters in English, Ex. 135
  Mohawk not type 2, 233-34
  pronouns and mathematical variables, 4, 54-55
  quantifiers in, 53-55, 59-61, Ex. 77-78
  as recursive set, 236, 294
  sentence connectives, 15, Ex. 45-46
    'and', 15-16
    'but', 16
    'if and only if', 22
    'if . . . then'. *See* 'If . . . then'
    'is a necessary and sufficient condition for', 22
    'is a necessary condition for', 21
    'is a sufficient condition for', 21-22
    'it is not the case that', 18
    'just if', 22
    'just in case that', 22
    'not', 17-18
    'only if', 21
    'or', inclusive and exclusive, 16
  sentences vs. propositions, 14

Natural language (*cont.*)
  as set of strings, 166, 207
  some phonological relations in, Ex. 134-36
  tautologies, 26
Necessary condition, 21
Negation:
  and absolute complementation, 98
  compared with 'not', 17-18
  definition, 17
  as singulary operation, 152
  truth table, 17
Nelson, R. J., 280
Node, in tree, 144
  daughter, 146
  leaf, 146, 150
  root, 146
  sister, 146, 149-50
Node admissibility condition, 218-19
Nonassociativity:
  of alternative denial, Ex. 48
  of Cartesian product, 107
  of relative complementation, 91
  of subtraction and division, 154
Noncommutativity:
  of Cartesian product, 107
  of composition of functions, 130, 154
  of composition of relations, 132
  of concatenation, 165
  of relative complementation, 91, 154
  of subtraction and division, 154
Nonconnexity, 114
Nondenumerability, 181-86. *See also* Denumerably infinite set
  of [0, 1], 184-86
  of power set of integers, 182-84
Nondeterministic automaton. *See* Finite automaton; Linear bounded automaton; Pushdown automaton; Turing machine
Nonidempotence, 91, 155
Nonrecursiveness of transformational languages, 293-96
Nonreflexivity (Def.), 111
  in diagram of relation, 116
Nonsymmetry (Def.), 112
Nontangling Condition, in tree, 148-49
Nontransitivity (Def.), 113
Null relation, 109
Null set, 2, Ex. 9-10, Ex. 86
  in Cartesian product, 107
  and contradiction, 98-99
  as identity element, 156
  as null relation, 109
  as subset of every set, 7, 45
  uniqueness, 6
  and universal set, 92

Null string, 164-66
  generation by formal grammar, 228-29

One-sided linear grammar, 222. *See also* Type 3 grammar
One-to-one correspondence, 128, 167-68, Ex. 172-73
  and equivalence of sets, 174-83
One-to-one function, 127-28, Ex. 135
Onto function, 126, Ex. 135
Operations, 152-57
  in mathematical configurations, 157-64
  notations for, 153
  properties of. *See* Associativity; Closure; Commutativity; Distributivity; Idempotence; Well-definition
  singulary, binary, ternary, etc., 152
  special elements in. *See* Identity element; Inverse element; Zero element
Order (of group), 161
Order (relation), 137-43
  diagrams of, 139-40
  linear, 141
  partial. *See* Partial order; Partially ordered set
  predecessor and successor in:
    immediate, 140
    strict (strong) vs. weak, 140
  preorder, 138
  strict (strong) vs. weak, 138-39
  total, 141
  totally ordered set, 141-42, 167
  transitivity of, 138
  as type of relation, 137-38
Ordered pairs:
  definition, 104
  equality of, 105-106
  and relations, 107-108
Ordered triples, quadruples, etc., 106

Paper, H. H., 135-36
Paradox:
  Grelling's, 87
  Russell's, 86, 183
Parenthesis-free notation. *See* Polish parenthesis-free notation
Partial function, 133, 259-60, 276
Partially ordered set, 141-42, Ex. 172, Ex. 220-21. *See also* Order (relation); Partial order
  greatest and least elements (Def.), 142-43
  immediate predecessor diagrams of, 142
  isomorphism of, 169-70

Partially ordered set (*cont.*)
  maximal and minimal elements (Def.), 142-43
Partial order, 141, Ex. 172-73. *See also* Order (relation)
  strict, precedence relation in tree as, 148-49
  weak, dominance relation in tree as, 145-46, 149
Partial recursive function, 278-80. *See also* Recursive function
Partition, 121-24, Ex. 134
  cell, 122
  induced by equivalence relation, 121-24
  refinement of, 270-71
Passive sentence, order of quantifiers in, 55
Passive transformation, 291-93
Path, in tree, 239
pda. *See* Pushdown automaton
Peano, G., 192
Peano's Axioms. *See* Axioms, Peano's
Performative, 14
Peters, P. S., 290, 293-95
Phone/Phoneme, Ex. 134
Phrase marker, 290. *See also* Tree
Phrase-structure tree. *See* Tree
Polish parenthesis-free notation, Ex. 46-47, Ex. 204, Ex. 206
Postal, P., 233-34
Power set, 8-9, Ex. 10, Ex. 103
  cardinality of, 181-84, Ex. 204
Precedence, in tree, 147-49
Predecessor. *See* Order, predecessor and successor in
Predicate, 52. *See also* Propositional function
  binary, ternary, etc., 53
  extension of, 59
  notation for, 52-53, 81-82
  set-theoretic, 81-82
Predicate notation for set, 4, Ex. 10, 59
Premise, 12, 34
  temporary, in conditional proof, 41, 43-44
Preorder, 138
Procedure, 254. *See also* Decision procedure; Algorithm
  and Turing machine, 279-80
Product, Cartesian. *See* Cartesian product
Product, set. *See* Set product
Production:
  in axiomatic system, 197
  in extended axiomatic system, 200
Production schema, 199
"Program", automaton, 255

Pronouns and variables, 4, 54-55
Proof:
of argument, 13, 40, Ex. 49-50, Ex. 78-79
in axiomatic system (Def.), 198
conditional. *See* Conditional proof
in extended axiomatic system (Def.), 200
indirect. *See* Indirect proof
by induction. *See* Mathematical induction
informal style in, 84-86
from recursive definition, 190
in semi-Thue system, 203
substitution of logical equivalences in, 41
Proper extended axiomatic system, 200
Proper inclusion/Proper subset, 7, Ex. 86, Ex. 134. *See also* Subset
definition, 85
transitivity of, Ex. 86
in Venn diagrams, 93-94
Proposition, 13-15. *See also* Predicate; Propositional function
complex, 22
contingent, 27
elementary. *See* Elementary proposition
expressed by sentence, 14
formed by instantiation, 52-54
formed by quantification, 53-57
in predicate calculus (Def.), 57
truth value of, 13-14
Propositional function, 52. *See also* Predicate; Proposition
instantiation by constants, 52-54
notation for, 52-53
quantification of, 53-55
in two or more variables, 54-55
Pushdown automaton:
acceptance of input, 282-83
acceptance of type 2 languages, 285
deterministic, 283-85, Ex. 288
"memory" of, 285
nondeterministic, 283-85
pushdown store in, 282-83

Quantification:
and domain of discourse, 58-59
and instantiation, 54, 58
Quantified expressions, English equivalents of, 53-55, 59-61, Ex. 77-78
Quantifier Distribution, Laws of (Quant. Distr.), 63-65, 72
Quantifier Negation, Laws of (Quant. Neg.), 60-61, 63
as generalized DeMorgan's Laws, 64

Quantifiers. *See also* Existential Generalization/Instantiation; Universal Generalization/Instantiation
existential, 53-55
and logical disjunction, 58, 64
Identical, Laws of (Ident. Quant.), 63-64
order of, 54-55
scope of, 56-57, Ex. 76
superfluous, 57
universal, 53-55
and logical conjunction, 58, 64

Rabin, M. O., 259
Range:
of function, 124-25
of relation, 108-109
Rational number, 184
Real number, 184
Recoverability of deletion, condition on, 292-95
Recursion, of recursive function, 260
Recursion step, in recursive definition, 189
Recursive definition, 188-93, Ex. 204, 266
base, 189
of integers, 192
of mirror-image language, 188-90
recursion step, 189
restriction, 189
of *wff*'s in propositional calculus, 190-92
Recursive enumeration, by Turing machine, 278-80
Recursive function, Ex. 204, 260
base, 260
partial, 278-80
recursion, 260
Recursively enumerable set, 213, 278-80. *See also* Recursive set
generated by transformational grammar, 293-96
vs. recursive set, 279-80
Recursive set, 235
and natural language, 236, 294
properly included in type 1 languages, 236-38
vs. recursively enumerable set, 279-80
Reductio ad absurdum. *See* Indirect proof
Reduction of type 2 grammars, 241-47
Refinement, of partition, 270-71
Reflexivity, 110-111, Ex. 135. *See also* Irreflexivity; Nonreflexivity
of complementary and inverse relations, 117-18, 120
in diagram of relation, 116

Reflexivity (*cont.*)
  of dominance relation in formal grammar, 208
  of dominance relation in tree, 145
  of weak order, 139
Regular grammar. *See* Type 3 grammar
Regular language. *See* Type 3 language
Regular set, 213
  accepted by finite automaton, 265-67
  definition, 226
  equivalent to type 3 languages, 265-67
  included in type 3 languages, 225-31
Reich, P. A., 223
Relation:
  binary, ternary, etc., 108
  complementary. *See* Complementary relations
  composition of, 132, Ex. 135
  diagrams of, 115-17
  domain, 108-109
  equivalence. *See* Equivalence relation
  from A to B, 108
  identity, 109, 130
    in composition, 132
  in A, 108
  inverse, 109-10, Ex. 134, Ex. 173
    properties of, 117-21
  notation for, 108
  null, 109
  properties of. *See* Connexity; Reflexivity; Symmetry; Transitivity
  range, 108-109
  as set of ordered pairs, 107-108
  universal, 109
Relative complementation, Ex. 102
  and absolute complementation, 92
  definition, 91
  nonassociativity of, 91
  noncommutativity of, 91, 154
  nonidempotence of, 91, 155
  right identity element for, 156
  Venn diagram, 96
Repeating decimal, 184
Representing expression, 231, Ex. 252
r.e. set. *See* Recursively enumerable set
Restriction:
  of function, 133
  in recursive definition, 189
Right identity element, 155-56
Right invariance, 269
Right inverse element, 156-57
Right-linear grammar/language. *See* Type 3 grammar/language
Right zero element, 157
Ritchie, R. W., 290, 293-95
Root node, 146

Rule, grammatical:
  in formal grammar, 207-208
  as node admissibility condition, 218-19
  transformational. *See* Transformational rule
Rule schema, 207-208. *See also* Rules of inference
Rules of inference, 38-41, 197
  in axiomatic system, 197
  in extended axiomatic system, 200
  involving quantifiers, 65-71
  Principle of Mathematical Induction, 193-97
  in propositional calculus (Table), 39
Russell, B., 86
Russell's Paradox, 86, 183

Scott, D., 259
Second coordinate, 104-105
Self-contradiction, 26. *See also* Contradiction
Semigroup, 157-58, 163-64, Ex. 173
  Abelian, 158
  with identity. *See* Monoid
Semi-Thue system, 202-204, Ex. 206
  definition, 202
  derivation (Def.), 203
  and formal grammar, 207-208
  proof, 203
  theorem, 203
  as type 0 grammar, 212
Sentence, 166, 174
  vs. proposition, 14
Sentence connectives. *See* Natural language, sentence connectives
Set:
  of all sets, 82
  cardinality of. *See* Cardinality; Cardinal number
  denumerable. *See* Denumerably infinite set
  equality of. *See* Equality
  equivalence of. *See* Equivalence
  inclusion. *See* Inclusion
  infinite. *See* Infinite set
  members of. *See* Membership of set
  nondenumerable. *See* Nondenumerability
  notation. *See* List notation for sets; Predicate notation for sets
  null. *See* Null set
  ordered. *See* Order (relation); Ordered pair; Partially ordered set
  power. *See* Power set
  recursive. *See* Recursive set
  recursively enumerable. *See* Recursively enumerable set

General Index

Set (cont.)
  regular. See Regular set
  subset. See Subset
  successor, 192
  universal. See Universal set
  unordered, 3, 104
Set operations. See Absolute complementation Cartesian product; Intersection; Relative complementation; Set product; Symmetric difference; Union
Set product, 225, Ex. 252
Set-theoretic equalities, 98-101
  relation to logical equivalences, 98-99
  table of, 99
  use in manipulating expressions, 100-101
Sieve of Eratosthenes, 254
Single Root Condition, 146, 149
Singleton, 2
Sister node, 146, 149-50
State, of automaton, 255
State diagram, for finite automaton, 257
String, 164-66, Ex. 173
  abbreviatory notation for, 211
  concatenation (Def.), 165
  as function, 164
  length of, 164
  null. See Null string
  occurrences or tokens in, 164
  terminal (Def.), 209-210
Strong generative capacity, 289, 295
Structural change:
  of passive transformation, 292-93
  of transformational rule, 291
Structural condition:
  of passive transformation, 291-92
  of transformational rule, 291
Subgroup, 160-61. See also Group
Subjunctive conditional, 19
Submonoid, 163. See also Monoid
Subset, 6-7, Ex. 9-10, 82, Ex. 134, 189, 192. See also Inclusion
  and equal sets, 83
  proper. See Proper inclusion/Proper subset
Substitution (elementary transformation), 291-92
Substitution instance, 34
Subtraction, 154-57
Subtree, 149. See also Tree
Successor. See Order, predecessor and successor
Successor set, 192
Sufficient condition, 21
Superset, 7. See also Subset
Surface structure, 290

Symmetric difference, Ex. 102-103, 154-55, Ex. 157, Ex. 173
Symmetry, 111-13, Ex. 135. See also Antisymmetry; Asymmetry; Nonsymmetry
  of complementary and inverse relations, 118-20
  in diagram of relation, 116

Tautologous conditional. See Logical implication
Tautology, 25-27
  and logical equivalence, 28-29, 31-32
  in predicate calculus, 62-63
  truth tables, 26-27
  uniform substitution in, 32
  and universal set, 98-99
Temporary premise, in conditional proof, 41, 43-44
Term:
  constant, 52
  in propositional function, 52
  variable, 52
Terminal string (Def.), 209-10
Terminal tree, 217
Terminated derivation, 209
Theorem, 118, 197
  in axiomatic system (Def.), 198
  in extended axiomatic system (Def.), 200
  in semi-Thue system, 203
Thue, A., 202
Thue-system, 203. See also Semi-Thue system
Tokens, in string, 164
Totally ordered set. See Order, totally ordered set
Total order. See Order, linear
Transformational cycle, 290-91, 295
Transformational grammar, 290-96
  base component, 290
  boundary symbol, 291
  context-free based, 294
  context-sensitive based, 293
  descriptive adequacy of, 295
  equivalence to type 0 grammar, 293-96
  filtering in, 291
  surface structure, 290
  theory of, 294-95
  transformational component, 290
  transformational cycle. See Transformational cycle
  transformational rule. See Transformational rule
Universal Base Hypothesis, 295
weak generative capacity, 295

Transformational language, nonrecursiveness of, 293-96
Transformational rule:
conjunction reduction, 292-93
elementary transformations, 291-92
Transformational rule (*cont.*)
imperative formation, 293
linear ordering of, 290
passive, 291-93
structural change, 291
structural condition, 291
Transformation (function), 126. *See also* Function
Transitivity, 113, Ex. 135
of complementary and inverse relations, 119-21
in diagram of relation, 116-17
of dominance relation in formal grammar, 208
of dominance relation in tree, 145
of inclusion, 83-84
of orders, 138
of precedence relation in tree, 147
of proper inclusion, Ex. 86
Tree, 144-52, 289-90
'belonging-to' relation in, 150-52
branch, 144
clause mates, 151-52, Ex. 173
command, 151-52, Ex. 173
daughter node, 146
definition, 149
from derivation, 214-17, 219-20
diagrams of, 144
dominance relation in, 145-46, 149
"empty", 146
Exclusivity Condition, 147, 149
"forest", 146
immediate dominance relation in, 146
'in construction with' relation in, 173
label, 144
labeling function, 148-49
leaf node, 146, 150
Nontangling Condition, 148-49
path, 239
precedence relation in, 147-49
root node, 146
Single Root Condition, 146
sister node, 146, 149-50
subtree, 149
terminal, 217
Tree derivation, 217
Truth functional connectives, 15
Truth table, 15-16, Ex. 46
for biconditional, 21
for checking validity of argument form, 35

Truth table (*cont.*)
for Complement Laws, 26, 28
for complex propositions, 23-25
for conditional, 18
for conjunction, 16
for contradiction, 26
demonstrating logical equivalences, 28-30
for DeMorgan's Laws, 28
for disjunction, 16
for Distributive laws, 30
for Idempotent Laws, 28
for negation, 17
shorter method of constructing, 24-25
steps in constructing, 23-25
for tautology, 26-27
Truth value, 13-14
uniform assignment of, 27-28
Turing, A. M., 274
Turing machine, 274-81, Ex. 287-88
acceptance and rejection of inputs, 274-75
and algorithm, 280
deterministic, 276
equivalence to type 0 grammar, 280-81
equivalent formulations of, 278-79
final states, 274, 276
halting of, 274-75
initial state, 274, 276
input alphabet, 276
instructions of, 274, 276
"memory" of, 285
move of, 277-78
next-move function, 276
nondeterministic, 278, 280
and procedure, 279-80
and recursively enumerable sets, 278-80
and recursive sets, 278-80
situation of, 277
Two-sided identity element, 155-56
Two-sided inverse element, 156-57
Two-sided zero element, 157
Two-valued logic, 13
Type 0 grammar, 212
equivalence to transformational grammar, 293-96
equivalence to Turing machine, 280-81
Type 0 language, 213
closure properties of (Table), 251
Type 1 grammar, Ex. 252
as base for transformational grammar, 293
definition, 212
enumeration of, 237
undecidability questions, 238

Type 1 language, 213
  accepted by nondeterministic lba, 286
  closure properties (Table), 251
  decision procedure for membership in, 234-36
  properly included in type 0, 281
  and recursive sets, 236-38
Type 2 grammar, Ex. 252
  as base for transformational grammar, 294
  Chomsky Normal Form, Ex. 252
  decision procedure for emptiness question, 238-41
  definition, 212
  reduced, 239, 241-47
Type 2 language, 213
  accepted by nondeterministic pushdown automaton, 285
  characterization theorem for, 239, 247-49
  closure properties, 239, 249-51, Ex. 252
  properly included in type 1, 249
Type 3 grammar, Ex. 251
  as base for transformational grammar, 295
  definition, 212
  equivalence to finite automaton, 261-64
  inadequacy for English, 289
Type 3 language, 213, Ex. 287
  accepted by finite automaton, 261-64
  closure properties:
    set product, 228
    "star", 228-30
    table of, 251
    union, 226-27
  equivalence to regular sets, 265-67
  regular sets included in, 225-31
  representing expression for, 231
Type 3.1 grammar, 223-25
  equivalence to finite automaton, 261-64
  equivalence to type 3, 223-25

Ullman, J. D., 259, 261, 280, 285
Undecidability, 238. *See also* Decision procedure
Uniform assignment, of truth values, 27-28
Uniform substitution:
  in argument form, 36-37
  in tautology, 32
Union:
  associativity of, 89, 99, 154
    proof by Venn diagrams, 97

Union (*cont.*)
  commutativity of, 89, 99, 154
  Complement Laws, 99, Ex. 157
  connections with subset, 90-91, 99
  definition, 87
  DeMorgan's Laws, 99
  Distributive Laws, 99, Ex. 102, 155, Ex. 173
  idempotence of, 89, 99, 154
  Identity Laws, 99, 156-57
  related to disjunction, 98
  as semigroup operation, Ex. 173
  in Venn diagrams, 96
Universal Base Hypothesis, 295
Universal Generalization (U.G.), 65-67
  and E. G., order of applying, 75-76
Universal Instantiation (U.I.), 65-66
  applied to multiply quantified propositions, 74-76
Universal quantifier, 53-55. *See also* Quantifier; Quantification
Universal relation, 109
Universal set:
  as identity element, 156-57
  and null set, 92
  and tautology, 98-99
  in Venn diagrams, 93
Universe of discourse. *See* Domain of discourse
Unrestricted rewriting system, 212. *See also* Type 0 grammar
urs. *See* Unrestricted rewriting system

Validity, 12-13, 35-37, Ex. 47-50, Ex. 78-79
  definition, 35
  shown by truth tables, 35
  and truth of premises, 37
Value, of function, 126
Variable:
  bound versus free, 56-57, Ex. 76
  instantiation by constant, conditions for, 52-53
  in propositional function, 52-53
  symbol, 4
Venn diagram, 92-98
  absolute complement, 93
  equality of sets, 93
  for four sets, 98
  inclusion, 93-94
  intersection:
    of three sets, 97
    of two sets, 93-94
  relative complementation, 96
  union, 96
Venn-Euler diagram. *See* Venn diagram

Vocabulary. *See also* Alphabet
   of formal grammar, 166, 207
   nonterminal and terminal, 207

Weak equivalence, of formal grammars, 209
Weak generative capacity, 289, 295
Well-definition (Def.), 153-54
Well-formed formula (*wff*):
   in Polish parenthesis-free notation. *See* Polish parenthesis-free notation

Well-formed formula (*wff*) (*cont.*)
   in propositional calculus, Ex. 205-206
   generated by axiomatic system, 199
   generated by extended axiomatic system, 201-202
   recursive definition of, 190-92
wff. *See* Well-formed formula
Word, 166

Zero, element, 157